A Free Church in A Free State

The Possibilities of Abraham Kuyper's Ecclesiology
for Japanese Evangelical Christians

Surya Harefa

ACADEMIC

In this groundbreaking book, Surya Harefa shows how Abraham Kuyper's ecclesiology, rooted in his robust theology of culture, can effectively address the uniquely Japanese understanding of "communal authority" – often seen as an obstacle to the spread of the gospel in Japan. As an additional benefit for those of us in the global neo-Calvinist movement, Harefa provides us with a much-needed wisdom regarding how to bring Kuyper's thought to non-Eurocentric contexts.

Richard Mouw, PhD
President Emeritus and Senior Professor of Faith and Public Life,
Fuller Theological Seminary, California, USA

Challenged by the political situation in Japan and the anonymous role of Japanese Christians in politics, Surya Harefa proposes in this thorough study of Abraham Kuyper's ecclesiology to equip Christians in Japan to engage in politics as Christians. By comparing the Dutch situation in which Kuyper developed his ecclesiology and the present Japanese context dominated by Shinto civil religion, he discusses the preference of Japanese Christians for a strict separation of religion and state. Surya disagrees and argues convincingly for another strategy, based on Kuyper's ecclesiology: by distancing all religions from the state and treating them in an equal way, for the best of a free and flourishing Japanese society.

George Harinck, PhD
Director of the Neo-Calvinism Research Institute (NRI), Kampen
Professor of History, Free University in Amsterdam

Dr. Surya Harefa grew up in Indonesia and had experience studying theology and pastoring churches in Japan. He understands Japanese church history objectively and existentially. Christianity is a minority in Japan, and thus, political involvement is difficult and tends to be defensive. The achievement of this book is showing how Christianity in Japan can have a sound political contribution by applying Kuyper's ecclesiology.

Yamaguchi Yoichi
President and Professor of Japanese Church History,
Tokyo Christian University, Japan

Although Abraham Kuyper's ecclesiological perspective was forged in the context of nineteenth-century Dutch Reformed church politics, academic theology, and pastoral ministry, his insights continue to have important resonance. Harefa's work illustrates the dynamism in Kuyper's thought, applying it fruitfully in a seemingly unlikely but ultimately entirely appropriate context – contemporary Japan. Harefa's work is a salutary model of intercultural and constructive theological retrieval, as he carefully examines Kuyper's thought in its original setting, and with sensitivity and wisdom applies insights gained from this study to the challenges facing Japanese Christians today.

Jordan Ballor, PhD
Kuyper Conference Coordinator and Director of Research,
The Center for Religion, Culture & Democracy

This book by the Indonesian theologian living in Japan, Surya Harefa, fits in with a trend. Notwithstanding that it is surprising at the same time. There is currently worldwide attention on the originally Dutch neo-Calvinist tradition. Abraham Kuyper is the central thinker within that tradition. Non-European evangelicals, in particular, expect his thoughts to provide inspiration to interpret and stimulate their Christian public responsibility. Several studies have been published that link elements of Kuyper's theology to the context of a specific country. Harefa's study is part of that nascent tradition because he makes Kuyper's ecclesiology fertile for the Japanese context.

At the same time, Harefa's study surprises because it avoids two risks that easily arise. In the first place, he avoids a direct transplantation of Kuyper's ideas to Japan without sufficient contextual awareness. He shows insight into the character of Kuyper's activities and thoughts, which are strongly related to the Dutch context. He accurately describes that context. At the same time, he offers a well-informed and instructive analysis of the Japanese context. This strong contextual awareness enables him to draw lessons in a nuanced way from Kuyper's thinking that can be of value in the Japanese context.

Second, non-Western Christians interested in Kuyper often belong to a relatively large Christian minority or substantial minority in their own country. This often means that they mainly use Kuyper's thinking to increase the Christian impact on their societies. Then even the risk arises that they will use public and political power to enhance this Christian influence. That causes tension with the priority to the gospel message which first wants to conquer hearts. After all, this has also proven a risk in the Netherlands itself since the secularizing context of the nineteenth century. Because of the number of Christians, then a cultural-Christian bridge between church and society could become possible, especially in former Christian societies of the West but elsewhere too. In Japan, however, Christians form a tiny segment of the population, while the public religion of the country is outspokenly non-Christian. The more cultural-Christian approach of neo-Calvinism would not be appropriate there, nor would it work. Harefa knows how to use Kuyper to equip the Christian public calling in an outspoken minority situation that turns out to be sometimes difficult for or even downright mistrustful of Christianity.

In addition, Harefa's analysis presents another surprise. While other theologians who reflect on a minority situation often tend to fall back on the church as an institution, Harefa considers Kuyper's view of the church as an organism to be of value. This emphasis on the church as an organism is usually considered appropriate in contexts where Christianity still has social impact. Harefa, however, shows that the church in Japan is so small and divided institutionally that it would be difficult for it to act effectively publicly. The realization that there are also forms of Christian community that are not directly ecclesial increases the possibilities for this. Here a difference emerges between recent theories for a minority situation that have developed in a Western context that is still Christian, and the views of a theologian who already lives in such a minority context.

In addition to these substantive reasons, I heartily recommend Harefa's study for its carefulness and clarity. It offers an excellent introduction to Kuyper's thinking about church and society and is written with momentum and conviction. Not only in Japan but in all contexts, Christians who reflect on their public vocation and Christians who feel related to neo-Calvinism can learn a lot from it.

Ad de Bruijne, PhD
Professor of Ethics and Spirituality,
Theological University of Kampen/Utrecht, Netherlands

© 2023 Surya Harefa

Published 2023 by Langham Academic (Previously Langham Monographs)
An imprint of Langham Publishing
www.langhampublishing.org

Langham Publishing and its imprints are a ministry of Langham Partnership

Langham Partnership
PO Box 296, Carlisle, Cumbria, CA3 9WZ, UK
www.langham.org

ISBNs:
978-1-83973-652-0 Print
978-1-83973-888-3 ePub
978-1-83973-889-0 PDF

Surya Harefa has asserted his right under the Copyright, Designs and Patents Act, 1988 to be identified as the Author of this work.

All rights reserved. No part of this publication may be reproduced, stored in a retrieval system or transmitted, in any form or by any means, electronic, mechanical, photocopying, recording or otherwise, without the prior written permission of the publisher or the Copyright Licensing Agency.

Requests to reuse content from Langham Publishing are processed through PLSclear. Please visit www.plsclear.com to complete your request.

Scripture quotations are from The Holy Bible, English Standard Version® (ESV®), copyright © 2001 by Crossway, a publishing ministry of Good News Publishers. Used by permission. All rights reserved.

British Library Cataloguing-in-Publication Data
A catalogue record for this book is available from the British Library

ISBN: 978-1-83973-652-0

Cover & Book Design: projectluz.com

Langham Partnership actively supports theological dialogue and an author's right to publish but does not necessarily endorse the views and opinions set forth here or in works referenced within this publication, nor can we guarantee technical and grammatical correctness. Langham Partnership does not accept any responsibility or liability to persons or property as a consequence of the reading, use or interpretation of its published content.

Contents

Acknowledgments xi

Chapter 1 1
Introduction
    1.1 Japanese Christians' Political Engagement and Ecclesiology 1
    1.2 Ecclesiology and Abraham Kuyper 6
    1.3 Appropriating Kuyper's Ecclesiology into the Japanese Context ... 9
    1.4 Research Methodology 12

Chapter 2 17
Christian Responses to Sociopolitical Issues in Contemporary Japan
    2.1 Yasukuni Shrine 18
        2.1.1 The Issue 18
        2.1.2 The Responses of Japanese Christians 25
        2.1.3 Evaluation of Christian Responses 35
    2.2 Constitutional Amendment 37
        2.2.1 The Issue 38
        2.2.2 The Responses of Japanese Christians 40
        2.2.3 Evaluation of Christian Responses 52
    2.3 The Countermeasures to the 2011 Great Eastern
        Japan Disaster 55
        2.3.1 The Issue 56
        2.3.2 The Response of Japanese Christians 60
        2.3.3 Evaluation of Christian Responses 71
    Conclusion 73

Chapter 3 77
The Context of Japanese Christians' Political Engagement
    3.1 Early Modern Period (Sixteenth to Early Nineteenth Century) 77
        3.1.1 Tendency Toward a National Church 78
        3.1.2 Persecution by the Authorities 80
        3.1.3 Between Martyrdom and Apostasy – Japanese
        Christianity 1 84
    3.2 Imperial Period (1868–1945) 88
        3.2.1 Denominationalism 89
        3.2.2 Nationalism 92
        3.2.3 Responses to Nationalism – Japanese Christianity 2 ... 99

    3.3 Post-war Period (1945–present) 101
        3.3.1 Top-Down Changes 102
        3.3.2 Denominationalism 105
        3.3.3 New Religions 110
    Conclusion..113

Chapter 4 117
    Kuyper's Concept of the Church
    4.1 The Organism-Institution Distinction 118
        4.1.1 The Church as Organism..118
        4.1.2 The Church as Institution..121
        4.1.3 Political Engagement in the Organism-Institution
            Model 122
        4.1.4 Marginalization of the Church as Institution 128
    4.2 The Believers' Church 140
        4.2.1 The Pure Church 140
        4.2.2 The Army of God 146
        4.2.3 The Office of Believers 148
        4.2.4 Infant Baptism 150
    4.3 A Free Church..153
        4.3.1 Freedom from the State 154
        4.3.2 Free from Ecclesiastical Hierarchy 164
        4.3.3 The Political Engagement of the Free Church 166
        4.3.4 Some Tensions in Kuyper's Free Church Ecclesiology 168
    4.4 The Pluriformity of the Church................................169
        4.4.1 Diversity..170
        4.4.2 Unity 174
        4.4.3 The Political Aspect of Pluriformity 179
        4.4.4 The Debate on the Pluriformity of the Church 182
    Conclusion..185

Chapter 5 187
    The Context of Kuyper's Ecclesiology
    5.1 The Church Elections 188
        5.1.1 The Complex Relationship between the Church and
            the State 190
        5.1.2 Diverse Theological Strands................................194
    5.2 The School Struggle..204
        5.2.1 Political Liberalism..207
        5.2.2 Conservatism 208
        5.2.3 Anti-Revolutionary 210

    5.2.4 Mass Mobilization 211
   5.3 The Doleantie of 1886 215
    5.3.1 The Church and the Synod..217
    5.3.2 The Church and the Free University...................................220
    5.3.3 The Union of 1892..222
   Conclusion...228

Chapter 6 233
  The Possibilities of Kuyper's Ecclesiology for Japanese Evangelical Christians
   6.1 The Organism-Institution Distinction 234
   6.2 The Believers' Church 243
   6.3 A Free Church...248
   6.4 The Pluriformity of the Church..253
   Conclusion...258

Bibliography..263

Acknowledgments

I want to express my sincere gratitude to those who supported me in completing this dissertation. Foremost, I am truly thankful to my first supervisor, Prof. Ad de Bruijne, for providing critical feedback patiently and heartening encouragements generously. I am impressed not only with his high intelligence but also with his humble diligence in serving as preacher, translator for international students, usher, and coffee server at Eudokia church. Furthermore, I thank Prof. Inagaki Hisakazu, my second supervisor, for unsparingly sharing his sophisticated insights and works that deepened my understanding of the complex Japanese context.

I wish to express my gratefulness to all faculty members and staff of Theological University Kampen. Prof. Roel Kuiper and Drs. Jan de Jong had allowed me to work in a cozy study room that also enabled me to connect with other workmates in the attic: Lee Chungman, Jasper Bosman, Koos Taminga, Arco den Heijer, Seo Junghun, Kim Eunkyu, Lim Moses, Jeon Aaron, Kang Byunghoon, and Dr. Myriam Klinker. I greatly appreciate Drs. Jos Colijn, who always responds swiftly and prudently. Without his aid and support from other International office staff, Jolanda van Gelder (as well as Hans, her husband, who later also became TU's staff), and Klaas Vroom, I could not have managed my residency in the Netherlands with my family. The Neo-Calvinism Research Institute (NRI) monthly research group meeting has been beneficial to me to date with the recent development of neo-Calvinism. Dr. Dmytro Bintsarovskyi has saved me a lot of time by creating online a complete Kuyper's bibliography and archive. Many thanks to Prof. George Harinck and Dr. Marinus de Jong, who gave thought-provoking comments on feasible directions and methods for my research at the NRI expert meeting. I appreciate members of the Netherlands School for Advanced Studies in Theology and

Religion (NOSTER) who gave critical feedback to my presentations at the research seminar and the Spring Conference.

I also want to thank faculty members and affiliates of Tokyo Christian University (TCU). I am truly grateful to the late Rev. Obata Susumu and Rev. Shimokawa Tomoya, who have encouraged me to pursue doctoral study on various occasions. Prof. Yamaguchi Yōichi has been wonderfully supportive through all the process. Dr. Shinohara Motoaki arranged warm hospitality and provided me thoughtful insights when I was collecting resources at TCU. The late Prof. Kobayashi Takanori, Prof. Kurasawa Masanori, Prof. Fujiwara Atsuyoshi, Rev. Asaoka Masaru, Dr. Saitō Isomi, Rev. Aoki Yoshinori, and Rev. Yamamoto Masato allocated their time to have meetings that were heartening for me.

I am indebted to leaders and members of the Reformed Evangelical movement in Indonesia. Rev. Stephen Tong had made me interested in Reformed theology since my teenage years and then in Abraham Kuyper through his endeavors in the so-called cultural mandate field. I will not forget his challenge to keep the balance between evangelism, pastoral works, and theological study. I learned how to answer that challlenge in a realistic way from Rev. Benyamin Intan, PhD. He honored me with enormous support from the beginning of my study at the International Reformed Evangelical Seminary. I received encouragement from Rev. Billy Kristianto, PhD, Rev. Liem Kok Han, Rev. Antonius Un, PhD, Rev. Audy Santoso, Vic. Jack Kawira, and Vic. Tirza Rachmadi when they came to Kampen.

This doctoral study was possible because of personal donations from members of the Indonesian Reformed Evangelical Church in Pondok Indah as well as scholarships from TCU (Ueda Method), Hulp Buitenlandse Studenten, Greijdanus-Kruithof Fonds, Jagtspoel Fonds, and Stichting Afbouw Kampen. I am grateful to Langham Partnership, who offered not only scholarship but also annual consultation conference, retreat, and scholar care program. The visits of Liz and Malcom McGregor as well as Dr. Parush Parushev to Kampen were beneficial not only to me but also for my entire family. Elizabeth Hitchcock has provided outstanding administrative guidance. I thank Rev. Ayub Mbuilima, Rev. Yustinus Hia, Jemmy Widjaja, and Todo Napitupulu for their generous gift. Many churches in the Netherlands funded this research indirectly by inviting me to preach. Delivering sermons almost every week at different churches was a privilege that helped me connect my study to church life.

I appreciate Dr. Albert Gootjes, who proofread all chapters and suggested helpful comments. I thank Vic. Verawati Halim, who designed the book cover readily. Corina Guijt has allocated her time to provide Dutch language coaching so that I could read a work of Kuyper in Dutch. I wish to extend my gratitude to members of the Lapian Family, who treat my family as their own family. We thank Roel and Ria Buit, Willem and Eveline Visser, Wim and Martha Kooiker, Choi Changjun, Lee Jonghoon, and Kim Junggi for their warm friendship and support. My deep appreciation goes to Vic. Erianto Chai, who is always ready to pray and help in excellent ways.

Finally, I would like to express my special thanks to my family. Foremost, I am genuinely thankful to my beloved wife, Yuko, for her graceful support and encouragement. She has managed all the numerous tasks of daily life amazingly so that I can concentrate on working. Our beloved children, Jun and Yuki, have always been lovely and made my day. I am also thankful to my parents, who are now with the Lord, my parents- and brother-in-law, my brothers Cahya and Satrya, and their families.

CHAPTER 1

Introduction

1.1 Japanese Christians' Political Engagement and Ecclesiology

Contemporary Japanese Christians have difficulties in engaging with politics as Christians. They do have freedom of religion as guaranteed by the constitution and in the course of time have succeeded in exercising significant influence on Japanese society, including the field of politics.[1] Some Japanese Christians have even managed to become prime minister.[2] However, they seem to keep their faith a private matter and in their political engagement prioritize their identity as Japanese. One famous example is Ōhira Masayoshi (1910–80), who served as prime minister from 1978 to 1980. He never brought his identity as a Christian to the fore and even ignored a letter from the National Council of Churches in Japan (NCCJ) urging an end to the practice of cabinet visits to Ise Shrine and Yasukuni Shrine. In response, Ōhira defended his worship at the shrines, emphasizing that it was his duty

---

1. Mullins, "Christianity in Contemporary Japanese," 140–41.
2. Their names, denominational affiliation, and terms of office are as follows: Hara Takashi, Catholic, 1918–21; Takahashi Korekiyo, Protestant, 1921–22; Yoshida Shigeru, Catholic, 1946–47 and 1948–54; Katayama Tetsu, Protestant, 1947–48; Hatoyama Ichirō, Protestant, 1955–56; Ōhira Masayoshi, Protestant, 1978–80; Asō Tarō, Catholic, 2008–9; Hatoyama Yukio, Protestant, 2009–10. Yoshida had his family baptized, but delayed his own baptism until his deathbed. Cf. Oliai, "Japanese and Christianity," 200–201; Doak, "Introduction," 4, 28, note 41.

as a Japanese.³ In contrast, other Japanese Christians, particularly those who belong to evangelical circles, tend to avoid political engagement altogether.⁴

There are many interrelated factors hindering Japanese Christians in their political engagement. Aike Rots identifies one significant factor in the anti-Christian discourse that has long existed in Japan and developed over the course of several centuries.⁵ As a result, Christians in Japan find it difficult to integrate their seemingly contradictory identities as Japanese and Christians. Even apart from the long persecutions during the Tokugawa period (1603–1868) and the military oppression of Christians during the first half of the Shōwa period (1931–45), William Steele finds another factor in the theological biases of individual redemption and piety. He likewise draws attention to a persistent, one-sided interpretation of Barthian theology, emphasizing that the church's mission is not to change the world but to be obedient to the word of God.⁶ In the same vein, Shinohara Motoaki argues that the missionaries' unbalanced emphasis on individual salvation and the patriotic spirit of Japanese people had impeded Japanese Christians from developing a robust ecclesiological concept that could confront the state's attempt to subjugate the church during the pre-1945 period.⁷ In sum, the difficulties for Japanese Christians to engage in politics seems to relate to, if not originate from, their ambiguous ecclesiological concepts.

The ecclesiological problem is observable from other issues as well. Mark Mullins thus points to "a serious dropout rate or an aversion to organized religion" in Christian churches in Japan.⁸ Although a 2001 Gallup Poll reported that 4 percent of the population was Christian, church membership data of *Kirisutokyō Nenkan* for 2008 indicated that only 0.9 percent of the population belonged to a church. While the former used random sampling through the telephone survey method, the latter used questionnaires filled

---

3. Steele, "Christianity and Politics," 367. For a brief biography of Ōhira, see Rothacher, *Japanese Power Elite*, 87–94. For a thorough biography, see Satō, Kōyama, and Kumon, *Postwar Politician*.

4. Sherrill, "Christian Churches," 169; Shinohara, "Church as God's Missionary," 250–51; Fujiwara, "Theology of Culture," 243. Wipf and Stock published Fujiwara's dissertation as a book with the same title in 2012.

5. Rots, "Ambiguous Identities," 311.

6. Steele, "Christianity and Politics," 360–61.

7. Shinohara, "Church as God's Missionary," 176–77.

8. Mullins, "Christianity in Contemporary Japanese," 138.

out by the Japanese churches. The discrepancy in the results indicates the possible existence of a group of people who self-identify as Christians but do not belong to any institutional church. Matsunaga asserts that Japanese Christians lack "the nurturing and training of individual Christians into the Body of Christ."[9] Thomas Hastings observes that missionaries in Japan considered the mission schools more relevant to Japanese society and hoped that they could be used to evangelize many Japanese. As a result, some schools achieved a high level of public recognition, but missionaries were forced to concentrate more on education than evangelism. Moreover, between 1890 and 1945, the Japanese government exerted pressure on the mission schools to move them in a direction serving national policy, leading to a severe weakening in or even rejection of their evangelism commitment. Consequently, so Hastings observes, there is virtually no synergic relationship between Christian schools and churches in Japanese Protestant circles.[10]

As mentioned briefly in the previous paragraph, the number of Christians in Japan is small. As of 31 December 2018, the Agency of Cultural Affairs (ACA) reported that the population of Christians in Japan was 1,921,484.[11] This figure is equal to 1.51 percent of 127,094,745, the total population reported by the 2015 National Census.[12] However, since the ACA did not implement strict reporting procedures from the registered religious bodies, the way of calculating and defining religious body members are different depending on each religious body. As a result, the total reported religious population, without the atheist population, is 181,329,376 persons, which is 54 million more than the total population. Trying to get the more actual condition, the Japan Missions Research (JMR) of Tokyo Christian University combined and scrutinized the annual data from the Catholic Central Council, Christ Newspaper, and Christian Newspaper. It reported that the number of Christians in 2018 was 1,044,733, which is equivalent to 0.83 percent of

---

9. Matsunaga, "Theological Education in Japan," 299. Matsunaga also pointed to the results of a study in one church, possibly the Ushigome Haraikatamachi Church of UCCJ Shinjuku, Tokyo, showing that the average length of membership in this church is only 2.8 years. Cf. http://www.revival.co.jp/rj/legwork-diary/2009/10/post-19.php, accessed 20 September 2017. See also Hastings, "Japan's Protestant Schools," 102; Mullins, "Christianity in Contemporary Japanese," 138.

10. Hastings, 102–5, 112–13, 116–17.

11. Bunka-chō [Agency for Cultural Affairs], *Shūkyō Nenkan Reiwa*, 35.

12. Statistics Bureau, Ministry of Internal Affairs and Communications, *Final Report*, 2.

the total population.¹³ The details are as follows: Catholic: 440,832 (0.35% of total population); Eastern Orthodox: 9,816 (0.01%); and Protestant: 594,085 (0.47%). The 2018 JMR Investigation Report also mentioned that as of 2018, there were 8,003 Protestant churches with 274,360 attendants in Sunday service. Those figures mean that the average number of church members in one Protestant church is 74.23 and the average number of Sunday service attendance is 34.23.

Evaluating this small number of Christians in Japan, Furuya Yasuo has suggested that Christianity will be able to grow in Japan by improvements in the church's condition. In his analysis, the churches in Japan: (1) lack an element of joy in their worship; (2) have become temporary places of study like schools; and (3) are trapped in dogmatism and fail to reflect on society.¹⁴ Furuya predicts that his church group, the United Church of Christ in Japan (UCCJ) along with other mainline churches will continue declining unless they learn to do evangelization like the evangelicals.¹⁵

In Japan, the term "mainline" or "ecumenical" churches refers to the churches belonging to the NCCJ, which is affiliated with the World Council of Churches.¹⁶ Generally, these churches welcome the influence of liberal or Barthian theology. In contrast, the "evangelical" churches maintain the belief that the Bible is written entirely by the inspiration of God and is the word of God without error.¹⁷ Many evangelicals join the Japan Evangelical Association (JEA), which has an affiliation with the World Evangelical Alliance.¹⁸ In the global context, the evangelicals have grown in numbers and have been

---

13. Yamaguchi and Shibata, *JMR Chōsa Repo-to*, 8, 15. On the one hand, they removed Christian groups that are difficult to be considered as Christians; on the other hand, they added the number of Christians that have not been recorded based on the estimation of previous years' data.

14. Furuya, "Naze Nihon ni Kirisutokyō," 167–71.

15. Furuya, "Nihon no Kyōkai," 33.

16. Some of the NCCJ's members are the UCCJ, the Anglican Church of Japan, the Japan Evangelical Lutheran Church, the Japan Baptist Convention, and the Korean Christian Church in Japan.

17. Nakamura, *Nihon ni Okeru Fukuin-ha*, 10; Izuta and Kim, *Nihon no Fukuin-ha*, 43; Cf. McGrath, *Evangelicalism*, 55–85.

18. The Presbyterian Church in Japan, the Japan Mennonite Brethren Conference, the Salvation Army, the Evangelical Free Church of Japan, the Japan Alliance Christ Church, the Japan Holiness Church, and the Japan Assemblies of God are some of the members of JEA.

predicted to shape the future of global Christianity.[19] Similarly, evangelicals in Japan also increase in number and activities.[20] Nevertheless, research on Japanese evangelical Christians is still rare.[21]

Although evangelical churches may solve the first and second problems analyzed by Furuya, the tendency to avoid political engagements remains problematic. As an evangelical Christian working in Japan, but originally from Indonesia and influenced by neo-Calvinism, I view the ecclesiological problems of Japanese evangelical Christians as precisely that which neo-Calvinism attempts to solve. According to the neo-Calvinist approach, since the beginning, God created and delighted in not only human beings, but also the world as a whole. Moreover, having created humankind in his image, God gives human beings the responsibility to be his representatives in developing this world to his glory.[22] Rather than abandoning this noble task after the fall, God repeated it in many forms. Sinful humanity could still develop this world, although it no longer directed this work to the glory of God.[23] The cross and resurrection of Jesus Christ extend not just to Christians, but to the whole creation. God's redemption enables Christians to head the development of the world in the right direction, namely for the glory of God.[24] At the second coming of Christ, some of these accomplished developments will somehow be brought into the New Jerusalem.[25] Thus, according to the neo-Calvinism understanding, Christians should be active not only in church life, but also actively engage as Christians in developing all aspects of life, including politics.

Would this neo-Calvinist understanding be of use for addressing the ecclesiological problem facing Japanese Christians? As I suggested earlier, evangelical Christians in Japan need to find concepts of the church that will

---

19. McGrath, Future of Christianity, 99; McGrath, Evangelicalism, 55–85.

20. Tsuchiya, "Nihon ni okeru Kirisutokyō," 84–87; Mullins, "Christianity in Contemporary Japanese," 148.

21. Nakamura, *Nihon ni Okeru Fukuin-ha*, 9; Tsuchiya, "Nihon ni okeru Kirisutokyō," 84–87; Mullins, "Christianity in Contemporary Japanese," 148.

22. Wolters, *Creation Regained*, 36.

23. Marshall, *Thine Is the Kingdom*, 23, 27; Wolters, *Creation Regained*, 47, 49; Plantinga, *Engaging God's World*, 53; Goheen and Bartholomew, *Living at the Crossroads*, 50.

24. Plantinga, 106–7, 119–20; Wolters, 60, 69; Colson and Pearcey, *How Now Shall We?*, 296; Walsh and Middleton, *Transforming Vision*, 86; Goheen and Bartholomew, 6.

25. Marshall, *Thine Is the Kingdom*, 34; Wolters, 41; Plantinga, 137–38; Mouw, *When the Kings Come*, 20, 24–25, 29–30, 32, 35, 37.

help them deal not only with their Japanese identity and their traumatic history with the state, but also with the institution of the church and with such Christian organizations as the Christian school. I will therefore argue that Japanese Christians can indeed draw useful insights from the ecclesiological concepts of the Dutch neo-Calvinist theologian Abraham Kuyper.

1.2 Ecclesiology and Abraham Kuyper

Ecclesiology was a lifelong issue for Abraham Kuyper (1837–1920). At the beginning of his study of theology at Leiden University, Kuyper wrote a thesis on papal power, in which he also discussed the position of the church in society and its relation to the state.[26] Later on, he participated in a prestigious national essay competition on the ecclesiology of John a Lasco and John Calvin.[27] In September 1862, Kuyper earned a doctorate from Leiden University with a revision of his prize-winning essay.[28] Having "profound interest in the Church question," Kuyper determined to devote his life to fighting the absence of a solid concept of the church and restoring the church to its position as the mother of believers.[29] After several years of pastoral ministry, Kuyper also became active as a journalist, educator, and politician, even serving as prime minister of the Netherlands between 1901 and 1905. Although Kuyper's career left him a legacy particularly in terms of his political engagement, he had a passion for ecclesial matters. As John Wood puts it,

> Kuyper's ecclesiology . . . was a lifelong theological concern of his and certainly an earlier one than his much discussed public theology. Ecclesiology bookended his professional career as a

---

26. Kuyper submitted his 150-page thesis entitled "The Development of Papal Power under Nicholas I" on 2 January 1859. Cf. Bruijn, *Abraham Kuyper*, 24; Vree and Zwaan, *Kuyper's Commentatio*, 22.

27. For this national student research competition launched by Groningen University's faculty of theology, Kuyper submitted an essay of 320 pages in April 1860. It was the only entry, but was deemed deserving of the gold medal. Bratt, *Abraham Kuyper*, 36.

28. Kuyper revised the first part of his essay and submitted it as his doctoral dissertation. Vree and Zwaan, *Kuyper's Commentatio*, 36.

29. Kuyper, "Confidentially [1873]," 46, 61: "The lack of a solid church concept had become, in spite of myself, the 'Carthago delenda' of my personality. And so, taking my own thirst as a measure of the inner needs of others, and longing with all my heart that they might also receive that supreme, calm commitment: for my own sake and for others', the restoration of 'a church that could be our Mother' had to become the goal of my life."

theologian, from his master's thesis and doctoral dissertation to his final theological study, "Concerning the Church," which ran sixty-eight chapters and which was only brought to an end by his death.[30]

In other words, Kuyper never abandoned his early interest and life goal. Rather, he developed a coherent ecclesiology that could encourage Christians to involve themselves actively in society and culture, including politics.

Following the recent revival of Kuyperian studies in North America, scholars started translation projects of his works, including the writings related to ecclesiology. For example, James Bratt included "Confidentially," "Conservatism and Orthodoxy: False and True Preservation," and "Uniformity: The Curse of Modern Life" in his *Abraham Kuyper: A Centennial Reader* (1998).[31] In 2013, the Abraham Kuyper Translation Society published *Rooted and Grounded*, a translation of Kuyper's work discussing the nature of the church and its position in the public sphere.[32] This translation anticipated the publication of a more extensive collection of ecclesiological writings, which appeared in November 2016.[33]

Prior to the revival of interest in Kuyper, scholarship on his ecclesiology had been by and large conducted in the Dutch context. The only comprehensive study of Kuyper's ecclesiology to appear in English was an article by Henry Zwaanstra published in 1974, which drew heavily on the older Dutch work of Petrus A. van Leeuwen.[34] Zwaanstra argued that ecclesiology forms the core of Kuyper's theology, and the church as organism the heart of his doctrine of the church.[35] Several decades later, however, English-language studies of Kuyper's ecclesiology began to emerge one after another. In 1998, Peter Heslam provided the background of Kuyper's ecclesiological formulas and described Kuyper's expectations from those formulas by way of a thorough analysis of the *Lectures on Calvinism*. According to Heslam, Kuyper's ecclesiology was designed "both to reserve a large place for his own social and

---

30. Wood, *Going Dutch*, 3; Cf. Bratt, *Abraham Kuyper*, 172, 187.
31. Bratt, *Kuyper: A Centennial Reader*.
32. Kuyper, *Rooted and Grounded*.
33. Kuyper, *On The Church*; Cf. Foreword by John H. Wood Jr., in Kuyper, *Rooted and Grounded*, xi.
34. Van Leeuwen, *Het Kerkbegrip*.
35. Zwaanstra, "Kuyper's Conception of the Church," 150.

cultural program and to accredit this program with ecclesiastical sanction" and "to oppose the idea of a state church."[36] In 2001, John Bolt argued for the appropriateness and feasibility of Kuyper's public theology for American evangelicals, devoting several pages to an elaboration of Kuyper's distinction between the church as organism and the church as institution.[37] With this model, Bolt suggested, American evangelicals can keep the church "true to her own spiritual purpose" and can positively "influence their society."[38] In 2005, Jasper Vree and Johan Zwaan published Kuyper's Latin essay on the ecclesiology of Calvin and a Lasco, together with historical and philological introductions in English.[39] Inspired by Kuyper's works, Richard Mouw has written several articles and books on his thought. He insists on the significance of Kuyper's concepts for this twenty-first century, while also suggesting a "compensatory strategy" for updating Kuyper's views on the church.[40]

A more thorough investigation of Kuyper's ecclesiology was undertaken by John Wood, who, working from a historical perspective, concluded that "Kuyper's public theology was a public theology designed to meet the needs of his free church [concept]."[41] He commends Kuyper as an example teaching us that "ecclesiology ought to be a first principle of public theology."[42] Similarly, in his comprehensive, chronological, and thematic biography of Kuyper, James Bratt acknowledges that Kuyper's "ecclesiology had central importance for Kuyper in its own right" and "marked the crossroads where his twin passions of divine sovereignty and social formation intersected."[43] However, Bratt also views Kuyper's ecclesiology as proposals to serve "the larger purposes," such as "the themes of cosmic renewal and personal salvation," "the kingship of Christ," and the "campaign against theological liberalism."[44]

Interestingly, in a 2014 article, Ad de Bruijne expressed his disagreement with certain common interpretations that consider Kuyper to have a

---

36. Heslam, *Creating a Christian Worldview*, 132–35.
37. Bolt, *Free Church*, 427–28.
38. Bolt, 427, 431.
39. Vree and Zwaan, Kuyper's Commentatio.
40. Mouw, "Culture, Church," 56–59; Mouw, *Abraham Kuyper*, 122.
41. Wood, *Going Dutch*, 174.
42. Wood, 175.
43. Bratt, *Abraham Kuyper*, 172.
44. Bratt, 173.

preference for the church as organism and to privatize the church institute.[45] He argues that although Kuyper seemed to propose that the church as institution should keep its distance from the public domain, ever since his conversion to Calvinism he believed that the church as organism could not exist without the institute.[46] While emphasizing that Kuyper himself had never intended to apply the so-called Kuyperian approach to all contexts, de Bruijne does believe that "Kuyper's ecclesiology could be helpful in finding more balance" for the forms of the church in today's postmodern climate.[47] De Bruijne's challenge to the conventional interpretation indicates that there is a significant task for future scholarship on Kuyper's ecclesiology, mainly to offer a more precise definition of the church's role in political engagement. The relevance of this task is also confirmed by the relatively small number of existing studies on Kuyper's ecclesiology.

1.3 Appropriating Kuyper's Ecclesiology into the Japanese Context

We have now seen that research on Kuyper's ecclesiology is significant both for developing the context of renewed scholarly attention for Kuyper and for considering its possibilities in equipping Japanese Christians in their political engagement as Christians.[48] However, some objections could be raised, resulting from the character of Kuyper's ecclesiology as a late nineteenth-century Dutch ecclesiology, which at first sight does not seem a natural fit for the needs of contemporary Japanese Christians. Indeed, contextual theology has shown that all theology, including Western theology, is contextually shaped.[49]

---

45. Bruijne, "'Colony of Heaven,'" 456, 460–64.

46. Bruijne, "Not without the Church," 76–91. See also Bruijne, "'Colony of Heaven,'" 445–90. For a detailed treatment of this discussion, see section 4.1.

47. Bruijne, "'Colony of Heaven,'" 471–72.

48. Cf. Wood, *Going Dutch*, 174–75. Wood argues that public theology depends on ecclesiology. Kuyper's public theology was a theology designed to meet the needs of his Free Church concept. He also argues for the reverse relationship, with public theology implying an ecclesiology. While contemporary public theology tends to be disconnected from the concrete Christian community, "Kuyper's example teaches that ecclesiology ought to be a first principle of public theology." See also Bruijne, "Not without the Church," 84, who argues that Kuyper's ecclesiology has implications for the public character of theology.

49. Cf. Bosch, *Transforming Mission*, 448–49; Bevans, *Models of Contextual Theology*, 1–4; Toren, "Can We See?," 94–95.

Kuyper's ecclesiology is no exception; it was a product to satisfy the needs of its particular time and region, while Japan's contemporary context differs widely from Kuyper's Dutch context. Moreover, recommending Kuyper's ecclesiology for Japanese Christians would run the risk of repeating the old mistakes of imposing Western theology onto non-Western worlds.

This objection can, however, be relativized and even turned into positive expectations regarding the value of Kuyper's ecclesiology. As Benno van den Toren puts it, the approach of intercultural theology enables a "conversation between different contextual theologies."[50] This insight means that Christians can benefit from Christians of different cultures and ages. Andrew Walls emphatically writes: "We need each other's vision to correct, enlarge and focus our own; only together we are complete in Christ."[51] The precondition for such an endeavor would be to develop and display sufficient contextual awareness and sensitivity. In doing so, we do well to use the method of "critical contextualization" suggested by Paul Hiebert.[52] Therefore, by critically investigating both the Japanese context and Kuyper's ecclesiology and its context, we can minimize the danger of imposing improper elements into one context and maximize the benefit of appropriating Kuyper's ecclesiology.

Several attempts have already been made to utilize elements from Kuyper's principles in different places. American evangelicals, for example, seem to take encouragement for their political and cultural engagement from Kuyper's life and works.[53] Timothy Keller and Jim Belcher have developed church practices that relate to Kuyper's ecclesiology.[54] In Canada, the Christian Reformed Church in North America has established hundreds of churches, as well as

---

50. Toren, "Intercultural Theology," 124. He admits that intercultural theology is a relatively new discipline and may refer to several different approaches.

51. Walls, "Ephesian Movement," 79. Cf. Bevans, *Models of Contextual Theology*, 14–15, who suggests that a person of another culture "can be more aware of a culture's weak, negative, or inconsistent aspects. . . . [T]he stranger can do a great service to the local culture and the local church."

52. Hiebert, *Anthropological Insights for Missionaries*, 183–92. Initially, critical contextualization was a proposal for missionaries in the mission field. It means one should neither reject nor accept old beliefs and customs without examination. These should rather be studied with regard to the meaning and place they have within their cultural setting and then evaluated in the light of biblical norms. Hiebert argues that his method can be used to deal not only with old beliefs and customs but also with new ones.

53. Bolt, *Free Church*, 127–29, 409.

54. Keller, *Center Church*, 46, 243, 297; Belcher, *Deep Church*, 191.

Christian schools, colleges, universities, labor associations, political parties, relief, and development organizations.[55] In Indonesia, Stephen Tong often refers to Kuyper in expounding his cultural mandate vision. Like Kuyper, he established not only a church and a seminary, but also Christian schools, a research center for religion and society, a Western and Eastern fine art museum, and a concert hall.[56] In South Korea, several of Kuyper's concepts, including his ecclesiology, seem to be have been fruitful fodder for the reflection of Korean Christians.[57]

In Japan, the earliest reference to Kuyper can be attributed to Takakura Tokutarō (1885–1934), a pastor and theologian of the Japan Christ Church.[58] In a 1923 work, he drew attention to Kuyper's *Lectures on Calvinism* as a proper analysis of the relation between Christianity and culture.[59] Takakura most likely read Kuyper's work during his study of theology in the UK (1921–24), at the University of Edinburgh and the University of Oxford. The first Japanese translation of Kuyper's *Lectures on Calvinism* was published in 1932. Founders of the Reformed Church in Japan (RCJ) adopted Kuyper's worldview as the first assertion of its 1946 Founding Declaration. They believed that this theistic worldview represented the only solid foundation for the establishment of a new Japan after its ruin during the Second World War.[60] Theologians of the RCJ established the Japan Calvinist Association (JCA) as a cultural organization to develop Christian activity.[61] Nevertheless, the interest in Kuyper remains limited to this small RCJ and JCA circle.[62]

---

55. Wagenman, "Kuyper and the Church," 126. Wagenman firmly believes that Kuyper's thought has helped the church in the twentieth century to "recover its mission to proclaim and embody the gospel in every aspect of life and in all institutions of culture, not only those directly ecclesial."

56. Subeno, *70 Years of Blessing*, 9–10; Cf. Lillback, "Interview of Dr. Stephen Tong," 292, 299.

57. Son, "Relevance of Sphere Sovereignty," 179–89; Chung, "Ecclesiology and Social Ethics," 168–69.

58. Inagaki, "Yakusha no Atogaki," 302.

59. Takakura, *Takakura Tokutarō Chosaku-shū*, 232.

60. Cf. Rekishi Shiryō Hensan Iinkai, *Nihon Kirisuto Kaikakuha*, 164. For the complete contents of the Founding Declaration, see http://www.rcj-net.org/resources/declaration/foundation.htm.

61. Ichikawa, "21 Seiki o Mukaeta," 414.

62. Inagaki, "Yakusha no Atogaki," 302.

One attempt to introduce Kuyper's principles to evangelical circles has been undertaken by Inagaki Hisakazu (b.1947), a professor of Christian Philosophy at Tokyo Christian University (TCU).[63] He did so by translating Peter Heslam's *Creating Christian Worldview* and Richard Mouw's *Abraham Kuyper: A Short and Personal Introduction* into Japanese.[64] As we will see in chapters 2 and 6, Inagaki also utilizes Kuyper's principles to seek solutions to several political problems in Japan and has attempted to introduce them also beyond evangelical Christian circles.[65] Even though Inagaki does also note the importance of the Kuyperian free church concept and the church as organism and institution distinction, his emphasis has been on Kuyper's concepts of common grace and sphere sovereignty for developing a public philosophy.[66] As a result, research is still needed, focusing more on the possibilities of Kuyper's ecclesiology for Japanese Christians.

1.4 Research Methodology

The main research question of the dissertation is: *How could Kuyper's concept of the church equip Japanese Christians in their political engagement as Christians?* To address this question, I will examine (1) the context of Japanese Christians and (2) the concept of Kuyper's ecclesiology. The first part will be investigated through the following subquestions: What kind of political issues do contemporary Japanese Christians face? How have Japanese Christians engaged these issues? What were their underlying ecclesiological concepts? How did the historical context of Japanese Christians influence their concept of ecclesiology? The subquestions for the second part are as follows: What are the elements of Kuyper's ecclesiology, and how should the church engage with political issues? What are the surrounding contexts of Kuyper's ecclesiology? The answers to these subquestions will yield material for addressing the main research question.

---

63. It is worth noting that although Inagaki is a member of the Tokyo Onchō Church of the RCJ as well as the JCA, he is neither a pastor of the RCJ nor a professor at the RCJ seminary (Kobe Reformed Theological Seminary).

64. Heslam, *Kindai Shugi to Kirisutokyō*; Mouw, *Aburahamu Kaipa- Nyūmon*.

65. Inagaki, "Kokumin-teki Fukushi to Heiwa," 7.

66. Inagaki, "Kyōkai no Jichi," 320–40.

To address the above research questions, this dissertation assumes the aforementioned notion of intercultural theology, according to which Christians can derive benefit from Christians of different cultures and ages by critically investigating both contexts. I also draw on the presuppositions of the synthetic model of contextualization, which Bevan explains as follows: (1) every culture or context has elements that are unique to it and elements that are held in common with other cultures or contexts; (2) most features of a culture are ambivalent: they can be good or bad, depending on how they are used and developed; (3) Christians are called to perfect their context; and (4) contextualization should start with the local culture, but also needs the presence of experts from outside.[67]

In my investigation, I do not consider Kuyper's ecclesiology as a set of timeless and boundless principles, but the product of a particular age and place. This makes an investigation of its surrounding context indispensable. The context of contemporary Japanese Christians and of Kuyper's time will be investigated by using a sympathetic, but critical historical approach. By comparing the issues facing Kuyper and Japanese Christians and how they dealt or deal with those issues, one can find essential similarities and differences between the two contexts and the ecclesiological concepts that are at work.[68] In analyzing the possibilities offered by Kuyper's concepts for Japanese Christians, I will also offer critical remarks on Kuyper's ecclesiology, thus showing its limitations and the need for adaptation. Nonetheless, given the purpose of this dissertation, more attention will be devoted to showing how Kuyper's ecclesiology can be used to address the continuing shortcomings in Japanese ecclesiological understandings.

A survey of Japanese contexts will investigate literature on Japanese Christians available in Japanese and English. This study will focus on several political issues in contemporary Japan and how the historical incidents shaped the contemporary characteristics of Japanese evangelical Christians' political engagement. Japanese names are given in Japanese order; family

---

67. Bevans, *Models of Contextual Theology*, 83–85. He elaborates five models of contextualization that are being used today: (1) translation model; (2) anthropological model; (3) praxis model; (4) synthetic model; and (5) transcendental model. The nature of this dissertation, which uses an outsider's concept while also respecting the inner context, means that it uses Bevans's fourth model.

68. Cf. Haight, "Comparative Ecclesiology," 393.

name precedes first name. The citations of and bibliography for Japanese literature follow this same order. However, for English literature written by a Japanese, the citations and bibliography are given in the order used for Western authors. Macrons are used for Japanese names and terms, with the exception of well-known names and places like Tokyo, Osaka, and Kobe.

For the study of Kuyper's ecclesiology and its context, I will investigate his ecclesiological works and the related secondary sources. I will mainly deal with the literature available in English, as Dutch scholarship was not accessible for me. Nonetheless, as noted in section 1.2, the recent revival of interest in Kuyper has yielded a significant number of secondary sources in English as well as translations of a reputable academic standard. In particular, the conscious selection of all of Kuyper's major works, together with some smaller publications, for English translation was intended to offer a credible representation of Kuyper's thought, including his ecclesiology. Since this study is not intended as a historical-theological engagement with existing Kuyper interpretations, but has the practical aim of appropriating Kuyper's ecclesiological concepts for the Japanese context, the potential disadvantages following from the absence of Dutch-language literature in this study are not insurmountable.

This dissertation is comprised of six chapters. The present chapter has introduced the background of this study, the research questions, and the methodology, and will conclude with a description of each chapter's contents.

In chapter 2, I will examine several political issues in contemporary Japan, focusing on the Yasukuni Shrine, constitutional amendment, and response to the 2011 Great Disaster. These issues are considerably long term, nationwide, and have the potency to affect religious life. With such characteristics, one can safely expect Japanese Christians to have known and responded to those issues. Thus, we can have enough resources to analyze how evangelicals in Japan react to those problems. Furthermore, as we will see in chapter 2, these three issues represent well the essence of other political issues in Japan, such as the Hinomaru flag and Kimigayo anthem, National Foundation Day, Regnal Year, New Emperor's Food-offering Ritual, emergency law, and collective self-defense right. After surveying the core of each issue and Japanese Christians' responses, especially the evangelicals, this chapter will evaluate them from an ecclesiological perspective. The next chapter investigates the context of Japanese Christians. Focusing on the nature of the relation between the church and the state in each period of Japanese Christian history, I will analyze several characteristics of Japanese Christians that shaped their political engagement as detailed in chapter 2.

In chapter 4, I will analyze Kuyper's concept of the church. Since Kuyper suggested several ecclesiological principles in a variety of separate works, this chapter attempts to offer a systematic elaboration of his distinction of the church as organism and institution, as well as his notions of the believers' church, the free church, and the pluriformity of the church. The discussion will elaborate the relationship of each suggestion with the role of the church in political engagement as well as corresponding debates on each of Kuyper's ecclesiological proposals.

Chapter 5 investigates the surrounding contexts of Kuyper's ecclesiology. By focusing on several crucial issues for which Kuyper fought, it will shed light on the historical contexts of his ecclesiology. It will provide materials for analyzing the similarities and differences between the political issues in Japan and the Netherlands, as well as the response of Christians in Japan and in Kuyper's time.

In chapter 6, I will construct the possibilities offered by the appropriation of Kuyper's concept of the church into the Japanese context. I will argue for parts of Kuyper's ecclesiology that can and should be appropriated for equipping Japanese Christians, particularly with regard to their political engagement. This final chapter will end with several conclusions and suggestions for further research.

To sum up, this doctoral thesis has a twofold aim. First, it intends to understand the complex ecclesiological problem of Japanese evangelical Christians in their political engagement. Second, it endeavors to explore Kuyper's vision for the church's role in political engagement. My sincere hope is that this study may contribute to the development of research on Kuyper's ecclesiology, and thus provide initial stimuli for equipping Japanese Christians in their political engagement as Christians.

CHAPTER 2

Christian Responses to Sociopolitical Issues in Contemporary Japan

Sociopolitical problems affect the lives of people, including their religious life, in many ways. Some issues may be advantageous for Christians, others harmful to the Christian life. It is only natural to assume that Japanese Christians would respond to issues that are considerably long term, nation-wide, and have the potency to affect religious life. To that end, this second chapter will discuss three recent contemporary issuess: the worship at the Yasukuni Shrine, the question of constitutional amendment, and the government responses to the 2011 Great Disaster. Since these issues are still ongoing, I have decided to limit my research to the developments up to the end of 2017, unless otherwise noted. After describing the issues, I will examine how Japanese Christians responded to them and conclude with ecclesiological evaluations of their engagements. Although my focus will be on the evangelicals who have published at least one work with the major evangelical publisher Inochi no Kotobasha,[1] I will also describe several non-evangelical responses in order to bring the position of these evangelical Christians into greater relief.

---

1. Since there are numerous evangelical denominations in Japan, the selection of figures who have published with this publisher ensures that they have attained fairly broad recognition in Japanese evangelical circles.

2.1 Yasukuni Shrine

After Abe Shinzō's official worship visit to the Yasukuni Shrine on 26 December 2013,[2] citizen groups in Osaka and Tokyo brought appeals against their premier before the corresponding district courts. Prior to that, the official worship of Koizumi Jun'ichirō in 2001–6 had likewise earned him criticism and led to protest demonstrations. After citizen groups in Fukuoka, Matsuyama, and Osaka sued the prime minister at their district courts, similar citizen groups in Tokyo and Chiba appealed to their respective district courts as well. Neighboring countries, particularly China and South Korea, also protested the premier's worship visit.[3] John Breen has rightly noted that the issue is "a problem of daunting complexity."[4] As we will see, it involves several interconnected aspects, including the constitution, historical perception, war criminals, commemoration, and war responsibility.

2.1.1 The Issue

Located in the center of Tokyo, the shrine was established on 28 June 1869 as Tokyo Shōkonsha, a shrine to memorialize the spirits of fallen soldiers who took the side of the emperor during the Boshin War.[5] Ten years later, the government renamed it the Yasukuni Shrine and designated it as a Special Government Shrine.[6] The rituals in this shrine represented an adoption of the custom of memorializing the war deads as conducted by the feudal rulers in Chōshū regions[7] into a Shinto-style and emperor-centered ritual.[8] From the beginning, the Yasukuni Shrine therefore had a unique position connecting the Shinto religion, the emperor, and the military.[9]

---

2. As of May 2020, the 2013 visit is the most recent official visit by a prime minister.

3. Protests had come from China since the prime minister's worship visit of Nakasone Yasuhiro in 1985. Cf. Breen, "Voices of Rage," 285–86; Steele, "Christianity and Politics," 366.

4. Breen, 278.

5. The Boshin War was a civil war lasting from 1868 to 1869 between the forces of the Tokugawa shogunate and the supporters of the imperial camp. With the victory of the latter, the war ended the Tokugawa period and ushered in the Meiji government.

6. The term "Yasukuni" literally means "pacifying the nation." John Breen prefers the translation "land of peace." Breen, "'Nation's Shrine,'" 137.

7. The present-day Yamaguchi Prefecture, located at the western end of Honshū island.

8. Takenaka, "Mobilizing Death in Imperial Japan," 5–8.

9. The building had Shinto attributes, and it was Shinto priests who conducted the first *shōkon* (summoning the spirits of the dead) ritual. At the same time, it was also decorated with the imperial sixteen petal chrysanthemum crest, and the emperor dispatched an imperial

Despite the use of Shinto sanctuaries and priests, and the adoption of Shinto worship style, the government insisted on the *Kokka Shinto* (State Shinto) as national ideology and on the Yasukuni Shrine as a non-religious national facility. The officials held forth enshrinement at this facility as the highest honor a Japanese could obtain. By spreading this belief, they managed to mobilize Japanese people to sacrifice their lives for the country. As a result, the vast majority of souls enshrined in Yasukuni are the war dead soldiers from the Pacific War (1941–45).[10]

After Japan surrendered to the Allied forces in 1945, General MacArthur, the Supreme Commander for the Allied Powers (SCAP) in Japan, ordered the disestablishment of the State Shinto with the so-called Shinto directives on 15 December 1945. This order diminished the special position of the Yasukuni Shrine to that of a mere religious corporation in 1946. However, once the Allied occupation government left Japan in 1952, many right-wing conservative[11] politicians and war-bereaved families attempted to revive the special status of the shrine. Due to protest movements, however, these efforts have to date not proved successful.

---

messenger to pay tribute at the shrine one day after the first ritual. The imperial princes regularly graced the Great Spring and Autumn rituals. The idea for and selection of the location came from the Army ministry, which together with the Navy ministry had the right to appoint the priests for the shrine and to organize the ritual performances as co-celebrants. For a detailed description of the Tokyo Shōkonsha, see Takenaka, 1–3; Breen, "'Nation's Shrine,'" 140; Breen, "Voices of Rage," 287.

10. The Yasukuni Shrine enshrined the spirits of the Japanese soldiers who had fallen in war since Japan's conflicts with Taiwan in the 1870s, but does not enshrine members of Japan's post-war Self Defence Forces (SDF). SDF's members, however, are enshrined at prefectural *Gokoku Jinja* (state protecting shrines) that was established in the Meiji period. Breen, 280, 300, note 7.

11. While "conservative" means having a desire to resist to, or at least a suspicion of, change, "progressive" alludes to accepting new values, usually with the values advocated by liberalism such as individualism, rationalism, freedom, justice, and toleration. Subsequently, "right-wing" refers to a political position that favors ideas such as authority, hierarchy, order, duty, tradition, reaction, and nationalism, whereas left-wingers prefer notions such as freedom, equality, fraternity, rights, progress, reform, and internationalism. Cf. Heywood, *Key Concepts in Politics*, 36, 119. In the Japanese context, as we will see in this chapter, right-wing conservatives would like to preserve or revive the nationalistic values developed during the imperial period. The progressives would like to maintain or develop more democratic values introduced after the defeat of Japan in 1945.

2.1.1.1 Constitution

One of the reasons motivating protests against official visits as well as the movement to renationalize the Yasukuni Shrine concerns the constitution. Article 20 reads as follows:

> (1) Freedom of religion is guaranteed to all. No religious organization shall receive any privileges from the State, nor exercise any political authority.
>
> (2) No person shall be compelled to take part in any religious act, celebration, rite or practice.
>
> (3) The State and its organs shall refrain from religious education or any other religious activity.

Furthermore, Article 89 stipulates:

> No public money or other property shall be expended or appropriated for the use, benefit or maintenance of any religious institution or association, or for any charitable, educational or benevolent enterprises not under the control of public authority.

For those who oppose the nationalization of Yasukuni, the prime ministerial official visit represents a way to smooth the path for renationalization. Renationalizing the shrine implies the use of public money for the Yasukuni Shrine and the revival of the obligation to worship there as in the imperial period. Hence, the movement is a violation of both the principle of religious freedom and the separation of state and religion as prescribed by Articles 20 and 89.

On the other hand, the proponents of Yasukuni attempt to interpret Article 20 as guaranteeing the prime minister's right to worship at a shrine. They also argue that worshiping at shrines is a non-religious practice of Japanese custom. In addition, because Yasukuni enshrines the war dead soldiers who fought for their country, it has been said that prime ministers should pay respect to their souls at Yasukuni. Accordingly, proponents insist on special treatment for the Yasukuni Shrine.

On the occasion of Abe's worship visit mentioned at the beginning of section 2.1, the district and high courts, in both Osaka and Tokyo, ruled against the citizen groups and avoided giving a verdict of unconstitutionality on prime ministerial worship visits.¹² Similarly, none of the trial courts ruled in favor of the citizen groups that had submitted lawsuits against Koizumi. Since there is no constitutional court in Japan, the citizens' groups could not sue the prime minister for unconstitutionality. They needed to base their appeal on other reasons, in this case the mental damage caused by the violation of religious freedom, religious human rights, and peaceful living rights. Such appeals led the judges to render a "no [sufficient] reasons for the damages claim" judgment.¹³ Only the judges in Fukuoka District Court and Osaka High Courts were of the opinion that the visit was unconstitutional for effectively promoting the Yasukuni Shrine and, consequently, Shintoism. However, since such opinions are not the decisions themselves, they have no binding authority.¹⁴ As a result, on the legal level, opposition to and support for prime ministerial visits to the Yasukuni Shrine remain ambiguous.

In order to bolster the legality of official worship at, and the renationalization of, the Yasukuni Shrine, the politicians of the long-ruling Liberal Democratic Party (LDP) submitted a bill in 1969 offering state support to the shrine. This bill elicited massive protests, from opposition parties down to several religious groups.¹⁵ The ruling party tabled the bill on five occasions in an attempt to have it pass, failing each time. Seeing that the 1947 Constitution represented the biggest hurdle to success, the LDP attempted to amend it. This issue of the amendment will be discussed separately in section 2.2.

2.1.1.2 *Historical Perception*

By amending the 1947 constitution, which was enacted while the Allied occupation government was in power, the LDP believes Japan will experience a return to its glory days.¹⁶ These are typically located in the imperial period

---

12. https://www.sankei.com/affairs/news/191125/afr1911250033-n1.html, accessed 16 June 2020.

13. For a more detailed description of the results of the lawsuits relating to the Yasukuni Shrine, see Breen, "Voices of Rage," 281–84.

14. Fukuoka Chihō Saibansho 7 April 2004, Heisei 13 (Wa) no. 3932, 5 Minji, https://www.courts.go.jp/app/files/hanrei_jp/141/008141_hanrei.pdf; Osaka Kōtō Saibansho, 30 September 2005, Heisei 16 (Ne) no. 1888, 13 Minji, https://www.courts.go.jp/app/files/hanrei_jp/273/002273_hanrei.pdf, accessed 21 March 2017.

15. The protesters held demonstrations, hunger strikes, protest rallies, and marches. They also managed a nation-wide campaign, gathering approximately four million signatures in opposition to the bill. See Steele, "Christianity and Politics," 366.

16. Mullins, "Neonationalism, Politics, and Religion," 108.

(1868–1945), when Japan adopted Western ideologies and methods, while utilizing Shinto doctrines that consider the Japanese emperor to hail from an unbroken imperial line descended from the goddess Amaterasu.[17] It was in this context of reviving the central position of the emperor that the government established the Yasukuni Shrine.[18]

To turn Japan into a modern country like the Western countries, the Meiji government enacted a constitution guaranteeing freedom of religion in 1889. At the same time, it positioned the emperor as the sovereign and Japanese people as his subjects, and used this relationship as a limitation on religious freedom.[19] As a result, Japan became a powerful nation both economically and militarily. It prevailed in military conflicts with Taiwan in the 1870s, with China in the 1890s, and, in the twentieth century, with Russia and many Asian nations. While the proponents of Yasukuni's renationalization emphasize this success story, the opponents point to the dark side of this period, namely imperialism and fascism. The latter thus prefer to locate the beginnings of modern Japan in the period after 1945.

As mentioned in section 2.1.1, in 1945, Japan surrendered to the Allied forces. The Allied occupation government reduced the status of the Yasukuni Shrine to that of a mere religious body, and announced a new draft of a constitution that was to become the present constitution, enacted in 1947. In a departure from the Meiji Constitution, the preamble of the 1947 constitution now identified the Japanese people as the sovereign, rather than the emperor's subjects. As noted, this new constitution prescribes freedom of religion and the separation of state and religion (Articles 20 and 89). Besides, it prescribes that the emperor is just the symbol of the nation (Article 1), and prohibits Japan from keeping military forces (Article 9).

For the proponents of Yasukuni, the post-1945 changes mark the loss of the heart of the glorious spirits and state ethics, as well as national morale.[20]

---

17. For a more detailed treatment of the imperial period, see section 3.2.

18. Takahashi, *Yasukuni Mondai*, 6–7.

19. https://www.ndl.go.jp/constitution/e/etc/c02.html#s2

Article 1: The Empire of Japan shall be reigned over and governed by a line of Emperors unbroken for ages eternal.

Article 3: The Emperor is sacred and inviolable.

Article 28: Japanese subjects shall, within limits not prejudicial to peace and order, and not antagonistic to their duties as subjects, enjoy freedom of religious belief.

20. Breen, "Voices of Rage," 294.

For the opponents of Yasukuni's renationalization, in contrast, a revival of its special status would mark a return to imperialist and fascist Japan. The latter fear that the government will use Yasukuni's status to encourage, if not coerce people to worship there and to mobilize its citizens to military service again. This concern has only increased as they note the present government's attempt to reinterpret Article 9 and to allow more military traits to the Japan Self-Defense Force.

2.1.1.3 Class-A War Criminals

The above concerns are also a worry to Japan's neighboring countries, victims of Japanese militarism and fascism. Significant to this diplomatic relation is the enshrinement of "class-A" war criminals, that is, those who planned, initiated, or waged war according to the classification maintained by the 1946 International Military Tribunal for the Far East. The Yasukuni Shrine enshrined the souls of these class-A war criminals on 17 October 1978, and granted them the exclusive title of "Martyrs of the (Emperor) Shōwa Period." This title was also granted to Tōjō Hideki (1884–1948), the military general and prime minister who was responsible for initiating the Asia-Pacific War and ordering the inhumane treatment of the prisoners of war.[21] In the eyes of the countries that suffered under the atrocities committed by the Japanese military, the class-A war criminals were the source of their suffering. The worship of their souls as glorious spirits therefore represents a painful denial of the brutalities which the war criminals inflicted on Asian countries.

Nevertheless, many right-wing conservatives and war-bereaved families believe that the 1946 tribunal was an unfair victor's trial, and understand the class-A war criminals to have died on duty for Japan.[22] Many LDP politicians would like to maintain the support of members of the Bereaved Society and the Shinto Association of Spiritual Leadership,[23] a powerful political organization of the Association of Shinto Shrines.

---

21. Steele, "Christianity and Politics," 367.
22. Mullins, "Neonationalism, Politics, and Religion," 107–9.
23. In Japanese, *Shinto Seiji Renmei*, abbreviated as *Shinseiren*, literally means Shinto Political Alliance.

Making the matter more complex, however, is the fact that not all Yasukuni proponents agreed with the enshrinement of the war criminals.[24] Emperor Hirohito (reigned 1926–89) never visited Yasukuni after their enshrinement.[25] Similarly, although Emperor Akihito (reigned 1989–2019) visited Yasukuni four times as crown prince, he has never visited it since his enthronement in 1989. In contrast, Akihito regularly attends the annual national rite of mourning for the war dead at Budōkan Hall in Tokyo, and has made multiple memorial visits to war-related sites such as Hiroshima, Nagasaki, Okinawa, the Ogasawara islands, Iōjima, and Saipan. These visits show that the emperor does hold much sympathy for the war deads, but is somewhat reluctant when it comes to Yasukuni.[26] The shrine's historical position as an imperial facility makes the emperor's reluctance to visit the sanctuary somewhat remarkable, leading several Yasukuni supporters to propose the removal of the fourteen class-A criminals, in the hope that the emperor will conduct official worship at Yasukuni again. Some believe that the removal of these war criminals will likewise work to restore the relationship with neighboring countries.[27] However, from the perspective of the Yasukuni Shrine, there is doctrinally no room for the souls of those who have been enshrined to be removed. Furthermore, the government cannot force their removal, since such a measure would impinge on the principle of religious freedom.

2.1.1.4 Commemoration and War Responsibility

Another critical angle to the Yasukuni issue is the need for commemoration. The war deads died on duty for their country. The bereaved family lost their beloved for the sake of the country. For Yasukuni apologists, the state should therefore provide recognition for the war dead and for their bereaved

---

24. Breen, "Voices of Rage," 296–98. Even though the Ministry of Health had urged enshrinement since 1958, Yasukuni's chief priest of the time, Tsukuba Fujimaro (1905–78), consistently refused the proposal during his tenure from 1946 to 1978. The famous Shinto figure Ashizu Uzuhiko (1909–92), the president of the Japan Society of the War Bereaved Koga Makoto, and two officer veterans likewise number among those who disagreed with the enshrinement of class-A war criminals.

25. Breen, 287–88, 301, note 27. The publication of the diary of the emperor's aides revealed that the enshrinement of war criminals was the reason for his absence.

26. Nonetheless, it is also important to note that although the emperor did not visit Yasukuni, the annual Great Spring and Autumn rituals always include the presence of imperial emissaries. Breen, 287.

27. Breen, 289, 296–98.

families. They also promote the *ishizue* (cornerstone) theory, which projects the war dead as the cornerstone for the peace and prosperity of post-war Japan. Accordingly, they argue that Japan needs Yasukuni to commemorate the bravery of those who sacrificed their lives for Japan. This narrative has been embraced by many senior LDP politicians and prime ministers, and is also narrated in the war museum located in the Yasukuni precinct, the Yūshūkan.[28]

Yasukuni's opponents, however, have countered that such a narrative is irresponsible, given the many dark sides to the war. As noted in the section on historical perception, they do not consider the wars to have been conducted for the peace of Japan, but for the invasion and colonization of other Asian countries. What the soldiers did was far from honorable. One notorious example is the cannibalism committed in New Guinea. Faced with starvation, the Japanese officers shot their comrades to consume their flesh.[29] The war museum in Yasukuni, however, describes the New Guinea campaign as a well-planned battle. There is no place there for the story of cannibalism, of starvation, or of reckless military leaders.

Without any reflection of such facts, Yasukuni rites transform the war deads into glorious spirits. The ceremony of remembrance at Yasukuni avoids, if not denies, the issue of the responsibility of the military commanders who initiated the New Guinea campaign. It recalls the war deads for their virtues of loyalty, patriotism, and self-sacrifice.[30] The rites decorate their deaths as glorious achievements to be celebrated, rather than recalling a tragedy to be mourned. Hence, many of the opponents of the Yasukuni Shrine prefer to have an alternate facility to answer the need for such commemoration.

2.1.2 The Responses of Japanese Christians

Japanese Christians were among the first to protest the movement to renationalize Yasukuni Shrine, sending letters to the prime minister, publishing protest statements, and filing lawsuits.[31] Although Christians represent a very small part of the Japanese population, their contributions are significant. To

---

28. Breen, 291–93.
29. Tanaka, *Hidden Horrors*, 124–26, 140.
30. Breen, "Voices of Rage," 290–91.
31. Tanaka, *Yasukuni no Sengoshi*, 86, 105, 110–11, 116–17, 119, 123–31, 132–36, 147, 156–57, 163, 176, 190–98.

analyze such contributions from an ecclesiological perspective, I will focus on the responses of four figures. The first two are not evangelicals, but their responses will serve to provide the bigger picture of the Japanese response and give greater clarity to the positions held by evangelical Christians.

2.1.2.1 Asō Tarō

Asō Tarō (b.1940) is a Japanese elite politician and a Roman Catholic believer. After working in several family businesses, he entered the political field in 1979 as a member of the House of Representatives. He later became the 92nd prime minister of Japan (2008–9), and currently serves as the deputy prime minister and minister of finance (December 2012–). While serving as minister for foreign affairs in 2006, he published an article entitled "Yasukuni ni Iyasaka Are! [Long Live Yasukuni!]"[32] The article came with a disclaimer specifying that Asō had not written the piece as a cabinet minister, but as an individual. For this reason, the article cannot be taken as representative of the views of Japanese Christians, not to mention evangelicals. Nevertheless, one of the main concerns of Asō's thesis is the problem of Japanese Christians engaging politics more as Japanese than as Christians. In chapter 1, I already noted how Ōhira Masayoshi, a Protestant prime minister, had defended his worship at Yasukuni by appealing to his duty as a Japanese citizen. Asō's treatment of the Yasukuni issue can therefore serve as a more detailed elaboration of Japanese Christians who prioritize identity as a Japanese citizen above that as a Christian, and is therefore worth treating in greater detail.

In his article, Asō argues for the restoration of Yasukuni's original position. Because Yasukuni has served as the collective memory of Japanese people ever since the Meiji period, Asō discards the proposal to establish an alternative facility. To his mind, the establishment of such a facility would turn Japan as a state into a person suffering from amnesia, who no longer understands its own identity. Asō furthermore claims that a state should pay the highest respect to citizens who sacrificed their lives for the sake of their country; this is a universal principle, and the least a state can promise her people. In the case of Japan, the Yasukuni Shrine was the promise between the emperor and the Japanese people. For that reason, Asō's strong wish is for the emperor to perform the worship visits as the fulfillment of that promise.

---

32. Asō, "Yasukuni ni Iyasaka Are!"

Asō seeks a third-way solution for the issue of Yasukuni. Since Yasukuni's status as a religious body represents a hindrance to his wish for imperial worship, he proposes that the Yasukuni Shrine dissolve itself and thereafter assume the status of *zaidan hōjin* (foundation corporation) or *tokushu hōjin* (special corporation). With this solution, Asō believes that Yasukuni will function again as the original Yasukuni did, that is, as a peaceful place for the propitiation of the war dead spirits, without breaching the principle of religious freedom and the separation of religion and state.

2.1.2.2 *Tomura Masahiro*

Tomura (1923–2003) was a minister of the United Church of Christ in Japan (UCCJ), the largest mainstream Protestant denomination in Japan. He graduated from Japan Christ Seminary, present-day Tokyo Union Theological Seminary. Although he is not an evangelical, his view can function as a bridge between Asō's emphases and the view of evangelicals detailed in the section 2.1.2.3 and 2.1.2.4. Tomura promoted the movement to confess war responsibility and to oppose the reestablishment of the enthronement day of the mythological Emperor Jinmu as the National Foundation Day.[33] He actively preached and gave seminars on Yasukuni all over Japan, and served as the chair of the UCCJ Yasukuni Issue Special Committee.

In contrast to Asō, Tomura criticized the direction nationalism had been taking in Japan as an extreme inwardness.[34] While the Protestant Prime Minister Ōhira defended the view that Japanese people had a good sense for balancing liberal and conservative nationalism, Tomura condemned what Ōhira called the liberal direction in Japanese nationalism as just another form of the conservative direction. According to Tomura, Japanese nationalism was unchangingly inward even in the Meiji period (1868–1912), when Japan ended its period of isolation and opened itself up to Western technology.[35]

---

33. According to Japanese mythology in the *Kojiki* and *Nihon Shoki*, Emperor Jinmu was the first ruler of Japan, reigning from 11 February 660 BC to 9 April 585 BC. His enthronement day was commemorated as the National Foundation Day beginning in 1873. This holiday was abolished in 1948 due to its close association with the emperor system, but reinstated in 1966.

34. Tomura, "Nihon no Nashonarizumu," 25.

35. Tomura, 12.

This nationalism has proved so strong that not even the war defeat could put a dent in the Japanese notion of the "non-religious shrine."[36]

Whereas Asō emphasized the importance of a solution pursuing the recovery of Yasukuni's original function, Tomura believed that this original function itself was the problem. He identified the purpose and arguments used by the Yasukuni proponents during the period from 1960 to 1980 as a "recapitulation" of the non-religious shrine doctrine popularized under the Meiji government. Along with their efforts to amend the present constitution, revise school textbooks, and establish emergency law, the Yasukuni proponents want to revive the system of the State Shinto.[37] In that system, war and emperor occupy a central position, and Yasukuni, with its festivals, was intended to retighten the bonds of the state which may have been loosened.[38]

Moreover, Tomura argued that the Yasukuni Shrine's practice of enshrining only those war deads who had fought on the emperor's side had the effect of brainwashing Japanese people with an oversimplified division between an imperial and a "rebel" army. Anyone who did not stand on the side of the emperor was therefore considered a "rebel."[39] Such discrimination, so Tomura noted, is still practiced today, albeit with different terms.[40] It leads Yasukuni's proponents to label their opponents as *hikokumin* (unpatriotic, or non-Japanese), who are to be expelled from Japan.[41] For Tomura, this brainwashing was very successful, so that even contemporary Japanese people still have not recovered from its aftereffects.[42]

Tomura also referred to the Japanese characteristics that fit group thinking, rather than independence as individuals.[43] In Japanese thought, the smallest and indivisible group unit is not an individual, but a family. Although the

---

36. Tomura, 12, 15.

37. Tomura, *Tennō-sei Kokka*, 329.

38. Tomura, "Aa Ware Yasukuni-bito," 189; Tomura, "'Yasukuni' to Fukuin," 203.

39. Tomura, "'Yasukuni' to Fukuin," 202, 206. The government discriminates the "rebels" in many ways, exiling them, treating them as minorities, and even truncating them. If a rebel shows even a small inclination to stand on the emperor's side, the government will treat him generously as an ally.

40. Tomura, 205. Tomura gives examples such as the distinction between "government and people (*kan to min*)" and "public and private (*kō / ōyake to shi / watakushi*)."

41. Tomura, 204.

42. Tomura, 202.

43. Tomura, "Aa Ware Yasukuni-bito," 189.

feudal system has long been dismantled, the *ie* (familial society) system is still the pattern of Japanese self-consciousness.[44] This way of thinking leads Japanese people to distinguish between insiders and outsiders, a distinction which in turn severely hinders the ability to acknowledge those in Japanese society who have a different identity or opinion. It is this inability that makes it difficult for Japanese people to reflect seriously on their war responsibility. Although the Meiji government had miraculously succeeded in turning the familial social system and clan loyalty into the state social system and imperial dedication, Japanese people could not and do not have a principle of loyalty higher than the emperor. In Tomura's eyes, this inward familial system is at the very root of the Yasukuni problem.[45]

In addition, Tomura explained that the combination of a culture of shame and familial society caused Japanese people to turn a blind eye to unfavorable things done by in-group collusion.[46] He associated Japanese familial society with what Romans 7 refers to as the deadly power of the flesh that exists in the human heart and fights against the power of God from the outside. For this reason, Japanese people need to be freed from this power.[47] Tomura has argued that by continuing their opposition to Yasukuni's proponents, Japanese Christians will be able to help their fellow Japanese to overcome the power of Yasukuni and to implement a more liberal nationalism.[48]

Interestingly enough, Tomura warned that the roots of the attempts to privilege the Yasukuni Shrine as a national facility could also be found among Japanese Christians.[49] Therefore, he reminded them that they are not merely fighting against the emperor, prime minister, and LDP officials, but also against such inclination inherent in themselves.[50]

Tomura likewise emphasized that the churches in Japan should be turning their church planting efforts into a struggle for freedom.[51] Evangelism

---

44. Tomura, 190.
45. Tomura, 194.
46. Tomura, 195.
47. Tomura, 197.
48. Tomura, "Nihon no Nashonarizumu," 25.
49. Tomura, "Aa Ware Yasukuni-bito," 188.
50. Tomura, "'Yasukuni' to Fukuin," 206–7.
51. Tomura, "Shibarareta Te," 180.

should be carried out in awareness of the social tide.[52] Noting that the concept of freedom is still underdeveloped in Japan, Tomura argued that this is an "honorable evangelism opportunity."[53] To his mind, Christian churches have the rare opportunity to be able to think, talk, and at times struggle together with society for freedom. It is not merely the church's social responsibility, but at a more fundamental level it also relates to the church's very existence. Tomura believed that it is at once a task and a blessing from God.[54]

2.1.2.3 *Nishikawa Shigenori*

Nishikawa (1927–2020) was a Christian journalist active in both church ministry and political engagement. He served long as an elder in the Reformed Church in Japan at Tokyo. Nishikawa also earned himself the nickname "the Nishikawa of Yasukuni" for his long and active involvement in the Yasukuni Shrine debates. He was the representative of the Gathering of Opposing Yasukuni Shrine Nationalization Evangelical Christians, and served in leadership positions in several other Christian related organizations as well.[55] He was also a member of a war-bereaved family, since his older brother was a soldier who died of illness during the war in then-Burma.

Nishikawa protested the movement to renationalize the Yasukuni Shrine in many ways. Besides conducting protest demonstrations at the site and writing protest statements, he wrote several articles for national newspapers and published a number of books. He also delivered seminars on Yasukuni throughout Japan.

Unique to Nishikawa's approach was his commitment to hearing the plenary and committee meetings of the national Diet. He came to realize the importance of this approach after the ruling party submitted the controversial Yasukuni Shrine Bill to the national Diet in 1969. Even though Parliament

---

52. Tomura, "Nihon no Nashonarizumu," 25.
53. Tomura, "Shibarareta Te," 180.
54. Tomura, 179.
55. Nishikawa, *Yūji Hōsei-ka*, 211. Nishikawa was the Executive Committee Chairperson of the Christian Bereaved Family Association, Executive Director of the National Council for Monitoring Violation of Religion-State Separation, Representative of the National Coordination Committee for Peaceful Bereaved Family Association, Executive Director of the Stop the Way to War! One Million Signature Collection Movement, Joint Representative of the Citizen Council for Realizing the War Damage Investigation Law, Executive Director of Solidarity for Chongqing Bombing Victims in Tokyo, and Lecturer of the Constitution Serial Course.

finally dropped the bill in 1974, the movement to revive the Yasukuni Shrine as a national and special corporation continued. Being aware of the nature of several other bills with consequences as severe as the Yasukuni Shrine Bill, Nishikawa decided in 1999 to hear the meetings of the Diet. After sitting in on the meetings for ten years, he concluded:

> By hearing the National Diet, I could understand that the present National Diet is acting in concert with the proponents [of the Yasukuni] movement outside the Diet which with their three pillars – the Constitution, Self-Defense Force, and Education – ignore the basic principles mentioned in the Constitution of Japan, such as Article 9 (War Renunciation), Article 19 (Freedom of Thought and Conscience), and Article 20 (Freedom of Religious Belief and Prohibition of Religious Activities of the State).[56]

Nishikawa's direct observation of the national Diet provided him historical evidence on the current situation and direction of current Diet members, which informed his reflection on the issue and had considerable appeal.[57]

While Tomura emphasized the importance of fighting the Japanese notion of an inward, familial society, whose roots he also found in the nation's Christians, Nishikawa suggested more practically and concretely that one should learn the historical facts from before and during the war period. He insisted on the importance of inquiring why the war happened, and what kind of damage Japan inflicted on its neighboring Asian countries. This, he believed, is of crucial importance for perceiving the absurdity of the official worship at the Yasukuni Shrine. He wrote:

> In conclusion, by learning the facts of the horrors caused by the [Pacific] war, one becomes unable to deny the war and post-war responsibilities of the emperor. It stands to reason that, if they [the bereaved families] perceive how unfair it is to regard their [war dead] family members, who were made "glorious spirits" by the worship of such [irresponsible] emperors, as subjects of "propitiation" and glorification, they will come to understand the

---

56. Nishikawa, i.
57. Nishikawa, 204, 207.

contradiction of their movement towards the realization of the emperor's public worship for which they had hitherto hoped.[58]

Nishikawa also shared his experience when he spoke before several members of the Japan Bereaved Association living in Tsukui City in the Kanagawa Prefecture. Although the Japan Bereaved Association had been one of the most passionate proponents of the Yasukuni Shrine, after listening to the actual historical facts, they could agree that official worship at the shrine would open the way for the Japanese government once again to mobilize the people for the horror of war.[59]

Nishikawa likewise suggested learning and practicing the basic principles of the constitution of Japan. For him, the present constitution clearly prescribes the principles of popular sovereignty, pacifism, separation of state and religion, and freedom of belief, thought, and consciousness. However, in practice, the government and the Diet members of the ruling party often ignore those principles in the name of patriotism or Japanese traditions and customs. Knowledge of the underlying principles determined by the constitution will enable one to recognize any unconstitutional attempts or practices on the part of the government and Diet members. Claiming that "constant caution is the price of freedom," he encouraged Japanese people to exercise their rights firmly in assessing and criticizing the government.[60] As for the problem of the Yasukuni Shrine, he insisted that it is important to strictly exercise the principle of the separation of state and religion. In line with this, Nishikawa also leveled sharp criticism against the official visits by cabinet members, Diet members, and the Tokyo governor, as well as the *hatsumōde* (New Year's Worship) at Yasukuni by the prime minister which was largely ignored in the media.

Following the above suggestions of learning historical facts and understanding the principles prescribed by the constitution, Nishikawa emphasizes the need to offer a sincere apology. He compared Japan with Germany, which was once in a similar position when it initiated war and inflicted terrible damage on neighboring countries. As he saw it, Germany was able to reconcile itself with neighboring countries because it had prioritized its relationship

---

58. Nishikawa, 169.
59. Nishikawa, 168.
60. Nishikawa, 43, 127.

with its neighbors and had done its best to apologize and to seek reconciliation. Nishikawa believed that if Japanese people were to be educated well in the history of the war and in the basic principles of the Japanese constitution, Japan could be successful like Germany in achieving reconciliation with its Asian victim countries.[61]

2.1.2.4 Inagaki Hisakazu

Inagaki Hisakazu (b.1947) is a member of Tokyo Onchō Church of the Reformed Church in Japan (RCJ), and a professor of Christian philosophy at Tokyo Christian University, an evangelical institution for theological education. He has also been a visiting scholar and visiting professor at the Free University of Amsterdam.

In contrast to other Yasukuni critics, Inagaki warns that even if the prime minister were to stop the official worship altogether and if the shrine were to remove the class-A war criminals from Yasukuni, the problem will still not be solved.[62] The controversial Yasukuni Shrine is not just a political and diplomatic problem, but also a problem of memory and reconciliation related closely to the core of Japanese traditional religion.[63] He writes:

> We must distinguish between what we should and should not forget. We must forget the Yasukuni ideology that calls for sacrificing oneself for the sake of the state. This is something that should be put behind us. However, we must remember the past [Pacific] War and the victims of that War. At the same time, we need to face the past scars of war as experienced by people with different perspectives.[64]

For him, the Yasukuni Shrine had two functions: (1) honoring the fallen soldiers by bestowing on them the status of heroic deities in war; and (2) offering a place of mourning for the massive numbers of those who died in war.[65]

---

61. Nishikawa, 145, 186.
62. Inagaki, *Yasukuni Jinja 'Kaihō'-ron*, 15.
63. Inagaki, "Kokumin-teki Fukushi to Heiwa," 7; Inagaki, "Memory and Reconciliation," 41–51. The latter is a revision of the English summary of Inagaki's *Yasukuni Jinja*. While this article utilizes the concept of sphere sovereignty, the article "Kokumin-teki Fukushi to Heiwa" approaches the question from the perspective of the doctrine of common grace.
64. Inagaki, "Memory and Reconciliation," 46; Inagaki, *Yasukuni Jinja*, 17.
65. Inagaki, "Memory and Reconciliation," 42.

These two functions must be taken into account in considering a solution to the Yasukuni issue. Accordingly, Inagaki suggests instituting public memorial places for recalling the horrors of war and for pledging not to commit the same foolish mistakes again. That facility should be a place for everyone, whether Japanese or non-Japanese, including both religious and non-religious people.[66] Consideration for the non-Japanese is necessary because the Asia-Pacific War had not only three million Japanese victims, but also twenty million non-Japanese.[67]

While Inagaki agrees with Yasukuni supporters who insist on pacifism and on the separation between Yasukuni and governmental activities, he disagrees with their claim that religious commemoration is merely a private matter.[68] Instead of making the new site free from religious rituals, he urges that "all religious and non-religious groups, national or international, can gather in this place according to their diverse practices and cultural expressions," and that this facility "should be funded with taxes paid by the Japanese people, but the Japanese Government should keep an equal distance from all groups."[69] Inagaki thus emphasizes the importance of religion in the public square for two reasons: first, because the Yasukuni issue is closely related to the uniqueness of Japanese religiosity; and second, because in his eyes the experience of spiritual conversion taught by the world's great religions will transform the nation's citizens into new people who value tolerance. To foster this tolerance, Inagaki recommends Kuyper's concept of sphere sovereignty for and between each religious group. To maintain the tolerance in a public space, the most crucial element is communication through dialogue.

Inagaki also suggests that the Japanese notion of *wa* (harmony) will be useful for establishing this dialogical element. People in Japan have already been practicing this notion since the sixth century, and the famous Japanese regent Shōtoku Taishi (574–622) had considered it the most respectable virtue. Originally, *wa* was one of the principles of Confucius, teaching harmony without uniformity. Therefore, this principle can be used to encourage the creation of harmony between those of different opinions, religions, and even

---

66. Inagaki, "Kokumin-teki Fukushi to Heiwa," 8.
67. Inagaki, 7.
68. Inagaki, "Memory and Reconciliation," 43.
69. Inagaki, 47.

nationalities. Chinese and Korean people, who suffered most under Japanese imperialism, will welcome this concept because they too are highly influenced by Confucianism.[70]

Inagaki concludes his argument by stating that it is meaningless just to protest the government system; rather, Japanese Christians should propose and put into practice a social movement, based on a Christian worldview, which can also transform the government system into a more democratic one that respects the role of religion in the public square. Drawing on Kuyper's doctrine of common grace, Inagaki encourages Christians to participate more actively in various life spheres.[71]

2.1.3 Evaluation of Christian Responses

Although Asō calls his solution a third-way solution, in the end it boils down to Yasukuni adherence. He does not provide a real answer to the danger of breaching the constitution. Instead, he gives privileges to the emperor and Shinto religion that are actually prohibited by the constitution. Although Asō refrained from official worship during his premiership, his article shows that he is a proponent of official worship. His arguments contradict the content of the protests against official visits of Prime Minister Mori and Prime Minister Koizumi raised by Japanese bishops in 2000 and 2005 respectively.[72] His reasonings are identical to those used by the Protestant Prime Minister Ōhira, as mentioned in chapter 1. From an ecclesiological perspective, it is no exaggeration to say that although Asō does not hide his identity as a Roman Catholic,[73] he still is a Christian who prioritizes his identity as a Japanese citizen. He allows the state to take precedence over his religion. Christianity is a private matter and should therefore not be brought into the public square.

Tomura conversely seeks that every Japanese, including Japanese Christians like Asō and Ōhira, be liberated from that inclination. With his thorough analysis, Tomura can help Japanese Christians to understand the complexity of the Yasukuni issue. In contrast to Asō who focuses only on

---

70. Inagaki, 41–42, 50; Inagaki, *Yasukuni Jinja*, 149.
71. Inagaki, "Kokumin-teki Fukushi to Heiwa," 13, 15.
72. Breen, "Popes, Bishops and War," 5.
73. Before he visited Italy for the G-8 Summit on 8–10 July 2009, Asō had requested to meet the Pope. During their meeting on 7 July, Asō unhesitatingly explained that his family had been Catholic since his grandfather's generation.

restoring Yasukuni to its original condition, Tomura sharply recognized the danger of Yasukuni and its surrounding Japanese cultural and ideological background. Tomura's arguments for the importance of pacifism and religious freedom are persuasive.

From the perspective of ecclesiology, we can conclude that Tomura raised awareness of the church's social responsibility. He influenced many Japanese Christians beyond his denomination, especially those who were members of the National Christian Council in Japan. Evangelical Christians also learned much from him.[74] However, they rejected his suggestion to redefine evangelism as a fight for freedom of religion. Japanese evangelical Christians have thus rejected the so-called social gospel implied in his proposal.

Nishikawa's works, on the other hand, might be of service for evangelical Christians to learn from Tomura without adopting the social gospel implications of his project. Nishikawa's efforts in actively engaging with church ministry and political problems are undeniably a real model for Japanese evangelical Christians in their engagement with both church and society. He started his unceasing struggle to protest the nationalization of the Yasukuni Shrine back in 1969. His approach in hearing all the meetings of the national Diet is unique, as he seems to be the only opponent of official Yasukuni Shrine worship to utilize this method. Hearing the meetings of the Diet has provided him actual and substantial facts about the conditions of Diet members that others do not clearly see.

However, it goes without saying that many of Nishikawa's arguments that depend on the present constitution will become invalid once Yasukuni supporters' attempts to amend the constitution succeed. In addition, since the discussions between opponents and proponents of the Yasukuni Shrine have failed to reach a satisfying conclusion even after decades of struggle, the feasibility of a solution based on protesting the nationalization of the Yasukuni Shrine and demanding a strict separation of state and religion is questionable.

Inagaki attempts to offer a third-way solution to the deadlock between Yasukuni's supporters and opponents. He does not just protest the movement of its opponents, but also provides a concrete alternative to the present Yasukuni Shrine. His proposal is very detailed, comprising both concepts for

---

74. For example, the following evangelical literature references Tomura's works: Idogaki, *Shinkyō no Jiyū*, 116; Ikejiri, "Oshiyoseru 'Kokka Shintō,'" 29.

and contents of the facility and even the way to run and maintain the site. He accommodates both the proponents' religious needs and the opponents' concerns regarding the violation of religious freedom and the separation of religion and state. His proposal not only sees to it that the state grants its fallen soldiers and victims their due honor, but also prevents the new facility from potentially becoming a tool of abuse for mobilizing people for war. He furthermore takes into consideration the traditional Japanese notion of *wa*, which has a much longer history than the Yasukuni practice.

From the perspective of ecclesiology, one might argue that while Tomura and Nishikawa emphasize the strict separation between religion and the state, Inagaki suggests the equal participation of religions in the public space. He rightly understands the dissatisfaction of Yasukuni's supporters with the strict separation between church and state. Inagaki derived his approach, which he named *kōkyō tetsugaku* (public philosophy), from the Kuyperian principles of common grace and sphere sovereignty. While recommending that Japanese Christians implement the Kuyperian distinction of the church as organism and institution into their sociopolitical engagement, he points out that Japanese churches are still not sufficiently mature to have a theological understanding of the organic church.[75]

As we have seen in chapter 1, Japanese Christians need a more robust ecclesiology. This makes it important to offer a more systematic and historical exploration of the other elements of Kuyper's ecclesiology, and thereafter to consider its possibilities for the Japanese context. These will be discussed in chapters 4 and 6. First, we still need to continue our investigation of the contemporary sociopolitical issues facing Japanese Christians.

2.2 Constitutional Amendment[76]

Although constitutional amendments are not uncommon in democratic countries, Japan has never amended its present constitution, the *Nihonkoku*

---

75. Inagaki, "Kyōkai no Jichi," 329.

76. An earlier version of this section has been published as Harefa, "Resistance to Japanese Nationalism," 330–44.

Kenpō (Constitution of Japan), since it took effect in 1947.[77] Amendments have been proposed, but have never gained the consensus required for passing.

Since its establishment in 1955, the Liberal Democratic Party (LDP) has propounded the view that the present constitution does not reflect Japanese values because it was drafted and imposed on Japan by the Allied occupation government of 1945–52. The party also insists that revisions are necessary to address new challenges facing Japan, especially with a view to the right of a self-defense force. However, several other parties and societal groups see the threat of fascist nationalism lurking behind some of the amendment efforts and have therefore offered powerful resistance against them.

2.2.1 The Issue

In December 2018, Prime Minister Abe Shinzō expressed his determination to see the Japanese constitution amended by 2020. He argued that revising the present constitution would restore Japan to its glory days. This declaration was not new, as Abe had made similar statements on several previous occasions. During his 2012 campaign, for example, Abe used the slogan *Nippon wo Torimodosu* (Taking Back Japan) and promoted constitutional revision as an important component in the LDP platform.

For the LDP, the present constitution represents a foreign imposition. After its surrender in 1945, Japan was occupied by the Allied occupation government until 1952. After rejecting a draft constitution written by a Japanese committee of constitutional scholars led by Matsumoto Jōji in February 1946, MacArthur, the supreme commander of the occupation government, presented an alternative draft within less than a week. This draft was implemented with only minor revisions.

Matsumoto's draft had sought to maintain the prescriptions of the 1889 *Dai-Nippon Teikoku Kenpō* (Constitution of the Empire of Great Japan),[78] which identified the emperor as the sovereign and the Japanese people as his subjects. MacArthur's draft, in contrast, established the Japanese people as

---

77. For example, since the end of the Second World War, the United States has ratified amendments in 1951, 1961, 1964, 1967, 1971, and 1992; France has amended its constitution at least twenty-four times.

78. This document was also known as the *Meiji Kenpō* (Meiji Constitution) or the *Kyū Kenpō* (Old Constitution). Its contents are available at www.ndl.go.jp/constitution/etc/j02.html (Japanese version) or www.ndl.go.jp/constitution/e/etc/c02.html (English version).

the sovereign and made the emperor only a symbol of the nation. Thus, from the perspective of supporters of the 1889 Constitution, the 1947 Constitution originating from MacArthur's draft is "new and bad," not based on the "old and good" values of Japan. Moreover, the occupation government's Civil Censorship Detachment (CCD), which exerted pre-publication censorship over about seventy daily newspapers, all books and magazines, and many other publications, reinforced this sense of coercion.

When Japan regained its sovereignty in 1952, the narrative of coercion soon surfaced. Ever since its establishment in 1955, the LDP has always insisted that the current constitution was imposed on the nation, and therefore included "revision of the current constitution" on its political agenda. For the LDP, amending the present constitution "will unshackle the country from the system established during the Occupation and make a truly sovereign state."[79]

In recent years, the LDP has taken several significant steps toward realizing its amendment agenda. Following the release of a first draft of proposed amendments in 2005, the party succeeded in gaining approval for an Act stipulating procedures for amending the constitution from both houses of the Diet in 2007. This Act was legally necessary because there had been no practical law to that date indicating how the constitution might be amended. Although the LDP lost the 2009 general election to the Democratic Party of Japan (DPJ), it did not give up its efforts; on the contrary, it released a second draft of proposed amendments, the *Nihonkokukenpō Kaisei Sōan* (Draft for the Amendment of the Constitution of Japan), on 27 April 2012.

Boasting that its amendment committee had reviewed and revised all articles of the 1947 Constitution, the LDP claimed that it was presenting "a draft of a revised constitution appropriate to the times and circumstances of Japan."[80] The party also appealed to the fact that if the draft were to be endorsed, it would be the first constitution in Japanese post-war history established without foreign intervention. The proposed revisions were substantial. Along with suggested changes in the preamble, the LDP offered 11 chapters and 110 articles, replacing the 10 chapters and 103 articles of the present constitution. It prescribed new provisions governing such matters as the national flag and anthem, the right of self-defense, emergency declarations,

---

79. "LDP Announces a New Draft."
80. "LDP Announces a New Draft."

and amendment procedure. The draft also includes clauses regarding the emperor as the head of the State and familial responsibility for ensuring a healthy economic situation.[81]

The proposed amendments were released a little more than a year after the great triple disaster (earthquake, tsunami, and nuclear reactor accident) which struck Japan in March 2011. During the intervening year, all of Japan had been preoccupied with relief and recovery activities. The LDP's ongoing work on the amendments thus shows its firm resolve to have the constitution changed.

In December 2012, the LDP regained a majority in the House of Representatives and became the ruling party again. Following this success, the party also won a majority of seats in the House of Councillors in July 2013. These electoral results have given the LDP a greater probability of winning approval from the Diet for its proposals, thus increasing the likelihood of constitutional amendment.

2.2.2 The Responses of Japanese Christians

There was no significant response from Christians when the LDP published its draft amendments in April 2012. This was not only because the country was focused first and foremost on recovering from the Great Disaster, but also because the LDP had not yet retaken its position as the ruling party.

A sense of crisis emerged as the 2012 general election approached. For one, many Japanese realized that the DPJ government was no more successful in its disaster response than the LDP had been. Moreover, they saw that Abe, who had suddenly resigned as prime minister in September 2007, seemed to have been reborn as a promising leader since winning the post of LDP president in September 2012.

In this context, some Christians started to raise concerns about the presence of nationalist tendencies in the LDP under Abe's leadership.[82] For example, the chairperson of the Japan Baptist Convention (JBC) sent a special message reminding members to use their voting rights in the election and to pray earnestly, as called for in 1 Timothy 2:1, since a movement for fundamental change in Japan was afoot. Three days before the election, the JBC

---

81. "LDP Announces a New Draft."
82. Neda, "Maegaki [Foreword]," 3.

held a voluntary "Emergency Prayer Meeting Due to Concerns about the Circumstances of Constitutional Amendment" in Tokyo. After the new year, the federation held a similar event in the Kyūshū region.

Several events held by Christians or Christian organizations in 2013 raised further awareness about an impending crisis. The *Christian Yearbook* reported four related events.[83] The *Christian Newspaper* also began to highlight the constitutional amendment issue with a series of twenty-five articles, from 14 April to 13 October 2013. The Social Committee of Japan Evangelical Association hosted an emergency prayer meeting. The Christian Student Fellowship held a prayer meeting for "Confessing Hope." And, in August 2013, the Church and State Committee of Japan Alliance Christ Church held a special prayer meeting at Nakano Church, Tokyo, that was attended by fifty people.

The main concerns of Japanese Christians related to the preservation of Article 9, known as Japan's pacifist article, as well as the provisions relating to the freedom of religion. Article 9 describes Japan as a peaceful country without any right to wage war, as follows (emphasis added):

1947 Constitution:

(1) Aspiring sincerely to an international peace based on justice and order, the Japanese people *forever* renounce war as a sovereign right of the nation and the threat or use of force as means of settling international disputes.

(2) In order to accomplish the aim of the preceding paragraph, land, sea, and air forces, as well as other war potential, *will never* be maintained. The right of belligerency of the state *will not* be recognized.

---

83. The four events are as follows: (1) On 27 May 2013, a seminar on "What Should Christians Do regarding the Amendment" at Keisen Baptist Church in Tokyo, held by the JBC, attended by sixty people; (2) On 29 May 2013, fifty religious figures from the Christian, Buddhist, and Shinto religions released a joint statement on opposing the amendment of Articles 9 and 96; (3) The "Wind of Fraternity Peace" organization and Aoyama Gakuin University Research Institute co-hosted a dialogue on the form of nation, attended by ninety people from both the revisionist camp and advocates of the present constitution on 23 June 2013; (4) The Christian Newspaper and the Christ Newspaper held an emergency symposium entitled "Where Will This Country Go!?" at Meiji Gakuin University, Tokyo. About 150 participants attended this symposium. Since the number of attendees exceeded the capacity of the building, the response surpassed the expectations of the host. See Kirisutokyō Nenkan Hensyūbu, *Kirisutokyō Nenkan 2014*, 10–16.

2012 Draft:

(1) Aspiring sincerely to an international peace based on justice and order, the Japanese people renounce war as a sovereign right of the nation and will not employ the threat and use of force as a means of settling international disputes.

(2) The provisions of the preceding paragraph *shall not prevent* the exercise of the right to self-defense.

Under the present constitution, Japan must seek to resolve disputes by means other than military action. The second clause reinforces this pacifist commitment by rejecting the nation's right to maintain military forces. However, the draft amendment omits the word "forever" in the first clause, and changes the meaning of the second clause by introducing a new provision concerning the right of self-defense. It also removes the statement abolishing the maintenance of all national forces.

Christians have similarly closely followed the efforts to revise Article 20, although mass media has paid less attention to this issue than it did to Article 9. The current text and the proposed revision read as follows (emphasis added):

1947 Constitution:

(1) Freedom of religion is guaranteed to all. No religious organization shall receive any privileges from the State, *nor exercise any political authority*.

(2) No person shall be compelled to take part in any religious act, celebration, rite or practice.

(3) The State and its organs shall refrain from religious education or any other religious activity.

2012 Draft:

(1) Freedom of religion is guaranteed. The State shall not grant privileges to any religious organization.

(2) No person shall be compelled to take part in any religious act, celebration, rite or practice.

(3) The State, local governments and other public entities shall refrain from particular religious education and other religious activities. *However, this provision shall not apply to activities that do not exceed the scope of social rituals or customary practices.*

In the first clause, the draft amendment omits the phrase "to all." It also weakens the prohibition regarding religious organization by omitting the words "nor exercise any political authority" in the first clause, and weakens the purvey of the third clause by excluding religious activities that can be classified as "social rituals or customary practices." This wording would make it possible for the government to treat worship at shrines as mere social rituals, rather than religious acts.

Long before the release of the 2012 draft amendments, several Japanese Christians had been involved in initiating movements to preserve Article 9 and to protest alleged violations of this article, as well as to protect the freedom of religion and the separation of religion and state.[84] They had participated, for example, in a lawsuit filed when the government used public funds to pay a contribution for rituals at a Shinto shrine, and when the prime minister worshiped at a shrine, not as a private individual but in his function as prime minister.

In what follows, we will consider how several evangelical figures have responded to the proposed constitutional amendments, and how they attempted to encourage other Christians to overcome their inclination to avoid political involvement.

2.2.2.1 *Watanabe Nobuo*

Watanabe Nobuo (1923–2020) was a pastor at the Tokyo Confession Church, belonging to the Japan Christ Church denomination of Presbyterian orientation. He held a doctorate in the ecclesiology of John Calvin from Kyoto University. Watanabe had been involved in the movement to defend Article 9 since the 1950s. In his seminars, he called on Christians to fight for the preservation of Article 9.

Watanabe articulated an essential principle for Japanese Christians engaging in the public square, believing Article 9 to be consistent with biblical

---

84. See Tanaka, *Kenpō Kyū-jō no*, 118–19, 149.

principles. However, he emphasized that his public advocacy was not based on this article's agreement with the teachings of the Bible.[85] Rather, the struggle is justified because this article is true – not only for Christians who believe in the Bible but also for non-Christians. Watanabe suggested focusing on the fact that if countries do not give up their right to establish military forces and to wage war, humanity will destroy itself.[86]

Watanabe criticized political leaders for lacking ideologies and beliefs that would equip them for resisting war. In his view, those leaders also failed to understand the principle of the separation of religion and state. He pointed out that religion is often used to justify war. For him, the attempt to revise Article 20 hides a latent desire among members of the present government to use religion to facilitate mobilization for war.

A firm believer in the separation of church and state, Watanabe affirmed that the church must not intervene in matters under the jurisdiction of the state. However, the church may ask the state to repent, especially in an emergency situation, where the state violates the religious sphere for the sake of its political agenda. He also contended that the failure of Japanese churches to resist the government during the imperialist and fascist periods was closely related to their vague understanding of faith.[87] For this reason, he suggested that Christians must clarify their understanding so as to have the confidence to stand up for what they believe in their heart.[88]

Watanabe stated that Christians must understand and identify the real beneficiaries of war. Every war is always detrimental to both the attacker and the attacked, and it is the arms industry alone that profits. Behind the LDP efforts to revise Article 9, he saw people who were trying to take advantage of the opportunity to manufacture and sell high-technology military weapons. Although many thought that right-wing politicians were leading the charge to amend Article 9, Watanabe believed that representatives of the weapons

---

85. Watanabe, "Kenpō Kyū-jō no."

86. It is interesting to note that although most Calvinists support just war theory, Watanabe supports pacifism. Drawing on his deeply impactful war experience as an officer in the Japanese imperial navy, he states that Christians should resist war absolutely. Christians must be willing to endure injustice rather than to fight with violence. For him, this does not imply a passive attitude, since Christians must also work actively for peace. Overall, pacifism seems to find unusually strong support among Japanese Christians.

87. Watanabe, "Daiichi no Haisen," 30, 33.

88. Watanabe, 17.

industry were using the power of the political right for their own purposes.[89] Building nuclear and other high-tech weapons, so Watanabe argued, endangers not only enemies but also the makers and users of the weapons themselves. Article 9 shows the path to growth for a country that has experienced the devestation of modern war. For these reasons, Watanabe called on Christians to defend Article 9.

The strong point in Watanabe's argument was his personal experience of war, which led him to study Calvin's ecclesiology. Since most Japanese Christians today have no war experience, Watanabe was able to influence them with his real-life stories about the horrors of war. This feature makes his arguments persuasive, and solidly grounded in Christian thought.

Through his account of the right of resistance, Watanabe made a significant contribution to evangelical Christian engagement with the threat of Japanese nationalism. He was also a source of inspiration for Asaoka Masaru (b.1968), an evangelical figure who also engages actively with this issue and others.[90] However, when it comes to the proposed amendments, Watanabe's focus was limited to Articles 9 and 20. The next figure we will discuss, however, has attempted to address other articles as well.

2.2.2.2 Nishikawa Shigenori

As we have seen in section 2.1.2, Nishikawa was a Christian journalist active in both church ministry and political engagement. Like Watanabe, he emphasized the importance of defending Article 9 and 20. However, he engaged with this issue in a unique and broader way, having attended and listened to all the meetings of the *Kenpō Chōsa-kai* (National Diet's Constitution Investigation Committee), lasting for five years from January 2000 to April 2005.[91] Although he was not a legal expert, Nishikawa could give a series of

---

89. Watanabe, "Sensō Seikan-sha."

90. Asaoka is a pastor of the Japan Alliance Christ Church in Tokumaru district, Tokyo. He responded to the situation in a unique way, considering this political development a "situation of confessing faith" similar to the situation German Christians faced in 1933. On 18 December 2012, he launched a Facebook group called "We Believe and Confess" as a forum to share information and arguments for Christians who have a similar view of the crisis. For his response to the amendment issue, see Asaoka, "'Shinjitayōni Ikiru,'" 10–23; Asaoka, *Ken o suki*. As we will see in section 2.3.2, he also served as the chair of the Japan Alliance Christ Church Disaster Countermeasures Headquarters and actively participated in relief and recovery work in the wake of the 2011 disaster.

91. Nishikawa, *Watashitachi no Kenpō*, 3.

lectures on the constitution and published a book explaining the meaning of every article in the 1947 Constitution.[92] He pointed to several problems in contemporary Japanese politicians' approaches to the amendment issue.

Nishikawa challenged the LDP's entire narrative regarding the importance of revising the 1947 Constitution. For him, the current constitution is not an imposed constitution. Before it was promulgated and came into effect, the constitution went through several democratic processes, such as the elections of the House of Representatives and the House of Councillors, to know the will of the Japanese people.[93] Nishikawa also showed that the content of the current constitution was not necessarily unknown to the Japanese people. In 1880, long before the Allied occupation began, a group of Japanese civil rights activists led by Chiba Takusaburō in Itsukaichi, Tokyo, had proposed a draft that had similarities with the constitution proposed by the occupation government.[94] In light of these historical facts, Nishikawa urged Christians to study history and to recognize how the Japanese government during its Great Japan Imperial period (1864–1945) had denied the freedom of religion by supporting the emperor system and the State Shinto. The government oppressed Christianity and Buddhism, and forced the people to worship at Shinto shrines, in particular the Yasukuni Shrine.[95] It also infringed on the freedom of assembly and association, as well as the freedom of press, by glorifying war.

In other words, Nishikawa argued, even though the Meiji Constitution of 1889 guaranteed the freedom of religion and expression, the Japanese authorities violated this principle by propagating the slogan "for the sake of the emperor and the country."[96] In his view, studying history, and in particular the atrocities committed by the Japanese imperial army on surrounding Asian countries, will help Japanese Christians to understand the dangers posed by

---

92. This work was published in 2005 and deals with the draft of 2005, but the arguments are valid for evaluating the draft of 2012 as well.

93. Nishikawa, *Watashitachi no Kenpō*, 112–13. General elections for the House of Representatives were held on 10 April 1946 (seven months before the promulgation of the constitution) and 25 April 1947 (one month before the constitution came into effect); the Election for the House of Councillors was held on 20 April 1947.

94. Nishikawa, 50–51.

95. Nishikawa, 29.

96. Nishikawa, 30.

the conservatives and their false claims. This historical awareness will also serve to increase the involvement of Japanese Christians in political issues.[97]

Nishikawa's dedication in attending all the meetings of the national Diet's Constitution Investigation Committee is unique. On the one hand, it enabled him to offer a lively account of the attempts to amend the constitution in the national Diet, and also served to lend extra strength to his arguments. On the other hand, it will be difficult for other Christians to continue his approach.

2.2.2.3 *Sasakawa Norikatsu*

Sasawa Norikatsu (b.1940) is a former law professor at Meiji University. In 2015, he published an academic article based on a seminar delivered on 15 October 2013 before the Nationwide Pastors' Meeting of Japan Christ Church – the same Presbyterian denomination of which Watanabe is a member – held in the Ōmori Church. Like Watanabe and Nishikawa, Sasakawa opposes the revision of Article 9.[98]

As a law professor, however, Sasakawa goes further, criticizing the 2012 draft as a destruction of the constitutional system. As the ruling party, he regards the LDP as a part of the government. Therefore, LDP politicians have the duty to respect and defend the existing constitution, which guarantees individual rights and limits the power of the government. However, in Sasakawa's estimation, the LDP is trying to revise precisely those constitutional sections that limit the government's power. The proposed provisions make an opening for the government to exert its power more freely.[99]

Sasakawa also highlights a problem in the way the LDP draft addresses the imperial system. The draft amendments do not return to the imperial system of the Meiji era, which made the emperor the ruler over all fields. Unlike the Meiji Constitution of 1889, the LDP draft restricts the emperor from having a role in the political arena. However, this restriction is not consistently observed, since the draft ascribes the emperor a status as head of state and affirms his involvement in government organizations. Here too there is no specific limitation on the expansion of the emperor's role.[100]

---

97. Nishikawa, 29.
98. Sasakawa, "Jimintō 'Kenpō Kaisei Sōan,'" 57.
99. Sasakawa, 58, 88.
100. Sasakawa, 88.

The 2012 draft differs from the 1947 Constitution with regard to its understanding of the terms of popular sovereignty. The first sentence of the preamble in the 1947 Constitution clearly denies all power and authority outside the constitutional system:

> We, the Japanese people, acting through our duly elected representatives in the National Diet, determined that we shall secure for ourselves and our posterity the fruits of peaceful cooperation with all nations and the blessings of liberty throughout this land, and resolved that never again shall we be visited with the horrors of war through the action of government, do proclaim that sovereign power resides with the people and do firmly establish this Constitution.

However, the proposed new preamble replaces those sentiments with the following:

> Japan is a nation with a long history and unique culture, receiving the emperor as the symbol of the unity of the people, governed based on the separation of the legislative, administrative and judicial powers subject to the sovereignty of the people.

Rather than recognizing the Japanese people as sovereign, the proposed amendment text declares that the nation receives the emperor regardless of consent by the people.[101] In this way, the LDP draft undermines the conception that the state belongs to the people.[102]

Sasakawa also criticizes the tendency of the 2012 draft amendments to limit freedom of thought and conscience in its statements on the national flag and anthem, its establishment of an imperial calendar system based on the year of the emperor's reign, and its positing of concerns for "public benefits and public order" as limits on freedom. He adds that the draft undermines the principle of the separation of state and religion, thus paving the way for the prime minister, cabinet members, and parliamentarians to perform public worship at Yasukuni and Gokoku shrines.[103]

---

101. Sasakawa, 76.
102. Sasakawa, 95.
103. Sasakawa, 89.

Sasakawa warns that the 2012 draft, if enacted, may severely affect Christians in Japan. Although no articles limit the church's functioning directly, history suggests that the emperor system, with its public worship rituals at Yasukuni and Gokoku shrines, would have negative consequences. Not only would it reinforce a tendency to consider faith as just an internal matter,[104] it would also result in many clashes between government policy and the beliefs of Christians, who regard worshiping at shrines as idolatry.[105]

As a law professor, Sasakawa has dedicated his expertise to engaging with the issue of constitutional revision. He has dealt courageously and candidly with the sensitive problem of the emperor system and clearly revealed the undertone of nationalism pervading the proposed amendments. However, like Watanabe and Nishikawa, he has failed to offer a solution to the deadlock. Some solutions have, however, been suggested by the fourth figure, to whom we will now turn.

2.2.2.4 Inagaki Hisakazu

As we have seen in section 2.1.2, Inagaki is a professor of Christian philosophy at Tokyo Christian University. Like Nishikawa and Sasakawa, he views the amendment movement as an attempt to make public worship at the Yasukuni Shrine constitutional and to allow the government to oppress those who hold different opinions or positions by invoking "the sake of public interest and public order." By reviving a stronger emperor system, Inagaki believes, the government is trying to foster nationalism and thus make it easier to mobilize Japanese people.[106]

Inagaki goes further than the figures we have already discussed earlier. He addresses the indifference of evangelical Christians toward this amendment issue as well as other interconnected matters of nationalism. For him, this indifference results from the absence of a properly conceived, robust Christian worldview, without which Christians have no proper interest in social engagement and are not equipped to fight such complex battles as the question of constitutional amendment. This theme requires an understanding

---

104. Sasakawa, 90.
105. Sasakawa, 91.
106. Inagaki, *Kaiken Mondai*, 51.

of history, ideology, politics, economy, society, and religion.[107] Since a particular worldview undergirds any constitution as well as proposed amendments thereof, a Christian worldview allows one not only to fight at the superficial level but also to dig deeper and investigate implicit competing worldviews, and, finally, to evaluate the appropriateness of proposed amendments based on that investigation.

Inagaki seeks not only to preserve the current constitution, but also to apply its provisions thoughtfully.[108] He does not simply indicate the danger of the term "public interest and public order" in the draft of 2012, but also contrasts it with the concept of "public welfare" in Articles 12 and 13 prescribing responsibility in using guaranteed freedom, and in Article 29 authorizing property rights. The relevant passages read as follows (emphasis added):

> Article 12:
>
> 1947 Constitution:
>
> The freedoms and rights guaranteed to the people by this Constitution shall be maintained by the constant endeavor of the people, who shall refrain from any abuse of these freedoms and rights and shall always be responsible for utilizing them for the *public welfare*.
>
> 2012 Draft:
>
> The freedoms and rights guaranteed to the people by this Constitution shall be maintained by the constant endeavor of the people. The people shall refrain from any abuse of these freedoms and rights, shall be aware of the fact that there are responsibilities and duties that accompany these freedoms and rights, and shall not infringe the *public interest and public order*.
>
> Article 13:
>
> 1947 Constitution:
>
> All of the people shall be respected as individuals. Their right to life, liberty, and the pursuit of happiness shall, to the extent

---

107. Inagaki, 8; See also Inagaki, "Kirisutokyō Sekaikan," 146–51.
108. Inagaki, *Kaiken Mondai*, 9, 29–30, 32.

that it does not interfere with the *public welfare*, be the supreme consideration in legislation and in other governmental affairs.

2012 Draft:

All of the people shall be respected as persons. Their right to life, liberty, and the pursuit of happiness shall, to the extent that it does not interfere with the *public interest and public order*, be the supreme consideration in legislation and in other governmental affairs.

Article 29.2:

1947 Constitution:

Property rights shall be defined by law, in conformity with the *public welfare*.

2012 Draft:

Property rights shall be defined by law, in conformity with the *public interest and public order*. In this case, with regard to intellectual property rights, consideration shall be given for contributing to the improvement of the intellectual creativity of the people.

The draft proposes to change the term *kōkyō fukushi* (public welfare) in the above three articles to *kōeki oyobi kō no chitsujo* (public interest and public order). Inagaki warns that, while the term *kō* in the draft amendment refers to the government, the term *kōkyō* in the 1947 Constitution implies all people in all of society.[109] Hence, under the proposed amendment, it is the government, not the people, that has the right to define public interest and public order. This understanding of "public" could lead to an authoritarian government, as had happened in Japan's imperial period. Rather than going back to that situation, Inagaki proposes to make positive use of the concept of public welfare, which is repeated several times in the current constitution. He calls this direction the new *kōkyōsei* (publicness), or *shimin no kōkyō* (citizen's publicness).

---

109. Inagaki, 30, 63–66.

After criticizing the weakness shown by Japanese churches in engaging with the concept of public welfare, Inagaki encourages Christian churches to use their considerable capacity to take leadership and to become role models for the wider society in promoting public welfare.[110] He urges Christians to cooperate with non-Christians toward this end, utilizing the concepts of diaconal work, common grace, sphere sovereignty, and the church as organism as articulated by Abraham Kuyper. With this Kuyperian approach, Inagaki attempts to extend the political engagement of Japanese evangelical Christians. He encourages them not just to protest against the government's threatening actions, but also to be a showcase for the government with regard to the creation of a better society based on the concept of public welfare. Inagaki believes that creating a civil society in this way can help Japanese people to solve many sociopolitical problems, including the problem of nationalism.[111]

2.2.3 Evaluation of Christian Responses

As we have seen, the amendment movement hides a nationalistic agenda. The proposed draft amendments of 2012 display similarities with the state in which Japan found itself during its imperial era, when the nation made rapid progress in technology and military power. During that time, Japan could motivate its citizens to die for their country and thus secured major victories for itself in conflicts with other Asian countries as well as Russia.

However, the 1947 Constitution prohibits Japan from having a military force. It also prescribes the principle of freedom of religion and the separation between religion and state. These principles make it more difficult for the government to mobilize people using religious narratives, as it did during its imperialistic period. Therefore, the politically conservative camp is attempting to revise the constitution partly to bring Japan back to its former glory days.

The responses of Japanese evangelical Christians to this return to a militaristic nationalism are admirable. Despite their small numbers and their usual inclination to avoid political engagement, Christians have generated various movements and produced several arguments in response to the amendment

---

110. Inagaki, 45–47. Inagaki explains that the insertion of the phrase "family responsibility" in the 2012 draft was intended to shift the responsibility for welfare from the state to the family. He also emphasizes the importance of freedom of association for creating citizen awareness. Inagaki, 30, 32, 44.

111. Inagaki, 33–34.

issue. The four figures discussed in this chapter applied their differing abilities – as pastor, journalist, law professor, and philosophy professor – to engage actively with this issue and to raise the awareness of many evangelical Christians regarding the potential danger of nationalism present in the efforts to amend the constitution.

Given the deadlock in the question of the proposed amendments, Inagaki's approach is deserving of special attention. As we have seen, the LDP has envisioned amending the constitution going as far back as 1955. On the one hand, the right-wing conservatives firmly hold to their position as *kaiken-ha* (revisionists); on the other hand, their opponents remain *goken-ha* (guardians) of the existing constitution. While the protest movements of many Japanese evangelical Christians can be classified as *goken-ha* movements, Inagaki's proposal of *katsuken* (using the current constitution in a positive way) to aid the building of Japanese civil society hints at a third-way solution.

For the guardian camp, at least, Inagaki's *katsuken* idea offers another way of engagement apart from merely protesting the revisionist camp. If one considers protest a negative action, then developing a civil society based on the concept of public welfare can be seen as a positive action. In fact, as will be noted later, Inagaki's ideas have gained support from several social welfare and cooperative circles. If this movement could actually yield visible, positive results in Japanese society, it is not inconceivable that the revisionist camp will reconsider its current articulated intention to change "public welfare" to "public interest and public order."

If we compare the attendance at events related to the constitutional amendment movement with other Christian events, one can see that the passion for this issue among Japanese evangelical Christians remains quite modest.[112] There clearly still is a large portion of the evangelical community that has failed to develop an interest in the topic. As Nishikawa has pointed out, this lack of interest may relate to the limited historical education received by Japanese students. The Japanese government does not provide history

---

112. Cf. Kirisutokyō Nenkan Hensyūbu, *Kirisutokyō Nenkan 2014*, 14–15. For example, there were 280 participants at the seminar to commemorate 450 years of Heidelberg Catechism on 30 September 2013, and 150 persons in attendance at the church hall dedication ceremony for Fujimi Church in Tokyo on 27 October 2013. The contrast is even greater if we compare it to attendance at the Christmas dinner held by the International VIP Club at Hotel New Otani Tokyo on 26 November 2013 (300 participants), or the ceremony for the hundredth anniversary of Sophia University on 1 November 2013 (4,200 attendees).

textbooks that honestly detail what the imperial army did to other Asian countries during the era of the Great Japan Empire. The absence of a proper historical understanding is exacerbated by the absence of a Christian worldview, as noted by Inagaki. Hence, equipping Japanese evangelical Christians to develop effective forms of Christian engagement is necessary.

From the perspective of ecclesiology, we can see that Watanabe engages with this issue based on the principle of the strict separation of religion and state. He warns of the potential danger in the government using religion to mobilize people for its own agenda. While advising the church not to intervene in the affairs of the state, Watanabe does insist on the right of the church to raise a prophetic voice, especially when the state is infringing, or about to infringe, on the religious sphere. Nishikawa's approach and suggestions are similar to Watanabe's. Both suggest that Christians must assume the role of a watchdog against the state. Inagaki goes further by suggesting a more dynamic role, that is, not only protesting but also actively participating in the building of civil society. It is no exaggeration to say that the indifference displayed by Christians in engaging with this issue is indicative of the need to develop and disseminate an ecclesiological understanding regarding the dynamic role of Christians in society.

It is worth noting that there are non-Christians who have shown some interest in Inagaki's Kuyperian approach. His suggestions for public philosophy and public welfare, which also relate to his research on Kagawa Toyohiko (1888–1960),[113] the founder of several consumer, agricultural, and fishing cooperatives (co-ops),[114] have been opening the way for him to engage with scholars in the field of public philosophy and public welfare, as well as leaders of several cooperatives. Besides publishing his work with various non-Christian publishers,[115] Inagaki has on several occasions also coordinated the

---

113. As a Japanese Christian social activist, Kagawa attempted to implement Christian principles in reforming society. He is famous for his determination to help the poor by moving to live in a slum area during his time of study at Kobe Theological Seminary. He is also a peace movement activist.

114. A cooperative is a jointly owned enterprise to address common economic, social, and cultural needs.

115. For example, *Shūkyō to Kōkyō Tetsugaku*; *Kokka, Kojin, Shūkyō*; *Jissen no Kōkyō Tetsugaku*; *Kōkyō Fukushi*; Ōsawa and Inagaki, *Kirisutokyō to*; "Nihon ni Sanka-gata," 2–12; "Hatarakukoto" no Tetsugaku.

Kagawa Symposium, which involves non-Christians.[116] This is an interesting development that the evangelicals in Japan would do well to follow.

2.3 The Countermeasures to the 2011 Great Eastern Japan Disaster

The 2011 Disaster was an unprecedented disaster of national scale. It started with a 9.0 magnitude earthquake, the largest in Japan's recorded history, which occurred at 14:46 on 11 March 2011, in the northwestern Pacific Ocean at a relatively shallow depth of 32 km. This quake caused liquefaction, sunken ground, and the collapse of dams and other infrastructure. The damage then cut off electricity, gas, and water supplies in Japan's northeast regions. Moreover, the earthquake triggered massive tsunami waves ranging from 3.5 to 17 meters in height and inundating over 400 km² of land.[117] The powerful tsunami wiped out dozens of communities in twenty prefectures along Japan's northeast coastline, and caused a loss of power at the Fukushima Daiichi Nuclear Power Plant, located approximately 240 km north of Tokyo. The power loss caused the cooling system to stop working, leading to the meltdown of the reactor and the release of large quantities of radiation. This hazardous radioactive leakage forced the evacuation of residents within a 20 km radius of the power plant.[118]

The triple disaster caused severe losses. As of 1 September 2014, the Japan Broadcasting Corporation reported that the official death toll of this series of disasters exceeded 19,000 persons; more than 2,600 remained missing and more than 6,000 people were injured.[119] It is no exaggeration to say that more will inevitably die in the years to come from injury and radiation sickness. More than 120,000 buildings were entirely destroyed, while another 257,000 partially collapsed. Over 340,000 people had to be evacuated and took

---

116. Symposia were held on 14 March 2015, 29 October 2016, 11 November 2017, 10 November 2018, and 9 November 2019.

117. Mori, Takahashi, and Joint Survey Group, "Post Event Survey," 2.

118. Samuels, *3.11 Disaster and Change*, ix; Arase, "Impact of 3/11 on Japan," 314–15.

119. "Disaster Overview," *NHK (Japan Broadcasting Corporation)*; See also Reconstruction Agency, "Hinanshasū no suii"; Fire and Disaster Management Agency, "Heisei 23 nen"; Cabinet Office, "Heisei 24 Nenban."

residence in the homes of relatives, public housing, and temporary housing, as well as evacuation centers.

The disaster affected both the national and local governments. Richard Samuels has rightly observed that "[the prefectures of] Miyagi, Iwate, and Fukushima had been hardest hit, . . . [but] the rest of Tōhoku [district] also suffered, as did parts of Kantō (the densely populated capital district) and the rest of the nation."[120] While the official name for the catastrophe is *Higashi Nihon Daishinsai* (The Great Eastern Japan Disaster), the common term used by Japanese people is "3.11 (*san ten ichi ichi*)." This brief moniker not only alludes to the March 11 date, but also recalls the series of terrorist attacks in the United States of America on 11 September 2001. Just as 9/11 (*kyū ten ichi ichi*) had been the primary issue on the forum at the national level in the United States, so "3.11 and its consequences refocused a long-standing national debate on the future of Japan."[121]

2.3.1 The Issue

The Japanese government promptly took several disaster management measures. It mobilized the Japan Self-Defense Forces to rescue the survivors as soon as possible.[122] The authorities also immediately sent teams to repair destroyed highways, as a vital measure for the transportation of relief supplies.[123] Together with aid organizations from Japan and 163 other countries, they offered various kinds of assistance, providing evacuation sites, relief goods, and volunteers to the disaster regions. The government also secured temporary housing for those who could not return to their homes. Public facilities such as transportation, markets, and airports were in many places able to resume operations quickly.

To some extent, the above measures were possible because the Japanese government had predicted the earthquake and tsunami disaster.[124] Given the scale of the earthquake and tsunami that had taken place in 1896 and in

---

120. Samuels, *3.11 Disaster and Change*, xiii.

121. Samuels, x.

122. For a more detailed report on the government's timely and effective acts in mobilizing the SDF and setting up crisis headquarters, see Samuels, 90, 107.

123. Cf. Samuels, 8.

124. The prediction, with 99% probability, had been for a 7.4 magnitude earthquake to occur within thirty years. Mori, Takahashi, and Joint Survey Group, "Post Event Survey," 2.

1933, along with smaller tsunamis every 10 to 50 years in the Tōhoku region as well as the Great Hanshin Awaji earthquake in Hyōgo Prefecture in 1995, both national and local governments had made preparations. The fact that the majority of buildings were destroyed due to the tsunami rather than the earthquake indicates the success of the government's attempt to implement the earthquake resistance building policy. As reported by a joint survey group of 299 researchers from 64 institutions throughout Japan, "Tohoku was an area highly prepared for a tsunami."[125]

Nevertheless, a longer-term evaluation indicates several concerns in the way the Japanese government coped with this catastrophe. These concerns can be classified into three categories: (1) slow recovery works; (2) leniency to the electric company; and (3) an ambitious nuclear program.[126]

First, in spite of the aforementioned achievements in disaster preparation and relief work, it can hardly be said that the entire recovery project proceeded smoothly. Samuels lists the following examples:

> Seven months after the disaster, less than two-thirds of the temporary housing for the displaced had been built, and nearly a full year later, only 5 percent of the voluminous debris left by the tsunami had been removed. More than half of the funds allocated for rebuilding Tohoku were still unspent.[127]

On the one hand, the delay resulted from the weak crisis management skills of Prime Minister Kan Naoto and his political party, the Democratic Party Japan (DPJ).[128] On the other hand, LDP politicians, seeing the weakness of Kan and DPJ as their chance to return as the ruling party, deliberately

---

125. Mori, Takahashi, and Joint Survey Group, 2.
126. Cf. Mullins and Nakano, "Introduction," 1.
127. Samuels, *3.11 Disaster and Change*, 8.
128. In addition to weak support from within the DPJ, Kan did not trust the career bureaucrats and tended to micromanage the numerous emergency task forces he had established. However, it is important to note that he had just assumed his premiership in June 2010, less than a year before the disaster occurred. The DPJ had also just become the ruling party by defeating the decade-long rule of the Liberal Democratic Party (LDP) in August 2009. The LDP had been continuously in power since 1955, with the exception of a short period between 1993 and 1994 and between 2009 and 2013.

refused the offer to form a large coalition government.[129] As a result, the government's action was delayed and inadequate.[130] In December 2012, the LDP succeeded in becoming the ruling party again. However, even then the recovery process did not improve significantly. In 2014, there still were 98,000 people living in temporary housing, without any idea of when they would be able to return to their homes. Many survivors felt abandoned by the Abe government when it shifted its attention and resources to preparing Tokyo to host the 2020 Summer Olympics.[131]

The second issue is formed by the inadequate measurements taken in relation to the Fukushima Daiichi Nuclear Power Plant accident. The plant operator, Tokyo Electric Power Company (TEPCO), gradually began to acknowledge a number of shocking facts. Prioritizing the interests of the company over national safety, the executives at the Tokyo headquarters had tried to stop emergency measures undertaken by the plant manager.[132] TEPCO also admitted releasing massive amounts of contaminated water into the ocean because the storage facilities were full. In August 2014, the company announced that the meltdown had started even before the tsunami came and that the reactor was far worse than initially estimated.[133] On 24 February 2015, TEPCO confessed that it was aware of the ongoing leakage of highly radioactive water, but kept silent.[134]

The disaster also revealed other problems surrounding TEPCO. The company had ignored international guidelines and made excuses instead of taking adequate safety measures.[135] Furthermore, many of the company's workers

---

129. Before approving the new taxes for reconstruction, LDP politicians set difficult conditions for DPJ by requiring it to abandon such popular programs as highway toll reductions and child allowances. See Samuels, *3.11 Disaster and Change*, 16.

130. Samuels, 10–11; Mullins and Nakano, "Introduction," 9.

131. Mullins and Nakano, 15; Kingston, "Downsizing Fukushima," 63.

132. The executives thought that the injection of saltwater by Yoshida Masao, the plant manager, would do irreparable damage to the reactors. Fortunately, the plant manager disobeyed their instructions to stop the injection of water and averted a far worse catastrophe. Cf. Samuels, *3.11 Disaster and Change*, 37, 45; Kingston, 59.

133. While NISA raised its evaluation to "level five," Koide Hiroaki, a dissident nuclear physicist of long standing, together with several colleagues, insisted that it was actually a much more severe "level six" or higher. IAEA assessed the event as a "level seven" disaster – the highest possible level. Samuels, *3.11 Disaster and Change*, 14; Cf. Kingston, 59.

134. Kingston, 60.

135. Samuels, *3.11 Disaster and Change*, 36.

had been "low-paid and exploited contract workers who had no other employment options."[136] At the same time, TEPCO was offering *amakudari*, that is, upper level post-retirement positions to retired government officers. This explained why the government had tolerated the electric company and given it privileges, despite its severe problems. Without giving any clear administrative penalties, the government injected aid into TEPCO to pay local governments for cleanup operations and to compensate displaced families for their losses. Moreover, while failing to implement sufficient solutions for preventing future human error, the government honored the company as an official sponsor of the 2020 Olympics.[137]

The third issue relates to the ambitions of the Abe government for developing nuclear power technology.[138] In April 2014, Prime Minister Abe laid down Japan's new national energy strategy. He proposed a "nuclear renaissance that involves downplaying risks, restarting reactors, building new ones, and exporting reactor technology and equipment."[139] With the support of LDP, he emphasized the renewed importance of nuclear energy as a key source of energy.[140] Noting that nuclear energy is a cheap alternative to imported fossil fuels, he stated that if Japan were to succeed in developing nuclear technology, it would enjoy a significant advantage by selling the technology in the global market.[141] He thus saw the program as an important step in making Japan a strong country in the fields of technology and the economy.

Regarding the safety concerns, Abe argued that the Nuclear Regulation Authority (NRA), the new nuclear watchdog agency, had created a new, stricter standard that was the most stringent in the world. Hence, he promoted the restart of existing nuclear plants as soon as they met the NRA requirements.

Many people, however, doubted the arguments of Abe, noting that his proposals were too ambitious and that his new guidelines lacked evacuation

---

136. Samuels, 45.
137. Mullins and Nakano, "Introduction," 16; Kingston, "Downsizing Fukushima," 61, 67–68.
138. This issue includes a much wider discussion concerning the pros and cons of nuclear power plants in general, particularly in Japan. Since this is a technical topic beyond the scope of this dissertation, I will not enter deeply into all the arguments.
139. Kingston, "Downsizing Fukushima," 78.
140. Kingston, 71.
141. Kingston, 64.

plans and preparations.[142] Kingston has argued that before 3.11, Japan had fifty-four reactors in operation, supplying nearly 30 percent of the nation's demand for electricity. The new safety standard limited the number of reactors to be restarted to just one-third of the original number, meaning that nuclear energy would cover no more than 10 percent of the national electricity supply. For Kingston, this is an indicator that the claim of the necessity of nuclear power as the base for supply is no longer valid.[143] He has also noted the presence of a hidden agenda, in terms of the potential of developing nuclear weapons.[144] These concerns prompted one hundred thousand people to flood the streets in protest against the revival of nuclear energy.[145]

2.3.2 The Response of Japanese Christians

2.3.2.1 Relief Work

Evangelical Christians in Japan responded to the 2011 Disaster mainly by conducting relief work. Using and asking information from the government, they also actively attempted to find and spread direct information from survivors in disaster areas. Moved by the vivid details they had gathered from the disaster areas, they undertook whatever relief work they could. Since it was difficult for the government to cover all the affected areas with the necessary relief, it is no exaggeration to say that the relief work performed by Japanese Christians played a significant role in the recovery efforts.

Since the responses came in many different forms, I will briefly describe them and for each response choose one figure who can be used to explain the theological motives involved in the issue at stake. The relief response can be divided into three categories based on the origin of the responder: (1) churches in the disaster areas; (2) churches outside the disaster areas; and (3) Christian organizations. After describing the actions undertaken by each category of responders, I will also note some representative points of views expressed by Japanese evangelical Christian leaders.

---

142. Mullins and Nakano, "Introduction," 17; Kingston, 71.
143. Kingston, 73.
144. Kingston, 66.
145. Kingston, 78.

First, the damage following from the 3.11 catastrophe affected Japanese churches as well.[146] Although the churches in disaster areas were victims of the catastrophe and needed relief supplies and support, many of them refused to wait passively for help. Instead, they themselves became a kind of relief supplies distribution center.[147] One famous example is Seaside Bible Church, which has already been mentioned in footnote 146. With support from CRASH Japan, a Japan-based Christian relief organization, the church rented the building of a former café and used it not only as a place for Sunday worship, but also as an open café for survivors to gather and receive relief supplies and mental healthcare. The supporting Christian relief organization used the second floor of the building as its sub-base camp.[148] While pastor Naitō Tomohiro emphasized that the basis of what the church ought to do – namely, to preach the word of God and to pray – did not change, his son Naitō Noah views the disaster as a plan from God providing Japanese Christians a better chance to share the gospel.[149]

In a similar situation, the entire building of Kesenuma First Bible Baptist Church was swept away by the tsunami, and the pastor was forced to live in a temporary house. Receiving relief supplies from churches outside the affected areas, this church distributed them to several evacuation centers and temporary housing sites. With support from the Samaritan's Purse, an American-based Christian relief organization, they erected two prefabricated buildings on the former church site and used it as a place of prayer as well as

---

146. For example, the tsunami swept away the entire building of the Seaside Bible Church (in Sendai, Miyagi Prefecture) and Kesenuma First Bible Baptist Church (in Kesenuma, Miyagi Prefecture). The entire congregation of Fukushima First Bible Baptist Church (in Futaba, Fukushima Prefecture) had to move to another place because its church building was located only five kilometers from the damaged Fukushima Daiichi Nuclear Power Plant. Many other churches were heavily destroyed, and numerous churches suffered partial damage. Akiyama, "Hisaisha Shien to Kyōkai," 7–48. Tōhoku Help created a list describing the condition of the churches in affected areas, which can be downloaded at http://tohokuhelp.com/network/dmg_ch/index.php, accessed 31 July 2017.

147. Alanna Foxwell-Barajas, "Tsunami Aftermath: Second Chances in Japan," *Christianity Today*, 16 March 2012, https://www.christianitytoday.com/ct/2012/march/tsunami-aftermath-japan.html, accessed 4 July 2017; Cf. Shinohara, "Church as God's Missionary," 249.

148. "Kamisama to no Majiwari, Yori Fukaku: Naitō Tomohiro Bokushi," *Christian Today*, 14 August 2011, http://www.christiantoday.co.jp/articles/9499/20110814/news.htm, accessed 4 July 2017.

149. "After Japan Quake, Church Finds New Purpose," *CBN News*, 24 June 2011, https://odysee.com/@JesusLoves日本:f/cbn-news-after-japan-quake-church-finds:9, accessed 3 July 2017.

a distribution center for relief supplies. The church also arranged for musical concerts and a food distribution program.[150] Pastor Minegishi Hiroshi views the disaster as a challenge from God for Japanese churches to become one in evangelization.[151] He reflected on his own way of evangelizing, and concluded that it had been too isolated and inwardly directed. Since the disaster, he has become more outward in his evangelism efforts.[152]

Other churches in disaster areas, such as Brethren Ishinomaki Christ Church, UCCJ Ishinomaki Eikō Church, Watari Bible Christ Church, Miyako Church, Ōfunato Church, Shinsei Kamaishi Church, and Shiogama Bible Baptist Church,[153] were also involved in various types, scales, and periods of relief work.[154]

Second, as we have already seen, churches in disaster areas could conduct and even develop various and long-term relief works because of the support of the Christians and churches outside the disaster areas. They gathered and sent a lot of relief supplies, donations, and volunteer teams to the affected areas.[155] Takahashi Kazuyoshi, the executive director of the Disaster Relief Christian Network (DRCnet) for the period from August 2011 to March 2013, compiled a rather detailed report on the relief activities undertaken by Japanese churches. He reported that Christians in Japan, including both Roman Catholics and Protestants, were all quick and active in responding to the disaster, conducting relief work and support activities in disaster areas.[156]

Christians started their involvement by confirming the safety of their churches and members in disaster areas and delivering relief supplies to the afflicted churches.[157] As soon as they had grasped the scale of the catastrophe,

---

150. "Uchinaru Koe ni Shitagau Kirisuto-sha e," *Christian Today*, 17 October 2012, http://www.christiantoday.co.jp/articles/11241/20121017/news.htm, accessed 25 July 2017.

151. "Kesen'numa no Bokushi ga Kōen: 3 11 Chōkyōha Kitō e," *Christian Today*, 12 July 2011, http://www.christiantoday.co.jp/articles/9415/20110712/news.htm, accessed 25 July 2017.

152. "Uchinaru Koe ni Shitagau Kirisuto-sha e," *Christian Today*, 17 October 2012, http://www.christiantoday.co.jp/articles/11241/20121017/news.htm, accessed 25 July 2017.

153. Shiogama Bible Baptist Church conducted a disaster relief project called Hope Miyagi. This project ended on 31 March 2017, but continues under the name *Inochi no Pan* (Bread of Life), which is an NPO for distributing food to the needy. https://www.breadoflife.jp.

154. Cf. Shinto no Tomo Henshūbu, *Sonotoki, Kyōkai Wa*; Akiyama, "Hisaisha Shien to Kyōkai," 22.

155. McLaughlin, "Wake of the Tsunami," 293–94.

156. Takahashi, "Kirisutokyō no Katsudō," 88–113.

157. Cf. Asaoka, "'Tsutaeru Kyōkai' kara," 37; Asaoka, "'Tsukaeru Kyōkai,'" 48–49.

they extended the scope of their coverage to all of society. Since most church denominations originated from outside Japan, Japanese churches along with their synods also received significant donations from overseas Christians, churches, and synods.[158] This allowed them to set up various kinds of long-term relief work. They established disaster response headquarters in their synod offices and opened several base camps in disaster areas. Along with these synods, Christian universities and seminaries also actively engaged in relief work, sending teacher and student volunteer teams to the affected areas in the summer vacation period.[159]

The catastrophe may well yield a development in the way Japanese Christians understand the church's ministry. Churches that had no experience in serving society could learn from the more experienced churches.[160] Asaoka Masaru[161] testifies that the disaster forced him to rethink his understanding of the gospel, faith, mission, church, its relationship to the world, and of how to live life and how to face death.[162] He concluded that the church should change its mindset, moving from a *tsutaeru* (teaching or preaching) church to a *tsukaeru* (serving) church. While the former refers to a church that focuses exclusively on preaching the Bible, inviting people to church, and growing its membership, the latter indicates a church that is also willing to snuggle[163] up to, listen to, and be sent to serve people, including non-Christians. Asaoka believes that this diaconal ministry has been an essential ministry since the time of the apostles. He asserts that the church should always help people in suffering, not only in times of disaster. The church should engage in both evangelism and diaconal activities. For this reason, Asaoka recommends Calvin's ecclesiology, which strikes a balance between

---

158. Cf. Takahashi, "Kirisutokyō no Katsudō," 91, 99, 102, 103. Takahashi gave the following breakdown of received donations (denomination name, amount in JPY from domestic donors, amount in JPY from overseas donors): Catholic (Caritas Japan): 681,660,109 and 586,645,543; Anglican: 177,369,458 and 119,738,284; UCCJ: 446,424,690 and 228,476,685; JACC: 57,961,538 and 12,107,932.

159. Examples included Tokyo Christian University, Ibaraki Christian University, Aoyama Gakuin University, Seigakuin University, Seinan Gakuin University, and Hokusei Gakuen University.

160. Takahashi, "Kirisutokyō no Katsudō," 109–10.

161. For more detailed information on Asaoka's profile, see footnote 90.

162. Asaoka, "'Tsutaeru Kyōkai' kara," 37; Asaoka, "'Tsukaeru Kyōkai,'" 46–47.

163. The Japanese term *yorisou* has become a famous keyword for relief and recovery work after the 2011 Great Disaster.

evangelism and diaconal ministry, as the solution to the oft-posed question regarding the position of relief work in church ministry. With this model, the Japanese church can leave behind its dualistic way of thinking, which forces a choice between "relief works or evangelism," and therefore always engage both ministries at once.[164] Asaoka also says that the catastrophe caused him to rethink the very foundations of his theological thought. He believes that the 3.11 disaster demands a total and radical reformation of Japan's churches.[165]

Third, the scale of the catastrophe and the dynamic conditions of the survivors in the disaster areas also triggered an awareness of the need for a network across synodical organizations and theological positions.[166] While large denominations may be able to conduct various kinds of assistance work, on a long-term basis, by themselves, other smaller denominations could indeed benefit from these networks. Several types of Christian disaster relief networks emerged in the wake of the disaster. The first category is networks of churches in disaster areas. Tōhoku Help, 3.11 Iwate Church Network, Fukushima Christian Communication Group, and Miyagi Mission Network are some examples.[167]

Among this first type, Tōhoku Help represents the biggest network, and was established on 18 March 2011 by the Sendai Christian Alliance, a fellowship organization of local Catholic and Protestant churches. Partnering with various religious bodies and other institutions, it conducted a wide range of activities, such as aid for affected churches and members, assistance for foreign victims, food radiation measurement, child education, a clinical pastoral training course, and anti-nuclear power protests.[168] Tōhoku Help has completed a total of 517 projects.[169] In January 2013, it became an authorized Non-Profit Organization (NPO). Like its parent organization, the Sendai Christian Alliance, Tōhoku Help is supported not only by the so-called

---

164. Asaoka, "'Tsutaeru Kyōkai' kara," 35–53; Asaoka, "'Tsukaeru Kyōkai,'" 45–78.

165. Asaoka, "'Tsukaeru Kyōkai,'" 46–47.

166. Takahashi, "Kirisutokyō no Katsudō," 101.

167. As of 1 August 2017, their websites are as follows: http://touhokuhelp.com (Tōhoku Help), http://311.ichurch.jp (Iwate Network) and http://www.mm-network.jp (Miyagi Mission Network).

168. Akiyama, "Hisaisha Shien to Kyōkai"; Kawakami, "Kyōkai no Minisutorī-," 49–118. For information on Tōhoku Help in English, see http://touhokuhelp.com/index_en.html, or Kawakami, "Cooperation of Christians," 103–4.

169. Kawakami, "Kyōkai no Minisutorī-," 84.

ecumenical denominations, but also by several evangelical denominations. In addition, executive director Kawakami Naoya is a pastor from an ecumenical denomination,[170] and had been working as an administrative staff member at Tokyo Christian University, an evangelical theological university. This experience seems to have opened the doors for cooperation from the evangelical side, despite its hesitation regarding some of Tōhoku Help's activities.[171]

The second type of network is composed of churches based outside the disaster areas. Agape Christian Global Network (Agape CGN), Aomori Church Network, Hokkaido Christians Mission Network (Hokumin), Serve for Others Live with One Another (SOLA), and Disaster Relief Christian Network (DRCnet) are some of the Christian networks and organizations established by churches outside the disaster areas in the wake of the catastrophe.[172] Unlike other organizations, the DRCnet focuses on being a hub facilitating connections between churches, relief organizations, and individuals that want to get involved in relief activities and the affected areas. It functions as a center that can collect, organize, and provide information regarding the latest needs of the disaster area, including the condition of churches there. As of July 2011, there were forty-two institutions, including evangelism organizations, NGOs, churches, and synods, that had become members of this network. As they wished, the members included so-called evangelicals, Pentecostals, and ecumenicals, making the network a Protestant structure of unprecedented scale.[173]

It is also important to note the existence of several Christian humanitarian aid organizations in Japan prior to the 2011 Disaster. These include World Vision Japan (WVJ), Japan International Food for the Hungry (JIFH), the

---

170. Sendai Townspeople Church, a church from the United Christ of Church Japan (UCCJ) denomination.

171. One example of such activity is prayer to the dead. Cf. Yamaguchi, "Hon Bukkuretto no Atogaki," 119.

172. Agape CGN was established by Wesleyan Holiness Yodobashi Church as an interdenominational disaster relief organization. The following is a list of their websites as of 1 August 2017: http://agapecgn.blogspot.com (Agape CGN), http://www.hocmin.net (Hokumin), http://drcnet.jp (DRCnet), https://kbcnet.wixsite.com/sola (SOLA). To some extent, Aomori and Hokkaidō also numbered among the affected areas. However, since Aomori Christian Network and Hokumin soon focused on helping those in Iwate, Miyagi, and Fukushima, I have classified them as being "outside disaster areas."

173. DRCnet pamphlet, http://drcnet.jp/_userdata/drcnet-bylaw20110415.pdf, accessed 26 June 2017.

Foundation for International Development/Relief (FIDR), and Christians Relief Assistance Support and Hope (CRASH) Japan.[174] These organizations also actively conducted relief work.

As an evangelical Christian organization specialized in disaster relief, CRASH is worth observing. Founded in 2005 by Jonathan Wilson, a missionary pastor ministering in the far west of Tokyo, CRASH aims to train and mobilize Christian volunteers to provide help and hope in the wake of natural disasters.[175] Wilson intentionally embedded "Hope" in the name of the organization because he believes that hope is intrinsic to the core of the gospel message. Furthermore,

> there is great need in Japanese society at this time for hope, not just with disaster survivors but also in families of bullied school children, isolated young people, suicidal adults, battered women, and elderly who are abandoned. Now is the time that we must stop calling them to come out of the world and into the church, but call the church to go to the suffering in the world with the compassion of Christ.[176]

In Wilson's eyes, Japanese churches are primarily concerned with their own membership and tend to be inward looking. Through CRASH, he tries to help them to become outward looking, not just during disaster times but also in normal times. In the wake of the catastrophe, numerous evangelical churches and individuals from Japan and abroad sent donations, relief supplies, and volunteers through this organization.[177] These enormous financial

---

174. https://www.worldvision.jp (WVJ), http://www.jifh.org/ (JIFH), http://www.fidr.or.jp (FIDR), and http://crashjapan.com (CRASH).

175. Cf. Timothy C. Morgan, "Don't Give Up on Japan," *Christianity Today*, 30 July 2013, www.christianitytoday.com/ct/2013/july-web-only/dont-give-up-on-japan.html, accessed 3 July 2017.

176. Wilson, "'Staying In,'" 81. It is interesting to note that other Japanese evangelical Christian figures who are actively involved in disaster relief and support works such as Asaoka Masaru and Kondō Yoshiya also consider the importance of bringing hope to Japanese people. Kondō, *Hisaichi kara no Tegami*; Asaoka, "'Tsukaeru Kyōkai,'" 73–76).

177. Founded by a missionary, CRASH enjoyed a close relationship with the Japan Evangelical Mission Association (JEMA), an association of Japan-based mission agencies, their personnel, and other missionaries. When the 2011 disaster occurred, JEMA's supporters (churches, missionary agency, individuals) could get fresh information about the catastrophe through the missionaries and disseminate the CRASH information to their other networks all over the world. Moreover, the Japan Evangelical Association (JEA), a fellowship of evangelical churches and institutions in Japan, decided to become engaged in relief work through CRASH

and human resources made it possible for CRASH to set up five bases in the disaster areas and to arrange various types of relief work, including clean-up, supply distribution, the rebuilding of destroyed buildings, mental healthcare for survivors, mobile cafés, and trauma care for children.[178] In August 2011, CRASH was able to register as an NPO, and with this official recognition from the Japanese government, it succeeded in gaining greater trust from Japanese Christians, non-Christians, local governments, and other NPOs in disaster areas. Under relief and support work arranged by CRASH, many Japanese Christian volunteers could meet and cooperate with other Japanese Christians from different denominations and from overseas. They could also reach and meet the needs of individuals in disaster areas that the government had not yet met.

2.3.2.2 Engagement with the Nuclear Program Issue

Along with conducting relief work, Japanese Christians also held seminars and symposiums. By inviting guest speakers who had theological knowledge or practical experience in relief works, participants learned how to respond better to the disaster both theologically and practically. Through seminars, they could avoid the extreme view according to which the 3.11 disaster is just a punishment from God. They were encouraged to get involved, out of a pure motive to help the survivors.[179] Seminars were also crucial in triggering Japanese Christians to engage with the government's nuclear program. In this section, I will discuss four Christian figures who have been actively involved in this arena.

The first figure worth noting is Ishiba Shigeru (b.1957), a senior Christian politician of the LDP. Although he is not an evangelical Christian, his political engagement and understanding of the nuclear plant issue can offer a good point of comparison. Ishiba has served in several high government positions, such as minister of defense (2007–8), minister of agriculture, forestry and fisheries (2008–9), secretary general of the LDP (2012–13), and minister of state for regional revitalization (2014–16). In an interview with

---

Japan. Hence, numerous Japanese evangelical churches and Christians (and their mother or sister churches overseas as well) sent their donations and volunteers through this organization.

178. http://crashjapan.com/en/about/, accessed 3 July 2017. Cf. Oliai, "Japanese and Christianity," 195.

179. Takahashi, "Kirisutokyō no Katsudō," 110.

Christian Today, he acknowledged, "I have been a Christian since I was born." He acknowledges that he has no faith awakening experience, but he also never went through a time when he doubted the existence of God. As a fourth-generation Christian, he is a great-grandson of Kanamori Michitomo (1857–1945), former president of Dōshisha Seminary (the predecessor of Dōshisha University Faculty of Theology) and honorary professor of Tokyo Bible Institute as well as Kashiwagi Bible Institute.[180] In a speech given before the 2017 national Diet Dinner and Prayer Meeting, he told the audience that he was a member of Tottori Church, in the United Church of Christ Japan (UCCJ) denomination. After graduating from junior high school, he moved to Tokyo and attended the then-Setagaya *Dendōsho*, that is, a mission post of the Church of Christ in Japan (CCJ). During his third year of senior high school, he studied the Bible passionately after becoming a temporary teacher of the church's Sunday school.[181]

Ishiba is a strong advocate of the use of nuclear power plants. As the secretary general of the LDP, he rejected the proposal of the DPJ ruling party to eliminate nuclear power plants. He was the only secretary general of Japan's political parties to oppose the proposal publicly.[182] Although he insisted there was no need for nuclear weapons, he argued that the nuclear plants should indeed continue to be used in order to show other nations that Japan has the potential to make nuclear weapons.[183] In other words, Ishiba supports the LDP's ambitious nuclear program to make Japan a strong country on the technological and economic levels.

From a totally different perspective, Watanabe Nobuo, a figure we have already encountered in section 2.2.2, sees affinities between the 2011 disaster

---

180. "Kono Hito ni Kiku (7) Ishiba Shigeru Kokumu Daijin 'Goyō no tame ni Omochi'i Kudasai': Inori to Negai o Kizande 'Shinjitsu' to Mukiau," *Christian Today*, 27 May 2016, http://www.christiantoday.co.jp/articles/21001/20160527/konohito-ni-kiku-ishiba-shigeru.htm, accessed 11 July 2017.

181. Uchida Shūsaku, "Jimintō no Ishiba Shigeru Moto Kanji-chō ga Aisatsu: Dai 17-kai Kokka Bansan Kitōkai (1)," *Christian Today*, 25 March 2017, http://www.christiantoday.co.jp/articles/23486/20170325/17th-national-prayer-meeting-1.htm, accessed 11 July 2017.

182. As of 1 July 2013, Ishiba was the only secretary general of Japan's political parties to publicly oppose the "Zero-Nuclear Power Goal" proposal. "LDP Alone in Fighting Nuclear Power Exit," *Japan Times*, 1 July 2013, https://lucian.uchicago.edu/blogs/atomicage/2013/06/30/ldp-alone-in-fighting-nuclear-power-exit-via-the-japan-times/, accessed 10 July 2017.

183. Okada Kōhei, "'Kaku no Senzai-teki Yokushi-ryoku Jūyō' Jimin Ishiba-shi Kaku Busō ni wa Hantai," *The Chugoku Shimbun - Hiroshima Peace Media Center*, 22 December 2011, https://www.hiroshimapeacemedia.jp/?p=5453, accessed 10 July 2017.

and the 1945 war defeat, and for that reason calls the 2011 disaster a second war defeat. The Asia-Pacific War was a tremendous human-made disaster that could have been stopped earlier, if only Japanese Christians and churches had raised their discontentment with the policy of the government. In the same way, the 2011 nuclear disaster brought to light the arrogance and greed of the government, which Japanese Christians and churches could have halted by voicing their concerns about the nuclear energy policy.[184] As it was, however, in both cases Japanese Christians and churches were defeated by the intimidation and brainwashing of the ruling power. For Watanabe, this happened because Japanese Christians had not sufficiently grasped the Christian faith and for that reason could not establish principles of life based on the Christian faith.[185] Therefore, having diagnosed this as the problem facing all Japanese churches, Watanabe strongly urges Japanese Christians and churches to foster their power of discernment, enabling them to identify the strange decisions of the ruling power as curious or incorrect.[186] He criticizes Japanese Christians and churches for their tendency to keep silent, even when they know in their hearts that what the government is doing is not the right thing.

Naitō Shingo (b.1961) has addressed the issue of nuclear power from a more technical perspective. He pastors in the Japan Evangelical Lutheran Church (JELC), and actively protested against the nuclear power plant long before the Fukushima accident. After graduating from Japan Luther Theological Seminary in 1991, he served in Nagoya Church (1991–2004), Kikukawa Church (2004–11) and, since 2011, in Minoridai Church. He began his protests against the nuclear power plant project in 1993, when he received a direct account of the inhumane working conditions from a day-hire worker at the plant. He is one of four officers of the "Society of Religious People Rethinking Nuclear Power Administration," and has written several books on nuclear power plants and Christianity.

Naitō has repeatedly asked the officers of the Nuclear and Industrial Safety Agency (NISA) to host an open debate between scholarly supporters and opponents of nuclear power. However, NISA just insisted that the nuclear

---

184. Watanabe, "Daiichi no Haisen," 33.
185. Watanabe, 17, 34.
186. Watanabe, 30, 34.

power plants were safe installations and never acceded to Naitō's request.[187] In his seminars, Naitō explains his reasons for opposing the nuclear power plant, even in the absence of an accident. He notes that the nuclear power plant project had severe problems even from the excavation stage. He also points to several limitations in today's nuclear technology.[188] In addition, Naitō has called for attention to the vulnerability of Japan's geographical situation. Japan is a country that lies on several active faults, causing it numerous earthquakes and tsunamis.[189] Arguing that Japan has an excellent ability to develop technology, he proposes alternative forms like gas and geothermal energy. Naitō asserts that although Christians are not saved by works, they should resist evil and think about what is truly useful for, and abundantly protects, others.[190]

Another figure who has addressed the political and nuclear issues of the 2011 Disaster is Mizukusa Shūji (b.1958). He attempts to view the nuclear disaster issue from a more theological perspective. A graduate of Tokyo Christian Theological Seminary (1985), Mizukusa has ministered to the Japan Alliance Christ Church (JACC) at Nerima (1985–94) and Koumi (1994–2016). While in pastoral ministry, he studied Augustine of Hippo at Tokyo Metropolitan University Graduate School. Since 2016, he has been the pastor of Tomakomai Church, and a lecturer of systematic theology at Hokkaidō Bible Institute.

Addressing biblical passages on the so-called cultural mandate, the fall, and the development of Cain's descendants, Mizukusa views the nuclear power plant project in Japan as a state policy that caused Japanese leaders to become greedy for wealth and power. The nuclear policy brought the political elites massive amounts of money, which in turn allowed them to establish

---

187. Naitō, "Kirisuto-sha toshite," 61–62. He made the same request to several municipalities which receive nuclear power plant subsidies in exchange for providing their land as plant site. Naitō was only successful with one municipality, the Shizuoka city. However, pro-nuclear scholars who dare to participate in the debate are hard to find. It took three–four years to find one, and during the debate, the arguments of the scholar who opposed the use of nuclear power were more convincing.

188. Naitō, 54–55, 71–72. Examples include the weakness of the Fast Breeder Reactor technology, which is the technology to store non-reprocessed spent fuel for one hundred thousand years and reprocessed spent fuel for one million years.

189. Naitō, 57–58.

190. Naitō, 74–75.

even more power.¹⁹¹ Even though they knew the dangers of the project, they ignored them and brainwashed the Japanese people to believe that the nuclear plants in Japan were safe. The misery of the 2011 nuclear disaster was not enough to make them change their minds. They were bound by the tools they had created.¹⁹² Mizukusa urges Japanese Christians to pray, speak, and act for a society that does not depend on nuclear power for its energy policy in the future.¹⁹³

2.3.3 Evaluation of Christian Responses

Other Japanese people, who were not Christians, also became involved in similar disaster relief volunteer work in response to the catastrophe.¹⁹⁴ However, considering the small numbers of the Christian population in Japan, it is no exaggeration to say that Japanese evangelical Christians had conducted impressive relief work. They helped the government reach those whom it had a hard time reaching, and provided certain information that the government did not have in detail. Some of the Christians focused on helping children or foreigners, who were often unintentionally marginalized in the government's relief measures.¹⁹⁵ A few of them even negotiated with the government to implement better countermeasures for the disaster victims.

Relief work responses show that the Great Disaster led evangelicals in Japan to implement the church's diaconal task in society. On the one hand, this shows how Japanese Christians have the potential to conduct diaconal ministry. On the other hand, it indicates that they do not have an ecclesiology enabling them to design and perform diaconal work for society when there is no disaster. The task is a difficult one, since the government of Japan, as a developed country, already has many social welfare policies in place. It is not easy to find a gap that has not yet been taken care of by the state.

Moreover, as Takahashi, Asaoka, and Akiyama noted, there were debates between Japanese Christians as to whether or not they should use the disaster

---

191. Mizukusa, "Seisho o Megane," 40.
192. Mizukusa, 21.
193. Mizukusa, 41.
194. Cf. Ambros, "Mobilizing Gratitude," 132–55; Graf, "Buddhist Responses," 156–81; McLaughlin, "Wake of the Tsunami," 292–96.
195. Cf. Satō, "Higashinihon Daishinsai," 103–26.

work as opportunities for spreading the gospel.[196] Many evangelical Christians considered the relief work as opportunities to bring the gospel to the disaster areas immediately or in the near future. Some others considered the relief activies a "seed sowing" ministry, and hoped that the seed would bear fruit in the future. Others preferred to conduct pure relief work, without relating it to evangelization. Kawakami notes that this kind of debate takes place not only in evangelical circles, but also within mainstream churches.[197] Although the debate may be a necessary process, it also indirectly highlights the absence of a clear position on diaconal ministry in the ecclesiology of Japanese Christians.

Relief work has also helped Japanese Christians to establish a more concrete, intensive, and synergic network across denominational walls.[198] The severity and geographical breadth of the disaster made the willingness to cooperate stronger and the adherence to one's own denomination weaker. Many Japanese Christians have experienced the benefit of cooperation with Christians from other denominations. However, once the disaster becomes a thing of the past and people forget, the synergic network may gradually weaken and eventually fade away.[199] Even when the disaster relief work was still at its peak, Akiyama reports that some longstanding church members in disaster areas felt they were losing their place in the church. The reason was the emergence of many volunteers in the church who from their perspective were "outsiders."[200] This shows that the church needs to fill the needs of church members, while also nurturing an understanding of the church's tasks in a way that enables members to welcome and cooperate actively with outsiders. In other words, what is needed is a more robust ecclesiology that weakens excessive adherence to one's own denomination and strengthens the diaconal ministry of the church so as to contribute to Japanese society.

---

196. Takahashi, "Kirisutokyō no Katsudō," 109; Akiyama, "Hisaisha Shien to Kyōkai," 42–43.

197. Kawakami, "Kyōkai no Minisutori-," 87.

198. Cf. Akiyama, "Hisaisha Shien to Kyōkai," 46.

199. Interestingly, after observing the 2011 Disaster in relation to Japanese politics, Samuels concludes that although "the catastrophe opened all of these possibilities and, in a famously conservative system, the first months that followed the quake, the tsunami, and the meltdown provided encouraging (if limited) signs of change," "it did not cause structural change to the Japanese body politic." Samuels, *3.11 Disaster and Change*, 200.

200. Akiyama, "Hisaisha Shien to Kyōkai," 37.

Japanese evangelical Christians were less engaged in the issue of nuclear power than disaster relief. This happened because the government had long been propagating only the advantages of nuclear power, without explaining its danger. Moreover, the nuclear question is a complicated one and requires knowledge of advanced science and technology. Nevertheless, three pastors tried to address this complex issue, from various perspectives. Watanabe used his experience as a Japanese imperial Navy officer to point to the similarity between the Japanese government's arrogance and greed in the nuclear program and during the Asia-Pacific War. Naitō devoted himself more to the technical issues in nuclear power plants and has been active in protest movements going back to 1993. Mizukusa attempted to offer an analysis of nuclear technology by combining biblical and systematic theology. Although Mizukusa does not mention it, his concept of cultural mandate does bear traces of influence from Kuyperian thought. These three figures all have concluded in similar fashion that Japanese leaders have struck out in the wrong direction and that Japanese Christians should therefore oppose the nuclear program.

Unlike Watanabe, Naitō, and Mizukusa, Ishiba supports the nuclear program. There is some similarity here with the case of Ōhira and Asō as described in chapter 1 and in chapter 2, section 2.1.2. Like them, Ishiba engaged actively with politics and held positions of high rank. Like them, he adopted a standpoint that, in the eyes of the evangelicals, prioritizes one's identity as Japanese over one's Christian identity. This phenomenon may corroborate the inclination of evangelicals to withdraw from political engagement altogether. From an ecclesiological perspective, this is indicative of the need for ecclesiological concepts that can encourage evangelicals to engage with politics without forsaking their commitment as Christians.

Conclusion

Our investigation of three contemporary issues revealed that Japanese Christians face complex problems. These problems ended up in a deadlock due to their connection with Japanese nationalism. The majority of politicians who comprise the ruling government are right-wing conservatives. Since 1955, they have not given up their agenda of restoring Japanese nationalism as in the imperial period. Even the case of the 2011 Great Disaster, particularly on the issue of the nuclear program, showed a relationship with nationalism.

Through the nuclear energy program, the right-wing conservatives would like to make Japan a strong country in terms of the economy as well as technology. Technology here relates not only to science, but also to potential military power in the ability to develop nuclear weapons. When it came to Yasukuni and the amendment, Japanese nationalism sought to build a strong Japan by using what they called Japanese traditions and customs. However, those traditions and customs proved to have a strong connection with the State Shinto as in the imperial period. Hence, the problem of nationalism in Japan is interconnected with the principles of religious freedom and the separation between state and religion. To make the problem more complicated, nationalism is oriented toward the building of a strong military power. This makes it a sensitive issue for the surrounding Asian countries which had been victimized by the Japanese military during the beginning and middle of the twentieth century. Japan's restoration to its former glory days through such nationalism is not about Japan alone, but also concerns other countries.

Engaging with such complex political issues is difficult. A critical position toward the government may be associated with an absence of nationalism. On the one hand, this is a result of the government's success in creating and propagating its beautiful narratives to its citizens. On the other hand, it reveals an ecclesiological weakness among Japanese evangelical Christians. They do not have robust ecclesiological concepts available to them that would help them become aware of the wrong direction taken by the government, even when it is successful in establishing stability in the economic field. Paradoxically, Japanese evangelical Christians also need a kind of ecclesiology that not only wakens them to the danger of the state, but also helps them to have a more positive view on government and state. Many Japanese, including Christians, based their protests on the constitution, decrying the government's movement as being out of harmony with the constitution. Although this is a sound protest, once the conservative politicians are successful in amending the constitution, Christians may lose the foundation for their protest. Hence, they need ecclesiological concepts that can also provide a solid foundation for them to continue their protest and to develop more positive Christian sociopolitical engagements.

The 2011 Great Disaster revealed that many Japanese evangelical Christians have the desire to engage with their society. Prior to the disaster, it had been difficult for them to mobilize themselves, in part because Japan is a developed country that already has an established, solid infrastructure for the social welfare of Japanese citizens at both the local and national levels. This indicates that evangelicals need ecclesiological insights to help them find needs that have not yet been handled well by the government. Since this difficulty is also a problem for Christians in other developed countries (even if in different forms), one can say that Japanese Christians need an ecclesiology that encourages them to share information and experiences mutually with other Christians across the border. As such, they may be stimulated to find creative and effective ways to implement the church's diaconal task to society, even when there is no disaster.

We have seen several Christians who have engaged passionately with the issues of Yasukuni, constitutional amendment, and the nuclear program. However, their acts are more individual acts than anything else. If their cooperation in engaging with the nuclear disaster is compared with their acts in relation to Yasukuni and the proposed constitutional amendment, the individual nature of the latter is brought into relief. It shows the need for an ecclesiology that encourages both the activist and other Christians to work together. To bolster the conclusion of this chapter, we need to explore the crucial events in the history of the Japanese church that led to these ecclesiological weaknesses. These will form the topic of discussion for the next chapter.

CHAPTER 3

The Context of Japanese Christians' Political Engagement

In the previous chapter, we saw responses of Japanese evangelical Christians to several contemporary political issues. Despite the protest efforts of a number of figures, most evangelical Christians remain indifferent to political engagement. Undoubtedly, the inherent traits of evangelicalism play a significant role in this. However, since such indifference can also be detected in other Japanese, evangelicalism is not the only cause. This chapter seeks to understand the historical background of this attitude of indifference. Using a historical approach, I will survey essential developments during the early modern, imperial, and post-war periods, in an attempt to uncover historical factors that have shaped the political attitude of most evangelical Christians in Japan.

3.1 Early Modern Period (Sixteenth to Early Nineteenth Century)

The first missionaries to land on Japanese soil did so in the mid-sixteenth century.[1] On 15 August 1549, Francis Xavier (1506–52) and several Jesuits

---

1. Although there are records of Nestorian Christianity in China sending missionaries to Japan in 736 AD, I prefer the position that establishes the arrival of Christian missionaries in the sixteenth century, since other theories still do not have adequate academic evidence. Cf. Mullins, "Japan," 198–99; Mullins, "Christianity in Contemporary Japanese," 134; Fujiwara, "Theology of Culture," 158. For arguments supporting the arrival of the Nestorians in Japan, see Lee, *Rediscovering Japan*, 59–87.

arrived in Kagoshima, the homeland of his Japanese companions.² Xavier attempted to use a method of cultural accommodation. He tried to learn the Japanese language, as well as Japanese culture.³ After several weeks, he read an explanation of the Ten Commandments in Japanese, prepared by his Japanese assistants. Xavier also made efforts to avoid cultural friction.⁴ As a result, he succeeded in converting 1,000 Japanese in just two years of mission work in Japan. He established churches in Hirado, Yamaguchi, and Bungo. Jesuit missionaries continued his work after his departure in 1551, and the number of Japanese Christians continued to increase. While there were 4,000 converts in 1553, by 1579 that number had reached 100,000. In 1614, there were 370,000 Christians, and by the early 1630s, Christians numbered 760,000 out of a total population of 12,000,000.⁵ Christianity spread rapidly throughout Japan, and for this reason the period from 1549 to 1644 is known as the *Kirishitan*⁶ *no Seiki* (Christian Century).⁷

3.1.1 Tendency Toward a National Church

Several factors had influence on the numbers of converts listed above. First, Xavier and his successors applied political approaches, too. They arranged to meet the local and national rulers not just for permission to preach, but also for their patronage. For that purpose, they represented themselves as enjoying economic and political power. When Xavier asked for permission

---

2. Kagoshima lies in southwestern Kyushu, the third largest island of Japan. It was an important port city. Xavier traveled with two Jesuits, Cosme de Torres and Juan Fernandez, as well as two body servants and three Japanese converts. The Japanese were Yajiro, his servant, and another compatriot. For a description of Xavier's journey to Japan, see Boxer, *Christian Century in Japan*, 36–40.

3. Abe, *Jesuit Mission*, 82–83.

4. Oliai, "Japanese and Christianity," 19–20. Cf. Higashibaba, *Christianity in Early Modern Japan*, 12–17; Abe, *Jesuit Mission*, 98–100. According to Higashibaba, this adaptation method became a "rule" of the Jesuit Society in Japan after the arrival of Alessandro Valignano (1539–1606). Abe adds that despite some minor differences, the Franciscans followed the method of the Jesuits.

5. Miyazaki, "Roman Catholic Mission," 7; Cf. Higashibaba, *Christianity in Early Modern Japan*, 12, who offers the following numbers: 1560: 6,000; 1569: 30,000; 1570s: 100,000.

6. This Japanese expression comes from *Cristão*, a Portuguese word that simply means Christian. Now it has become a technical term for referring to Roman Catholic Christians in early modern Japan.

7. Miyazaki, "Roman Catholic Mission," 4. He uses the 1549 arrival of Francis Xavier and the 1644 martyrdom of Mantio Konishi, the last missionary to remain in Japan, to mark the beginning and end of the period.

to preach in Yamaguchi, he offered the feudal lord luxurious gifts on behalf of the Goa bishop and as the ambassador of the Portuguese Indian governor. In turn, the feudal lord not only gave him permission to preach, but also offered him a dwelling place. In this way, Xavier succeeded in gaining favor from several feudal lords who then converted to Christianity and forced their people to do the same.[8] This explains why Xavier could report the baptism of one hundred converts in Kagoshima, another hundred in Hirado, and more than five hundred in Yamaguchi.[9] The later Jesuit missionaries saw the value of this political approach, so that "the vital matter in Japan was determining whom to approach for patronage rather than considering whether the missionaries should preach to the young or the old."[10]

A second factor was formed by philanthropical work. The missionaries established hospitals as well as philanthropic confraternities. Members of the Jesuits who had medical knowledge shared it with Japanese physicians. Such opportunities for gaining medical treatments and knowledge were attractive to the Japanese.[11]

Third, the Jesuit missionaries were also active in education. They conducted two types of education: (1) fundamental Christian doctrines; and (2) training for future priests. They also decided to provide elementary education in order to prevent parents from sending their children to Buddhist temples, which up to that time had been the place where children learned to read and write. The education program for children was effective in attracting the children's parents to Christianity.[12] Furthermore, the missionaries established a seminary as early as 1579, and another one in 1580. However, they also accommodated the children or younger brothers of the warlords and their retainers at the seminaries. By doing so, they secured the patronage of the local elites.[13]

---

8. Miyazaki, 7.
9. Abe, *Jesuit Mission*, 96.
10. Abe, 91.
11. However, the Jesuits' headquarters came to prohibit its members from direct involvement in the medical field in 1558. This change of policy, which reached Japan in 1560, caused the Jesuits to stop their work in the establishment of hospitals and clinics. See Abe, 93.
12. Abe, 95.
13. Abe, 96.

To sum up, the first Catholic missionaries were actively engaged in sociopolitical matters. As a result, they were successful in many places, baptizing almost all kinds of people, from high and low status, old and young, men and women. As noted above, however, from the side of Japanese people, the local elites welcomed Christianity in the expectation of benefits from the missionaries. It is hard to determine how many from the above numbers became Christians out of personal conviction. While they conducted Christian rituals, there was no guarantee that they sufficiently understood what they were doing. Hence, while this also happened in other Catholic mission fields, the pursuit of what we now call the "national church" (rather than the believers' church) had been taking place from the very beginning of the history of Christianity in Japan.[14]

Although the political approach brought many advantages to the mission work, it also came with many disadvantages. The missionaries became part political figures. Even if they did not depend on the local or national rulers for most of their work, the priority they gave to this political approach kept them from being fully focused on the spiritual work. When a large number of people became Christians because their local rulers had forced them to, the missionaries failed to instruct them properly, both before and after the mass baptism. As Tsukada concludes, "from the very beginning of Christian history in Japan the contradiction of 'serving two masters' had never been treated seriously."[15] The missionaries attempted to use the rulers for their purposes. However, the rulers also attempted to use the missionaries, and, as we will see in the following section, they prioritized their own interests over those of the missionaries.

3.1.2 Persecution by the Authorities

The increasing number of Christians in Japan did not mean that all Japanese people welcomed Christianity. Many Buddhist priests hated the nascent,

---

14. As I will show in greater detail in chapter 4, the national church is a concept of church establishment that embraces the entire membership of a nation or ethnic group. A believers' church, by way of contrast, refers to a church that consists of believers only.

15. John Jutaro Tsukada, "Whose Politics?," 144.

growing influence of the missionaries.[16] Their aversion only increased when Christians in several regions destroyed the Buddhist sites. The priests then persuaded common people as well as leaders to preserve Buddhism, rather than adopting a foreign religion. Animosity also came from the feudal lords who failed to get military or economic advantages from the Portuguese merchants. Even though the national rulers had initially been happy with the benefits from Western influences, they later started to see Christianity as a threat. They came to understand that Christians, with their teaching of the sovereignty of God, would not submit to them absolutely. The missionaries' relationships with their sending countries and their kings, as well as their allegiance to the Pope, rendered the sense of threat even more complex.

For this reason, the rulers started persecuting Christians from the second half of the Christian Century onwards. In July 1587, Toyotomi Hideyoshi (1537–98), the actual national leader at the time,[17] suddenly abandoned his favorable disposition toward the Christian faith. On 25 July, he issued the Missionaries Expulsion Edict. This edict led to the confiscation of several Christian buildings as well as the expulsion of female Christian servants from the castle of Hideyoshi. The missionaries responded by avoiding activities that could catch the public eye. For a while, Hideyoshi tolerated this strategy and allowed ordinary Christians to continue practicing their faith.[18] Nine years later, Hideyoshi tightened the prohibition on Christianity and ordered the executions of Christian leaders in Kyoto and Osaka.

There were several possible background for Hideyoshi's persecution against Christians. One can be found in the threatening words of a dismayed captain, who stated that the king of Spain would soon come to conquer Japan and that the missionaries were preparing Japanese Christians to support the king. The captain in question was angry because Hideyoshi had justified the seizure of the luxurious cargo of his ship which had been wrecked in Japanese territory. Another probable trigger was the group of Franciscan missionaries,

---

16. Buddhism was officially brought to Japan by Buddhist monks from Korea around the middle of the sixth century and became a dominant religion alongside the Shinto tradition. Cf. Sonoda and Brown, "Early Buddha Worship," 372, 412–14.

17. Although Japan had an emperor system, the military leader was the actual national leader.

18. Miyazaki, "Roman Catholic Mission," 10; Higashibaba, *Christianity in Early Modern Japan*, 133–4.

who had just arrived in Japan and preached in public despite the first edict.[19] The existing hostilites between Jesuits and Franciscans may likewise have been a disturbance to Hideyoshi. Whatever the case may be, the adversarial policy he adopted against Christianity was undoubtedly a strategy to secure his hegemony.[20]

The national leader after Hideyoshi, Tokugawa Ieyasu (1543–1616), established the Tokugawa Shogunate (feudal military government) in 1603. During its first ten years, this government allowed the growth of Christians in order to maintain its good trading relationship with Portugal and Spain.[21] However, when the shogunate established a solid trading relationship with England and the Dutch who had no agenda to send missionaries to Japan, shogun Tokugawa Hidetada (1579–1632) issued the Christians Expulsion Statement on 27 January 1614. This edict demanded the immediate deportation of all foreign missionaries and commanded feudal lords to destroy Christian churches. The edict banned Christianity and labeled it as a *jakyō* (evil religion) that was threatening a great catastrophe to Japan's social order. The government persecuted Japanese Christians and forced them to return to their original religions.[22] The persecutors gradually intensified their method and shifted from killing to forced apostasy. Miyazaki describes the persecution as follows:

> Diverse methods of torture were invented and applied to the Kirishitan. In the beginning the rather simple methods of beheading, crucifixion, and burning at the stake were used, but they moved the hearts of the onlookers, and far from instilling fear these methods produced the counter effect of stirring people's faith. For that reason methods of torture were more and more designed to prolong the suffering, and to have the victims renounce their faith rather than to kill them. The most severe form of torture was suspension in a pit. To prevent early death a small hole was made at the temple which allowed the

---

19. Miyazaki, 10–11; Higashibaba, 134–35; Oliai, "Japanese and Christianity," 21–22.

20. For more detailed discussions, see Fujiwara, "Theology of Culture," 162–63; Higashibaba, *Christianity in Early Modern Japan*, 127–31.

21. Miyazaki, "Roman Catholic Mission," 12; Higashibaba, 136–37.

22. Higashibaba, 139.

blood to drip out when the victim was hung head down from a scaffold, and the body was tightly bound with a rope to prevent the intestines from turning over. The head was lowered into a pit dug in the ground, and care was taken to have no light enter it in order to frighten the victim also psychologically.[23]

In 1637, a revolt took place at Hara Castle in Minamishimabara, Nagasaki. Seeing the determination of the rebels, who were only 37,000 in number and mostly consisted of peasants, the shogunate sent 125,000 soldiers to suppress it. After a long siege of the castle, lasting from 17 December 1637 to 15 April 1638, the shogunate troops defeated the rebels and spared no lives.[24] Although the main reason for the revolt was discontentment with the high taxes levied by the regional ruler, most of the rebels were Christians. This fact, together with the determination of the insurgents, surprised the shogunate and led to the policy of eradicating all Christians from the country.[25]

The third Shogun, Tokugawa Iemitsu (1604–51), imposed various measures to effect a thorough eradication of all Christians. The most famous measure is the so-called *Sakoku* (National Isolation) policy.[26] Other measures included the following: (1) denouncer remuneration, by which rewards were bestowed on those who denounced their Christian faith or prizes given to those who reported missionaries, and later also lay Christians and those who revoked their apostasy; (2) allegiance tests, as Christians were ordered to tread on the sacred image of Mary or Jesus; (3) the five households group system: if one member of a five-family group reported someone within the group for being Christians, the remaining four households would not be censured; however, if the report came from another group, all members of that five-family group would be executed; (4) a written oath of apostasy, which had to be confirmed by the village headman and the priest of the Buddhist temple; and (5) lists of the family groups of Christian martyrs, for close surveillance. The authorities imposed these measures in a very systematic way.

---

23. Miyazaki, "Roman Catholic Mission," 12; See also Higashibaba, 139–40.

24. Worth noting for Dutch readers is the fact that a Dutch ship, *De Rijp*, assisted the shogunate side in bombarding the castle.

25. Tsukada, "Whose Politics?," 144.

26. Iemitsu issued several edicts from 1633 to 1639 prohibiting foreigners from coming to Japan, with the exception of Chinese and Dutch merchants who were permitted in Nagasaki. This policy lasted until 1853.

For example, they repeated the *fumie* (allegiance test by treading on sacred image) every year, even after a person had renounced the faith.[27]

3.1.3 Between Martyrdom and Apostasy – Japanese Christianity 1

In many places, the persecutions resulted in martyrdom. Almost all of the missionaries determined to remain in Japan despite the expulsion edict. They went underground and were ready to sacrifice themselves as martyrs. They also recommended Japanese Christians to do the same.[28] The first and most famous incident was the martyrdom of twenty-six Christians in Nagasaki. As mentioned in the previous section, Hideyoshi renewed his prohibition on Christianity in 1596, and ordered the execution of Christian leaders in Kyoto and Osaka. Hideyoshi gave the command that their ears be cut off, and paraded the leaders as a warning for the people to obey his edict. Afterward, he sent them to Nagasaki and had them crucified on 5 February 1597. Instead of accepting the chance to denounce their faith, the leaders showed a passion for dying for their faith. This martyrdom encouraged Japanese Christians to hold on to their faith despite the edict. Until the prohibition of Christianity was overturned in 1873, Miyazaki reports, the number of martyrs whose names are known reached 4,045 individuals, while the number of unknown martyrs is estimated to be as high as 40,000.[29]

However, martyrdom was not the only response to the persecution.[30] As noted in the previous section, the authorities arranged for many methods of torture that were not intended to kill, but to cause Christians to apostatize. They developed a massive, systematic, and structured system of persecution that lasted for more than two centuries. In this way, the persecutions

---

27. Miyazaki, "Roman Catholic Mission," 14–15; Miyazaki, "Kakure Kirishitan Tradition," 20. For a detailed chronology of the persecution, see Higashibaba, *Christianity in Early Modern Japan*, 143–48.

28. Higashibaba, 148–54; See also Fujiwara, "Theology of Culture," 176–77. Two documents circulating among the Christians, "Recommendation of Martyrdom" and "Instructions on Martyrdom," glorify death resulting from confession of one's faith.

29. Miyazaki, "Roman Catholic Mission," 13. Cf. Higashibaba, *Christianity in Early Modern Japan*, 154; Fujiwara, 159.

30. There were also Japanese Christians who surrendered all their property in Japan and fled to a foreign country, including the famous Christian feudal lord Takayama Ukon.

caused a large number of Japanese Christians to renounce their faith.[31] The persecutions were so fierce that even Cristovão Ferreira (1571–1649), the head of the Jesuits in Japan, renounced his faith and cooperated in seducing Christians to apostasy.[32]

Confronted with two choices between martyrdom and apostasy, Japanese Christians developed a third-way alternative. They acted like non-Christians in public, while practicing Christian rituals in secret. These *kakure kirishitan* (Hidden Christians) transformed the figure of the Virgin Mary into a statue of Buddha and adapted the recitation of Christian prayers to sound like Buddhist chants. Higashibaba describes the rationale of Hidden Christians as follows:

> Hiding Kirishitan faith by external apostasy was reasonable for them, because it enabled them to continue their faith in this world. Whichever they might choose, whether apostasy or martyrdom, they could no longer continue to practice Kirishitan faith. Therefore, they created another option for themselves – to apostatize but not to abandon their faith – in order to live and continue their Kirishitan faith and practice. Although this option disobeyed the instruction of the Church, perhaps as much as real apostasy, it was the most reasonable and practical conclusion if people wanted to continue their faith.[33]

Although the Hidden Christians invented numerous means to avoid the attentive eye of the officials, the government was successful in rounding them up on several occasions, arresting at least 10,628 Hidden Christians.[34] After the national government lifted the prohibition on Christianity in 1873, some

---

31. Given the length of the persecution, it is difficult to determine the number of those who renounced their faith. What we do know, as mentioned in section 3.1, is that by the early 1630s there were 760,000 Christians, and, as will be described at the end of this section, there were presumably 50,000 to 60,000 Hidden Christians by the time the persecutions ended. The persecution period therefore saw a decrease by 700,000.

32. Miyazaki, "Roman Catholic Mission," 13.

33. Higashibaba, *Christianity in Early Modern Japan*, 155.

34. Miyazaki, "Kakure Kirishitan Tradition," 20–21; Miyazaki, "Roman Catholic Mission," 16–17. He lists the place, year, and numbers for rounded-up Christians as follows: Kōri: 1657, 608; Bungo: 1660–82, 220; Binō: 1661, at least 996; Amakusa: 1805, 5,200; Urakami: 1790–1867 (four times), more than 3,414; Gotō: 1868, 190.

25,000–30,000 Hidden Christians were estimated to have revealed themselves and joined the Catholic Church.[35]

However, a significant number of Hidden Christians chose to continue as Hidden Christians. During the persecutions, which lasted more than 250 years, their doctrines and practices had come to deviate from Catholic teachings. This happened because they relied on oral tradition during that period, without the existence of official Catholic clergy. When they found that their Hidden Christian practices and doctrines were different, they wanted to preserve them. Miyazaki suggests that the number of Hidden Christians was about 30,000 in the 1930s, and that more than 1,000 of them still remained in the 1990s.[36] When, in the 1990s, many remaining groups of Hidden Christians were dissolved for lack of successors, most former members became Buddhists or Shinto parishioners. Only a small number turned to the Catholic Church. Notably, even after their Hidden Christian groups were dissolved and they joined other religious groups, it was common for them to continue their old Hidden Christian practices, such as the annual memorial services and prayer recitation.[37]

To sum up, many Japanese Christians remained loyal to the faith during the persecution period. They showed a strong attitude, resisting the ungodly rulers by their martyrdom. A similarly powerful stance can be detected in the Hidden Christians. Considering the notoriety and length of the persecution by the authorities, it is clear that being a Hidden Christian was never an easy option. Miyazaki rightly states that surviving such systematic and unceasing persecution is a "truly astonishing fact."[38]

Notwithstanding, the fact that a significant number of Hidden Christians preferred to continue their identity as Hidden Christians rather than rejoin the Catholic Church calls for us to examine the characteristic of that loyalty more deeply. In "Instructions on Martyrdom," a document that circulated among the Christians at that time, several teachings can be found allowing Christians to hide their Christian identity to avoid arrest and to keep the faith.

---

35. Cf. Fujiwara, "Theology of Culture," 164, f.n. 612. Although Fujiwara warned that there was no accurate data for this assumption, he probably mistakenly doubled the number who returned to the Catholic Church when he noted the figure 50,000–60,000.

36. Miyazaki, "Kakure Kirishitan Tradition," 22–23.

37. Miyazaki, 32.

38. Miyazaki, "Roman Catholic Mission," 17.

However, the one condition it stipulated was that one could never act like a heathen.[39] For this reason, we must conclude that neither the missionaries nor the "Instructions" ever prescribed a strategy of public apostasy combined with secret Christian observance. Neither did they recommend the choice to continue as Hidden Christians after the persecutions ended.

This fact indicates the existence of a non-theological element which played a significant role in the history of the Hidden Christians. For Miyazaki, behind the decision to continue as Hidden Christians after 1873 lies the loyalty of descendants to their ancestors.[40] Similarly, Fujiwara writes that it was a "loyalty to their ancestors, who kept their faith even by risking their lives, rather than a loyalty to God."[41] Apart from a sense of responsibility for keeping the faith of one's ancestors, Higashibaba argues that the communal aspect, rather than the faith itself, also enabled Japanese Christians to hide their beliefs during the brutal persecutions: "If the Kirishitan decided together to apostatize or to hide their faith, their decision for martyrdom must have also been made together. An individual probably could not apostatize while the rest of the villagers secretly kept their Kirishitan practice."[42] Oliai goes even further, stating that this kind of loyalty is one of "the hallmarks of the Japanese character."[43] Thus, rather than being theologically motivated, the loyalty of Hidden Christians amounted to a decision to continue customs that they had already been conducting. It was a loyalty to communal authority.

This loyalty to communal authority can be used to explain many things. First, it accounts for the persistence of Hidden Christians in continuing their rituals instead of rejoining the Catholic Church once the persecutions had ended. Second, it complements our understanding of their decision to become Hidden Christians during the persecutions. In previous paragraphs, we saw that being Hidden Christians was a third-way solution for them between martyrdom and apostasy. Now we can frame this choice also as a third-way

---

39. Higashibaba, *Christianity in Early Modern Japan*, 148–54; Fujiwara, "Theology of Culture," 176–77.

40. Miyazaki, "Kakure Kirishitan Tradition," 31.

41. Fujiwara, "Theology of Culture," 164; Cf. Miyazaki, "Kakure Kirishitan Tradition," 21–22; Miyazaki, "Roman Catholic Mission," 17. Miyazaki finds that they exhibit "multilayered beliefs, ancestor worship, orientation towards worldly benefits, and ritualism," and that they therefore "should be regarded as another form or expression of Japanese folk religion."

42. Higashibaba, *Christianity in Early Modern Japan*, 157–60; See also Fujiwara, 193.

43. Oliai, "Japanese and Christianity," 23.

solution between loyalty to their Christian ancestors and their present rulers. Third, without intending to underestimate their martyrdom, we might even suggest that their willingness to martyrdom likewise was related to this loyalty to communal authority. Fourth, if we regard this loyalty to communal authority as a Japanese characteristic, we can see how strong the influence of Japaneseness was on Japanese Christians in the early modern period. This Japaneseness caused them to adapt Christianity in such a way that it departed from its origin, and over the course of time the Hidden Christians preferred the adapted version to the original faith. Fifth, to some extent, loyalty to communal authority is also reflected in the character of the Japanese officials' demands. To persuade someone to apostatize, the officials used the phrase *katachi dake* (only formality). This meant, on the one hand, that they demanded thorough obedience from their subjects, requiring Christians to apostatize. On the other hand, they did not care what actually lived in the hearts of their subjects.

The actual object of this loyalty to communal authority appears to have changed in the course of time. Until the early modern period, that object was the ancestors or the village leader. In the modern period, the object became the emperor or the state of Japan. It is to this period that we will now turn.

3.2 Imperial Period (1868–1945)

In 1853, Commodore Matthew C. Perry (1794–1858) arrived at the bay of Edo (present-day Tokyo).[44] Within one year, he succeeded in obtaining an agreement with Japan for opening Shimoda and Hakodate ports to American ships. Although the Treaty of Kanagawa (1854) was detrimental to Japan, the nation's leaders had no other choice. They realized that Japan lagged far behind America and other Western countries in terms of military capacities.[45] The Japanese government felt the need to receive influence from abroad in order to conduct military reform and to modernize the nation. This 1854

---

44. The US government sent Perry for the following purposes: (1) to make Japan a coaling base for American ships; (2) to open a trade channel with Japan; and (3) to secure proper treatment for shipwrecked American sailors in Japan. Cf. Lee, *Rediscovering Japan*, 133.

45. Murayama-Cain, "Bible in Imperial Japan," 29–30.

treaty paved the way for later agreements with the US and several other Western countries.⁴⁶

3.2.1 Denominationalism

The Amity and Commerce treaties allowed foreigners to live and practice their own religion in Japan. Using this long-awaited chance, mission bodies sent their missionaries to Japan, with six of them arriving in Japan in 1859.⁴⁷ These first missionaries came from different denominations: the Protestant Episcopal Church, the Presbyterian Church in the USA, and the Dutch Reformed Church in America.⁴⁸ Although they were restricted to the areas designated for foreigners, they attempted to reach Japanese people by learning their language, developing a dictionary, translating the Bible, distributing Christian literature, offering private lessons, and providing medical treatment.⁴⁹

However, since the government did not abolish the prohibition on Christianity until 1873, Japanese who became Christians were persecuted by the authorities. Similar experiences, or even worse, overcame the Hidden Christians. The arrival of Catholic missionaries from France led some of the Hidden Christians to stop concealing their identity as Christians. They even started refusing the compulsory Buddhist funeral for family members who had died. As a result, the government arrested them and attempted to convert them by persecution.

---

46. For example, the Treaty of Shimoda in 1855 with Russia; the Treaty of Amity and Commerce with the US in 1856, and with The Netherlands, Russia, Great Britain, and France in 1858.

47. That was why Japan celebrated 150 years of Protestant missionaries entering Japan in 2009. Strictly speaking, the first Protestant missionary actually came in 1846. Bernard J. Bettelheim (1811–70), a missionary of the Loochoo Naval Mission (Loochoo refers to the Ryūkyū islands in the present-day Okinawa Prefecture), arrived in Naha, Okinawa, and lived there for seven years. Neither his ministry nor that of his successors was successful. After Morton, Bettelheim's successor, left Okinawa in 1856, the Loochoo Naval Mission ended its endeavor. However, the recognition of the arrival of the missionary Bettelheim in Okinawa is essential, because it concerns the identification of Okinawa as a part of Japan. The people in Okinawa have often experienced unequal and unfair treatment from the central government of Japan. For a detailed description of the ministry of Bettelheim in Okinawa, see Cary, *History of Christianity in Japan* 18–27; Dohi, *Nihon Purotesutanto Kirisutokyō-shi* 10; Kerr, *Okinawa*, 279–96, 337–41.

48. For a list of mission bodies that sent missionaries to Japan, see Dohi, *Nihon Purotesutanto Kirisutokyō-shi*, 11–14.

49. Dohi, 11.

The persecutions to which Christians were subjected incited the representatives of Western countries to protest to the Japanese government. Initially, the Japanese government replied by stating that it concerned a domestic issue and that foreigners had no right to interfere. They defended their actions as punishments on Japanese people who had violated Japanese law, and not because they were Christians. Not satisfied with such reasoning, the Western representatives continued to protest against the arrest and torture of Japanese Christians. They expressed their disappointment and asked the Japanese government to release the arrested Christians and to secure the freedom of religion as a requirement for a civilized country.[50] In Japan, the principle of religious freedom was therefore not established in recognition of the goodness of the principle by Japanese leaders, but rather as a result of outside pressures from Western countries. It is worth noting that the pressures did not just come from one Western country, but from several Western countries. As we will see in the following paragraphs, these countries would contribute to the plurality of denominations in Japan.

After the government revoked the ban on Christianity in 1873, more missionaries started making their way to Japan. Since they came from various denominations, the number of denominations in Japan also increased as a result. In his "List of Major Foreign Missions," Dohi identifies thirty-one Protestant mission bodies that produced twenty-two church denominations in Japan.[51] Although America was the biggest sending country, other Western countries such as Canada, England, and Germany, as well as Scandinavian countries all appeared on the list. Dohi divides the church denominations in Japan into six large groups: Anglican-Episcopal, Japan Christ Church, Congregational, Baptist, Methodist, and others. This final group includes the Unitarians, Universalists, Plymouth Brethren, Salvation Army, Seventh Day Adventists, and evangelical churches.[52] Therefore, although other countries

---

50. Protests continued, even when the government had shifted from the Shogunate to the emperor system. When the Japanese delegation visited European countries for the purpose of studying Western systems, their presence was protested by people in the countries they visited. Finally, the Japanese government lifted the prohibition on Christianity in 1873. Moreover, as we discussed in chapter 2 sections 2.1.1.2 and 2.2.1, it arranged (limited) religious freedom through the promulgation of the Meiji Constitution of 1889.

51. Dohi, *Nihon Purotesutanto Kirisutokyō-shi*, 11–14.

52. Following this list, Dohi classifies the theological understanding of the missionaries to Japan into three categories: (1) evangelicalism; (2) liberalism; and (3) pure gospel. While

too have a variety of denominations, Japan's denominationalism is unique in the sense that it has neither a major denomination nor a single sending country. The denominations came to Japan at virtually the same time, and a single denomination could also come from several different sending countries.

The missionaries attempted to minimalize the potential negative effects of denominationalism. Although missionaries from Anglican-Episcopal churches were sent from three different mission bodies, they agreed to cooperate in Japan and therefore only established a single denomination, the Japan Anglican-Episcopal Church. Missionaries from different Methodist mission bodies also agreed to establish just one denomination, that is, the Japan Methodist Church. Similarly, missionaries from several Reformed and Presbyterian mission bodies agreed to merge into the United Church of Christ in Japan in 1877, which later in 1890 became the Church of Christ in Japan.[53]

In spite of these efforts, a plurality of denominations was inevitable. The clash between missionaries and Japanese Christians contributed more to the increase of denominations. Moreover, the responses to the influx of liberal theology from the German modernist camp and from American Unitarianism caused splits and frictions.[54] Reunification only happened after the militaristic government forced the merger of all denominations through the revision of the Religious Body Law in 1940. When the occupation government abolished this law in 1946, many denominations withdrew from the united churches. There have therefore been many denominations in Japan from the beginning of Protestantism. This pluriformity of denominations has become one of the characteristics of contemporary Christianity in Japan.

---

placing the first missionaries, who were from Episcopal, Presbyterian, and Dutch Reformed, as well as congregational, denominations, into the first category, Dohi identifies Barclay F. Buxton as a missionary of the third category. In contrast with Dohi, Nakamura uses a broader framework for understanding the evangelicals in Japan. His criterion for evangelicalism is acceptance of the plenary inspiration of the Bible, and thus includes not only the first and third categories of Dohi, but also the Salvation Army. See Dohi, 17–25; Nakamura, *Nihon ni Okeru Fukuin-ha*, 10.

53. Dohi, 29–30.

54. This confusion caused many Japanese Christians to be divided into one of three major positions: liberal, evangelical, and a middle position (which accepts higher criticism, while maintaining biblical authority and the divinity of Jesus). The mediating theologians welcomed Barthian theology in the 1930s, since they saw his criticism on liberal theology as a solution for their confusion. After extensive debates, liberals too came to accept Barthianism as a sort of compromise.

As part of their ministries, missionaries in Japan engaged with various social issues. Catholic missionaries from France focused on rural areas, attempting to direct the underground Christians back to Roman Catholicism and working among the disadvantaged, particularly poor and abandoned children. Their general trend was to ignore political developments and movements for social reform in favor of building a community of believers centered on the priesthood, thereby isolating themselves from mainstream society.[55] Protestant missionaries were active in the urban areas, and they, together with their converts, had a great impact on Japanese mainstream society. They put great efforts into educational work as a tool for evangelism, particularly at the secondary level and higher.[56] They established Christian schools, schools for girls, and hospitals. They also sought permission to educate prisoners. As Lee has put it, Christianity in the Meiji era contributed to Japanese society in three areas: education, feminism, and charity.[57] Worth noting are the two types of Protestant missionaries. The first type were sent by churches or mission bodies. There were also missionaries who received an invitation from the government to teach English and Western science. They shared their faith at work in such a way that many Japanese around them came to believe and were baptized. These sociopolitical engagements were effective in attracting many Japanese people to the faith. The period 1883–88 thus saw the rapid development of Christianity. At that time, the missionaries believed Japan would soon become a Christian country.[58]

3.2.2 Nationalism

However, in the period 1889–1900, the growth was no longer as it had been before. One reason for the declining growth came from the side of Christianity. As has been noted, the advent of liberal theology caused confusion and frictions among Christians in Japan. Another reason for the decline was the opposition from Japanese people, who received powerful ammunition for their attacks from the criticism of liberal Christians on orthodox Christianity and mission work. There were several parties in Japan that resented Christianity's

---

55. Ballhatchet, "Modern Missionary Movement," 40–42; Oliai, "Japanese and Christianity," 103.
56. Ballhatchet, 44; Hastings, "Japan's Protestant Schools," 111.
57. Lee, *Rediscovering Japan*, 139.
58. Hastings, "Japan's Protestant Schools," 110–11.

growing influence. The first were the Buddhist priests. Buddhism had received privileges as the state religion during the Tokugawa period. The Buddhist priests persuaded people and government to prevent the continuing growth of Christianity in Japan and to restore the privileges for Buddhism.[59] Another party was composed of those who ran brothels. They too persuaded the people to oppose Christianity, because many Christian leaders were pursuing the elimination of licensed prostitution.

The most vigorous resistance against Christianity, however, came from the camp of the nationalists. In the beginning, there were two views on how to build Japan into a powerful nation. While the first proposed to absorb Western technology without Christianity, the second emphasized the need to adopt both Western technology and Christianity together. The former ended up becoming the dominant view.[60] Its proponents used the motto *wakon yōsai* (Japanese Spirit with Western Technology). Instead of the Christian faith, which had become the backbone of modern Western countries, Japan's nationalist leaders chose to establish the so-called *Kokka Shinto* (State Shinto), which attempted to build a strong nation centered on the emperor system.

The nationalist group originated from local leaders who felt discontentment with the foreign policy of the Tokugawa government after the arrival of Commodore Perry. They considered the shogunate incapable of protecting Japan from the foreign nations. Apart from the disadvantageous treaties that the shogunate had made, they also hated the Westerners who came to reside in Japan and were spreading foreign religions that in their eyes despised the emperor and other Japanese traditional values. To solve these problems,

---

59. It is worth noting, however, that many Japanese people, including the government, did not show much sympathy for Buddhist priests. For them, many priests had become lazy and money-oriented people, who chanted mantras that common folk did not understand (and the priest themselves probably did not, either). As a result, although the priests themselves were part of the problem, they preferred to blame Christianity as its root. Since the priests held a unique status in society, their position was of some influence.

60. While one prominent proponent of the first view was Fukuzawa Yukichi, the founder of Keio University in Tokyo, an adherent of the second view was Niijima Jō, the founder of Dōshisha University in Kyoto.

the scholars of the Mito school[61] proposed reviving the emperor system[62] to strengthen Japan and so to keep out the foreigner threat.

At the outset, the Tokugawa government opposed this movement. However, after experiencing several defeats, the groups on the emperor's side succeeded in defeating the opposition.[63] In light of the above developments, shogun Tokugawa Yoshinobu (1837–1913) voluntarily surrendered his power to the Meiji emperor (1852–1912)[64] on 9 November 1867. His resignation marked the end of the shogunate system and the beginning of the restoration of the imperial system in Japan, the so-called Meiji Restoration of 1868.

The restoration of the imperialist system also marked the beginning of nationalism in Japan. Up to that time, Japan had been a feudal country where the loyalty of the people was directed more at the *daimyo* (feudal leaders) than the national leader. To make Japan as strong as Western countries, the new leaders believed that they needed to unite all Japanese people. By urging loyalty to the state and the emperor, the leaders were able to mobilize the people for industrialization and centralization. They propagated two slogans: "rich nation with strong army" and "catch up and surpass."[65]

As was mentioned in chapter 2, the Japanese government promulgated the Meiji Constitution in 1889. This constitution was the work of Itō Hirobumi (1841–1909)[66] and others who had previously traveled to Europe to investigate the constitutional form most suitable for Japan.[67] They chose the German con-

---

61. The Mito school was a gathering of scholars commissioned by Tokugawa Mitsukuni (1628–1701), the feudal lord of the Mito domain (the middle and northern parts of the present-day Ibaraki Prefecture), for compiling a history of Japan that focused on the emperor.

62. Although the traditional Japanese accounts of the *Kojiki* and *Nihon Shoki* say that the emperor system has existed in Japan going back to 660 BC, as a matter of fact the emperor rarely enjoyed significant, concrete political power after the establishment of the shogunate government in 1192. The emperor did have the nominal right to appoint the Shogun. In practice, however, the Shoguns were the actual rulers of Japan until 1868.

63. This Boshin War was the trigger for the establishment of the Shōkonsha Shrine (which is how the Yasukuni Shrine used to be called) discussed in chapter 2. The facility enshrined the war deads on the side of the emperor.

64. The Meiji emperor reigned from 3 February 1867 to 30 July 1912.

65. Lee, *Rediscovering Japan*, 135.

66. Later he became prime minister several times during the following period: 1885–88, 1892–96, 1898, and 1900–1901.

67. As we saw in the previous paragraphs, when Itō and his compatriots visited Europe, they encountered many protests due to the arrests and persecutions of Christians in Japan. These protests became one of the driving forces leading to the overturning of the prohibition on Christianity in Japan.

stitution (i.e. the Prussian Constitution of 1850) as their model, and therefore gave extensive power to the emperor, while still guaranteeing the rights of the people to some extent.

The Meiji government sought to establish a nation around the emperor based on an ideology that later the Allied occupation named the State Shinto.[68] Shinto originally was one of Japan's animistic religions. It evolved around a myth explaining the birth of Japan as a creation of the gods. The highest god is the *Amaterasu Ōmikami* (Sun goddess), the ancestor of the emperors. Shinto also includes the notion of the superiority of the Japanese race.[69] The leaders of the Meiji government developed those traditional Shinto ideas into the State Shinto. Establishing the State Shinto as national policy, the new Japanese leaders made the emperor the sovereign and the Japanese people his subjects. The Japanese were to be loyal to the emperor, being willing even to go to war and die for him. Realizing that the State Shinto was not in line with the principle of the separation of religion and state, which the West considered one of the hallmarks of a modern state, the leaders called it a non-religious or super-religious cult of national morality and patriotism.[70] Those who disagreed with the State Shinto came to be labeled *hikokumin* (non-patriotic person). To some extent, the new situation resembled the persecutions of the early modern period. During the early modern period, Japanese people had come to consider Christianity an evil religion; now they regarded Christians as non-patriotic people.

As in the early modern period, the appeal to Japaneseness proved effective. The nation's leaders could convince Japanese people that the State Shinto was non-religious, and even the mark of the Japanese. However, since the State Shinto used Shinto shrines, priests, and rituals, many Christians saw it as a religion that was being forced on every Japanese.[71] Initially, many Christians opposed the non-religious narrative.[72] However, harsh oppression from the

---

68. Hastings, "Japan's Protestant Schools," 112; Cf. Ion, "Cross under Imperial Sun," 83; Murayama-Cain, "Bible in Imperial Japan," 40.

69. Murayama-Cain, 31–32.

70. Murayama-Cain, 31.

71. Fujiwara, "Theology of Culture," 212, 215; Ion, "Cross under Imperial Sun," 85.

72. Fujiwara, 222; Ion, 85. For example, in 1932, some students of Sophia University refused to worship at Yasukuni Shrine. As a result, the authorities had a series of churches destroyed and furthermore expelled missionaries. In 1936, the Japanese Catholic Church allowed its members to worship at State Shinto shrines. They accepted the explanation of the

side of the authorities and condemnation by other Japanese forced many of them to accept the narrative of a non-religious State Shinto. They even went so far as to support the government's fascist agenda in order to show their Japaneseness.

One event that triggered the Christians' need to show their Japaneseness was the so-called blasphemy incident of 1891. As part of the national education system, the emperor issued the *Kyōiku ni kansuru Chokugo* (Imperial Rescript on Education) in 1890. This edict set an inviolate imperial household at the core of Japanese personal, familial, communal, educational, vocational, and national piety, and served as the sacred national creed from 1890 to 1945. The government distributed the edict in schools and ordered all teachers and students to bow down to the edict. When a Christian teacher, Uchimura Kanzō (1861–1930), hesitated to bow down and then only lowered his head in homage, the newspaper reported this 1891 incident nationally. The nationalists then seized on the event to emphasize the incompatibility of the imperial rescript with Christianity.[73]

Meanwhile, various advances achieved in a short span of time encouraged the Japanese government to seek to expand its territory. The victories in the war against China (the First Sino-Japanese War of 1894–95) and Russia (the Russo-Japanese War of 1904–5) bolstered that ambition. During the First World War, Japan declared war on Germany in 1914, and succeeded in occupying German territories in China (Shandong, Manchuria, and Inner Mongolia) and the Pacific Ocean (Mariana, Caroline, and the Marshall Islands). The growth of Japan's power was escalated by the collapse of the Russian Empire in 1917. Japan's partisanship in the victorious alliance of the First World War secured its position in the eyes of the world as a powerful country. Japan became one of the "Big Five" and received a permanent seat in the Council of the League of Nations.[74] This development contributed to the increased confidence of the Japanese government in its militaristic and fascist policy.

---

government claiming that such ritual activity was a civic duty and should not be regarded as a religious act.

73. Ono, *Nihon Purotesutanto Dendō-shi*, 30.
74. The other members of the "Big Five" were the US, Great Britain, France, and Italy.

After a somewhat more democratic era under the reign of Emperor Yoshihito (1912–26), Japan entered a period of political totalitarianism, ultranationalism, and fascism during the first half of the reign of Emperor Hirohito (1926–45). This resulted in a series of wars such as the Manchurian Incident (1931), the Shanghai Incident (1932), the Second Sino-Japanese War (1937–45), and, finally, the Pacific War (1941–45). The government suppressed all views that it considered dangerous to the unity of Japan. One such view was communism. Afterwards, the government also regarded various socialist movements as incompatible with national ideology. Within the Christian camp, hatred toward Christian socialists also increased following the growth of nationalism. The government recruited regional leaders, teachers, and Shinto priests to indoctrinate Japanese citizens with ultranationalist ideology. The State Shinto became considerably stronger and more severe.[75]

The oppression was systematic. In 1939, the government enacted the Religious Organizations Law as part of its overall policy of national mobilization for war. According to this law, the Ministry of Education only recognized Christian denominations that had at least fifty churches and no fewer than 5,000 members.[76] This regulation meant that recognition would only be granted to less than ten of the forty or more Protestant denominations. In August 1940, the authorities were prepared to arrest Christians believed to have strong ties with foreign countries.[77] The threat of imprisonment gave impetus to the Protestant leaders to form the *Nihon Kirisuto Kyōdan* (United Church of Christ Japan/UCCJ). After the establishment of the UCCJ, its representatives went to the Grand Shrine of Ise to report its establishment to the sun goddess.[78] The Japanese Catholic Church was also forced to make major changes, incorporating into the *Nihon Tenshu Kōkyō Kyōdan*, revising the catechism, and removing Westerners from leadership positions in churches and schools.[79] Furthermore, all Japanese schoolchildren were systematically indoctrinated with militaristic and fascist nationalism from 1942 until the end of the war in 1945. Even the mission schools and the church's Sunday schools

---

75. Fujiwara, "Theology of Culture," 221.
76. For a detailed description of this law, see Kramer, "Beyond the Dark Valley," 184–87.
77. Ion, "Cross under Imperial Sun," 89–91.
78. Steele, "Christianity and Politics," 361; Kramer, "Beyond the Dark Valley," 188–202.
79. Kramer, 92, 188–97.

had to shift their focus from evangelism to the moral education demanded by the government.[80]

When the national leaders propagated the concept of the Greater East Asian Co-Prosperity Sphere,[81] some Japanese Christian leaders went further by supporting the government's invasion program.[82] Not long after the annexation of Korea in 1910, the Congregational Church in Japan formed a mission body, which also received funds from certain government officials for educating Korean people. Ebina Danjō (1856–1937), one of the most prominent Japanese Christian figures from this denomination, numbered among those who supported the invasion program.[83] Only a few Christian figures criticized such cooperation with the Japanese invasion program of other countries.[84] The government sent Japanese Christian leaders to Japanese colonies in order to convince Christians there to serve the Japanese emperor.[85] This "missionary work" matched the interests of the colonial authorities, so that they regarded Japanese Christianity as a means for controlling their colonial subjects and therefore offered financial support to the Japanese missionaries.[86] In the stream of Japanese fascist nationalism, wars became the

---

80. Hastings, "Japan's Protestant Schools," 113, 116.

81. According to this view, Asian countries were to follow the example of Japan in order to confront the dangers of the expansion of the Western countries. In reality, however, it was Japan that expanded into Asian countries and carried out various atrocities of war crime category there. These included experiments involving living human bodies, the use of chemical and biological weapons, and mass murder in Nanjing in 1937.

82. Cf. Ion, "Cross under Imperial Sun," 77, 79.

83. Dohi, *Nihon Purotesutanto Kirisutokyō-shi*, 32. He interestingly suggests that the thought of using Christianity for civilizing people on the mission field could be found among American Christians, too. American missionaries to Japan believed that Christianity represented the ideal resource for making Japan a strong and flourishing country.

84. Murayama-Cain, "Bible in Imperial Japan," 47, 49. She listed the following examples: (1) Kashiwagi Gien (1860–1938), who stated that assisting the imperialist program was not evangelism at all; (2) Satō Shigehiko (1887–1935), who criticized the Japanese missionaries to Korea for having no love for Korea or its people, such that their attitude was, in the eyes of the Koreans, the same as that of Japanese government officials; (3) Suggesting pacifism, Uchimura Kanzō (1861–1930) expressed grief over the invasion and encouraged conscripts of the imperial army to die to show the futility of war; (4) While Uemura Masahisa (1858–1925) did not directly criticize government programs, he never agreed with the collaboration of Christians in the government's invasion program.

85. Ion, "Cross under Imperial Sun," 88–89.

86. Ion, 80.

medium through which Japanese Christians could most visibly show that they were as patriotic and nationalistic as their non-Christian fellow citizens.[87]

3.2.3 Responses to Nationalism – Japanese Christianity 2

In this modern period, several factors can be detected for the difficulties Japanese Christians faced in their engagement with the political issues described in chapter 2. First, the government had indoctrinated a fascist nationalism to all Japanese. Since the indoctrination placed this nationalism above all areas of life, including the spiritual realm, all Japanese, regardless of their beliefs, were mobilized to be willing to die for the emperor and Japan. If we compare the reasoning of this nationalism with the arguments applied by the Japanese Christians who defended worship at the Yasukuni Shrine as the duty of a Japanese (cf. chapters 1 and 2), several similarities emerge. This shows how the indoctrination succeeded in penetrating the mind of Japanese people, including Christians.

Against those who questioned the Christians' loyalty to Japan, Christian leaders argued that it was precisely by adopting the Christian faith that Christians became loyal citizens to Japan.[88] They also attempted to show that they did not depend on the missionaries, who were Westerners. The trustees at Christian schools adjusted the basic principles of the school to be in harmony with the Education Edict. Some Japanese Christian figures distanced themselves from Western Christianity and stressed a *Nipponteki Kirisutokyō* (Japanese Christianity) that was compatible with the ambitions of the government.

While it must be acknowledged that Japanese Christians found themselves in an extremely difficult situation during this time of oppression, it is also important to be critical of Japanese Christianity. As Fujiwara puts it, by attempting to harmonize Christianity and Japan, "the church became a religious servant to the nation" and "was taking the trajectory of a state church."[89] The Christian leaders came to identify serving the Japanese emperor with serving the kingdom of God.[90] Their nationalism seemed to trump their Christian

---

87. Murayama-Cain, "Bible in Imperial Japan," 183; Ion, 71–72.
88. Ono, *Nihon Purotesutanto Dendō-shi*, 30.
89. Fujiwara, "Theology of Culture," 222.
90. Fujiwara, 242.

faith. Ion supports this view by arguing that some Christians, including the Catholic Archbishop Doi Tatsuo and the Protestant Superintendent (UCCJ leader) Tomita Mitsuru, became mouthpieces for Japanese wartime propaganda because they were all sincere nationalists.[91]

Second, the Japanese government at this time exerted considerable pressure on those whom it considered a threat to the unity of the country. At such time, there were Christians who bravely opposed the program of Japanese nationalism. Although they knew the horrible consequences of their refusal, they were firm in their commitment.[92] The Mino Mission and the *Iesu Kirisuto no Shinyaku Kyōkai* opposed the *Kokumin Girei* (Citizen Ritual), in which they detected elements of idolatry. These groups, along with pastors of the Holiness denomination who refused to change the doctrine of Christ's second coming as the king of kings, suffered torture from the authorities.[93] There were also individuals who resisted the pressure of the government, such as Yuasa Hachirō, the president of Dōshisha University in Kyoto, and Yanaihara Tadao, a professor at the University of Tokyo. As a result, they had to step down from their prestigious positions.[94]

It is no exaggeration to say that such oppression traumatized the rest of Japanese Christians. They realized that having an alternative view on the government could cause bad things to happen to them and their families. If we relate this traumatic experience to the persecutions suffered during the early modern period as detailed in section 3.1, this renewed suppression by the Japanese government shows itself to be a second experience. Since both experiences were extremely intense, they caused a double trauma. In view of the successful indoctrination of nationalism on all Japanese people as described in the preceding section, Japanese Christians were doubly indoctrinated. It is no wonder that the desire and ability to be critical of the government could become very weak, if not disappear. Japanese Christians tend to avoid opinions diverging from those of their ruler – in part because

---

91. Ion, "Cross under Imperial Sun," 93.

92. Interestingly, Fujiwara asserts that those who resisted the oppression shared two common characteristics: biblical orthodoxy and minority consciousness. These helped them to avoid "Magisterial Christianity" and to remain faithful to the Christian message during the oppression period. Fujiwara, "Theology of Culture," 245.

93. Nakamura, *Nihon ni Okeru Fukuin-ha*, 147–52, cited from Shinohara, "Church as God's Missionary," 175, f.n. 1. See also Fujiwara, 244; Ion, "Cross under Imperial Sun," 93.

94. Steele, "Christianity and Politics," 360.

of the nationalism imposed by the government, and in part because of their fear of government persecution. Steele goes further when he calls it a real possibility that Japanese Christians had an unconscious aversion toward the government.[95] In addition, the inheritance of evangelicalism may have caused them to consider Christianity a merely private matter, which has nothing to do with the state.[96]

Third, Japanese Christian leaders took a position of supporting the government's imperialist program. They even went to other countries invaded by Japan to convince local Christians that the worship of the emperor was not a religious act, and thus not idolatry. As we will see in the following section, it was to take rather long for Christian leaders to reflect on their responsibilities.

3.3 Post-war Period (1945–present)

Beginning in June 1944, the Allied forces, which came from the US, Britain, and China, conducted attacks on and around the Japanese islands. While these attacks inflicted heavy damage on Japanese infrastructure and caused the deaths of hundreds of thousands of Japanese, the losses on the Allied side remained low. On 26 July 1945, the Allied forces called for unconditional surrender in the Potsdam Declaration.[97] Following the Japanese public statement indicating the intention to continue fighting, the US detonated atomic bombs over Hiroshima on 6 August and over Nagasaki on 9 August. One day before the bombing of Nagasaki, the Soviet Union joined the list of nations to declare war on Japan. This series of events caused Emperor Hirohito (1901–89)[98] to broadcast the acceptance of the Potsdam Declaration on 15 August 1945. Although the emperor did not mention it clearly, the broadcast implied that Japan was stopping the war and surrendering to the Allied forces.

---

95. Steele, 360–61.

96. Shinohara, "Church as God's Missionary," 176–77.

97. The full text can be downloaded at www.ndl.go.jp/constitution/e/etc/c06.html, accessed 21 May 2019.

98. Hirohito reigned as emperor of Japan from 1926 to 1989. While the first half of his reign (1926–45) is known as the early Shōwa, the second half is commonly called the later Shōwa era.

3.3.1 Top-Down Changes

Before we proceed to other developments during the post-war period, it is important to consider the characteristic of Japan's surrender. Prior to the announcement of the emperor's decision, Japanese people were ready to fight for him to the last drop of blood. Surrender was not an option for them. Watanabe rightly notes that although many Japanese people had realized that they could not win the war against the Allied forces, they did not dare to suggest or even think to stop the war.[99] Even after the atom bombs struck Hiroshima and Nagasaki, Japanese soldiers were ready to die rather than surrender. However, once the emperor announced the decision to stop, they surrendered. From this perspective, the surrender represented a top-down change for the Japanese people. It was not because of the Allied forces that they stopped fighting, but because of the emperor. Thus, although the surrender was indeed a big change, at the emotional level it was not a change, but an act of continued obedience to the emperor. The people surrendered just as they had obeyed the order to go to war. This explains why Japanese people welcomed the Allied forces, their former enemies, as if they were welcoming heroes. It was an act of obedience to the emperor.

Having said that, the emperor's decision ushered in a new era for Japan, transitioning from the imperial period to the period of Allied occupation (1945–52). For the first time in its history, Japan found itself under the government of a foreign power. The US-led alliance appointed General Douglas MacArthur (1880–1964) to be the Supreme Commander for the Allied Powers (SCAP). Despite the full authority extended to him as the supreme leader of the occupation government, MacArthur decided to exercise his rule by using the existing Japanese government system, including the emperor. Thus, even after MacArthur's arrival in September 1945, Japan could maintain the emperor as well as the majority of Parliament and cabinet members. MacArthur did not send the emperor or other members of the imperial household who could have been considered war criminals to trial. The SCAP did put some military leaders before the war crimes tribunal, as required by the Potsdam Declaration. But the emperor's exemption from trial was no doubt intended to avoid unwanted reactions from the side of the Japanese population.

---

99. Cf. Watanabe, "Daiichi no Haisen," 20.

The SCAP also abolished many Japanese regulations that were not in accordance with the democratic system, including the Peace Preservation Law and the Religious Organization Law. MacArthur ordered the disestablishment of the State Shinto and had the Diet pass a new bill annulling the Imperial Rescripts on Education. In this way, the SCAP attempted to remove the State Shinto as well as aggressive and ultranationalist elements from public institutions.[100] The SCAP also stripped the emperor of his former position as the supreme commander of the military and turned him into a symbol of peace and democracy. The SCAP asked the emperor to deny his divinity, and Emperor Hirohito declared his humanity on 1 January 1946.[101] The occupation government secured these changes by presenting a draft for a new constitution, which was to become the 1947 Constitution. This constitution prescribes, among others, the principles of pacifism, human rights, and the separation of state and religion, as discussed in chapter 2.

The changes initiated by the SCAP had a significant effect on Japan's entire structure. On the one hand, the government and the people accepted and cooperated in implementing the changes. On the other hand, it cannot be denied that the process was imposed top-down. The changes were not the fruit of the struggle of Japanese people. As we saw in chapter 2, although the concepts in MacArthurs's draft were already known and had even been disseminated by some Japanese scholars before the occupation government's arrival, some officials preferred to continue the prescriptions of the 1889 Constitution. From their perspective, the changes made by the SCAP represented coercion by the US military. As Dohi has observed, there was a contradiction in that the occupation government demilitarized Japan using powerful military forces and democratized Japan without depending on the hand of Japanese people.[102] This contradiction became more apparent when the occupation government, which had demilitarized Japan, arranged a kind of military force for Japan with a view to keeping it and other Asian countries

---

100. Mullins, "Japanese Responses," 148.

101. However, even though the occupation government as well as the US government were satisfied with the emperor's declaration, it is essential to note that it had little impact for the Japanese. The humanity declaration was not the central part of the speech. Furthermore, the term "divine" in Japanese, *kami*, does not refer to a personal and absolute God as in the West. Cf. Murayama-Cain, "Bible in Imperial Japan," 57.

102. Dohi, *Nihon Purotesutanto Kirisutokyō-shi*, 412.

free of communist influence. This arrangement led Japan to sign the Security Treaty with the US in 1951.

When Japan regained its sovereignty in 1952, right-wing conservative political leaders soon began to exaggerate the top-down nature of the changes, framing them as an "imposed" element and appealing to their movements to revive Shinto by promoting nationalism and the dignity of the emperor.[103] Some Japanese, who were aware of the dangerous side to the Imperial period and of the sigificance of the aforementioned changes, protested the nationalist movement of the right-wing conservative camp. This resistance forms the background to the issues of the Yasukuni Shrine and constitutional revision discussed in the previous chapter.[104]

The top-down nature of the change also manifested itself in Christian circles. As noted in section 3.2, many church leaders called on Christians to support the war during pre-war and war times. However, soon after the announcement of surrender, most church leaders reversed their stance, calling on Japanese Christians to support the peace movement. Article 9 of the the 1947 Constitution, forbidding the nation to maintain armed forces and to engage in war, supports Japanese Christians in their resolve to pacifism, even though the denominations to which they belong usually support just war theory in their sending countries.

The turn from fascism to pacifism taken by the early post-war UCCJ leaders did not come from deep reflection on their actions during the imperialistic period. They did not acknowledge their support of imperialism and fascism as a mistake that needed to be confessed, nor did they offer an apology. Along with their tendency to support the emperor's decision to surrender, their appeal to the SCAP not to bring the emperor before the war tribunal in recognition of his contribution in bringing the war to an end likewise showed that they remained firmly on his side.[105] Nakamura identifies two factors that caused the lack of awareness regarding the responsibility for war: (1) the SCAP did not bring the church leaders who supported the war and promoted the invasion of Asian countries before the war tribunal; and (2) the booming

---

103. Mullins, "Japanese Responses," 148, 152.

104. This is also the background to other nationalist undertakings, such as the creation of new textbooks, the use of the Hinomaru flag and Kimigayo anthem, as well as the *gengō* (calendar system based on the emperor's regnal year). For more details, see Mullins, 155–57.

105. Tsukada, "Whose Politics?," 230–32.

growth of interest in Christianity during the occupation period.¹⁰⁶ Due to these two factors, the church leaders, and subsequently the rest of Japanese Christians, did not have sufficient time or occasion to reflect critically on their war responsibilities. Tsukada even goes so far as to argue that the absence of self-reflection is a result of: (1) the so-called "old layer" pattern of thinking inherent in Japanese people that caused church leaders to identify historical and cultural developments, including Japanese fascism and imperialism, with God's work and will; and (2) the influence of liberal Protestant theology on Japanese Christian leaders during the imperial period. These two elements led the UCCJ leaders to regard the war for the emperor as a holy war that was in harmony with the will of God. As in Europe, theological liberalism had turned the church in Japan into an obedient servant of the nation-state.¹⁰⁷

3.3.2 Denominationalism

As we have already noted, the Allied occupation government abolished the discriminating Religious Organization Law. Many churches welcomed this move and used it as a chance to separate from the UCCJ and reestablish their own denominations.¹⁰⁸ Worth noting is the fact that this separation decision came from the Japanese Christians themselves, not their missionaries. The missionaries chose to keep some distance and pledged their support, regardless of a decision to separate from or remain in the UCCJ. Those who remained regarded the establishment of UCCJ as a providential act of God for the unification of the Japanese churches. In contrast, those who left the UCCJ considered the unification an act of compromise to the government and therefore wanted to return to their former denomination. The Salvation Army and many Holiness denominations were among the first to separate. Remarkably, a group of churches related to the American Southern Presbyterian Mission formed the Reformed Church in Japan (RCJ). As mentioned in section 1.3, this denomination adopted Kuyper's worldview principle and included it in

---

106. Nakamura, *Nihon Kirisutokyō Senkyō-shi*, 293–94.
107. Tsukada, "Whose Politics?," 234–36. Tsukada uses the concept of "old layer" introduced by the Japanese political philosopher Maruyama Masao (1914–96).
108. By 1947, the UCC had lost a total of around 33% of its members, shrinking from 199,462 to 133,057. For details, see Sherrill, "Christian Churches," 163; Nakamura, *Nihon Kirisutokyō Senkyō-shi*, 298–99.

the preamble to its church constitution.[109] This group also formed the Japan Calvinist Association (JCA), which still discusses various topics related to neo-Calvinism even today. However, as Inagaki points out, this group is still small and its influence is limited.[110]

Apart from the churches that separated from the UCCJ, there were also newcomers. MacArthur believed that Japan needed Christianity and saw the current situation as an excellent opportunity for missionary work in Japan. For that reason, he encouraged American churches to send missionaries and made the application procedure for them to come to Japan easier. Churches and mission agencies in North America and Europe responded positively and quickly.[111] The majority of incoming missionaries were evangelicals from the US, Canada, Germany, Norway, and Sweden.[112] The number of evangelical missionaries soon exceeded the missionaries from mainline churches, and the rate of growth for evangelical churches likewise exceeded that of the mainline churches.[113]

Post-war evangelical missionaries were very conservative in their biblical interpretation and missionary work. They were suspicious of any manifestation of liberal theology and communism. These characteristics made it difficult for Japanese Christians to cooperate with those from other denominations. The reluctance to cooperate with other churches or denominations became stronger in the 1960s. Rapid economic and technological developments made it possible for Christians to attend church far from home. This had a twofold effect. For one, it extended the geographical coverage of the churches. At the same time, it escalated the spirit of competition between churches in the same region. Being protective of their members, churches did not recommend members who moved to join a church closer to their new home. As for the members, they felt a sense of loyalty to the pastor who had baptized them or to the first church to which they had belonged.[114]

---

109. For a detailed historical description, see Rekishi Shiryō Hensan Iinkai, *Nihon Kirisuto Kaikakuha*, 47–83.

110. Cf. Inagaki, "Yakusha no Atogaki," 302.

111. Cf. Mullins, "Christianity in Contemporary Japanese," 136. He notes that between 1949 and 1953, more than 1,500 missionaries came into Japan.

112. Nakamura, *Nihon Kirisutokyō Senkyō-shi*, 305–6.

113. In the period 1949–53, evangelical denominations grew by 92.1%, while mainline churches experienced only 6.5% growth. Sherrill, "Christian Churches," 164–65.

114. Sherrill, 170.

The post-war missionaries gave priority to the evangelism of intellectual elites, who were easier to reach because they were less bound to tradition and society. Consequently, Christians in Japan became a group of elite individuals isolated from the rest of society. Moreover, these elites tended to consider faith a private matter.[115] The missionaries were also inclined to classify things into spiritual and physical matters. Their soteriology emphasized individual salvation. Inagaki interestingly considers these teachings similar to the *Jōdo* (Pure Land Buddhism) teachings, which could already be found in Japanese society since the Kamakura period (1185–1333). Those who became Christians therefore did not actually experience a transformation in worldview. They kept viewing this world through the lens of Pure Land Buddhism teachings, namely as a corrupted world, and thus aspired to move to the pure land, or to use a more Christian term, to paradise. According to Inagaki, such acceptance of Christianity happened not only during the post-war period, but also in the early modern and imperial periods.[116]

The boom of Christianity only lasted until 1947. After this year, many Japanese people adopted anti-American sentiments and lost their interest in the Christian faith.[117] Mullins observes that after 1947, many churches reported a decline in baptisms, church attendance, clergy membership, and Sunday school enrolment.[118] One of the reasons for this development is that, although the occupation government took a neutral stance toward all religions, some missionaries did use the facilities of the SCAP and received special treatment from MacArthur. As Nakamura remarks, this had a detrimental effect on the image of Christianity in the eyes of the Japanese population.[119]

At the same time, Christianity did make essential contributions to Japanese society. Although Christianity did not show impressive growth in terms of numbers, many scholars suggest that its impact should not be evaluated numerically. The Pacific War had depleted many resources in Japan. As a result, most people lacked adequate food, housing, and medical care. This situation paved the way for churches in Japan to play a vital role in society.

---

115. Sherrill, 166–67.
116. Inagaki, "Kami no Kuni," 159–60.
117. Murayama-Cain, "Bible in Imperial Japan," 57.
118. Mullins, "Christianity in Contemporary Japanese," 136–37. However, the newer evangelical, Pentecostal, and independent churches showed modest growth.
119. Nakamura, *Nihon Kirisutokyō Senkyō-shi*, 304.

As Christians received support from Christian organizations abroad, mainly the US and Canada, they used it to provide for the needs of the Japanese people. Missionaries and Japanese Christians in the early post-war period thus became pioneers in social welfare, medical work, and education. Mullins thus states that Christian influence in these fields extended far beyond the growth in church membership.[120] Oliai goes even further, claiming that, in terms of influence, Christianity "can be considered successful."[121]

As we have seen in chapter 2, the government announced the Yasukuni Bill in 1969. As an attempt to renationalize the Yasukuni Shrine, it triggered many protests all over Japan. The UCCJ published a protest statement, arguing for the principle of separation of religion and state. On the one hand, this movement fostered ecumenical cooperation between Christian denominations. On the other hand, it led to polarization between those who favored the importance of Christian social action and those who prioritized strictly church-related activities.[122] Notably, within the UCCJ, this polarization led to the establishment of the so-called *shakai-ha* (social action faction) and *kyōkai-ha* (church-centered faction).

The tensions between the two factions grew in the 1970s. When the government hosted an International Expo in Osaka, it invited the church to organize a Christian pavilion. From the perspective of the social action faction, accepting the invitation amounted to cooperation with imperialism and capitalism. When students of Tokyo Union Theological Seminary (TUTS) protested and barricaded their campus, TUTS leaders from the church-centered faction called on the police to suppress the students. This confrontation between the two factions within the UCCJ continued for years and left deep scars. As a result, more than 8 percent of its membership ended up leaving the UCCJ.[123]

As we saw in section 3.3.1, following Japan's surrender in 1945, many church leaders failed to reflect sufficiently on their war responsibilities. But in

---

120. Mullins, "Japan," 204.
121. Oliai, "Japanese and Christianity," 214–15.
122. Sherrill, "Christian Churches," 169.
123. Sherrill, 171. From 1970 to 1978, the UCCJ membership declined from 205,051 to 188,409.

1967, the UCCJ made a confession of war responsibility.[124] It acknowledged that the church had committed mistakes both before and during the war years. Nevertheless, Murayama-Cain has criticized the ambiguity of this confession, noting that it "does not specify what kind of mistakes the Church made and why they were mistakes."[125] Similarly, although Nakamura commends this confession as something learned from the confession made by the churches in Germany and as the first confession acknowledging war responsibility to be made among religious, philosophical, and journalistic groups, he does point out that the former UCCJ leaders protested against this confession and did not accept their responsibility.[126] Theological students were frustrated when they saw the lack of integrity among their church leaders.[127]

It was not until 1986 that the UCCJ offered an apology to forty-six Holiness ministers who had been put in prison during the war. The UCCJ acknowledged its mistake in failing to support the adherents of the Holiness churches when they found themselves in a difficult situation for refusing to support the militaristic and fascist agenda of the government.[128] The UCCJ also started addressing injustice issues in countries victimized by imperialist Japan. It established ecumenical cooperation on several fronts, both within Japan and with other Asian churches. Together with the Roman Catholic Church, the UCCJ protested the use of public funds for conducting Shinto rituals that were part of a series of events which took place in 1990, relating to the burial of Emperor Hirohito and the enthronement of Emperor Akihito. It also actively protested the attempts to renationalize the Yasukuni Shrine.[129] Furthermore, the UCCJ became more aware of and engaged with issues of racial discrimination against Koreans, *burakumin* (outcasts), and immigrant laborers.[130]

---

124. The content of the confession can be viewed at http://uccj.org/confession, accessed 21 May 2019.

125. Murayama-Cain, "Bible in Imperial Japan," 58.

126. Nakamura, *Nihon Kirisutokyō Senkyō-shi*, 318–20.

127. Sherrill, "Christian Churches," 167–68.

128. Sherrill, 173. Sherrill also notes that this awareness of war responsibility allowed the UCCJ to regain its loss of membership. In 1987 its membership had increased to 201,063, and by 1997 reached 206,002.

129. Mikkel, "Contemporary Christian Response," 134; Mullins, "Japan," 211.

130. Mullins, 205.

In contrast with the decreasing numbers in UCCJ's membership, the evangelical denominations enjoyed an increase of 29.6 percent.[131] According to Sherrill, the evangelical camp did not experience the kind of turbulence seen in the UCCJ because of its avoidance of political issues.[132] The evangelicals kept themselves aloof from ecumenical denominations or churches, which they regarded as liberal for changing the traditional gospel to the social gospel. In 1968, they established the Japan Evangelical Association (JEA). While this development offered the evangelicals links within their own camp, it at the same time served to increase their distance from the ecumenical denominations. Even though the 1974 Lausanne Congress may have raised the awareness of Japanese evangelicals on the importance of conducting both evangelism and Christian social responsibility, in reality they still found it difficult to engage with political issues.

3.3.3 New Religions

As we have pointed out in section 3.3.1 as well as in chapter 2, the 1947 Constitution prescribes religious freedom. This opened the way for missionaries and churches in Japan to conduct evangelism and church planting. However, Christianity was not the only religion to enjoy religious freedom. Mullins observes that the constitution "created a free-market religious economy for the first time in Japanese history."[133] Accordingly, many new indigenous Japanese religions came to flourish during this post-war period. Unlike Christianity, these new religions did not experience the disadvantages of association with American or Western culture. This probably explains why new indigenous Japanese religions grew faster and became more prominent than Christianity, reaching almost 10 percent of the population.[134]

Furthermore, the new religions tended to emphasize spiritual experiences such as mediums, healing, and exorcism.[135] As such, they challenged the rationalistic and anti-magical spirit of modernism and answered the needs of the postmodern society that started to emerge in Japan during the 1980s. The

---

131. Sherrill, "Christian Churches," 171.
132. Sherrill, 169.
133. Mullins, "Japan," 203; Mullins, "Christianity in Contemporary Japanese," 136.
134. Mullins, "Japanese Responses," 149; See also, Mullins, "Japan," 203.
135. Reid, *New Wine*, 31, cited from Sherrill, "Christian Churches," 171.

ready acceptance of these new religions highlights the reluctance of Japanese people toward the rational, conservative, and Western side of Christianity.[136]

Most of the new religions combined the teachings of Shinto, Buddhism, and Christianity. This means that the Japanese have also been significant actors in reshaping the received traditions, including Christianity, through the formation of independent movements.[137] On the one hand, this indicates the willingness of Japanese people to accept outside influence, also in the religious sphere. On the other hand, it shows how difficult and complex the acceptance of Christianity in Japan really has been.

The situation became more complex after 1995. On 20 March of that year, Japan experienced a traumatic religion-related event. Some of the members of a new religion, the Aum Shinrikyō, carried out a sarin gas attack on the Tokyo subway, killing 13 passengers, seriously injuring 54, and further affecting another 980. This incident caused many Japanese people to think that religious membership may cause a person to conduct harmful events. As a result, Japanese Christians were even more inclined to keep their faith private.

This tendency to keep religion away from the public space can also be observed in the discrepancy between church statistics and the survey mentioned in chapter 1 (section 1.1).[138] There are some similarities here with the "Hidden Christians" of the end of the early modern period, who refused to join the Catholic Church after the ban on Christianity was lifted. The postwar version of "Hidden Christians" preferred to remain outside all church institutions.[139] At the same time, he flourishing of the new religions which usually involved affiliation with the organized institution, show that there is room for Christian churches to improve in bringing the "Hidden Christians" into the church institution.

A few months before the sarin gas attack, an earthquake of 6.9 magnitude occurred in the southern Hyogo prefecture, which was to remain the greatest post-war natural disaster until the 2011 Great Disaster. This Great Hanshin-Awaji earthquake disaster affected wide areas in western Japan, including metropolitan cities such as Kobe, Osaka, and Kyoto. It left 6,434

---

136. Sherrill, 172, 174.

137. Mullins, "Japan," 197; Mullins, "Christianity in Contemporary Japanese," 155.

138. Mullins, "Christianity in Contemporary Japanese," 138; Cf. Matsunaga, "Theological Education in Japan," 299.

139. Mullins, "Japan," 198.

dead and 43,792 wounded, and destroyed 639,686 houses as well as 41,496 non-residential buildings.[140] The disaster triggered many Japanese to become involved in volunteer relief work.

Along with the sarin gas attack, the 1995 disaster had a significant impact on Japanese society. Mullins goes so far as to suggest a resurgence in nationalism in the wake of the social crisis following these two events.[141] From a different perspective, Sherrill has argued that the earthquake and attack triggered a sense of self-doubt and crisis of identity in many Japanese people.[142] Unfortunately, Sherrill observes, post-war Japanese churches were still struggling to find an effective way to answer the needs of the Japanese people. The churches continued to be preoccupied with internal issues. Their concern to maintain the orthodoxy and intellectualism caused Japanese churches to fail to connect the gospel with the daily life and need of Japanese people. Instead of providing the relational redemption that they sought, the churches, as they firmly stood on their tradition, continued preaching only personal salvation. They often looked with suspicion on the world outside the church.[143] The churches were in part encouraged in this by a dualist distinction between the "sacred church" and the "sinful world." They were also partly influenced by the insider-outsider mentality inherent in Japanese culture. Thus, Japanese people considered the church an outsider because of its Western style; at the same time, churches considered Japanese people outsiders because Japanese people are not Christians.

Japanese Christians need to find a way to deal with this insider-outsider dichotomy, which is becoming ever more pressing as an issue due to global migration. As Japanese society has started to age, it needed labor forces, such as factory workers and caregiver nurses, from other countries. These migrants came to Japan bringing their own cultures and religions. It has been a challenge for Japanese society to live harmoniously with the migrant workers and their family members, not only in factories and nursing homes, but also in residential areas, schools, and other public facilities. Since a significant number of migrants were Christians, the situation also represented a challenge

---

140. http://web.pref.hyogo.lg.jp/kk42/pa20_000000015.html, accessed 29 June 2020. Cf. http://www.bousai.go.jp/kyoiku/kyokun/pdf/101.pdf.

141. Mullins, "Japanese Responses," 155.

142. Sherrill, "Christian Churches," 174.

143. Sherrill, 175–77.

to the churches. Mullins observes that Catholic migrants have been filling the empty pews of Catholic churches across Japan, particularly in Tokyo, Saitama, Nagoya, and Osaka. By 2005, the number of foreign Catholics in Japan had even surpassed that of Japanese Catholics.[144] Although the statistics on evangelical migrants are not yet available, evangelical churches will no doubt have to address a similar challenge in the near future.

Conclusion

In chapter 2, we saw how Japanese evangelical Christians experienced difficulties engaging with the issues related to Japanese nationalism. While most of them tended to withdraw from political issues, several figures did respond through the protest movement. This current chapter attempted to shed light on the historical contexts behind these withdrawal and protest attitudes by dividing Japan's Christian history into early modern, imperial, and post-war periods.

First, we examined the complex relationship between the state and religion in Japan. When it comes to the state, one can see how the Japanese government attempted to subjugate religions for its own purposes. While it used Buddhism in the early modern period, during the imperial period it created the State Shinto. At the beginning of both periods, the rulers welcomed Christianity in order to take advantage from the missionaries and their sending countries. When the rulers found ways to gain those same benefits without Christianity, their attitude turned to hostility once they understood that Christians would not fully submit to human rulers. From this perspective, it is no exaggeration to say that the Japanese government in the early modern and imperial periods shared totalitarian characteristics. In the post-war period, these characteristics did not manifest themselves very clearly due to the democratic system and the pacifism prescribed by the 1947 Constitution. However, at the deeper level, the power of the rulers did not fade. They still exercised a top-down authority, albeit implemented in more subtle ways.

As for the Christians, they on their part also sought to use the state for their advantage. At the beginning of each period, we saw Japanese Christians

---

144. While Japanese Catholics numbered 449,925, there were 529,452 foreign Catholics. Mullins, "Christianity in Contemporary Japanese," 153.

attempting to gain privileges from the political powers. Following a short period of certain privileges, however, the rulers turned to persecute Christians who believed that God is elevated above the rulers and those who had relations with foreigners. The Japanese authorities were successful in instilling Japanese people with a strong sense of loyalty to communal authority. In the early modern period, communal authority referred mainly to household and local leaders, but during the imperial period that authority was transferred to the Japanese state with the emperor at the top. After Japan's surrender, the workplace and its leaders became the objects of this loyalty to communal authority. For Christians, this meant Christian communities, both local churches and the denomination, together with its leaders.

When Christians found themselves in conflicts with the local or national authorities, Japanese Christians attempted to find a third-way solution. In the early modern period, they practiced Hidden Christianity, acting as non-Christian in public while practicing Christian rituals in secret. In the imperial period, they articulated a Japanese Christianity that was willing to worship at State Shinto shrines and support the imperialistic and fascist programs of the state. In the early post-war period, Christians, notwithstanding a change from war supporters to peace advocates, still displayed a form of support for the emperor, who gave the order to build a new and peaceful Japan. Like their Japanese fellow citizens, they continued carrying out the ideology of *messhi hōkō* (self-annihilation for the sake of one's country) in various forms.

Even though the 1974 Lausanne Congress raised awareness of social responsibility, in evangelical circles the influence of teachings regarding narrow individual salvation and a dualism between the sacred and the secular still inclined them to withdraw from sociopolitical engagement. This inclination was only strengthened by the lengthy friction between the social action and church-centered factions in mainstream church circles. Moreover, the plurality of denominations in Japan also made it more difficult to engage with political issues, since such engagement requires cooperation among Christians.

In sum, Japanese Christians need ecclesiological concepts that can help them to establish sound cooperation amongst themselves, while allowing them to remain in their own denominations. Such room for allowing people to remain in their own denominations is vital because, as we have seen, Christians in Japan have an inherent loyalty to communal authority. They also need theological principles that encourage them to engage with political issues, while keeping themselves from becoming servants of the state. For that purpose, chapter 4 will discuss the ecclesiological suggestions of Abraham Kuyper.

CHAPTER 4

Kuyper's Concept of the Church

This chapter and the next chapter will explore ecclesiological concepts in the thought of Abraham Kuyper. As mentioned in the introductory chapter, Kuyper was a theologian with a great passion for the church. With this passion, he wanted the church to stay faithful to its original and pure position. At the same time, he also hoped the church would respond to the new challenges of its time. These intentions led Kuyper to reflect continuously on the church and to write numerous works on ecclesial matters. Each work was written in response to specific conditions and for specific purposes. Furthermore, the primary goal of his writings was not to offer theoretical concepts, but to mobilize his readers to embody his proposals. Hence, it is important to investigate both the content and the context of his ecclesiology. Understanding the context of Kuyper's ecclesiology is also necessary for considering its appropriation in Japan.

In that line, chapter 4 will attempt to offer a systematic analysis of the contents of Kuyper's ecclesiology, while chapter 5 will focus on the historical context of his ecclesiological thinking. The present chapter will therefore focus on the "what" of Kuyper's ecclesiological concepts, while chapter 5 will focus on the "why" of the reasons for those concepts. Since Kuyper suggested several ecclesiological concepts, this chapter will discuss each of them separately: the distinction between the organic and the institutional church, the believers' church, a free church, and the pluriformity of the church.[1] With a

---

1. Cf. Wood, *Going Dutch*, 40–113. Bruijne, "Volume Introduction," xxxii–xxxvi; Wagenman, "Kuyper and the Church," 128; Heslam, *Creating a Christian Worldview*, 133–39. Wood elaborates on the notion of the free church, sacramental ecclesiology, and the believers' church from a historical perspective. De Bruijne discusses Kuyper's concept of the church as

view to the purpose of this dissertation, I will pay attention to the implications of those concepts for Christian political engagement. I will also engage with the raging debates surrounding them.

4.1 The Organism-Institution Distinction

First of all, Kuyper distinguished between the church as organism and the church as institution. This distinction is the most prominent element in his concept of the church, as Henry Zwaanstra identifies it as "the heart" of Kuyper's ecclesiology.[2] The organism-institution model enabled Kuyper to combine his passion for the ecclesial and sociopolitical realms. Peter Heslam observes that the distinction represents "a unifying link between the church and the world which would serve his [Kuyper's] twin aims of social and ecclesiastical renewal."[3] Similarly, John Bolt states that the distinction between organism and institution was "a cornerstone of Kuyper's public theology."[4]

4.1.1 The Church as Organism

For Kuyper, "the Church is a spiritual organism."[5] With the term "spiritual," he sought to emphasize the heavenly character of the church. The starting-point and the center of the church are in heaven.[6] This means that the church is "not of this world but from heaven, not from below but from above."[7] The basis for this concept is Kuyper's christological understanding. For him, Christ, who has ascended into heaven, is the founder, protector, and sustainer of the church. It, "with Him, around Him, and in Him, our Head, is the real

---

organism-institution and pluriformity. Wagenman summarizes Kuyper's thought under the headings creation, unity and diversity, covenant, and institute/organism. Heslam explains the ecclesiological ideas of Kuyper using the three divisions organic, democratic, and multiform; the first relates to the essence of the church, and the second and the third to its form. See also Eglinton, *Trinity and Organism*, 196. Eglinton deals with Kuyper's organic motif, as well as the pluriformity of the church.

2. Zwaanstra, "Kuyper's Conception of the Church," 150.
3. Heslam, *Creating a Christian Worldview*, 135.
4. Bolt, *Free Church*, 427.
5. Kuyper, *Lectures on Calvinism*, 59.
6. Kuyper, 59, 62.
7. Kuyper, "Lord's Day 21 [1893]," 322–23.

Church, the real and essential sanctuary of our salvation."[8] Thus, the church fully depends on the law of life of its heavenly founder.[9]

Kuyper defined the term "organism" as anything "which its vital parts have produced on their own and which, subject to changes in its form, perpetuates and enlarges its own life."[10] Although Kuyper adopted the term from Schleiermacher and Rothe,[11] his use of it was based on a biblical understanding. He observed that the parable of the tree with spreading branches that grew from a mustard seed (Matt 13:31; Mark 4:31; Luke 13:19), the true vine (John 15:1–3), the yeast (Matt 13:33; Luke 13:21), and the body (Rom 12:4–5; 1 Cor 12:12) all point to the organic nature of the church.[12] Kuyper often used the term organism to refer to the body of Christ in which Christ is the head and all the believers are the members. The believers are bound together by their mystical union with Christ.[13] Hence, the church is

> an *organism* insofar as we view it in its hidden unity as the mystical body of Christ existing partly in heaven, partly on earth, partly unborn, having penetrated all peoples and nations, possessing Christ as its natural and glorious head, and living by the Holy Spirit who as a life-engendering and life-maintaining force animates both head and members.[14]

Kuyper also used the term to explain the unity and connectedness of believers. These do not come about because the individuals come into a relationship

---

8. Kuyper, *Lectures on Calvinism*, 62; Cf. Wagenman, "Kuyper and the Church," 131.
9. Kuyper, "Lord's Day 21," 323.
10. Kuyper, "Common Grace," 187.
11. Both Friedrich Schleiermacher (1768–1834) and Richard Rothe (1799–1867) were German theologians, and had derived the terms from the German Romantic philosopher Friedrich Schelling (1775–1854). For a more detailed treatment of the origin of this term, see Heslam, *Creating a Christian Worldview*, 133. See also chapter 5 (section 5.1.2) for a discussion of how Schleiermacher influenced Kuyper's view of the church.
12. Kuyper, "Rooted and Grounded," 50. For the basis of the concept of the church as institution, Kuyper referred to a constructed house, which is consecrated by the Lord's Spirit to be his temple (1 Cor 3:16; Eph 2:21), and later expanding it to the dimensions of an entire city (Heb 12:22; Rev 3:12).
13. Kuyper, *Lectures on Calvinism*, 59; Kuyper, *Pro Rege 2*, II.1.§1, 108.
14. Kuyper, "Common Grace," 187. Emphasis original. Cf. Kuyper, *Common Grace 2*, 33.§1, 283.

with each other, but because of "a unity and an organic connectedness" already in existence before those individuals came into existence.[15]

Kuyper had three reasons for defining the church as an organism: (1) it bears a unique life within itself; (2) it lives according to its own rule and law; and (3) its later development is already supplied within its seed.[16] This organism is "the heart of the church" and the "vital seed" every missionary should bring into the mission field.[17] Kuyper also used the term organism to allude to the whole human race. Since all human beings are a single organism, Christ saved not just certain individuals but also the entire human race as one organism. Describing the human race as a tree, Kuyper asserted that "many branches and leaves fell off," but "the tree itself shall be saved."[18] This statement on branches and leaves that fell off means that in Kuyper's view there are individuals who are not saved. As such, his position is not suggestive of universal salvation.

In sum, Kuyper utilized this concept of organism to support his emphasis on the heavenly nature of the church and its essence. Although on the present earth there "is found, at most, one generation of believers at a time,"[19] the body of Christ includes all of the elect from all over the world and from all times.[20] Thus, for Kuyper, that organic body, which originates in God's sovereign election, is the essence of the church.[21]

The church as organism proved to be a rich concept in Kuyper's hands. With it, he developed the doctrine of the priesthood of all believers into his concepts of the believers' church and the pluriformity of the church, which will be discussed later on in sections 4.2 and 4.4.[22] Apart from using it to refer to the whole mystical body of Christ, Kuyper also utilized the concept of the organism in two other senses. First, he used it for the local churches as the primary manifestation of the church of Christ. Being a part of the organism,

---

15. Kuyper, "Common Grace," 188. Cf. Kuyper, *Pro Rege 1*, III.28.§4, 479.
16. Kuyper, "Rooted and Grounded," 54.
17. Kuyper, 54.
18. Kuyper, 59.
19. Kuyper, 61; Cf. Kuyper, "Twofold Fatherland," 286; Kuyper, "Tract on the Reformation," §14, 114.
20. Kuyper, "Twofold Fatherland," 286; Kuyper, *Lectures on Calvinism*, 61.
21. Kuyper, "Tract on the Reformation," §19, 129.
22. Cf. Vree and Zwaan, *Kuyper's Commentatio*, 53, 56.

each local church has the nature of the entire organism stamped on it. Second, Kuyper used it also to express the natural relationship between each local church.[23] This reference to the local church brings us to his understanding of the church as institution.

4.1.2 The Church as Institution

Having established the organism of the church as the church's essence, Kuyper continued by emphasizing the need for an institution. From the beginning of the New Testament church, the apostles had made several arrangements and regulations for it. By doing so, Kuyper insisted, the apostles gave the church a form that was to safeguard its existence.[24] He argued that just as "all life among human beings needs analysis and arrangement," so the church institution was indispensable.[25] Moreover, since the church gives a task to all believers together, "there must be an organization that regulates the mandate for everything that happens in the name of everyone."[26]

The institution is a means supplied by God for feeding and expanding the organism. Kuyper puts it as follows:

> Behold, on Pentecost the Holy Spirit descended – I do not say without preparation, but still immediately – and he created the church among men who could never have brought it forth. But after that miraculous creation, things were different. From now on, it is the church itself through which the Holy Spirit, who dwells within it, expands and unfolds that church. From now on, there is mutual interpenetration, a reciprocal influence. From the organism the institution is born, but also through the institution the organism is fed.[27]

As an example, Kuyper referred to Matthew 28:19–20, and argued that since teaching and baptizing presuppose human conscious arrangement, those

---

23. Kuyper, "Tract on the Reformation," §15, 116.
24. Kuyper, "Rooted and Grounded," 55.
25. Kuyper, 55. Kuyper observed that the case of the church was similar to the case of God's revelation, which was organic in essence but "still could not dispense with the institution of Israel or the form of document and writing." Christ himself also manifested his life "in human particularity through the incarnation."
26. Kuyper, "Rooted and Grounded," 55.
27. Kuyper, 56.

actions are not organic operations, and that human institution is needed to implement those actions. Therefore, the preaching of the word and the administration of the sacraments require the institutional church. The institution is the mechanical part of the church.

For Kuyper, the church is at once an organism and an institution. He believed that the church, as the body of Christ, had an inner organic life that flows directly from the Spirit of God. Nevertheless, the church is not only a body but also a house, founded and built by human hands. This building has a solid outward form that shapes and protects the inner organism. One should not separate these two aspects because they exist in "mutual interpenetration, a reciprocal influence."[28] Using the expression of Ephesians 3:17, Kuyper asserted that the church is "*[f]irst* rooted, *then* grounded, but both bound *together* at their most inner core!"[29] "Rooted" is the description of the organic life of the church, which "arises not through human artistry but immediately from the hand of the Creator." "Grounded" is the requirement of the institution, which is "drawn not from nature but the work of human hands."[30] For Kuyper, "there is no nurture where there is no regularity, no nursery where there is no order. Every sphere of nurture involves organism and institution."[31] For this reason, both organic and institutional aspects of the church are important.

4.1.3 Political Engagement in the Organism-Institution Model

Before discussing Kuyper's use of the organism-institution distinction for political engagement, it is crucial to understand his view on the church's purpose and tasks. The purpose and tasks of the church determine the content and the way of the church's engagement with the world, including the political sphere.

---

28. Kuyper, 56.
29. Kuyper, 58. Emphasis original.
30. Kuyper, 50.
31. Kuyper, 57.

Kuyper stated that the church on earth "exists merely *for the sake of God.*"[32] From beginning to end, its purpose is and remains to magnify God's glory.[33] The origin of the church is in God and the form of its manifestation is also from God. Hence, the church is not to be a human-centered church. For Kuyper, the redemption of Christ delivers believers from the world, but this is not intended to take them out of this world.[34] He refuted the idea that the purpose of the earthly church is to prepare the believers to enter heaven, since a regenerated child, dying in infancy, goes straight to heaven without any further preparation. Moreover, Kuyper asserted that regeneration alone would not be enough to satisfy the glory of God in his work among human beings.[35] Regeneration should be followed by a conversion that "radiates the light from the Church into the world."[36] To accomplish that purpose, the church should make every effort to do the following: (1) contribute to conversion by preaching; (2) brighten the lofty character of the believers by the communion of the saints and the administration of the sacraments; (3) exercise church discipline; and (4) practice church philanthropy.[37]

Although Kuyper listed the diaconal task as the fourth task, he had a high view of this ministry. He emphasized that the church institution should implement this ministry in the context of glorifying God, as with the other three tasks.[38] On other occasions, Kuyper even included the diaconal ministry as a part of the ministry of the word.[39] Furthermore, when he listed the three callings of the church to "what lies outside of the church," Kuyper

---

32. Kuyper, *Lectures on Calvinism*, 66. Emphasis original; Cf. Kuyper, "Twofold Fatherland," 293.

33. Kuyper, *Lectures on Calvinism*, 68; Cf. Kuyper, "Tract on the Reformation," §2, 85; §21, 137.

34. Kuyper, "Twofold Fatherland," 294.

35. Kuyper often used the term *palingenesis*, the original Greek word for "regeneration," to maintain the meaning of "both personal rebirth (Titus 3:5) and re-creation of heaven and earth (Matt 19:28)." Kuyper, "Blurring of Boundaries," 398, f.n. 63.

36. Kuyper, *Lectures on Calvinism*, 66; Cf. Kuyper, "Common Grace," 194.

37. Kuyper, *Lectures on Calvinism*, 66–67.

38. Kuyper, 67.

39. Kuyper, "Lord's Day 21," 349. After confirming that the sole purpose of the church as institution is the ministry of the word, Kuyper added that what he meant by the ministry of the word referred not only to preaching, but also to: (1) the administration of the sacraments; (2) the response to God's word in prayers and songs of praise; (3) church discipline; (4) mission in one's hometown as well as in distant lands; (5) the gathering of offerings; and (6) the work of love for the poor.

put the diaconal calling in the first place, ahead of evangelism and mission.[40] Moreover, he condemned the views that regard diaconal ministry as a lower level ministry as a false dichotomy.[41] Kuyper called the office of deacons "a high spiritual office" because they "must also work spiritually with the congregation by teaching it," apart from offering help to those in financial and material need.[42] He even called the diaconal ministry a "battle against sin."[43] This work of compassion must arise from "the awareness of communal guilt as the source of communal misery."[44] For this reason, it is also not a program to "obtain a good reputation among the people."[45] It is a long-term and continual program that every local church has to engage seriously.

To establish a significant diaconal ministry, Kuyper suggested electing deacons from those who have a stable social status and are in a position to offer the institutional church a connection with the government.[46] When a church understands and develops this ministry well, so that the deacons need to work full-time, he unhesitantly stated that "there would be no objection against providing for the needs of these deacons and their families, just as in the case of ministers – provided that the funds to do this are not taken from the alms but are paid by the church."[47] Kuyper was also open to giving an opportunity for deacons from different churches to collaborate in carrying out their ministry. In Kuyper's view, church philanthropy is not an additional task of the church.

Kuyper admitted that the deformation of the work of love and mercy relates to the expression of the church's life rather than its essence. He compared diaconal work with the flowers and fruit of a tree, not the root. However, he asserted that "the blossoms and fruit are seldom lacking if the life in the root is

---

40. Kuyper, "Tract on the Reformation," §33, 160.

41. Kuyper, §25, 145–46. In Kuyper's view, the diaconal ministry was partially corrupted in the early Christian church and entirely in the medieval period. This ministry was only partly restored during the Reformation period.

42. Kuyper, §25, 146.

43. Kuyper, "Rooted and Grounded," 69.

44. Kuyper, "Tract on the Reformation," §33, 160.

45. Kuyper, §33, 160.

46. Kuyper, §25, 146.

47. Kuyper, §25, 147.

not diseased," and condemned the deformation of the work of love and mercy as a "gruesome evil" that is connected to the very deformation of the church.[48]

Closely related to the aforementioned tasks is the understanding of the relationship between the church and the world. In Kuyper's view, the church is not against the whole world, but only the evil world, that is, the kingdom of Satan.[49] It is the sinful nature of the world that opposes the church.[50] However, the church should neither abandon nor avoid the world itself. The church stands in the life of the world and is called to develop the world to be in harmony with God's ordinance.[51] God desires that spiritual power be put on display for the world through and in his church. Firmly believing in the efficacy of the Christian faith, Kuyper claimed that Christianity alone has in it the germ of life that can regenerate the world. Christians are called to bring that life to the world. They have the fiery medicine in their hands which can heal the fatally sick world.[52] The battlefield is not the church, but the marketplace of the world.[53]

More specifically, Kuyper considered the government and the church to be connected. Identifying the nation or the state as the earthly fatherland, Kuyper emphasized that the church "should nurture virtue and subjection to the earthly fatherland, while the earthly fatherland, by giving free rein to the course of the Gospel, should serve the heavenly."[54] Hence, Kuyper's standard position was to agree with subjection to the government, because for him the members of a church are also citizens of a particular country. They should be "subject to the rule and authority of the government."[55]

However, Kuyper also emphasized the difference between church and the government.[56] Their authorities are "completely different with respect to their origin, essence, nature, and purpose":

---

48. Kuyper, §45, 186.
49. Kuyper, "Twofold Fatherland," 294.
50. Kuyper, "Tract on the Reformation," §2, 85.
51. Kuyper, *Pro Rege 1*, III.28. §4, 479; Kuyper, *Lectures on Calvinism*, 73.
52. Kuyper, "Conservatism and Orthodoxy," 81.
53. Kuyper, "Rooted and Grounded," 62.
54. Kuyper, "Twofold Fatherland," 308.
55. Kuyper, "Tract on the Reformation," §21, 137.
56. For a discussion of Kuyper's view on the separation of church and state, see the section on the Free Church (4.3).

> With respect to origin, because government authority springs directly from the sovereignty of the Triune God; ecclesiastical authority comes from the Mediator as the Head of his church. With respect to essence, because government authority concerns the external life of body, right, and possession; ecclesiastical authority concerns the inner person, in one's spiritual existence. With respect to nature, because government authority is an authority of power, which compels by violence; ecclesiastical authority is never more than an official or ministerial authority, before Christ as well as believers. Finally, with respect to purpose, because government authority purports to maintain the righteousness and honor of God in this life; ecclesiastical authority aims to glorify God in bringing the elect to their heavenly blessedness.[57]

Kuyper was also aware that an ideal harmony between the church and the government was rare. It is more common for the government to assume an opposing position against the church of God.[58] Therefore, the church's usual attitude toward the government is to subject to it, regardless of the religion of the magistrates.[59] However, in extreme situations, such as when the worship of God is prohibited, the people of God should "forsake our earthly fatherland so as not to give up our heavenly."[60] There are two options, Kuyper said: "if the antithesis should arise again, God's people should immediately apply the fixed rule: those who can, flee far across the border, and for those whose flight is prevented, the honor of the martyr's crown beckons."[61]

In case the government's opposition against the people of God does not reach that extreme, Kuyper proposed that Christians take "a real prophetic isolation."[62] He believed that the biblical figures and the earlier Calvinists prac-

---

57. Kuyper, "Tract on the Reformation," §21, 136–37.
58. Kuyper, "Twofold Fatherland," 309. Kuyper was fair in his admission that the conflict was caused not only from the side of the government, but also by the church. The conflict arises when "the church appropriates what belongs to Caesar, or if Caesar demands for himself what belongs to the church." Kuyper, "Tract on the Reformation," §21, 137.
59. Kuyper, "Tract on the Reformation," §21, 137.
60. Kuyper, "Twofold Fatherland," 301.
61. Kuyper, 302.
62. Kuyper, 311.

ticed this type of isolation.[63] Accordingly, Kuyper emphasized that Christians in the present time should follow the same pattern. Isolation here does not mean withdrawal from public life, since it is an isolation amid, not outside, society, and since it aims at the well-being of society. Kuyper wrote:

> You find such a prophetic group wrestling in the stream of national life, not outside of it. Such a group prays; they suffer for the distress of their fatherland; they sigh and weep for their heavenly Jerusalem; their hope is for hope against hope; *Luctor et emergo* [I struggle and I emerge] is their life's motto. Knowing that their people and nation cannot have a future unless they turn back to the Lord's Word, they dare, despite the evidence, to prophesy a better future for their dear fatherland and, enraptured by that prospect, they call king and people back to the law and the testimony.[64]

Thus, while isolating themselves in Christian groups, those groups should "throw themselves into the life of the nation, take part in the debate of the people, and make themselves heard in the public square."[65]

Kuyper also provided some examples. By establishing a separate Christian political party, Christians can strive "against and with all other political parties for such a regulation of law and justice that the freedom of everyone can run its free course unhindered, but still according to God's Word."[66] Similarly, there ought to be separate youth societies for nurturing "young people with the societal concern when the common association in society threatened to secularize the spirit of our young people"; a Christian press for protesting and providing "access to better ideas than the principally false concepts"; Christian schools for enabling Christians to take first place "in the development of society"; and the Free University so that the fear of God will not "die out in our national learning."[67]

This way of engagement through Christian organizations is closely related to Kuyper's doctrine of common grace. In contrast to particular grace, which

---

63. Kuyper, 309.
64. Kuyper, 310–11.
65. Kuyper, 310.
66. Kuyper, 311.
67. Kuyper, 311–12.

saves and is bestowed on the elect only, common grace is given to all people, regardless of their election, and does not relate to salvation.[68] This grace maintains the life of the world, relaxes the curse that rests upon the world, arrests the process of the world's corruption, and allows the development of human beings.[69] Relating common grace to the church as organism and particular grace to the church as institution, Kuyper restricted the church as institution from direct engagement with society, arguing that "the church of Christ can never exert influence on civil society directly, only indirectly."[70] The goals of the church institution should remain as follows: (1) to assure the church's freedom to maintain its own unique character; (2) to prevent the incorporation of pagan concepts into the country's laws in place of the Christian ones; and (3) to expand nobler and purer ideas in civil society by the courageous action of its members in every area of life.[71] As a result, public opinion, the general mindset, the ruling ideas, the moral norms, the laws, and the customs would be indicative of the influence of the Christian faith. Through this, Kuyper hoped the following:

> This influence leads to the abolition of slavery in the laws and life of a country, to the improved position of women, to the maintenance of public virtue, respect for the Sabbath, compassion for the poor, consistent regard for the ideal over the material, and – even in manner – the elevation of all that is human from its sunken state to a higher standpoint.[72]

In short, Kuyper proposed an indirect method of engagement for the church as institution, while allocating direct engagement to the church as organism.

4.1.4 Marginalization of the Church as Institution[73]

Kuyper's proposal of indirect engagement for the church as institution has led many scholars to argue that Kuyper privileged the church as organism

---

68. Kuyper, "Common Grace," 168; Kuyper, *Lectures on Calvinism*, 52, 123–24.
69. Kuyper, *Lectures on Calvinism*, 30.
70. Kuyper, "Common Grace," 197.
71. Kuyper, 197.
72. Kuyper, 199.
73. An earlier version of this section has been published as Harefa, "First Rooted, Then Grounded," 25–40.

and thus marginalized the institutional church.⁷⁴ One recent example is John Wood, who in 2013 published a thorough analysis of Kuyper's ecclesiology from a historical perspective. He praises Kuyper for his success in opening the way for the organic church to contribute to society. However, says Wood, Kuyper removed all direct public responsibilities from the institution and limited it to mere indirect engagement of the world.⁷⁵ He concludes:

> There is also a negative lesson to draw from Kuyper's ecclesiology. Kuyper's private church, grounded as it was in conscience, circumscribed by group identity and relativized as a modern organization, obscured the public mandate that the institutional church does have. Kuyper's proposal marginalized the institutional church, yet this church is the church for the world. Its mandate cannot be truncated by any social arrangements, modern or ancient. The preaching of the Word and the sacraments of the Lord, not Christian political parties or colleges or school systems, proclaim a message of hope to the world, the announcement of a light to lighten the Gentiles and the glory of the people Israel – a public mission if ever there was one.⁷⁶

In short, Wood concludes that Kuyper ended up marginalizing the institutional church by his institution-organism distinction.

Wood also argues that a change can be detected in Kuyper's thought in his later life, suggesting that he amended the reciprocal influence between organism and institution as originally found in his 1870 sermon. Later on, so Wood argues, Kuyper made this a one-way relation; the institution comes from the organism and not the other way around.⁷⁷ Beginning in 1883, Kuyper started introducing a concept of the visible organic church.⁷⁸ This term opened the

---

74. Cf. Chapter 1, section 1.2.
75. Wood, *Going Dutch*, 172.
76. Wood, 175.
77. Wood, 92.
78. "Visible organic church" was a middle term between the church as organism and the church as institution. According to Wood, Kuyper proposed that the visible church on earth might exist in two forms: (1) as an institution; and (2) as a pre-institutional and extra-institutional gathering of believers existing in organic connection. While Vree dates this term to the 1894 Encyclopedia, and Leeuwen to a series of articles from 1887, Wood believes the concept of the visible organism was already present earlier, going at least as far back as the 1883 Tract. Wood, 86–87.

way for Kuyper to make room for a person to leave their corrupted institutional church. He elaborated how believers could move from one church institution to another, or, if needed, to form an altogether new institution.

Wood compares the institution in Kuyper's organism-institution ecclesiology to the clothing of a body, as opposed to the body itself. When this clothing fails to serve its intended purpose, it can be exchanged for new clothing.[79] Thus, the institution is not the "being" of the church, but its "well-being." Further, for Wood, Kuyper distinguished the church institution from other religious societies that lack the will to manifest an ecclesiastical formation.[80] Therefore, the church could exist in some forms, even a visible form, without the church institution. The institution is necessary but not essential to the church.

Prior to Wood, Heslam had argued that the distinction between the church as institution and the church as organism is a theological justification to "restrict the activity of the church as institute to its ecclesiastical offices," and to "lay stress on the far broader task of the church as organism, which was the transformation of human society by bringing it into harmony with the insights provided by the Christian faith."[81] At almost the same time, Bratt asserted that the church that Kuyper valued was the organic church.[82] Vree and Zwaan observe that in the *Commentatio*, "[p]articularly remarkable is the primacy of the church as an organism over the church as an institute."[83] This marginalization view on the church as institution can likewise be found in Richard Mouw, who suggests a "compensatory strategy" to update Kuyper's views on the church.[84]

The question is whether this interpretation does justice to the concept of the church as institution in Kuyper's thought. On the face of it, one can indeed

---

79. Wood, 90.

80. Wood, 88–89. For Wood, this concept leads to the understanding that the difference between the visible organic church and the institution was located in the will to form a church, not in the means of grace.

81. Heslam, *Creating a Christian Worldview*, 132–35.

82. Bratt, "Kuyper: His World and Work," 11. However, Bratt also admitted that "Kuyper regarded it [the church as institution] as a crucial means nonetheless. Only if the church-institute's word was pure and strong, its ministry undefiled by error or half-heartedness, could the church organic be made vital for its mission in society and culture."

83. Vree and Zwaan, *Kuyper's Commentatio*, 2.

84. Mouw, "Culture, Church," 56–59; Mouw, *Abraham Kuyper*, 122.

find Kuyper writing statements and conducting actions that seem to set the scene for him to marginalize the church as institution. His account of the church as organism (section 4.1.1) and his proposal for indirect engagement (section 4.1.3) may indeed lead readers to the above interpretation.

Kuyper also wrote that the earthly church is merely a "silhouette that can be dimly discerned,"[85] and even that "no child of God should imagine that the real Church is here on earth."[86] In line with that warning, he insisted:

> supposing that the institution of the Word or the Reformed church would be the visible church . . . has resulted in the evil that many are content to be joined to an organized church without having any appreciation for the communion of saints. People then fall into a narrow ecclesiastical attitude – one that bans and bars others and breaks off from them without ever realizing what the communion of saints requires of every brother and every sister.[87]

For that reason, he asserted that the visible church "must be distinguished clearly from the organized church or institution."[88]

Although Kuyper did not deny the existence of the church on earth, he did state that the earthly church is the imperfect form of the true and perfect one in heaven. The church institution is

> an *apparatus*, a local and temporally constructed *institution* grounded in human choices, decisions, and acts of the will, consisting of members, offices, and useful supplies. As such it is a phenomenon in the external, visible, and perceptible world. . . . [It has the] real substance only insofar as the mystical body of Christ lies behind it and manifests itself through it, however imperfectly. When that ceases to be the case, the institute is no longer a church except in appearance, a false church.[89]

---

85. Kuyper, *Lectures on Calvinism*, 60. Here Kuyper added the following description of the heavenly sanctuary: The Altar of Atonement, the incense-Altar of Prayer, and Christ, the High Priest at the Altar.
86. Kuyper, 61–62.
87. Kuyper, "Lord's Day 21," 362.
88. Kuyper, 363.
89. Kuyper, "Common Grace," 187–88.

Kuyper continued by asserting that the church organism existed before the institution of the church. The organism provides the substance and value for the institution.[90] With the church institution as the visible church in mind, he stated that the "essence of a visible church is and always remains the invisible church."[91] Therefore, it cannot be denied that Kuyper indeed privileged the church organism. The organism is the essence, and the institution is the form.

Further evidence for Kuyper's apparent marginalization of the institutional church might be found in his decision in 1874 to resign from the pastorate and to involve himself in many areas of the church organism. Indeed, Kuyper used the concept of the organic church to explain his actions. This serves to corroborate the interpretation according to which Kuyper developed the organism principle to develop his vision of a free church and the pluriformity of the church and to convince his followers of it.[92]

Nonetheless, if we revisit Kuyper's works on the church as institution from his later life, several factors may lead us to a revised interpretation.[93] Three factors that emerge are: (1) a consistent emphasis on the importance of the church institution; (2) a broad perspective on the ministry of the institutional church; and (3) a vision for the enhancement of the church institution.

First, nearly ten years after his resignation from pastoral ministry, Kuyper can still be found emphasizing the importance of the church as institution. In *Tract of the Reformation*, the work that Wood used to show Kuyper's shift toward the marginalization of the church institution, Kuyper still stressed that although the organism is the essence of the church, it should be followed by "the will and desire to bring their communion to fuller and purer ecclesiastical manifestation as soon as the opportunity arises."[94] It is the institution that brings the potential essence into its actuality. From this perspective, Kuyper said, "the essence of the church cannot be separated from ecclesiastical office

---

90. Kuyper, 195.

91. Kuyper, "Tract on the Reformation," §14, 111.

92. Cf. Eglinton, *Trinity and Organism*, 196, 200–203.

93. Although there are different ways to periodize Kuyper's life, since this section deals with his turn to the marginalization of the church institution, I use a moment that can be considered Kuyper's turn in life, namely his resignation from the pastoral ministry in 1874. Accordingly, I describe the period preceding his resignation as Kuyper's early life, and the period that followed it – that is, after he took seat in Parliament – as his later life.

94. Kuyper, "Tract on the Reformation," §14, 111.

or the means of grace."⁹⁵ The essence of a church "consists, on the one hand, of the group of believers, and on the other hand, of the administration of the means of grace."⁹⁶ Therefore, in Kuyper's view, a mere gathering of believers without the institution of the church is not an ideal visible church.

Kuyper's description of the organism as essence and the institution as form did not mean he despised the institutional church. Indeed, he asserted that the institutional church could become deformed, and that believers should therefore stand for a reformation of the church.⁹⁷ Having said this, Kuyper reminded his audience of the need to take such decisions cautiously. While rebuking those who continue to live in a degenerated church, Kuyper warned that "it would also be terrible if we would leave or separate ourselves from a church that was still a manifestation of Jesus' body, and thus condemn as synagogue of Satan that which was still an instrument of the Holy Spirit."⁹⁸ As long as the church still preaches the word and administers the sacraments, one should stay and make efforts for the reformation of that church. Even in case of idolatry, Kuyper wrote,

> I need only to ask: Does the church in which I live, my church, still provide me with the preaching of the Word and the administration of the sacraments, with such a degree of purity that the essence of both means of grace is still present in them? The fact that idolatry exists alongside this tolerably pure administration of the means of grace does not remove the essence of the church. While it does present the consistory with the obligation to cut off this abomination, it does not require a member of the church to leave it.⁹⁹

Furthermore, where separation from an institutional church was unavoidable, Kuyper urged the need to find or establish a new church institution: "You may not remain on your own. Unless it becomes evident that no church of Christ can manifest itself in your town, you must seek that church; and if it

---

95. Kuyper, §14, 114.
96. Kuyper, §15, 116.
97. Kuyper, §58, 236–37.
98. Kuyper, §58, 237.
99. Kuyper, §59, 253.

is not there, you must try with God's help to bring it to manifestation."[100] This is why the association of Kuyper's resignation from pastoral ministry and his involvement in many areas of the church as organism as evidence for his marginalization of the institutional church fails to do justice to his thought. He consistently attached great value to the institutional church.

The interrelated function of the church as institution and organism also appears in Kuyper's Stone Lectures from 1898. Using the biblical metaphors of a city on a hill and the salt of the earth, Kuyper explained the concentrating role of the church as institution and the radiating or penetrating role of the church as organism.[101] Wagenman rightly elaborates the inseparable nature of these two functions as follows:

> If the light remains hidden within the city walls or if the salt remains in the shaker, they are of no effect. Likewise, if the source of the light is extinguished, its rays may travel but will soon fade away; if the storehouse of salt runs empty, the salt which has been used up will lose its saltiness and no longer perform its necessary function. Therefore both concentration and extension must take place in a living, dynamic rhythm for the image to work and the meaning to remain intact.[102]

Thus, since for Kuyper this gathering and sending role should exist together and continuously, the church as institution and organism should likewise exist together and continuously.

In *Common Grace*, written as a series of articles from 1895 to 1901, Kuyper insisted that while common grace prepares the way for particular grace, in turn wherever particular grace begins to exercise its influence, common grace yields strong development. Common grace cannot itself perform this development; only Christian faith can release the forces of common grace. As such, common grace is an emanation of particular grace that reaches the areas outside the church.[103] Kuyper stated that the circumference of the church as organism is "determined by the length of the ray that shines out from the

---

100. Kuyper, §58, 240–41.
101. Kuyper, *Lectures on Calvinism*, 53.
102. Cf. Wagenman, "Kuyper and the Church," 137.
103. Kuyper, "Common Grace," 169–71.

church institute over the life of people and nation."[104] This statement shows how Kuyper later consistently emphasized the importance of the church institution. The success of the church as organism is not independent of the church as institution.

Furthermore, Kuyper asserted the importance of the church institution in his *Pro Rege*, originally written between January 1907 and January 1911 as articles for the weekly *De Heraut*. He maintained that the church institution is "the essential manifestation" of Christ's body, as long as "it does full justice to this internal presence and indwelling of Christ in us."[105] Hence, although Kuyper sounded severe warnings about the possibility for a church institution to be no longer a church, he consistently valued the institutional church that is still related to Christ as its head.[106] A similar concern on the church institution is observable in *Our Worship*, a work on the church's liturgy. While Kuyper had already written more than half of the contents between 1897 and 1901, he completed the rest of the fifty articles in 1911. Although he was already seventy-four years old, his passion for recovering the vitality of the church institution did not fade away.[107] In the same vein, as I will elaborate in greater detail in section 4.3.1, although Kuyper in his 1916 "State and Church" showed a high view of the state by insisting that the church institution always be subject to the rules determined by the state, he expressed the hope that politicians would respect the church as an entity higher than the state.[108]

One can also see similar great concern on the church institution in his 1911 *Our Worship*. While more than half of the contents were written between 1897 and 1901, the rest of the fifty articles were written in 1911. His passion to recover the vitality of the church institution is undoubtable.

Before proceeding to the next section, we also need to note how Kuyper had already emphasized the importance of the church as organism from his early days on. In his 1858 work on the development of papal power, Kuyper had concluded that the institutional church was outdated. He observed that the church as institution was indispensable only when religion still existed in

---

104. Kuyper, 195.
105. Kuyper, *Pro Rege 2*, II.7.§4, 165.
106. Cf. Kuyper, *Pro Rege 2*, II.9.§1–2, 175–80.
107. Kuyper, *Our Worship*, 3.
108. Kuyper, "State and Church," 379.

its lower level of development, as was the case during the Middle Ages. For the modern era, it therefore became superfluous.[109] In his 1860 *Commentatio*, written for an essay competition during his doctoral study, Kuyper defined the church as "a spiritual brotherhood of the children of God."[110] He established Christ as the "lively center of the whole organism of the church."[111] He furthermore argued that Christ established his church according to the eternal counsel and good pleasure of God without any particular visible, external form. Hence, the church "has no external marks or characteristics but is recognized . . . by the way that they [the children of God] mutually embrace each other with the love of a friend."[112] Kuyper used the expression also to refer to the spiritual life kindled by the Spirit of Christ, which was why the members of the church "renounced whatever things are vile and vicious."[113] Thus, Kuyper had already been privileging the organism of the church over the institution since the 1860s.[114] His emphasis on the organism was not a new concept that Kuyper adopted later on in life.

Therefore, the significant shift that occurred in Kuyper's life was not an emphasis from institution to organism, but from organism to institution. Kuyper confirmed this ecclesiological change in a work published in 1873. Recalling his conversion to Calvinism during his ministry in Beesd (1863–67), Kuyper praised Calvin's use of the expression "the church as the mother of the believers."[115] He commended this phrase as a beautiful image that gives expression to both the organic and the institutional aspect of the church in

---

109. Vree and Zwaan, *Kuyper's Commentatio*, 22–23, 39.

110. Kuyper, "Commentatio," 13.

111. Kuyper, 23. Vree and Zwaan believe that the use of the term "organism" in the "Commentatio" indicated that Kuyper's model of church was something "new to the Netherlands," because "[n]ot only is the word 'organism' completely lacking in the work of the others, but also, none of them had thought so systematically about the role of the members of the congregation as such." Vree and Zwaan, *Kuyper's Commentatio*, 56–57.

112. Kuyper, "Commentatio," 13; Cf. Vree and Zwaan, 52. For Kuyper, the visible congregation of Christ is a *spiritual* community. Here, spiritual means "an elucidation about Jesus Christ as the binding and all-stimulating force within the church." Hence, the church does not need the "body of sacred doctrines" to hold it together.

113. Kuyper, "Commentatio," 28.

114. Cf. Vree and Zwaan, *Kuyper's Commentatio*, 2. Vree and Zwan point out that in *Commentatio*, "[p]articularly remarkable is the primacy of the church as an organism over the church as an institute."

115. Cf. Calvin, *Institutes of the Christian Religion*, 4.1.4. Calvin himself took this expression from Cyprian. Calvin, 1012, f.n.3.

an attractive way.[116] He firmly believed that his life goal was to restore the church in its position as "our mother." It is precisely this motherly nurturing character that renders the institution indispensable. After this shift, Kuyper consistently emphasized the church as organism, yet without denigrating the importance of the church institution.

Second, although Kuyper kept the institutional church from direct political engagement, he had a broad view on the ministry of the church as institution. Kuyper did assert that the institutional church should restrict itself to the ministry of the word. However, his concept of that ministry was far from narrow. As we saw in section 4.1.3, Kuyper emphasized the diaconal task as part of the ministry of the word. Placing it ahead of evangelism and mission, he allocated many pages to this task in his 1883 *Tract of the Reformation of the Churches*. Kuyper reiterated his broad perspective on the ministry of the church institution in his commentary on the Heidelberg Catechism, written as a series of articles for the weekly *De Heraut* from 1886 to 1894, as well as in his 1898 *Lectures on Calvinism*. This indicates that the limitations he imposed on the church as institution were no restriction confining the church to the private sphere alone. His restriction on the institutional church's direct involvement in society did not imply withdrawal from public life. Far from it, the church as institution can and must carry out its public responsibilities through diaconal work.

Moreover, Kuyper recommended establishing a special committee under the consistory to supervise the management of the church's assets.[117] Furthermore, when discussing the relation between school and church, Kuyper prohibited the church from taking direct charge of the schools. However, he did require the church to "be involved with the school" by (1) establishing, nurturing, and maintaining schools wherever no school could be found in accordance with the word of God; (2) making sure that all poor church members could receive a proper education; and (3) watching the school, to ensure whether it conducts education properly, "in the purity of

---

116. Later, Kuyper said that "Calvin had *founded a church*, and through his *fixed church form* he succeeded in spreading blessings and peace to receptive hearts among all the nations of Europe and across the sea, in town and village, even among the poor and the lowly." Kuyper, "Confidentially," 59–61. Emphasis original.

117. Kuyper, "Tract on the Reformation," §27, 150.

the truth, according to the Word of God."[118] This means that the institutional church in Kuyper's ecclesiology has a sort of responsibility for the situation of society. By limiting the church as institution to the ministry of the word, Kuyper did not mean to downplay its importance. The institutional church has many things to do, including engagement with broader society through diaconal work.

Ad de Bruijne interestingly argues that in Kuyper's view, the church as institution also forms a sphere with public features. Thus, "it cannot be reduced to the private sphere."[119] Since the term institution is a specifically modern concept, with roots in the nineteenth-century emergence of civil society, De Bruijne argues that Kuyper suggested the institutional church as an alternative public community.[120] De Bruijne also argues that the distinction between private and public itself does not fit the basic structure of Kuyper's theology. Kuyper recognizes only one life, which gradually unfolds in a multitude of spheres, all placed under the direct authority of God.[121]

Third, Kuyper envisioned the enhancement of the church as institution. As we will see in section 4.3.1.2, Kuyper rejected the concept of a national church. Instead, he longed for a robust confessional church. In his *Lectures on Calvinism* (1898), Kuyper emphasized the abnormality of the present human condition. Hence, "religion must necessarily assume a soteriological character."[122] In line with Calvin, he insisted on the holiness of God and the destructive power of sin. Sin is not merely an incomplete stage; human beings need both regeneration and revelation.[123] Therefore, as we will see in section 4.2.1, Kuyper urged the church to become a congregation of believers.[124] Accordingly, the church cannot embrace all people in a nation. Yet Kuyper added an interesting disclaimer: "Not one single state, but the *whole world* is its domain."[125] While rejecting the national church concept, Kuyper opened

---

118. Kuyper, §34, 161–62.
119. Bruijne, "'Colony of Heaven,'" 465; Bruijne, "Not without the Church," 77–78.
120. Bruijne, "'Colony of Heaven,'" 464.
121. Bruijne, 464.
122. Kuyper, *Lectures on Calvinism*, 54.
123. Kuyper, 55–56.
124. Kuyper, 65. However, in line with the Calvinist concept of the covenant, Kuyper did not exclude the children of believers. Infant baptism incorporates children in the communion of the church until they become confessors or "sever themselves from the church by their unbelief."
125. Kuyper, 65. Emphasis added.

the way for the institution of the church to envision something much bigger than a national church.

Furthermore, Kuyper's vision for the institutional church was for it to be a solid training facility. As we will elaborate in section 4.2.2, Kuyper stated in his commentary on the Heidelberg Catechism that the church is the army gathered by Christ to fight Satan for the establishment of the kingdom of God.[126] He depicted the institutional church as a military camp which is necessary for the success of the battle. This shows Kuyper's concern for a militant church institution. Limiting the institutional church to the ministry of the word is on purpose, so that the church can focus on accomplishing its task of training its members as a capable army of Christ.

Worth noting in this context is Kuyper's distinction between four terrains of common grace in his *Common Grace*: (1) common grace without particular grace; (2) particular grace without common grace; (3) common grace illuminated by particular grace; and (4) particular grace utilizing common grace. In the fourth terrain, Kuyper remarked, the institutional church could use the development resulting from common grace for the sake of the propagation of particular grace. It is this propagation of particular grace that Kuyper regarded as the "original and primary goal."[127] Therefore, when this vision is placed in the context of the distinction between the church as organism and institution, it is no exaggeration to say that Kuyper also aspired to see the enhancement of the church as institution through the church as organism's engagement with society.

In sum, saying that Kuyper marginalized the institution of the church fails to do justice to his ecclesiology. Indeed, Kuyper did privilege the church as organism as the essence of the church. He also set several restrictions on the institutional church. However, this does not mean that Kuyper disdained the church as institution. While emphasizing the importance of the church as organism, he consistently attached great value to the church as institution, even after his resignation from pastoral ministry. Kuyper consistently entrusted the church as institution with a wide-ranging notion of the ministry of the word. In Kuyper's thought, the church as institution is an active and sovereign church. His limitation on the church as institution is intended such

---

126. Kuyper, "Lord's Day 21," 326.
127. Kuyper, "Common Grace," 170, 185, 199.

that "the lamp of the gospel is allowed to shine more brightly and clearly in the church institute."[128] It is a step toward a higher goal, namely the strengthening of the institutional church. His rejection of the concept of a national church was intended to make sure that the church institution conducts its function properly. This conclusion leads us to the next section on Kuyper's concept of the believers' church.

4.2 The Believers' Church

To strengthen the institution of the church, Kuyper firmly believed the principle of the believers' church to be indispensable. He used several phrases to elaborate this principle. This section will discuss his emphasis on the concepts of the pure church, the church as the army of God, and the office of believers. While Kuyper proposed the concept of the believers' church, he also defended the practice of infant baptism. For this reason, he tabled the controversial concept of presumptive regeneration, which will be discussed at the end of this section as well.

4.2.1 The Pure Church

In *Lectures on Calvinism*, Kuyper defined the church on earth as a gathering of "*regenerated and confessing individuals*, who in accordance with the Scriptural command, and under the influence of the social element of all religion, have formed a society, and are endeavoring to live together in subordination to Christ as their king."[129] From this definition, it is evident that Kuyper put a special emphasis on the condition of the church's members: they must be regenerated members.[130] This emphasis is in line with his insistence on the earthly church as a manifestation of the heavenly church.

This does not mean that the earthly church must consist of morally perfect individuals. Kuyper wrote:

> Do not misunderstand me. I do not say: The Church consists of pious persons united in groups for religious purposes. That, in itself, would have nothing in common with the Church. The real,

---

128. Kuyper, 194.
129. Kuyper, *Lectures on Calvinism*, 62. Emphasis original.
130. Kuyper, *Pro Rege 1*, III.28.§4, 479.

heavenly, invisible Church must manifest itself *in* the earthly Church. If not, you will have a society, but no church. Now the real essential Church is and remains the body of Christ, of which regenerate persons are members. Therefore the Church on earth consists only of those who have been incorporated into Christ, who bow before Him, live in His Word, and adhere to His ordinances; and for this reason the Church on earth has to preach the Word, to administer the sacraments, and to exercise discipline, and in everything to stand before the face of God.[131]

With this concept of the believers' church, Kuyper did not intend to establish a perfect church. He was fully aware of the constant possibility of the children of the devil being mixed with the children of God. Kuyper also acknowledged that the children of God, including the office-bearers, "will always be guilty of various acts of faithlessness." He concluded that "it is sadly and painfully inevitable that the institution of the visible church can manifest itself only in an imperfect condition."[132]

Kuyper connected the principle of the believers' church to the doctrine of the communion of saints. For him, this represents the link between the invisible church and the visible church. Communion of saints does not only refer to sharing in Christ and his treasures in the invisible realm, but also to the communal possession of the gifts in the visible realm. Christians must use their gifts for the sake of other members of the visible church.[133] This implies a church life as follows:

> all Christian people are called to investigate which gifts of the Holy Spirit have been given to them: gifts of a general nature, such as faith and hope and love – expanded further in terms of humility, meekness, patience, and humble compassion; but also gifts of a special nature, such as gifts of prayer, praise and thanksgiving, prophecy, of discerning spirits, and of the soul-piercing word – manifested in counseling, admonition, and consolation. . . . [Y]ou may not keep them for yourself but are

---

131. Kuyper, *Lectures on Calvinism*, 62–63. Emphasis original.
132. Kuyper, "Lord's Day 21," 352.
133. Kuyper, 363.

called to employ them in your context, to the extent that you find opportunity, for the benefit and salvation of the other members of the same body of the Lord.

Finally, it follows that you must seek out those others, that you must make yourself known to others, that you must foster fellowship with others, not only to be a blessing to them, but also to receive a blessing from them. In this way, through the confession of personal faith and through the manifestation of personal gifts, the members of the body of Christ become known and visible to each other, and the church becomes visible to them.[134]

Given such a requirement for church life, it would be difficult, if not possible, for unbelievers to follow this kind of church life. This kind of church is the communion of saints and should therefore be the believers' church.

Kuyper agreed with the distinction between the invisible and the visible church. He emphasized that the two terms do not refer to different entities, because "the church that becomes visible is that very same church that remains spiritually invisible."[135] Kuyper was unhesitating in his insistence that there is no forgiveness of sins outside the invisible body of Christ.[136] However, it is important to note that Kuyper also insisted on the necessity of distinguishing the invisible from the visible church. He said,

> We may not for a moment lose sight of the profound distinction between this spiritual or *invisible church* – which is an object of faith and whose existence is confessed in the articles of our faith and explained by the Catechism in Lord's Day 21 – and that

---

134. Kuyper, 363.

135. Kuyper, "Lord's Day 21, 357; Cf. Kuyper, "State and Church," §23, 420. As we will see in more detail in the next section, Kuyper saw abuses against this doctrine which led to the practice of the national church. He argued that "this doctrine effectively made church discipline more lax ... if this doctrine were emphasized too much, it could give occasion to worry less about the state of the visible church, and to be less annoyed when the government intervened in ecclesiastical affairs somewhat more than it should do in principle." Kuyper, "Lord's Day 21," §12, 396.

136. Kuyper, "Lord's Day 21," 368. He added, "Luther did not maintain this connection, however, and later Lutherans in particular made the forgiveness of sins far too much a personal matter between God and one's heart, apart from affiliation with the body of Christ.... The reaction against the error of Rome had led in turn to an opposite imbalance."

very different phenomenon that we are calling the institution of the *visible church*.[137]

The invisible side of the church, explained Kuyper, never becomes visible. Using the illustration of the human soul, which can never become visible, Kuyper argued that a spiritual being or spiritual function will never be visible, and that the spiritual side of the invisible church will therefore never be observed by the human senses.[138]

Accordingly, Kuyper asserted that the decisive element was the existence of believers:

> As soon as there are any individuals who openly confess the Lord Jesus, and who show this among themselves and to others, anyone who pays attention can observe that the church of Jesus is also present in this place. The church is the body of Christ, and as soon as there are as few as two or three people in a certain locale who belong to this body, then this body exists not only elsewhere but also in that place; and as soon as these two or three persons gather in his name, he is among them, and in their confession the body of the Lord becomes manifest or visible.[139]

The essence of the visible church is not the ministry of the word, but the believers. The visible church is "an institution ordained by this King for his church – to gather, protect, and sustain this church."[140] Although the ministry of the word will cease when "everything on earth comes to its end," the body of Christ which consists of the believers will continue.[141]

From a historical perspective, it is worth noting that Kuyper had already emphasized the spiritual character of the church ever since his time as a doctoral student. Vree and Zwaan view this emphasis as the reason why Kuyper was critical of Calvin's plea for the fixity of rites in church.[142] They note that Kuyper had a high view of the work of Christ's Spirit so that the

---

137. Kuyper, 347.
138. Kuyper, 358.
139. Kuyper, "Lord's Day 21." As we saw in section 4.1, the "external institution belongs to the well-being, not to the being or essence of the visible church." Kuyper, 359.
140. Kuyper, "Lord's Day 21," 357.
141. Kuyper, 358–59.
142. Vree and Zwaan, *Kuyper's Commentatio*, 54.

boundaries of the church are not marked by baptism or the confession of the true doctrine, but "by the answer to the question whether people in their lives show signs of the basic principles of the new life, ignited by the Spirit."[143] In his *Commentatio*, Kuyper evaluated the ecclesiology of Calvin and a Lasco using the following standard:

> the Christian church, according to the thought of the gospel, is a spiritual brotherhood of the children of God – or rather, a religious and moral society founded by Christ according to God's eternal counsel and good pleasure. Without any particular visible external form, it appears only under the form of a friendly association and, therefore, has no external marks or characteristics but is recognized by a new principle and method of perception, thought, and will; by eagerness for pursuing truth and virtue; and, at the very least, by the way that they mutually embrace each other with the love of a friend.[144]

Calling it "a fraternal fellowship," Kuyper described the kingdom of heaven as "a vast family, whose *paterfamilias* is God himself. He decreed through Christ our older brother to closely unite Christ's younger brethren to himself."[145] Hence, Christ is both the center and the primary bond of the church.[146]

Kuyper continued holding to this concept during the first phase of his pastoral activity. According to Wood, Kuyper's early sermons at the church in Beesd (1863–67) indicated that he upheld a subjective inner piety. He disavowed such forms of the church as the liturgy and the sacraments.[147] For example, in his inaugural sermon "A Walk in the Light: The Foundation of All Communion in the Church of Christ," he stressed "the importance of holiness of life and love, walking in the light, as the bond of the church community."[148] Kuyper's sermon on Lord's Day 21 of the Heidelberg Catechism in Beesd also emphasized that the church "was supposed to be a pure, holy church."[149]

---

143. Vree and Zwaan, 55.
144. Kuyper, "Commentatio," 13.
145. Kuyper, 22.
146. Kuyper, 23–24.
147. Wood, *Going Dutch*, 40.
148. Wood, 42.
149. Wood, 42.

Although Kuyper did not consider his denomination, the *Nederlandse Hervormde Kerk* (Dutch Reformed Church/DRC),[150] a pure church, he chose to remain in it during his first years in Beesd because he "acknowledged that a good deal of chaff was mixed in with the wheat."[151] However, by the end of his time in that congregation, Kuyper showed himself more critical. He criticized the DRC for having become impure by its accommodation to a modernity that denies the spiritual traits. He insisted that there were times when Christendom must withdraw from a corrupt society rather than become corrupted itself.[152] He called for a separation of the communities of believers and unbelievers, determined in this by his antithetical principle of the "consecrated and unconsecrated." In an 1873 work, Kuyper writes that after reading the novel *The Heir of Redclyffe*, he experienced a conversion and "from then on I have longed with all my soul for a *sanctified Church* wherein my soul and those of my loved ones can enjoy the quiet refreshment of peace, far from all confusion, under its firm, lasting, and authoritative guidance."[153]

To safeguard the purity of the church, Kuyper reconceived church membership, connecting it to election.[154] For him, election is the origin of the invisible organic church. After electing Christ, God elected the church in Christ. Afterward, God elected the individual member of the church. Since the election of the people of Israel preceded the election of particular people in Israel, election to the church corporate is preparatory to the election of the church members.[155] Hence, one's relationship to Christ is determined by one's relationship to the church.[156]

With this pure church concept, Kuyper rejected the concept of a national church. A national church is a church comprising only a single nation, and that nation entirely. Kuyper's rejection of this concept will be discussed in detail in 4.3.1.2. Suffice it to say here that for Kuyper, the church – in contrast to a national church which comprises only a single nation – should not be

---

150. For a more detailed elaboration on the DRC, see chapter 5.
151. Wood, *Going Dutch*, 44.
152. Kuyper, *Lectures on Calvinism*, 65; Cf. Wood, *Going Dutch*, 47, 51.
153. Kuyper, "Confidentially," 55. Emphasis added.
154. Kuyper, "Rooted and Grounded," 54, 69; Kuyper, "Tract on the Reformation," §19, 129; Kuyper, "Lord's Day 21," 341.
155. Kuyper, "De Uitverkiezing," 170, cited from Wood, *Going Dutch*, 67.
156. Kuyper, *Common Grace 2*, 33.§1, 283.

limited to a single nation. Furthermore, while the national church concept attempts to embrace all inhabitants of a country, the church is not intended to comprise the entire people of a nation. As we have seen, Kuyper thought it was better to have a smaller, but purer church.

4.2.2 The Army of God

Building and maintaining such a pure church requires committed members. In his commentary on the Heidelberg Catechism, Kuyper stated that the church was the army gathered by Christ to fight against Satan in order to establish the kingdom of God. He summarized as follows:

> Christ gathers his church as a holy army of the living God. He gathers his church in order to establish the kingdom of God through it as his army. That is why this army is called church, that is, *ecclesia* or called-out, select troops. The church of Christ is his glorious bodyguard, the unit of his personal bodyguards, incorporated under him as the Head of all.[157]

This concept of the church as the army of God is identical with the doctrine of the militant church. However, in Kuyper's view, the term "militant church" had become a narrow reference to the struggle of believers against sin during their life on earth. For him, sin is "only one of" the battles, "not the main battle": "The church's actual battle is being fought against a much more powerful enemy who hides behind all these and many other sins and merely exerts his power in these sins."[158] One should understand the concept of the militant church in terms of the battle against the world, "not by individuals but by the church of Christ viewed as a whole."[159]

This battle against Satan is a never-ending one: "And whenever it seems to be otherwise, that is only because part of the people have become unfaithful, have deserted the cause of their Lord, and have gone over to the enemy."[160] The church has the calling to be a militant church on earth:

---

157. Kuyper, "Lord's Day 21," 326.
158. Kuyper, 339.
159. Kuyper, 328.
160. Kuyper, 331.

The idea of the battle or the war that we are to wage must, therefore, play a central role in every discussion of the doctrine of the church. If you omit this principle of our battle from the concept of church, then you will miss your active, driving force, and your resilience as a church will be less. In that case, there is no good reason for once godless but now regenerated sinners to remain on the earth.[161]

Kuyper stated that the battle extends to the believers' entire life. One should wage war "every day and every night" and "in heart, in households, in families, in conversations, in public opinion, in trade and work, in industry and profession, in science and art, at the cradle, and at the grave." However, Kuyper at the same time reminds us that the battle is "never fought by anyone but Jesus himself."[162] This is the guarantee of the victory of the battle, which will happen at the second coming of Christ.

Moreover, the concept of the church as the army of God is inseparable from the concept of the church as the people of God. Since the battle is a perpetual one, the people are the whole army, and the army is the whole people. Hence, the church has a twofold character: (1) an army under Jesus as its head for waging the battle against Satan; and (2) "a people destined to enjoy life under Jesus as its King."[163] Since the army and the people fully coincide, the distinction between people and church becomes irrelevant.[164] In addition, the semantics of the term *ecclesia* also corroborates the concept of the church as God's army. The church, according to Kuyper, is "the multitude of those called out, of those called to war."[165] From the perspective of the never-ending war, the terms "church," "people of God," and "army of God" all refer to the same entity.[166] This characteristic of the church as the army of God and the people of God implies a twofold task for the church. It must

---

161. Kuyper, 335; Cf. Kuyper, 341: "it is and remains the task and high calling of that church, in a world whose entire structure is full of Satan's dominion, to stand up courageously against that dominion, to strap on the sword against that dominion; and without retreat or cease-fire, restlessly and ceaselessly, now and forever until the Lord's return, to continue the struggle, the fight, the war involving life and death waged against this Satanic dominion."

162. Kuyper, 347.
163. Kuyper, 354.
164. Kuyper, 333.
165. Kuyper, 332.
166. Kuyper, 333.

prepare its members for war and it also should make sure that its members live for the glory of God, their king.[167]

For the visible institution church, Kuyper used the illustration of a military camp. It is a place where Christ as the head or commander of the church gathers and continually "feeds, arms, and trains" the members of his body.[168] Accordingly, Kuyper warned that the camp is not the actual battlefield. The real fight begins "only when we leave the camp and approach the enemy on the battlefield." The distinction between camp and battlefield helps one to avoid the danger of both churchism and churchlessness.[169] While the former overvalues the visible church institution, the latter underestimates it.

4.2.3 The Office of Believers

In Kuyper's concept of the pure church and the church as the army of God, his emphasis on the importance of the doctrine of the priesthood of all believers clearly comes to the fore. One implication of this doctrine is Kuyper's endorsement of the notion of the office of believers, as mentioned in Article 30 of the Belgic Confession.[170] For him, all members of the church also have a public calling to an office in the institutional church.[171] The general office of believers flows from the bond which the Holy Spirit forms between believers and Christ, and it is the foundation of the institution of the visible church.[172]

The most important function of this general office is the election of special officers. According to Kuyper, in a sinless world, Christ would work directly through all believers. However, because of sin, there must be a small group of officers: ministers, elders, and deacons. Believers could form a new church where there is none or also reform an existing institution wherever necessary. If their church has already become corrupt, they must join a true church or form a new one.[173] In either case, the special office-bearers must carry out their function by the Spirit of Christ. When they preach or administer the sacraments, they must let Christ himself preach and administer the sacraments.

---

167. Kuyper, 354.
168. Kuyper, 347.
169. Kuyper, 347.
170. Kuyper, "Tract on the Reformation," §26, 147.
171. Kuyper, "Lord's Day 21," 360.
172. Kuyper, "Tract on the Reformation," §12, 105–6.
173. Kuyper, §12, 106.

Their authority must always be ministerial. Kuyper asserted that "the office of believers and the office of ministers stand on the same level."[174] He insisted:

> in the church of Christ, every person who acts as bishop, member of synod, classical leader, or in whatever function, is as sinful and unworthy as any member of the church, and there is no reason in their persons why the members of the church should render to them reverence or obedience.[175]

In other words, submission to the special offices must be purely voluntary.[176] Believers may, and in fact have the responsibility to, leave when special office-bearers have deviated from the word of God.[177] Similarly, Vree and Zwaan have noted Kuyper's thinking on the ability of the believers through the Spirit to choose their own special office-bearers. They see Kuyper as being ahead of his contemporaries in awarding the right to vote also to women believers.[178]

Kuyper established two mechanisms for the office of all believers. First, the passive and negative function, which is to take over the duty of the special offices when the office-bearers go astray. The second duty is more active and positive. It is a "duty to proclaim the gospel where this is not occurring, or occurs only in appearance, as soon as the Lord God grants the gift to do so."[179] With this believers' church ecclesiology, Kuyper tried to empower and encourage all believers to participate actively in church life. Believers are to recognize and utilize their gifts for carrying out their responsibility to the visible church institution.[180] By perennially making sure that the institutional church provides them with a training ground for their fight against Satan and its influences, they can continue waging the spiritual war for Christ to establish the kingdom of God.

---

174. Kuyper, §18, 124.
175. Kuyper, §61, 258.
176. Kuyper, *Separatie en Doleantie*, 9–10.
177. Cf. Vree and Zwaan, *Kuyper's Commentatio*, 56. They observe that Kuyper had already held this concept in his *Commentatio*, and that this was one of the reasons for his preference for the ecclesiology of a Lasco.
178. Vree and Zwaan, *Kuyper's Commentatio*, 60.
179. Kuyper, "Tract on the Reformation," §26, 148–49.
180. See also Kuyper, §26, 150. Kuyper even acknowledged the possibility for someone who had no academic training for the ministry but had been granted extraordinary gifts by God to become a minister of the word.

4.2.4 Infant Baptism

Nevertheless, Kuyper also wanted to preserve the practice of infant baptism. Becoming a believer does not mean cutting through one's natural bonds with one's offspring.[181] Rather, believers consecrate the bond and incorporate their children in the communion of their church by infant baptism.[182] The children of believers are kept in church until they become confessors themselves, or else separate themselves from the church by their unbelief. As Kuyper wrote, "*Covenant* and Church are inseparable – the Covenant binding the Church to the race, and God Himself sealing in it the connection between the life of grace and the life of nature."[183] Kuyper was aware that the presence of unconverted children, who nevertheless may belong to the elect, could worsen the already imperfect condition of the church. For him, the visible church experiences difficulties caused by the mixture of unbelievers in the visible church, the faithlessness of the children of God, and acts of denial committed by the office-bearers.[184]

Kuyper viewed infant baptism as a seal of the forgiveness of sins that began in the church. It is the possession of the forgiveness of sins that distinguishes the members of the church from those outside the church. This forgiveness of sins is a grace because believers do nothing for it.[185] Knowing for certain that our sins are forgiven gives great comfort and is thus decisive for the flourishing of ecclesiastical life.[186]

Kuyper defined infant baptism as following on and presuming the prior inner work of grace. This was his concept of "presumptive regeneration." According to Wood, by prioritizing the inner and therefore private work of the Spirit as a precondition for baptism, Kuyper rejected the concept of the external covenant, which he considered an invention of adherents of the concept of the national church. Thus, Kuyper's theology of baptism was a part

---

181. Kuyper, *Lectures on Calvinism*, 65.
182. Kuyper, "State and Church," §31, 435. Although Kuyper's concept of the believers' church resembled the Anabaptist concept, the two differ because he maintained an approach "based not on a regeneration that cannot possibly be determined externally, but on holy baptism, and maintaining its holy character through admonition and discipline among these baptized members."
183. Kuyper, *Lectures on Calvinism*, 65. Emphasis original.
184. Kuyper, "Lord's Day 21," 353.
185. Kuyper, 370.
186. Kuyper, 371.

of his rejection of the national church concept.[187] Moreover, this doctrine of presumptive regeneration also was a result of the hard reality of infant mortality.[188] Kuyper argued that the parents who lost their young children could have comfort, not because their loved ones were not without a sinful nature but because they may be presumed to be regenerated.[189]

Wood observes a development in Kuyper's thought on infant baptism.[190] Before the 1886 Separation from the Dutch Reformed Church, Kuyper set the objective ecclesial community as the warrant for infant baptism.[191] After the Doleantie, Kuyper revised his theological view and proposed the concept of presumptive regeneration. This means that the basis of baptism is "the subjective spiritual life of the individual believer."[192] Kuyper thus changed his position from the shared faith of the congregation to the faith of the person being baptized; from baptism as a preparing grace to baptism as following an immediate regenerating work of the Holy Spirit.[193] However, baptism is also a means of grace. Children are not baptized because they choose God; they are baptized because God chooses them.[194]

Wood concludes that Kuyper's revision of baptism theology, even after the separation of church and state, means that baptism can be a public event. Through baptism, God let humanity see that this child belongs to God. Baptism speaks not only to the church but also to the world. It is a

---

187. Wood, *Going Dutch*, 115.

188. Wood, 127; Egmond, "Kuyper's Dogmatic Theology," 87. Wood summarizes Kuyper's personal experiences with child mortality as follows: "Four of Kuyper's sisters had died young; in 1872 his wife, Jo, suffered a miscarriage; and later, in 1892, one of his sons, Levinus Willem Christiaan Kuyper, died at age nine." Egmond notes that in the Netherlands, 45% of those who died in 1886 were younger than seven years old.

189. Kuyper, "Wedergeboorte en bekeering," 47–48; Wood, *Going Dutch*, 127. For a more detailed treatment of this issue by Reformed theologians, including Kuyper, see Mouw, "Baptism and Salvific Status," 238–54.

190. Cf. Wood, *Going Dutch*, 84–85. For Wood, Kuyper's believers' church ecclesiology represents a revision of his sacramental ecclesiology. As we saw in the previous section, Kuyper distinguished the church as organism and the church as institution. In Wood's view, Kuyper's ecclesiology is sacramental because he described the institution as a divinely instituted means of grace. With such a concept, Kuyper found it hard to leave the corrupted institutional church and to establish a new one. However, his newer concept allowed Kuyper to define the church primarily by the subjective participation of believers, rather than by an objective structure.

191. Wood, 127.

192. Wood, 132.

193. Wood, 133.

194. Wood, 138.

communal identity marker.[195] This theology of baptism helped Kuyper explain how Reformed Protestants could retain their practice of infant baptism in a world that otherwise threatened to undo it. Baptism, the seal of the covenant, was administered based on the subjective work of the Spirit in regeneration. This work of the Spirit might be known, or at least presumed, through the external and objective measure found in the covenantal family.[196]

At the same time, says Wood, by retracting the external covenant from the church's undergirding, Kuyper changed the position of the institutional church from the mother of the elect to their chambermaid.[197] As we have seen in section 4.1.4, this sort of interpretation fails to do justice to Kuyper's high view on the institutional church. His elaboration of regeneration reflects a similar understanding. Kuyper stated that regeneration "happens supernaturally through the Holy Spirit in a manner that we cannot understand."[198] Without the Spirit, every word is powerless. Nonetheless, the work of the Spirit "is not enough" and "has no effect" without the ministry of the word.[199] Therefore, although Kuyper at the outset stated that the Spirit implants the ability to believe supernaturally apart from the word, he afterward wrote that the Spirit activates that ability through the word. He did not set the Spirit's work apart from the ministry of the word.

As a theological position, Kuyper's notion of presumptive regeneration became the ground for the administration of infant baptism. Since in Kuyper's view only the elect receive the covenant, he emphasized the importance of assuming that the baptized infant is not only a covenant receiver but also numbers among the elect, until time should prove that this is not the case.[200] Other orthodox Calvinists, particularly those who had joined the 1834 Secession, could not agree with this Kuyperian understanding of infant baptism and its underlying view of the covenant.[201] For them, baptism ought to be grounded in God's promise and ordinance. In 1905, the Utrecht Synod accommodated

---

195. Wood, 137.
196. Wood, 136.
197. Wood, 137.
198. Kuyper, "Lord's Day 21," 345.
199. Kuyper, 346.
200. Cf. Mouw, "Baptism and Salvific Status," 247.
201. For a comparison of the positions of the Kuyperian and Secession groups, see Hanko, *For Thy Truth's Sake*, 264–65.

both positions by stating that, on the one hand, the seed of the covenant is to be considered a regenerated one, and, on the other hand, baptism should be grounded on the command and promise of God.[202] This compromising decision failed to settle the debate. Klaas Schilder (1890–1952) emphasized the need to separate baptism and election. He suggested viewing the baptized infant as the real receiver of the covenant, while keeping election a mystery.[203] Mouw rightly observes that Schilder's perspective is representative of the majority of the Reformed tradition.[204] Schilder reminds us to make the mystery of election God's mystery, and to observe the promise and demand of the covenant as the responsibility of its recipients.[205]

4.3 A Free Church

To thrive in the church institution, Kuyper firmly believed that a free church concept was indispensable. The term itself is not original to Kuyper.[206] However, the originality of Kuyper becomes evident when we compare his concept to that of earlier proponents of the free church concept, especially to the extent that it endeavors to answer some of the challenges of theological modernism and modern society. Heslam commends this ecclesiology as a third-way solution beyond the solutions of the Roman Catholics and the proponents of the national church concept.[207] In the same vein, Wood regards Kuyper's concept of the free church as an adjustment of Calvinism

---

202. http://rscottclark.org/2012/09/the-conclusions-of-synod-utrecht-1905/, accessed 29 July 2020.

203. Schilder, "Main Points of Doctrine."

204. Mouw, "Baptism and Salvific Status," 251.

205. See chapter 5 (section 5.3.3) for the historical context of the merger between these two groups.

206. As we will see later on in this section, Kuyper himself referred to the free churches in many places, including the Netherlands. Kuyper, "State and Church," §14–17, 401–8; §31, 435; Cf. Kärkkäinen, *Introduction to Ecclesiology*, 60; Olson, "Free Church Ecclesiology," 169. Kärkkäinen noted that although there are various free church ecclesiologies, most theologians regard the Radical Reformation and emerging Anabaptism as the origins of the free church mentality. Later on, Baptists like John Smyth developed the concept. Similarly, Olson believes that the medieval Waldensians in northern Italy had practiced an initial pattern of free church ecclesiology, which was later developed by the sixteenth-century Anabaptists and seventeenth-century Puritans.

207. Heslam, *Creating a Christian Worldview*, 138–39. As we will see in section 4.3.2 and 4.3.3, while Catholics chose to reinforce the institutional authority of the church, the supporters of the national church preferred to strengthen its legal status.

to modern society, which was characterized by the separation of church and state, religious pluralism, and democracy. It was a "revolutionary call" in the Netherlands, as it attempted to sever "the framework that had oriented Western society since Constantine and that the Reformation had not overturned."[208] At the same time, it was also an endeavor "to reconcile the separation of church and state with the church's role in Christianity's universal social implications."[209]

A concise account of the free church principle can be found in Kuyper's "Rooted and Grounded," where he summed up his position as follows: "Let the church be free from the state, free from the money purse, and free from the pressure of office."[210] However, since this issue was closely related to the issue of the separation of church and state, which remained a crucial one throughout Kuyper's entire career, one can also find numerous articles, speeches, and pamphlets relating to this concept of the free church.[211] As we saw in section 4.1.3, Kuyper was aware that it is no easy task to establish a proper relationship between church and state. Each side had contributed to the complexity of the relationship by attempting to extend its powers beyond legitimate boundaries. To use Kuyper's own words, "history shows how very difficult it is to define the correct relationship between the two."[212] For this reason, in treating his suggestion of freedom from the state, I will allocate some space to a discussion of his view on the state and his rejection of the concept of the national church. After dealing with his proposal for freedom from ecclesiastical hierarchy, I will deal with the political engagement in this free church ecclesiology and conclude with some remarks on its tensions.

4.3.1 Freedom from the State

As we saw in the previous section, Kuyper mentioned freedom from the state first on his list of the church's freedom. The second element, namely

---

208. Wood, *Going Dutch*, 141–44. For Wood's treatment of the way Kuyper defended his position and distinguished it from the French Revolution, see pp. 151–52.
209. Wood, 52.
210. Kuyper, "Rooted and Grounded," 66.
211. Cf. Heslam, *Creating a Christian Worldview*, 138, 161. Heslam believes that Kuyper had already advocated the concept of a free church as early as 1867 in his *De menswording God's, het levensbeginsel der kerk*.
212. Kuyper, "State and Church," §4, 383.

the money purse, refers to government support in terms of funds for church buildings and the salaries of church ministers. This means that freedom from the money purse is related closely to freedom from the state, to the extent that we will discuss both together in this section.

Kuyper acknowledged that the church needs money, but he was also aware that money could threaten the freedom of faith. Challenging the church to disdain the "gold" in favor of the "goldmine," he encouraged people to trust God who provides the gold as the fruit of faith, rather than seeking help from the government.[213] Dependence on the government's support for material issues, such as church buildings and the salaries of the ministers, had left the church unable to maintain its confession.[214] In Kuyper's view, the love of money had caused the Reformation churches to choose the path of becoming state-sponsored churches. They had become an organization, just like other organizations that were under the control of the government.[215]

Kuyper, in contrast, believed that the churches that had decided to be faithful instead of compromising for the sake of material support were able to survive. This had happened in the free churches in Scotland, England, Netherlands, and Germany.[216] For this reason, he challenged the church to be courageous in reforming itself and separating itself from all bonds.[217] It is worth noting that Kuyper had already made this argument in his 1860 "Commentatio," saying that all church members together should see to it that their church workers are paid.[218]

Kuyper contended for the church's freedom from the state. One reason for this assertion was Kuyper's awareness of the fundamental opposition between the church and the world. This opposition had existed from the outset of the church's establishment. For example, Abraham was called to leave his

---

213. Kuyper, "Rooted and Grounded," 66–67.
214. Kuyper, "State and Church," §13, 400; §28, 429–31.
215. Kuyper, §28, 430–31.
216. Kuyper, §31, 435.
217. Kuyper, "Tract on the Reformation," 81–82; Cf. Kuyper, "State and Church," §32, 435–36. It is interesting to see here that Kuyper also warned his followers not to offend others who could not accept his challenge.
218. Kuyper, "Commentatio," §182, 27. Referring to "Commentatio," §75, §85, §182, §196, and §34, Vree and Zwaan concluded that in Kuyper's view, "property and moneys are a matter for all members of the congregation, and not as in Geneva three centuries previously wholly (and in the Netherlands of the day chiefly) a matter for the public authorities." Vree and Zwaan, *Kuyper's Commentatio*, 58, f.n. 200.

land for the land that God would show him. Kuyper stated without hesitation that the church was not of the world. As he put it: "It was established not in cooperation with the world, but after breaking the world's fierce and fundamental opposition."[219]

For Kuyper, the free church concept represented a potential solution to the age-old conflict between church and world.[220] The concept could also solve the problems of both the Roman Catholic Church's paralysis and the spiritualist's drought.[221] On the one hand, the Roman Catholic Church "forged a double bond: of the human conscience to the church and of the church to state."[222] On the other hand, although the Reformation churches set the human conscience free, they did not sever the church's bond to the state. This was a serious failure, because it was like the act of separating the body of the church from its soul, and thus caused both the institutional church and the Christian spirit to lose their influence.[223] Nevertheless, people were not aware of this after-effect, being convinced that the problem between the church and the world had already been solved. Even when they saw the new phenomenon of the emerging free churches, they did not realize the importance of the free church concept itself.[224]

Kuyper believed that it was through the free church concept alone that the church could flourish best. Comparing the church to a river, which dissipates if its banks are demolished, he argued that the great stream of the church could not be produced until the congregations flowed together. Only an independent congregation can have a strictly administrative church government.[225] For him, the establishment between the church and the state would obstruct the healthy propagation of God's word.[226] Kuyper believed that the

---

219. Kuyper, "Lord's Day 21," 322.

220. Kuyper was aware that other people did not see the potential of the free church concept. As he put it, "when the 'free church' emerged as a new phenomenon, . . . no one dares guess the importance that this reborn power might well achieve in the future." Kuyper, "Conservatism and Orthodoxy," 67. In other works, he asserted that "the only good way out is what was realized in America: a wholly free church that is not connected to the state or dependent on it." Kuyper, "State and Church," §20, 413.

221. Kuyper, "Rooted and Grounded," 49.

222. Kuyper, "Conservatism and Orthodoxy," 67–68.

223. Kuyper, 68.

224. Kuyper, 67.

225. Kuyper, "Rooted and Grounded," 68.

226. Kuyper, *Our Program*, §300, 353; §301, 354.

church flourished most richly when allowed to live from its own strength on the principle of freedom. The sovereignty of the church finds its natural limitation in the sovereignty of other spheres. The church has no power over those who live outside of the sphere of the church.[227] Kuyper developed this notion of sphere sovereignty and applied it to various other spheres of life, such as education, the arts, and science.

In his 1916 "State and Church," Kuyper allocated several pages to a description of the practice of free church ecclesiology in America. He observed the following advantages: (1) receiving nothing from the state did not weaken the churches; instead, they grew and flourished better than the churches in Europe;[228] (2) the church members developed a greater sense of belonging and responsibility for maintaining the church;[229] and (3) paying no tax for a church to which one does not belong improved the relationship between different denominations.[230]

Kuyper was unequivocal in his claim regarding the legitimacy of the concept of the free church. First, he argued that the churches in the New Testament period practiced separation between church and state. Although they did honor the government as God's servant in civil and political life, "no mention is made of the government except in prayers," and they sought "so little financial aid from the government."[231]

Second, Kuyper insisted that his principle was in line with pristine Calvinism. He admitted that his claim is not without difficulty given certain historical facts in which the Calvinists had intervened and for which they

---

227. Cf. Kuyper, *Lectures on Calvinism*, 99, 104, 106, 108.

228. Kuyper, "State and Church," §14, 402. Kuyper stated that the churches in America were "better supplied, in every respect, with what a church needs. Nothing pertaining to the church is skimpy or minimal. All that is church-related grows and flourishes there." He added that there were some differences between the "luxury" in America and Europe. In Europe, especially in its southern parts, church buildings were monumental and furnished with first-class paintings as well as high-quality sculptures. In contrast, in America, "[t]he church buildings are designed to be practical. You will not be cold in church, and you will enjoy good lighting. The seating is arranged well, easily accessible, and nicely finished. From almost any seat you can easily listen to what the minister has to say.... Often, the church building is a place for education, for sport and even food, for the sake of those who come from afar and wish to stay for the evening service." "State and Church," §16, 405.

229. Kuyper, "State and Church," §15–16, 404–5.

230. Kuyper, §17, 407.

231. Kuyper, §23, 419–20.

had received support from the government.²³² He argued, however, that it was inevitable for the Calvinists (and the Lutherans) to do so. There was severe oppression from the government, which supported Roman Catholicism. Calvinists therefore needed governmental power to secure their daily and church life. Nevertheless, Kuyper contended that the real form of Calvinist church life was that of a self-governing and self-directing congregation.²³³

Before proceeding to the next section, it is worth noting that Kuyper did not suggest a strict separation between the church and the state. He argued that if the two become strangers to each other, there would be various clashes between the state and the church. Hence, Kuyper suggested the two to keep correspondence.²³⁴ On the one hand, the church should report its faith statement, pray for the state, fulfill the legal requirements, and ask necessary advice from the government. On the other hand, the government is obliged to keep orderliness at and around the sanctuary during the time of worship. However, Kuyper warned that the correspondence between the church and the state should maintain each other's freedom and must not have any bonding force with each other. The relation between the state and the church must be on an equal footing. Furthermore, the government should do justice to every denomination by giving no privileges to any church group.²³⁵

4.3.1.1 High View of the State

Thus, Kuyper's suggestion of separation between the church and the state does not mean that he had a low view of the state. Instead, he regarded both state and government as being of divine institution. Referring to John 19:11 and Romans 13:1–7, Kuyper believed that the authority of the government came from God.²³⁶ As such, there is no difference between a Christian and a non-Christian nation:

---

232. Kuyper, *Lectures on Calvinism*, 99–106. Here Kuyper mentioned the following facts: (1) Calvin's approval of the burning of Servetus and the government's intervention in religious matters; (2) the denial of certain rights and liberties of Roman Catholics in Calvinist Netherlands for centuries; and (3) Article 36 of the Belgic Confession.

233. Kuyper, "Rooted and Grounded," 68.

234. Kuyper, *Our Program*, §301, 354–§302, 355; §303, 357.

235. Kuyper, §305, 357; §304, 357, §311, 362–63.

236. Kuyper, *Our Program*, §301, 354; Kuyper, "State and Church," §21, 414.

just as a kitchen or a laboratory remains the same when its managers are in Christ or outside of Christ, the same is true here. Even under pagan rulers there were excellent governors, and many Christian princes fell short in the performance of their calling. The government builds and sustains the state in its own terrain, and common grace provides it with everything it needs for ruling rightly.[237]

Such a state concept was not compatible with an ecclesiology that understood the church "merely as a spiritually intended outward expression of faith." Such an ecclesiology would lead to the implication that the church must submit to the state in practical social life.[238]

In contrast, a church concept that views the church as an organization, not the people, of Christ would believe that the kingdom of God includes not only spiritual life, but also social as well as political life. Since the church on earth is a foreshadowing of that coming kingdom of God, it is directly related to that all-encompassing, worldwide kingdom.[239] Kuyper believed that such an ecclesiology would cause politicians to "esteem the church to be much higher than the state – even when it comes to that part of human society that is currently entrusted to the care of the state."[240] However, this does not mean he allowed the church to subjugate the state.

As both churchman and statesman, Kuyper maintained the sovereignty of both church and state. He emphasized the motto of "a free Church in a free State."[241] For him, the government has to judge and decide independently, not as an appendix to the church, nor as its pupil. Kuyper identified the origin of the government not only in terms of a remedy to the fall into sin, but he rather located that origin also in creation itself. Even in a sinless world, a sinless pattern of government would be necessary.[242]

---

237. Kuyper, "State and Church," §21, 415.
238. Kuyper, §1, 377.
239. Kuyper, §1, 378.
240. Kuyper, §1, 379.
241. Kuyper, *Lectures on Calvinism*, 99, 106. See also Kuyper, "State and Church," 421, f.n. 50: "This formula coined in reference to movements against established churches in Europe and particularly with the Italian statesman Count Cavour (1810–61), became a watchword for independents and Baptists in America."
242. Kuyper, *Lectures on Calvinism*, 92; Cf. Mouw, "Culture, Church," 54.

Kuyper did not exempt Christians from their responsibility toward the state to which they belong. He asserted without hesitation that all church members, as citizens of a nation, should submit themselves to the authorities. This obligation is applicable regardless of whether the government in question confesses or opposes the truth. However, since the authority of a government relates not to the internally human but only to the externally human, that obligation expires when the government may "overshoot its goal or oppress consciences."[243]

Kuyper had a high view of the state since his early life. In his 1860 "Commentatio," he discussed the relationship between the church and the state. Discarding the church's independence from human sin, Kuyper contended that because of human sinfulness, the state was "undeniably required" and "must never die" on the present earth.[244] Hence, the church members are to obey the laws of the state by free will (not from fear of the law), and to pay the highest respect to the government as long as it conducts itself in a right manner.[245] As such, Kuyper betrayed a position of non-resistance, which he would later on revise.[246] When the government no longer respects God or prioritizes the welfare of its citizen, "then the members of the church are called – in order to reveal the power of the Holy Spirit in themselves – to endure the cruelest punishments and tortures with a cheerful heart, rather than renounce the divine power."[247]

Before we move on to the next topic, it is also important to note that Kuyper did not overestimate the importance of the state. Comparing church and state, Kuyper observed that

> the state is little more than the scaffolding erected on the building site where the church is busy laying the foundation for the palace in which Christ will one day establish his royal throne. The state is a surgical implement to come to the aid of human

---

243. Kuyper, "Tract on the Reformation," §21, 137.
244. Kuyper, "Commentatio," §205, 34.
245. Kuyper, "Commentatio." In this work, since the gospel has nothing to say about the place of the state within the church, Kuyper judged that both Calvin and a Lasco had granted the state too much authority in the church.
246. See, for example, Kuyper, "Tract on the Reformation," §21, 137.
247. Kuyper, "Commentatio," §205, 35.

society in its situation of bondage . . . when the final hour arrives . . . the state will disappear forever.[248]

Kuyper continued by describing the church as bearing the seed of new life growing in the womb of the body. In this illustration, he suggested that one should consider the state as "the cloak wrapped around the body," not the body itself. He warned that once people think of the state as the body, then the church will be "reduced to a private organization for satisfying a certain mystical need." [249] He also warned that the state had a dangerous tendency to subjugate the church.[250] This observation leads us to the discussion of Kuyper's rejection of all attempts to identify the church with the state.

4.3.1.2 Rejection of the Concept of a National Church

Kuyper's proposal of the free church represented a critique of the concept of the national church. As we saw in section 4.2.1, he also rejected the concept of the national church using his notion of the believers' church. "A national church is not the church," he stated.[251] To Kuyper's mind, this concept overlooked the universal scale of sin, as well as the redemptive work of God. Since it was humankind, not one nation, that despised God, the victory of God's redemption must also be revealed to humankind, not one nation.[252]

As noted in the section 4.3.1, Kuyper admitted that cooperation with the state was inevitable for Lutherans and Calvinists during the Reformation era. Since "the Roman Catholics continually required the government to uphold the Roman Catholic organization over against the emerging Reformation, with force if necessary. The result was that great questions either had to be decided on the battlefield or be compelled by means of the gallows."[253] The Calvinists thus chose to "erect another government in opposition to the ruling [Catholic] government."[254]

---

248. Kuyper, "State and Church," §1, 378; Cf. Kuyper, "Commentatio," §205, 34.
249. Kuyper, "State and Church," §1, 379.
250. Kuyper, §8–10, 390–94.
251. Kuyper, *Pro Rege 2*, II.8.§3, 174.
252. Kuyper, "Tract on the Reformation," §2, 86.
253. Kuyper, "State and Church," §24, 421.
254. Kuyper, §24, 422.

Nevertheless, Kuyper also showed himself critical of that strategy. The cost for protection from the government was very high. Although the Reformation churches were successful in liberating themselves from the Roman Catholic hierarchy, the church lost its autonomous character and had to submit itself to the state.[255] Once the church and its ministers enjoyed the protection, support, and power of the state, it became difficult to relinquish those privileges.[256] In addition, the church lost its contact with the worldwide church and came to identify itself as the national church.[257]

From a broader church historical perspective, this tendency to rely on the support of the government for protection had existed since the conversion of Constantine.[258] This was why in Russia, Serbia, and Bulgaria, the Eastern Orthodox Church eventually came under the authority of the government.[259] In his exposition of the Heidelberg Catechism, Kuyper did not hesitate to describe Constantine as a figure who brought "serious harm to Christ's church."[260] He added:

> That is why it was so easy for the revolutionary rulers in the late eighteenth century to abolish the ruling church in the Netherlands and why there was so little resistance when in 1816 King William I incorporated the entire church into a state organization.... Many believers still held on to the false idea of Emperor Constantine, and there is still too little spiritual enthusiasm to fight the battle, as the people of the Lord, for the cause of God's kingdom.... The cause of all this misery was that the church of Christ had lost sight of the battle that it was to fight.[261]

Furthermore, Kuyper condemned the shift to the establishment of a national church as the work of Satan. He wrote, Satan "was not content to draw the *hearts* of people away from God, but he invaded the organic system of our human life. He breathed his spirit into all the institutions and customs and

---

255. Kuyper, §8–10, 390–94.
256. Kuyper, §13, 400; §28, 429–31.
257. Kuyper, §5, 385–86; §11, 395.
258. Kuyper, *Lectures on Calvinism*, 100; Cf. Heslam, *Creating a Christian Worldview*, 162.
259. Kuyper, "State and Church," §27, 427–28; §29, 431.
260. Kuyper, "Lord's Day 21," 337.
261. Kuyper, 338.

habits of life. He invaded all those influences and powers and energies that rule our human life."[262]

Apart from historical factors, Kuyper also mentioned several theological factors that had inclined people to the national church concept. Its proponents had thus argued that the Old Testament placed both tables of the law under the oversight of the rulers.[263] They generalized "the wholly unique and special position of Israel as covenant people to the church of Christ,"[264] and identified the calling of the Israelite government with the Christian government. Thus, for them, the government was to protect Christian ministry and to prevent all idolatry.[265] In Kuyper's thought, however, because the church did not resist the government's attempt to extend its supremacy beyond the church, ironically, "precisely in this form of a national church, it lost all of its independence and was forced to bow to the powerful arm of the government."[266]

Kuyper likewise pointed to the doctrine of the visible and invisible church as a cause for the flourishing of this practice of the national church. An overemphasis on this concept "could give occasion to worry less about the state of the visible church, and to be less annoyed when the government intervened in ecclesiastical affairs somewhat more than it should do in principle."[267] Kuyper also criticized the thought that considered the national church concept as a way to prevent the state from being a power against God.[268]

In contrast to the proponents of the national church concept, Kuyper paid respect to the Roman Catholic church for insisting on its independence from the state. He stated that it "must be openly admitted that the bishops of Rome are the ones who prevented the church from being swallowed up in the state, as was the threat back then."[269] However, Kuyper disagreed with the ways in which Roman Catholics had established the autonomy of the church. First, they tried to subjugate the government to the church. Second, they sought

---

262. Kuyper, 341.
263. Kuyper regarded their appeal to several verses of the Old Testament as "extremely weak." For his evaluation of those biblical verses, see Kuyper, "State and Church," §26, 425–27.
264. Kuyper, §25, 422.
265. Kuyper, §25, 422–24.
266. Kuyper, §25, 425.
267. Kuyper, §12, 396.
268. Kuyper, §18, 409.
269. Kuyper, §27, 428.

to "make all the churches of the world dependent on its bishops."[270] Kuyper's first point of disagreement has already been discussed, and so I will continue with the second in the following section. Kuyper articulated this second point by insisting on freedom from ecclesiastical hierarchy.

4.3.2 Free from Ecclesiastical Hierarchy

In Kuyper's view, establishing ecclesiastical hierarchy meant sacrificing the freedom within the church. Such a hierarchy might be useful for outward organizational unity, but not for spiritual harmony.[271] As noted in section 4.2.3, the church must be free from any ecclesiastical hierarchy because all believers, not only the teachers-pastors, share a common priesthood.[272] Kuyper argued that nobody should force others to obey him or her:

> Every man is sinful and has therefore forfeited any claim to respect for his person. The father has as little value as the child, and the father as a person does not inherently possess a single reason why the child should obey him. Every king is as sinful as the least of his subjects, and accordingly, there is in his person no reason why his subjects should submit to him. Likewise in the church of Christ, every person who acts as bishop, member of synod, classical leader, or in whatever function, is as sinful and unworthy as any member of the church, and there is no reason in their persons why the members of the church should render them reverence or obedience.[273]

He concluded that one must give God absolute obedience because he is the creator, sustainer, owner, and redeemer. However, one never owes absolute obedience to other human beings. Obedience to others exists "only if, and only as long as and to the extent that, the Lord God indeed and in truth orders and commands me to render to certain people, in his name, the obedience that is due to him."[274]

---

270. Kuyper, §27, 428–29.
271. Kuyper, §27, 428–29.
272. Cf. Kuyper, "Rooted and Grounded," 66–67.
273. Kuyper, "Tract on the Reformation," §61, 258.
274. Kuyper, §61, 259; Cf. Bratt, *Abraham Kuyper*, 151–52.

For Kuyper, the equality of all believers implies the presbyterian form of church government. However, he did not think the presbyters can stand above other members of the church. No human being should govern the church but Christ himself, through the Holy Spirit. Kuyper remarked:

> Therefore, all being equal under Him, there can be no distinctions of rank among believers; there are only ministers, who serve, lead and regulate; a thoroughly Presbyterian form of government; the Church power descending directly from Christ Himself, into the congregation, concentrated from congregation in the ministers, and by them being administered unto the brethren. So the sovereignty of Christ remains absolutely monarchial, but the government of the Church on earth becomes democratic to its bones and marrow; a system leading logically to this other sequence, that all believers and all congregations being of an equal standing, no Church may exercise any dominion over another, but that all local churches are of equal rank, and as manifestations of one and the same body, can only be united synodically, i.e., by way of *confederation*.[275]

Thus, Kuyper insisted that each local church is a full church and must be an autonomous church.

Furthermore, the office-bearers in every church were independently "instituted and held."[276] As Kuyper put it:

> In general the newly founded churches live in local independence and without external compulsory authority, and only in fraternal fellowship with other churches. The government has no authority over it. It honors the government as being a servant of God in civil and political life, but in the churches no mention is made of the government except in prayers, prayers lifted up for pagan governments as well.[277]

Each local church was free, not only from the state but also from other churches or particular leaders. This assertion from Kuyper, as Zwaanstra

---

275. Kuyper, *Lectures on Calvinism*, 63. Emphasis original.
276. Kuyper, "State and Church," §23, 419.
277. Kuyper, §23, 420.

has indicated, was influenced by a Lasco, who had emphasized that any coercion from outside one's local church was inconsistent with the essence of the church.[278]

Kuyper regarded his concept of the free church as the Calvinist approach. For him, one can distinguish Calvinism from five other approaches: (1) the Roman Catholic Church, which separated clergy and laity and destroyed the freedom of local churches; (2) the Greek Orthodox Church and (3) Lutheran churches, which submit themselves under the tyranny of the government; (4) the Collegial System, which denaturalized the church and reduced it to a pious society; and (5) Anabaptism, which withdrew from the world and thought it could determine who are the saints.[279] Kuyper also argued that in the New Testament, there was "hardly any trace of an organization that connects the individual local churches into one entity and allows for corporate action."[280] Even the synod of Jerusalem described in Acts 15 was not such a meeting to which the delegates of all churches were called. Rather, the assembly discussed a matter raised by Paul and Barnabas, who had been sent by the church of Antioch. They made the decision not by a majority vote but unanimously. It was "not in the same spirit as what in America and Scotland is called the *general assembly* of all churches together."[281] Kuyper believed that although the apostles might have exerted some authority in the local churches, basically every church acted as an independent organization.

4.3.3 The Political Engagement of the Free Church

While promoting the separation of the church from the state, Kuyper did assert that the church should also influence public life. However, he imposed a restriction on the way this influence was to be exercised. Kuyper provided the church a third alternative that neither admitted the world into the church nor withdrew the church from the world. In this third alternative, the church can separate from the state while continuing to influence the world.[282] The church may exercise direct influence on its members alone. In turn, the members

---

278. Zwaanstra, "Kuyper's Conception of the Church," 154.
279. Kuyper, "State and Church," §31, 435.
280. Kuyper, §23, 419.
281. Kuyper, §23, 419. Emphasis original.
282. Cf. Wood, *Going Dutch*, 166. Wood also views this as a third alternative to "church" and "sect" in Ernst Troeltsch's typology.

exercise their influence in "the press and the public opinion, and then in the nation's elected officials."[283] We have discussed this way of indirect political engagement through the organic church in section 4.1.3. In this section, we only need to add that the influence "must come to expression along the constitutional route."[284] For Kuyper, this was the democratic route.[285] In exerting its influence, the church should not hinder the state in any way, but respect its autonomy and independence.[286]

Kuyper advised a two-sided motivation, as two sides of the same coin: "on the one hand, the motivation to keep your church free from the state; and on the other hand, as members of Christ's church to influence the state and its government."[287] As a concrete example, Kuyper pointed out how in Europe, the church was able to introduce better morals and to improve national character, thereby positively influencing the government.[288] Kuyper also took America as another example. The church inspired the nation with the Christian spirit so as to abolish the slavery system.[289] Kuyper provided yet another example in his own person. According to Mouw, Kuyper's decision to resign from his position as pastor was "motivated in large part by his deep opposition to even the appearance of using the mantle of ecclesiastical office to influence life in another sphere. He wanted to make it clear that the exercise of authority within political life is different from the exercise of authority in the church."[290]

It is important to note that Kuyper did not abolish the government's responsibility to protect the true church. The church may ask the government to protect it. However, the way to protect the church is to give it "complete detachment."[291] The church should do this not only when it has a minority position, but also when it has already become the majority or when many church members have come to occupy strategic positions in the government.

---

283. Kuyper, "State and Church," §30, 432.
284. Kuyper, §21, 415.
285. Kuyper, §32, 437.
286. Kuyper, §23, 417; Cf. Bruijne, "'Colony of Heaven,'" 455.
287. Kuyper, §32, 436.
288. Kuyper, §21, 415.
289. Kuyper, §22, 417.
290. Mouw, *Abraham Kuyper*, 56.
291. Kuyper, "Tract on the Reformation," §21, 138.

The same principle applies whenever the church sees idolatry or heresy. The government has no capacity to intervene and determine which church is the true church. The church should not demand that the government oppress so-called heresy. Kuyper warned:

> But human nature is such that violence against moral error is ineffective; the nature of idolatry and heresy rather causes people to gain impetus when opposed; the government, according to the testimony of history, has almost always erred by viewing the truth as being heresy and condemning the truth as being idolatry. Therefore ... the government should be admonished not to try to remove heresy in any other way than to leave the true church free, and thereby to equip it for fuller development of its spiritual power.[292]

In other words, Kuyper did not recommend the church to seek privileges from the government. Instead, the church must encourage the government to keep its distance from all religious organizations, including the Christian church.[293]

4.3.4 Some Tensions in Kuyper's Free Church Ecclesiology

Nonetheless, Wood is right in seeing some tensions in Kuyper's free church concept.[294] His first sermons at Beesd Church (1863–67) indicate that Kuyper had a preference for rather little distance between church and state. However, by the end of his years there, he had changed his mind, favoring disestablishment.[295] Afterward, he sometimes allowed for a particular governmental influence in the church. Kuyper argued that the authorities as church members should be honored especially due to their office in the earthly homeland. He also accepted certain conditions for the possibility of financial support from the government to the church.[296]

Similarly, Kuyper initially demanded that the government be subject to divine commands. Since the government is the servant of God, it ought not to take human knowledge alone into consideration. Later, however, Kuyper

---

292. Kuyper, "Tract on the Reformation," §21, 140.
293. Kuyper, *Our Program*, §305, 357; §304, 357, §311, 362–63.
294. Wood, *Going Dutch*, 73–77.
295. Wood, 41.
296. Wood, 146; Cf. Bruijne, "'Colony of Heaven,'" 455.

changed his mind, asserting that the government could only act on human knowledge since it would always be surrounded by various conditions that made it impossible for the government to submit to biblical commands. Finally, by the time of the Stone Lectures, Kuyper reverted to his former position. However, he now suggested an indirect way of subjection, namely through the consciences of government officials.[297]

Furthermore, one can observe a tension with regard to the political role of the church. As we have seen, Kuyper insisted on indirect influence on the government, with the church focusing on influencing the consciences of government people. However, at times he also used expressions with a stronger import, as when he called the church the nation's custodian or caretaker.[298]

Another tension emerged between Kuyper's emphasis on the voluntary character of the free church and his assertion on the church as a divine matter. Wood is right in pointing to a naivety in Kuyper when he suggested that believers, not the ecclesiastical bureaucracy, choose their own forms of confessions. However, the fact of the matter is that even a relatively small synod of trained pastors have difficulties reaching a satisfying consensus on the forms. Furthermore, Kuyper insisted on the importance of the confessions, and for that reason required all ministers to subscribe wholeheartedly to every detail of the articles of faith.[299] At the same time, he admitted that other denominations might have different confessions and suggested that the civil government ought to tolerate these various positions and denominations.[300] This suggestion is part of his principle of the pluriformity of the church, which forms the topic of the following section.

4.4 The Pluriformity of the Church

Pluriformity is one of Kuyper's favorite terms and part of the "neo-" in his Calvinism.[301] Kuyper borrowed the idea of pluriformity from Johannes H.

---

297. Kuyper, *Lectures on Calvinism*, 103; Cf. Heslam, *Creating a Christian Worldview*, 164.
298. Wood, *Going Dutch*, 58, 78.
299. Wood, 74.
300. Kuyper, *Lectures on Calvinism*, 103-4; Cf. Heslam, *Creating a Christian Worldview*, 162.
301. Mouw, *Abraham Kuyper*, 16, 17.

Gunning Jr. (1829–1905).[302] The concept proved a controversial one for many, including some Calvinists. Klaas Schilder, for example, whom I already mentioned in section 4.2.4, showed his hesitance in stating that he was "not happy at all" with this concept.[303] On the contrary, Gerrit Berkouwer, while insisting on the call to unity and fellowship, assessed the pluriformity of the church as "a remarkable and suggestive ecclesiological theory."[304] After discussing what Kuyper meant by the pluriformity of the church and its implications for Christian political engagement, I will address some of the debates it elicited.

Kuyper explained that the pluriformity of the church is "another most important consequence" of the principle of the believers' church principle, free from ecclesiastical hierarchy.[305] Since there is diversity among human beings, as well as differences in climate, nation, historical experience, and disposition of mind, Kuyper believed that "widely variegating influence, and multiformity in ecclesiastical matters must be the result."[306] This multiformity places all visible earthly churches side by side, differing in degree of purity, but remaining in some way a manifestation of the one heavenly church. In other words, pluriformity is a concept of unity in diversity.

4.4.1 Diversity

Kuyper strongly believed diversity to be a part of God's will. He asserted that God had revealed this will in the Scriptures and also throughout the entire creation.[307] He boldly asked, "Where in God's entire creation do you encounter

---

302. Heslam, *Creating a Christian Worldview*, 137. However, different from Kuyper, Gunning himself did not say multiformity was an inevitable result. As we will see also in chapter 5 (section 5.1.2), Gunning was a student of Daniel Chantepie de la Saussaye (1818–74), the father of ethical theology, which adopted the Germanic organic thought of Schleiermacher.

303. Schilder, *The Church*, 19.

304. Berkouwer, *The Church*, 51, 62. Berkouwer argued that, in contrast with previous attempts, this theory is "neither to shift the unity of the Church into the future nor to make everything dependent on the already present, but hidden, unity of the invisible Church; rather it seeks to examine the concrete, visible Church, and does so by placing her in the light of pluriformity." The pluriformity of the church can both maintain the view on the church as Christ's one flock and admit the reality of its multiplicity.

305. Kuyper, *Lectures on Calvinism*, 63.

306. Kuyper, 64; Cf. Bolt, *Free Church*, 428; Heslam, *Creating a Christian Worldview*, 136. Heslam observes that Kuyper's belief in the democratic form of church government and his perception of the natural diversity of the material and spiritual world are the spring for his notion of the pluriformity of the church (p. 137).

307. Kuyper, "Uniformity," 35.

life that does not display the unmistakable hallmark of life precisely in the multiplicity of its colors and dimensions, in the capriciousness of its ever-changing forms?"[308] He argued that diversity can be found in both the angelic and human realms. He also argued that all life should multiply according to its kind.[309] Kuyper furthermore pointed out that in revealing his word, God applied variegation, using Isaiah and Amos, Paul and James. Even in Paul, one can see variety in the way he addresses the churches in Rome, Ephesus, and Corinth.[310]

The church is not merely a human organization, but rooted in the creational order. As such, for Kuyper, it is only natural and inevitable for us to find diversity in its historical development.[311] Wagenman points out that for Kuyper, the redeeming grace of God works hand in hand with the created natural world. Hence, just as the rest of creation produces diversity, so the church yields a diversity of expression, even in theology and worship.[312]

Furthermore, since the truth of God and salvation in Christ are so rich, Kuyper believed that the church inevitably and necessarily came to reveal itself in more than one form:

> But theology as such could never dismiss the problem of how this multiformity was to be brought into harmony with the unity of the body of Christ. It had already been seen that the truth of God was too rich and the great salvation in Christ too aboundingly precious, by reason of the Divine character exhibited in both, for them to be able to reach their full expression in one human form.[313]

Accordingly, Kuyper appealed to the limits of human knowledge in comprehending and articulating divine matters, which are without limit. Here the

---

308. Kuyper, 34.

309. Kuyper, 34. Kuyper also added that every believer would receive a new name on the last day.

310. Berkouwer, *The Church*, 57.

311. Cf. Wagenman, "Kuyper and the Church," 128, 130. Having compared the ecclesiological thought of Calvin and Kuyper, Wagenman concludes that by insisting more emphatically on the church as a part of creation, Kuyper made "a significant development from Calvin." The church "is not merely a post-Fall religious institution for the redemption of human persons."

312. Wagenman, "Kuyper and the Church," 132–33.

313. Kuyper, *Encyclopedia of Sacred Theology*, §104, 664.

epistemological motives in his doctrine of pluriformity are clear.[314] Kuyper viewed pluriformity as a phase of development at which the church of Christ must arrive.[315]

Kuyper viewed disunity as more than just a result of the human fall. Although he admitted that even within the Calvinist denomination, the emergence of numerous sects and denominations "unavoidably led to much unholy rivalry, and even to sinful errors of conduct," he also argued that

> after an experience of three centuries it must be confessed that this multiformity, which is inseparably connected with the fundamental thought of Calvinism, has been much more favourable to the growth and prosperity of religious life than the compulsory uniformity in which others sought the very basis of its strength.[316]

Kuyper regarded the pluriformity of the church like the division among the human nations. The pluriformity of the church is protection from God for his fallen creation against an evil unification that would affect the original creational diversity.[317] Kuyper would "dare far more than his opponents to suppose that there is a divine plan behind the reality of ecclesial plurality."[318] Kuyper believed that in this sinful world, a unity based in the uniformity of the church is harmful to the church itself. The true unity of the church will only be realized at the second coming of Christ.[319] This was why Kuyper regarded the disunity of the church not only as a result of the human fall, but at the same time also as a historical necessity, an inevitability, and as the unfolding of pluriformity.[320]

---

314. Brinkman, "Kuyper's Pluriformity," 116. See also Berkouwer, *The Church*, 58. Berkouwer evaluates this Kuyperian epistemology as being more anthropological than biblical, and thus insists that it does not suffice. For Berkouwer, it is "the core of Kuyper's ecclesiological epistemology."

315. Kuyper, *Encyclopedia of Sacred Theology*, §104, 662; Kuyper, *De Gemeene Gratie*, 3, 32.20, 231.

316. Kuyper, *Lectures on Calvinism*, 64–65.

317. Bruijne, "'Colony of Heaven,'" 468; See also, Bruijne, "Volume Introduction," xxxv–xxxvi. De Bruijne states that "with his theory of pluriformity, Kuyper allows for a trace of common grace within the ecclesial reality, though the church itself is part of particular grace."

318. Bruijne, "Volume Introduction," xxxvi.

319. Kuyper, "Uniformity," 21.

320. Berkouwer, *The Church*, 57.

As we have seen, Kuyper argued that while the invisible church had existed since creation, the institution of the church was a new creation at Pentecost. From the beginning, the institutional church had never been a single institutional unit, nor would it ever be. He argued:

> The Javanese are a different race than us; they live in a different region; they stand on a wholly different level of development; they are created differently in their inner life; they have a wholly different past behind them; and they have grown up in wholly different ideas. To expect of them that they should find the fitting expression of their faith in our Confession and in our Catechism is therefore absurd.[321]

For Kuyper, diversity in the institutional church is part of the beauty of human life, rather than a problem.

In Kuyper's thought, the concept of pluriformity also related to the concept of the church as organism and institution. Wood regards the pluriformity of the church as a primary consequence of Kuyper's organism-institution distinction and argues that Kuyper with that distinction shifted the traditional ecclesiological marks of unity and catholicity from the church as institution to the invisible organic church.[322] Eglinton similarly describes the doctrine of pluriformity as an application of the church as organism principle.[323] For him, Kuyper and Bavinck also believed that pluriformity has an analogy in the doctrine of the Trinity.[324]

---

321. Kuyper, *De Gemeene Gratie 3*, 32.20, 233; English translation cited from Wood, *Going Dutch*, 145.

322. Wood, *Going Dutch*, 151.

323. Eglinton, *Trinity and Organism*, 196, 200. For Eglinton, the role of the organic church in broader society and the pluriformity of the church are two consequences of the organism-institution model. When it comes to the Trinity, Kuyper and Bavinck admitted that the pluriformity of the church involves many disagreements, while within the Trinity there is no disagreement in the diversity. However, they considered those disagreements also beneficial and important for the church, since Christ will take them all into his service and adorn the church with them, just as many races and languages will be brought into the church and preserved for eternity.

324. Eglinton, *Trinity and Organism*, 201–2.

4.4.2 Unity

As we have seen, while emphasizing the inevitability of diversity, Kuyper also insisted on the unity of the church. Although the varieties of church differ from one another, those varieties do have one and the same organic aspect. He illustrated this with a family picture, in which each child may have different thoughts and feelings, but still be connected by one and the same family bond.[325] Kuyper was unhesitating in his insistence on the oneness of the church as the body of Christ. Although one can divide the church into the invisible and visible church, that visible and invisible church are not two churches but one:

> There is not one visible Church and another invisible; but one Church, invisible in the spiritual, and visible in the material world. And as God cares both for body and soul, so does Christ govern the external affairs of the Church just as certainly as with His grace He nourishes it internally. . . . Christ is the Lord; Lord not only of the soul, but before He can be that He must be Lord of the Church as a whole.[326]

Despite its various manifestations, the church is one in all the earth.[327]

Furthermore, Kuyper limited church division by requiring churches of the same confession to become one federation, while still allowing for pluriformity within that church federation.[328] With his doctrine of the multiformity of the church, he rejected the notion of an international church superstructure, and rather urged various churches to strive toward forms of mutual communion across national boundaries. The church in one country only forms the church of Christ together with the churches in other nations.[329] Considering that, as we will see in chapter 5 (section 5.3.3), Kuyper himself also implemented this concept by uniting his Doleantie group with the 1834 Secession group, Kuyper can be said to have been ahead of the later ecumenical movement.

---

325. Kuyper, *De Gemeene Gratie 3*, 32.20, 234.
326. Kuyper, *Work of the Holy Spirit*, 197.
327. Kuyper, 196.
328. Kuyper, "Tract on the Reformation," §57, 232.
329. Kuyper, *Lectures on Calvinism*, 64; Kuyper, *Tractaat*, 7, 33, cited from Bruijne, "'Colony of Heaven,'" 469, 488, f.n. 108.

What Kuyper refuted was uniformity, not unity, and not only for the church, but for all spheres of life. Kuyper thus distinguished between unity and uniformity. While the former is divine, the latter is worldly or satanic. Disunity is a result of satanic work.[330] Kuyper was convinced that God will restore the original broken unity. His 1867 speech "Uniformity" confirmed his belief in unity as the ultimate goal of God's ways. The unity of believers represents one of the petitions in the prayer of Christ, and it will be fulfilled at the second coming of Christ.[331] In the meantime, however, Satan offered uniformity, a corrupted version of unity which human beings pursue in their sinfulness.[332] The difference between God's original and Satan's plagiarism is as follows:

> In God's plan vital unity develops by internal strength precisely from the diversity of nations and races; but sin, by a reckless leveling and the elimination of all diversity, seeks a false, deceptive unity, the uniformity of death. The unity of God is written in the blueprint of the foundations; the unity of the world is merely painted on the walls. The Lord's unity is like the organic strength which holds together the fibers of the oak tree; the world's unity is like the spider web which upholds tenuous tissue in between. Organically one or an aggregate, a natural growth or a synthetic formation, become or made, nature or art – there, in a word, lies the profound difference distinguishing the spurious unity of the world from the life-unity designed by God.[333]

With this same perspective, Kuyper also contended that the French Revolution was a false unity. By seeking to inscribe the slogan of "liberty, equality, and fraternity" in the constitutions of the nations, the revolution attempted to eliminate the national diversity of ethnic groups.[334] For Kuyper, one should seek the unity of humanity in its origin and destiny, instead of in its developmental phases. God had determined to send forth humanity in various directions, rather than on one road. Therefore, the oneness of a body, not the

---

330. *De Heraut*, 20 May 1900, cited from Berkouwer, *The Church*, 56.
331. Kuyper, "Uniformity," 21.
332. Kuyper, 22–23.
333. Kuyper, 23–24.
334. Kuyper, 24.

sameness of a model, is the basis for God-intended unity. Far from removing diversity, this unity defines diversity more sharply.[335]

Kuyper admitted that the problem of unity emerged in church life earlier and more sharply than it did in societal life. He said that the question could be asked in terms of "how the unity which in principle it [the church] already possessed in Christ could emerge from the rich diversity of powerful Spirit-shaped personalities."[336] For Kuyper, the Roman Catholic Church attempted to solve this issue by establishing one model for its belief system, government, and liturgy, as well as language. Kuyper criticized this solution because it "opted not for a unity that would develop organically but for one that had been preconceived and simply demanded conformity."[337] Under this measure, Rome silenced every free expression of life and condemned those other expressions as either sectarians or heretics. In the same vein, Kuyper criticized the endeavor of the Reformation churches, arguing that they were doing the same thing as the Roman Catholic Church, but in a different way. They imposed uniformity in confession, piety, liturgy, and church government. The unity in the churches of the Reformation did not develop organically. Moreover, by localizing at the national level, the Reformation also broke the ecclesiastical unity with other churches in other countries.[338]

As a countermeasure, Kuyper suggested the concept of pluriformity. Pluriformity avoids all forced uniformity. Instead, the church pursues unity organically, which means it should

> first of all completely purge away the curse of uniformity, which is the mother of lies. Nothing should be forced and nothing united which is not organically one.... Thus, with complete autonomy let groups and circles unite who know what they want, know what they confess, and possess an actual, not merely a nominal, unity. If here and there such circles exist which share a common life-trait, let them become conscious of their unity

---

335. Kuyper, 35.
336. Kuyper, 37.
337. Kuyper, 37.
338. Kuyper, 37–38. Kuyper was no doubt referring to the churches of the later Reformation, which implemented the national church system.

and display it before the eyes of the world, but let it be only that feature and no other bond that unites them.[339]

In the place of clericalism and congregationalism, Kuyper proposed a confederative system. He required churches with the same confession to join into federations by their common confession, government, and history. However, such confederation is to be based on voluntary will, and has temporary, loose, and elastic characteristics.[340] In other words, the confederation should never eliminate the freedom of conscience at either the individual or congregational level.[341] He believed this was "the only way to combine freedom and unity without violating the truth and to lay the groundwork for a future in which the form is not artificially created but grows by the power of the Spirit from one's own corporate life."[342]

Kuyper believed that uniformity was not in harmony with the ordinance of God. It will lead to the destruction of life. Accordingly, he called uniformity a curse of modern life triggered by the French Revolution.[343] The pursuit of such uniformity was the reason why modern life was "almost totally devoid of artistic talent of any kind, poverty-stricken in aesthetic vitality, and totally destitute of great artistic creations."[344] Kuyper condemned those who oppose pluriformity for holding a dualism that does not allow the gospel to penetrate the fabric of life. This dualism hinders them from discerning the pluriformity existing in the relationship between Christians from different races, nations, and traditions. When this dualism is overcome, one can understand that although the objective truth is only one, its subjective application and confession should vary.[345]

Nevertheless, Kuyper did not agree with the concept of doctrinal liberty which allowed everything without any restriction or definition. He argued that "such formlessness block[s] all expression of the life."[346] Thus, Kuyper rejected the idea of congregationalism because it "fail[s] to appreciate the

---

339. Kuyper, 39.
340. Kuyper, *Tractaat*, 7, 33, cited from Bruijne, "'Colony of Heaven,'" 469.
341. Wood, *Going Dutch*, 176–78.
342. Kuyper, "Uniformity," 39; Cf. Kuyper, *Lectures on Calvinism*, 63.
343. Cf. Kuyper, "Uniformity," 24.
344. Kuyper, 36.
345. Kuyper, *De Gemeene Gratie* 3, 233.
346. Kuyper, "Uniformity," 38–39.

living bond between human spirits and nullif[ies] the community of people that has grown out of the root of Christ."[347] He encouraged believers to seek a purer revelation of the body of Christ. Hence, Kuyper was not promoting an ecclesiastical relativism.[348] On the contrary, while resisting confessional absolutism, Kuyper encouraged one to have a firm conviction in one's own confession, even to the extent of sacrificing one's life for it.[349] He allowed each person to judge whether or not a particular church has the marks of the true church.

Nevertheless, Kuyper emphasized the importance of appreciating other churches and denominations. He believed that Christ's church on earth consisted not only of his own church, but also other churches.[350] Kuyper remarked:

> our Protestant principle includes the open recognition of the correlation of the other churches with ours. No single confessional group claims to be *all* the church. We rather confess that the unity of the body of Christ extends far beyond our confessional boundaries. The theological gifts that operate outside of our circle may supply what we lack, and self-sufficient narrow-mindedness alone will refuse such benefit.[351]

Kuyper recognized that other churches might understand truths of God that his own church cannot grasp. This made it inevitable for him to accept the existence of other, different churches.

Kuyper therefore suggested a twofold attitude: firmness in one's own conviction, and, at the same time, tolerance. Brinkman rightly considers these two motives of anti-sectarianism and ecumenism to be two principal motives for the development of Kuyper's concept of the pluriformity of the church.[352] Kuyper resisted all forms of religious relativism and individualism. While stressing the importance of human consciousness, he also insisted on the role of the church in interpreting Scripture. This is the most substantial tension in Kuyper's doctrine of pluriformity. Brinkman puts it as follows:

---

347. Kuyper, 39.
348. Kuyper, *De Gemeene Gratie 3*, 37.25, 268–70.
349. Kuyper, *Encyclopedia of Sacred Theology*, §64, 323–24.
350. Kuyper, *De Gemeene Gratie 3*, 34.22, 245.
351. Kuyper, *Encyclopedia of Sacred Theology*, §64, 325–26.
352. Brinkman, "Kuyper's Pluriformity," 111, 115, 117.

On the hand, he wants to give prominence to the historicity of human existence, and therefore also of church traditions. That is the dynamic element in Kuyper's thought. On the other hand, however, he speaks – as mentioned above – about the "already fixed parts of truth." That is the more static element in his thought.[353]

In departure from the Roman Catholic model which locates the church outside the historical phenomenon, Kuyper positioned the church beyond the historical phenomenon but not outside of it. However, he added that the Holy Spirit is the one who protects the church from succumbing to the temporality of history.[354] History unfolds the development of God's creational variegation. Since Kuyper also recognized the human fall into sin as a cause of disunity, an ambivalence in his concept becomes visible here. The historical development of variety relates to both creation and fall.[355]

4.4.3 The Political Aspect of Pluriformity

To some extent, the pluriformity doctrine was an extension of Kuyper's distinction between the respective natures and roles of church and state. In his account, Kuyper applies his doctrine of common and particular grace as well as the sovereignty of Christ.[356] The state is an institution of common grace, and the church is an institution of particular grace. The church is and should be grounded in special revelation and regeneration. However, although special revelation too can provide many valuable directions for guiding the administration of the state, the state is not strictly necessarily regulated by special revelation.[357] While it is better for the state to have particular grace and the church, it can exist without them.[358] As to the sovereignty of Christ, Kuyper warns that we should not confuse Christ as the mediator of redemption and Christ as the mediator of creation. The former applies only to the elect,

---

353. Brinkman, "Kuyper's Pluriformity," 119.
354. Brinkman, "Kuyper's Pluriformity," 119.
355. Brinkman, "Kuyper's Pluriformity," 116.
356. Wood, *Going Dutch*, 142.
357. Kuyper, *De Gemeene Gratie 3*, 14.2, 100.
358. Kuyper, 18.6, 126–32.

whereas the latter applies to all people. Confusion will lead to either the state usurping the church, or else to the church subjecting the state.³⁵⁹

For Kuyper, the conviction that the church on earth "could express itself only in one form and as one institution" directly occasioned the practice of bringing religious matters into the jurisdiction of the government.³⁶⁰ In a country with a close relationship between church and state, this conviction erroneously gave the state the power to decide whether or not a particular denomination is heresy. However, the state is not competent to decide which church is the one true church and which churches ought to be removed and destroyed. Hence, the state was not to judge which confession or church was true, but to provide freedom for the churches under the state. This was also Kuyper's motive in proposing the revision of Article 36 of the Belgic Confession. Since Calvin still regarded the protection of the true church as a task of the government, Mouw is right to comment that Kuyper's notion of pluriformity represents a significant "neo-" in his Calvinism.³⁶¹ Although Kuyper believed that Calvin himself had already set this development in motion,³⁶² he also argued that people in Reformation times had not yet come to appreciate the concept of pluriformity. They were accustomed to thinking that absolute truth should manifest itself in a unity of form and content.³⁶³

Furthermore, the sphere of the state is observable in natural life, whereas the church deals with the heart. While the former uses coercive means, the latter depends on spiritual means. The state is an institution with an authority that can even extend over life and death. For instance, the state can call one to go to war. The church, on the other hand, is a voluntary institution and therefore cannot force anyone to become a member.³⁶⁴

In his 1869 lecture "Uniformity," Kuyper praised his audience, affiliated with the Christian-Historical school,³⁶⁵ because it "strives toward the unity

---

359. Kuyper, 17.5, 119–21.
360. Kuyper, *Lectures on Calvinism*, 100–101.
361. Mouw, *Abraham Kuyper*, 17.
362. Kuyper, *Lectures on Calvinism*, 63–64.
363. Kuyper, *Encyclopedia of Sacred Theology*, §104, 659–60.
364. Kuyper, *Lectures on Calvinism*, 105–6; Cf. Wood, *Going Dutch*, 146–48.
365. This conservative school emphasized Christianity as the historical identity of Dutch people, and therefore opposed the attempt of the government to remove Christianity from the education system. For a more detailed treatment of this movement, see chapter 5, section 5.2.2.

that is in *Christ* precisely through the free unfolding of *historically* developed life."[366] Opposing all-homogenizing centralism, Kuyper proposed a historical autonomy for persons, cities, and regions. He recommended the slogan "a distinct form of government for a distinct way of life."[367] Applying this slogan to the government of Dutch colonies, Kuyper asserted that the Dutch government should not impose the Dutch style of government on Javanese people (a tribe in present-day Indonesia). At the same time, Kuyper opposed excessive attachment to one's existing cultural system. Since the vitality of life could outgrow the form, he recommended introducing the gospel to the people in the Dutch colonies.[368] However, in doing so, as noted in section 4..4.1, Kuyper did not want the Javanese people to become like Dutch Christians. Javanese who become Christians should become Javanese Christians.

In other words, Kuyper did not think that Dutch culture was higher than other cultures, including those of the Dutch colonies. He did, however, think that the gospel should influence the existing system of culture. He placed all cultures in an equal position toward one another, and in a place under the gospel. Kuyper attributed that superiority not to the West as such, but to the gospel, which in his view was best elaborated in Calvinism. The gospel is not a means to change the culture, but to make the people of that culture become Christian with the character and form of that culture. Kuyper was convinced of the importance of religion, especially Christianity, for one's country. For him, history taught that "[w]ithout religion there can be no patriotism; where religion is most intense, there the love of country and people is most robust.[369] Scripture can give one the strength to live and the courage to die.[370]

Since the introduction of the gospel is the task of the church and not the state, Kuyper undoubtedly understood the church to have a role in influencing a nation by the introduction of the gospel to the people of that nation. The church should spread the gospel not by force, but by the voluntary decision of the people. In Kuyper's view, to be equal and to do justice to every life-expression is a basic principle for every Christian in his or her political

---

366. Kuyper, "Uniformity," 40.
367. Kuyper, 40.
368. Kuyper, 40.
369. Kuyper, 43.
370. Kuyper, 44.

engagement.[371] The church can encourage its members to political engagement with this understanding and direction, namely, that they should fight against uniformity and false unity, and promote unity in diversity.

4.4.4 The Debate on the Pluriformity of the Church

In the Netherlands, Klaas Schilder probably represents the most thorough critic of Kuyper's notion of the pluriformity of the church. In his view, Kuyper had built this doctrine from experience rather than Holy Scripture.[372] Condemning such method as Barthian, ethical, and modernistic, Schilder contended that the doctrine of the pluriformity of the church ought to be rejected.[373] While admitting that "in this world everything is different," Schilder regarded the churches that lived in contradiction with one another as a separate case.[374] He thus asserted that "God doesn't say yes and no at the same time."[375] Furthermore, Schilder believed that pluriformity hid a pagan notion regarding the essence as abstract and the forms as concrete. Instead of this extra-biblical idea, he suggested what he called a more biblical concept, that is, to "make visible what God has made invisible."[376] This means that one should strive to put church unity in the visible arena, rather than locating it in the invisible realm.[377]

---

371. Kuyper, 41.

372. Schilder, *The Church*, 6.

373. Schilder, 7. It is worth noting that Schilder also rejected the distinction between the militant and triumphant church and the visible and invisible church, as well as the church as organism and institution. For him, the militant-triumphant model actually is a Roman Catholic, scholastic distinction, and made on the ground of human experience. Although the ultimate victory will happen only after the second coming of Christ, Schilder believed that the church on earth not only fights but is also triumphant. He also thought that the church has invisible elements, such as faith, love, and prayer, and at the same time visible elements, such as the ministry of the word, prayer, and liturgy. Hence, there is no such thing as a visible church and an invisible church. Instead, there is only one church, with both visible and invisible elements. The church on earth should make the invisible element visible. With regard to the organic-institution model, Schilder rejected it because: (1) Kuyper had adopted the term organism from Friedrich Schelling, who had done so much wrong in Germany; (2) The model led to the degradation of the institutional church; (3) In a love relationship within the judicial context (e.g. the marriage institution), the organism-institution distinction is not valid and may lead to patented fornication. Schilder, 15–20.

374. Schilder, 20.

375. Schilder, 21.

376. Schilder, 20.

377. For a recent and thorough elaboration of Schilder's critique of pluriformity, see Jong, "Church Is the Means," 126–31, 164–70.

Kuyper's thought was subjected to similar criticism during his lifetime by Theodorus Bensdorp (1860–1917), a Dutch Catholic priest. Brinkman has rightly summarized the central point of the debate as follows: "Kuyper's doctrine of pluriformity eventually leads to the fact that several truths alongside one another will have to be recognized with the correspondence-concept of truth upheld by him."[378] When Bensdorp asked how contradictory confessions can be forms of one revealed truth, Kuyper answered that those different formulations are limited human attempts to understand the same reality. For instance, Kuyper did not mean that both the doctrine of transubstantiation and consubstantiation were correct. What he meant was that both doctrines were human attempts to understand the same reality of mystical communion with Christ in the sacrament. However, the human cannot express that communion adequately.[379] In line with Calvin's distinction between fundamental and non-fundamental matters,[380] Kuyper allowed diversity proportionate to the place a doctrine has in its relation to other doctrines.[381]

Berkouwer acknowledges the importance of the critiques on the pluriformity of the church.[382] He does not regard Schilder's criticism as a return to churchism.[383] He rather agrees that it is impossible to say that the disunity among churches is the manifold wisdom of God, given the biblical verses that express God's criticism on disunity (Eph 3:10; 1 Pet 4:10).[384] For Berkouwer, the vast variations of human subjectivity do not necessarily lead to church pluriformity. Instead, he comes to the following, different conclusion: "precisely when plurality becomes more visible than ever before, the call to unity and fellowship gains more force. The stress on inadequacy and incompleteness

---

378. Brinkman, "Kuyper's Pluriformity," 113.

379. *De Heraut*, 17 February 1901, included in Bensdorp, *De Pluriformiteit der Waarheid*, 1916, 69, cited from Berkouwer, *The Church*, 60, f.n. 35.

380. Calvin, *Institutes of the Christian Religion*, 4.1.12.

381. Brinkman, "Kuyper's Pluriformity," 119; Eglinton, *Trinity and Organism*, 202.

382. Berkouwer, *The Church*, 52–53. Berkouwer mentions four criticisms: (1) the concept eliminates the actual problem in the disunity of the churches, since a broken vase is hardly a "pluriform" vase; (2) one cannot justify the division of the church by using the multiformity of God's revelation; (3) the different forms of the church are neither harmonious with each other, nor directed at the well-being and building-up of the body of Christ; and (4) the doctrine does not take seriously enough the great danger of church division.

383. Berkouwer, 52. In footnote 8, Berkouwer mentions Valentine Hepp as one who considered Schilder's position as a return to churchism.

384. Berkouwer, 52–53.

does not legitimize the pluriformity of the Church, but rejects it because of the necessity of unity in Christ."[385] Instead of appealing to psychological, historical, or sociological factors, Berkouwer insists that true listening to the voice of Christ is the foundation of the church. With this, he believes that the church "cannot rest in the status quo or the 'riches' of pluriformity as a name for the division."[386] Kuyper's fascinating image of pluriformity "must be preserved and protected in the reality of an unassailable fellowship."[387] Although he does not agree with the view that simply holds church division to conflict with God's design, Berkouwer prefers the argument of Herman Bavinck, who appealed to the providence of God so as to argue that although disunity was a result of sin, there still is something good in that dividedness.[388]

Nevertheless, as mentioned above, Berkouwer still shows appreciation for the doctrine of pluriformity. For him, it is a rich concept that allows for variegation and distinction, and can therefore avert churchism.[389] He appreciates the element of unfolding development and human subjectivity in it.[390] Kuyper saw a distance between absolute truth and the truth assimilated in the subjective perception of a human being. While the former is perfect and complete, the latter is always imperfect and inadequate. Berkouwer also considers Kuyper's anti-dualism to be irrefutable.[391]

As we will see in chapter 5, Kuyper worked to unify churches with the same confessions in 1892. This union involved hundreds of thousands of Christians.[392] From this perspective, it is obvious that Kuyper's understanding of the pluriformity of the church was no reason to glorify division. For Kuyper, every Christian must strive for external unity wherever possible.[393]

---

385. Berkouwer, 62. In Berkouwer's view, a pluriformity whose form is division, disunity, and contradiction, does not fit the framework of biblical love (1 Cor 13; Eph 3:17).

386. Berkouwer, 74.

387. Berkouwer, 76.

388. Berkouwer, 55.

389. Berkouwer, 52.

390. Berkouwer, 55, 61.

391. Berkouwer, 62.

392. Brinkman, "Kuyper's Pluriformity," 115; See also Bruijne, "'Colony of Heaven,'" 475. For a more detailed account of Kuyper's endeavor for the 1892 Church Union, see chapter 5 (section 5.3.3).

393. Kuyper, "Tract on the Reformation," §16, 118, §31, 157–60; Kuyper, *Separatie en Doleantie*, 12.

Brinkman rightly concludes that although it was not fully successful, Kuyper more than others attempted to harmonize the tension between God's eternal truths and human knowledge of the truth.

Conclusion

In this chapter, I attempted to offer a systematize elaboration of Kuyper's ecclesiological concepts and their implications for Christian political engagement, under four categories: (1) the organism-institution distinction; (2) the believers' church; (3) the free church; and (4) the pluriformity of the church. While the church institution should focus on preaching, the administration of the sacraments, church discipline, and diaconal ministry, the church as organism can and should establish Christian organizations in all spheres of life. This organism-institution distinction was intended to strengthen the institution, rather than marginalizing it. Kuyper emphasized the need for the institution to be a gathering of regenerated and confessing individuals who form a society to live in submission to Christ as their king and reject the concept of a national church. For him, the genuine way for the church to flourish is by securing a church free from ecclesiastical hierarchy and the state. However, Kuyper neither despised the state nor encouraged Christians to withdraw from political engagement. Instead, he urged the church to influence society by nurturing the conscience of its members. Kuyper developed the concept of unity in diversity, not only for the relationship between churches but also as a model for Christians in their political engagement.

Although none of those concepts were original to Kuyper, he utilized and developed them in unique ways. He used each concept to help the church to participate in its engagement with society through the church as organism without endangering the existence and the implementation of the tasks of the church as institution.

With this understanding of Kuyper's ecclesiological concepts, we have moved one step forward toward our goal of considering the possibilities for the appropriation of his ecclesiology in the Japanese context. However, to that end, an understanding of the contexts of his ecclesiology is also indispensable. As we have seen, Kuyper's ecclesiological views can be found spread over numerous works, and they cover a long range of time. This means that his ecclesiology amounts to a series of suggestions for answering particular challenges that emerged in his time. The next task is therefore to investigate the historical background of Kuyper's ecclesiological concepts, which will form the focus of the next chapter.

CHAPTER 5

The Context of Kuyper's Ecclesiology

The investigation into the content of Kuyper's ecclesiology in the preceding chapter may already have brought to mind several possibilities for its application in the Japanese Christian context. However, as we noted in chapter 1, every theology is a context-shaped theology. Thus, investigating the historical context is indispensable for doing justice to a particular theology and for imagining its possibilities for application in other contexts. This fifth chapter will therefore explore the historical contexts that influenced Kuyper in developing and implementing his ecclesiological concepts. This process will not only deepen our understanding of his ecclesiology, but also enable us to analyze the potential of Kuyper's ecclesiology in the Japanese context in chapter 6.

Since Kuyper lived in a period of Dutch church history filled with interrelated upheavals, I have divided this chapter under the following three main headings, which help us to uncover other related topics from nineteenth-century Dutch church history: (1) church elections; (2) the School Struggle; and (3) the Doleantie. While the first issue is primarily concerned with church-state relations and the various theological strands that emerged in that time, the second deals with how the church engaged with sociopolitical problems. The third heading treats the church's relationship with the ecclesiastical hierarchies. This chapter will attempt to analyze the connections between these events and Kuyper's ecclesiological concepts as well as the responses of Dutch Christians.

5.1 The Church Elections

In 1852, King William II announced a new regulation[1] for the *Nederlandse Hervormde Kerk* (Dutch Reformed Church/DRC).[2] This royal decree was a consequence of the revision of the constitution in 1848. Since the new constitution had changed the political system from an aristocratic monarchy to a democratic monarchy, the General Regulations of 1852 also introduced a more democratic system to the church. Article 23 established the right for a congregation to appoint elders and deacons and to call ministers. In other words, it gave greater freedom to the church for deciding on the constitution of its own consistory. The church could now adopt democracy as its governance system.

This election system was new to the DRC. Up to that time, the right to vote had been restricted to consistory members who themselves elected their fellow members. The regular church members therefore had no right to choose consistory members or to call a minister.

The new system confused the DRC members, who seemed for the most part to have preferred the old system. They found it difficult to decide on consistory members and on the appointment of ministers by themselves. For more than a decade, the DRC did not implement the new election system, but maintained the old practice. It was not until 1866 that the General Synod finally decided to start implementing the new system, beginning 1 March 1867.[3] In the meantime, how the elections would work in reality continued to be a matter of nation-wide debate, which was carried out in pamphlets and church papers.

---

1. The *Algemeen Reglement voor de Hervormde Kerk van het Koninkrijk der Nederlanden* (General Regulations for the Reformed Church of the Kingdom of the Netherlands) can be downloaded at https://resolver.kb.nl/resolve?urn=MMTUK01:000000337:pdf, accessed 10 July 2020.

2. Although Allan Janssen and David McKay translate the name as the "Netherlands Reformed Church," I prefer to follow the more common translation, namely "Dutch Reformed Church." Cf. Blei, *Netherlands Reformed Church*, 56; Bos, *Servants of the Kingdom*, 14.

3. Vandenberg, *Abraham Kuyper*, 41, 42; Praamsma, *Let Christ Be King*, 50; Bruijn, *Abraham Kuyper*, 55. Vandenberg describes the content as follows: "In congregations of less than one hundred qualified voters these voters shall choose the consistory members and the ministers. In congregations of one hundred or more qualified voters these voters shall elect the officers themselves or the officers shall be chosen by an electoral commission."

In April 1867, Kuyper joined the discussion with the publication of a pamphlet of his own.[4] He encouraged the church to implement the new church election system.[5] The basis for his affirmation was more pragmatic than theological in nature. Theologically, Kuyper did not agree with popular sovereignty in the church. For him, the sovereign was God, through his word. In his eyes, Article 23 suggested general suffrage, a product of modern individualism.[6] Kuyer therefore saw Article 23 only as a temporary instrument to bring the church back to its proper condition, prior to the enforcement of the 1816 General Regulation. The church, he argued, should use Article 23 to recover its autonomy. The new church election system could thus be useful for liberating the church from the intervention of both state and synod.

Another angle to the matter concerned the dominance of liberal church leaders. When Kuyper became a pastor in the DRC, only 500 of the DRC's 1,600 ministers were orthodox.[7] However, at the grassroots level, there were many conservative lay members. These members were not satisfied with their non-orthodox leaders, but were unable to do anything about the situation. Some had shown their disagreement by refusing to attend services led by modernist ministers or by postponing the baptism of their children.[8] If they used the right granted them under Article 23 to vote for a conservative leader, the composition of the church's leadership would gradually change. This new and more democratic church election system therefore had the potential to remove, or at least reduce, the liberal influence in the church.

Many orthodox people welcomed Kuyper's suggestion. While many orthodox members were elected into the consistory during the church elections of 1867 and 1868, many liberals failed to be elected or re-elected. This happened in many churches, including the church in Amsterdam. The Amsterdam

---

4. The title of the pamphlet was: Wat moeten wij doen, het stemrecht aan ons zelven houden of den kerkeraad machtigen? Vraag bij de uitvoering van Art. 23 toegelicht [What should we do? Keep the right to vote for ourselves or empower the consistory? The question of carrying out Article 23 clarified].

5. Cf. Bruijn, *Abraham Kuyper*, 55–56; Vandenberg, *Abraham Kuyper*, 43.

6. When many orthodox believers came to appreciate Article 23, Kuyper wrote another brochure on it in January 1869. He repeated his warning that the church should not adopt popular sovereignty. Kuyper regarded the democratic system in the church as admissible only within a situation of confessional homogeneity.

7. Bratt, *Abraham Kuyper*, 59; Vandenberg, *Abraham Kuyper*, 49.

8. Kuyper, "Confidentially," 55–61; Bos, *Servants of the Kingdom*, 57–58.

church was one of the congregations that had long been dominated by theological modernism and had not called an orthodox minister for around twenty years. After the change in the election rules, it started to issue calls to orthodox ministers again.[9]

However, the implementation of Article 23 did not mean that everyone wanted to recover the autonomy of the DRC. For many of its leaders, close relations with the state still represented an attractive option. They were worried that disestablishment with the state would return the church to its miserable condition under the French occupation (1795–1815), which had disestablished the relationship between the church and the state. The church still sought the patronage of the state and favored the hierarchical system.[10] Furthermore, the implementation of the new electoral system was itself to some extent also an intervention by the state in church matters. It was a freedom granted by the state, not a freedom claimed or fought for by the church. The disestablishment therefore came from the side of the state, not the church.

This issue of church elections led Kuyper to embark on his first attempt to reform the church.[11] It can also serve as an introduction to two other significant factors in nineteenth-century Dutch church history, namely (1) the complex relationship between the DRC and the state; and (2) the diverse theological strands in the DRC.

5.1.1 The Complex Relationship between the Church and the State

In the early nineteenth century, the relationship between the church and the state in the Netherlands was quite complex. From the side of the state, there was a tendency to control all sectors, including religious life.[12] After the establishment of the Kingdom of the Netherlands in 1815, William I enjoyed full

---

9. Bratt, *Abraham Kuyper*, 59; Vandenberg, *Abraham Kuyper*, 50; Bos, *Servants of the Kingdom*, 330, 352. Bos argues that, while before the implementation of the new election system DRC ministers had been independent of the congregation members, after its introduction they had to consider their desires.

10. Since many prominent figures of the DRC considered the way of Kuyper's struggle as being excessively radical if not brutal, the reluctance displayed toward his concept was a complex issue. Nevertheless, it cannot be denied that many were afraid of losing the financial support of the state.

11. Vandenberg, *Abraham Kuyper*, 43.

12. Wintle, *Pillars of Piety*, 11.

power which he could exercise through royal decrees. In 1816, he announced a royal decree called the 1816 General Regulations.[13] This decree changed the name of the *Nederduitsche Gereformeerde Kerk* to *Nederlandsche Hervormde Kerk* (DRC),[14] and gave the king the power to appoint the officials of the national synod.[15] In the same vein, Wiliam I gave power to the provincial government to designate officials for the church boards at the provincial and classical levels.[16]

Even though the DRC under this regulation was not officially a state church, in reality it did assume many such traits. The church could thus receive support and privileges from the state, including provisions for the salaries of its ministers. However, the church also lost its autonomy, even for deciding on internal ecclesial matters. While the local congregations were to obey the decisions of the synod, the synod was to follow the decrees of the state. The state appointed the members of the General Synod Committee. The synod could decide on many ecclesial matters but could not convene for deciding doctrinal matters.[17] The presbyterian system of church government had become a centralized synodical system – from the bottom-up hierarchy to a top-down hierarchy.

It is worth noting that some did protest the 1816 General Regulations and the increasing dominance of theological modernism within the DRC.[18] When the synod did not accommodate their criticisms, a number of pastors and members separated from the DRC. The nation-wide schism that followed

---

13. The *Algemeen Reglement voor het Bestuur der Hervormde Kerk in het Koninrijk der Nederlanden* (General Regulation for the Administration of the Reformed Church in the Kingdom of the Netherlands) is available at https://resolver.kb.nl/resolve?urn=MMUBVU02: 000006162:pdf, accessed 10 July 2020.

14. *Nederduitsche* is an obsolete term for "Dutch." Theodore Plantinga translates *Nederduitse* as Low-German, as opposed to High-German (*hoogduits*). In this case, it is important to note that the term Low German here refers to the Netherlands, without any part of Germany. Bouma, *Secession, Doleantie, and Union*, 107.

Both *Hervormde* and *Gereformeerde* mean "Reformed." As we will see in section 5.3, orthodox Calvinists preferred to use the latter term to indicate faithfulness to the church of the Reformation. Cf. Blei, *Netherlands Reformed Church*, 2, f.n. 3.

15. Blei, 56–57.

16. Praamsma, *Let Christ Be King*, 50.

17. Wintle, *Pillars of Piety*, 67; Blei, *Netherlands Reformed Church*, 57–58.

18. For a discussion of the liberal strands within the DRC, see section 5.1.1. For a more detailed description of the protest against the regulation and the Secession of 1834, see Wintle, *Pillars of Piety*, 18, 26–30.

is known as the *Afscheiding* (Secession) of 1834.[19] By their separation, these church members not only lost the privilege of state support but also suffered persecutions from the state. Nevertheless, the new denomination that emerged in the wake of the schism grew steadily, so that Kuyper used it as an example of the benefits of not receiving state subsidies for the church.[20] As we will see later on in section 5.3, a large number of the adherents of this group later ended up merging with the Doleantie group of 1886 in 1892.

Apart from the opposition mentioned above, there was no resistance of any significance to the king's decree. Not only the majority of political elites, but also most church leaders welcomed the state's involvement in church matters. The occupation by the French from 1795 to 1815 had produced a kind of fear for the movement to diminish religious institutions. This is why, from the perspective of Dutch church leaders, the king's decree represented a strong guarantee securing the church's existence. At that time, the basic attitude for the church was to subjugate itself to the patronage of the state.

The above conditions pointed to several ecclesiological weaknesses in Kuyper's time. For one, the church did not yet have a solid foundation for resisting the state's attempt to control it. Moreover, the church did not have strong principles for checking its inclination to enjoy special privileges from the state.[21]

Kuyper pointed to the ecclesiological weaknesses in the Netherlands many times. He described the church where his father served as a minister as follows: "In Leiden, under the liberal regime of the time, a most pitiful situation prevailed, and the deceit, the hypocrisy, the unspiritual routine that sap the lifeblood of our whole ecclesiastical fellowship were most lamentably

---

19. The Secession of 1834 was a church split involving orthodox Reformed people under the influence of Hendrik de Cock (1801–42), a minister in Ulrum in the Province of Groningen. For a detailed and chronological description of the 1834 Secession, see De Jong, "Dawn of a New Day," 237–54; Blei, *Netherlands Reformed Church*, 64–66.

20. Kuyper compared the DRC congregation in Amsterdam to the 1834 Secession group. The former received a large subsidy from the state and had 140,000 members, but could only maintain 14 buildings and 27 pastors. The latter received no subsidy and had only 100,000 members, but it had 200 buildings and 220 pastors. Kuyper, *Confidentie*, 85–86; Cf. Bratt, *Abraham Kuyper*, 155; Wood, *Going Dutch*, 72.

21. Cf. Wintle, *Pillars of Piety*, 19, who suggests that the supposedly strong Dutch Calvinists accepted the new system because of: (1) the need for a united front, due to their minority status since the inclusion of the Catholic southern region in 1814; (2) the desire for a stable life after the crisis of the French occupation from 1795 to 1813; and (3) the influence of rationalism and humanism.

prevalent in the old university town."[22] In his "Commentatio" written in 1860, Kuyper stated that ecclesiology had not been developed well in his time.[23] Kuyper also considered there to be no church worthy of the name of a church in 1867.[24] Although Kuyper in 1870 did appreciate some of the changes made by high-level politicians and in popular thinking, he wrote that many people had still not come to a proper understanding of the concept of the free church.[25]

In Kuyper's view, all of the church's miserable circumstances related in one way or another to the acceptance of the 1816 General Regulation.[26] However, it is worth noting that he also admitted that the church's lethargy in his time followed partly from the decisions taken by the church in the Reformation era. The Reformation churches had needed the protection of the state to escape the hierarchical power of Rome. Kuyper acknowledged that "it was impossible to attain a peaceful position in the Netherlands without protection from the magistrate," adding that the Dutch government fortunately "did not claim for itself a spiritual character, as usually happened with caesaropapism."[27] Nevertheless, he still emphasized that the church paid for the state's support and protection with the loss of its autonomy and freedom.[28] He added that "the Reformed Churches in the Netherlands from 1619 to 1798 – that is, for a century and a half – were not able to gather as a general synod because the

---

22. Kuyper, "Confidentially," 46.

23. Since Kuyper wrote it for an essay competition on ecclesiology, he may have been trying to bolster the importance of his essay. However, the fact that the theme of ecclesiology had been picked by the committee also witnesses to the fact that many theologians of the time did not consider ecclesiology a primary concern, so that the competition could elicit new interest and development. Indeed, the essay contest was a part of the attempt of the Groningen movement to confirm the ecclesiology proper to the context of the Netherlands. The competition also revealed the presence of different theological positions. For a discussion of these theological strands in the Netherlands, see section 5.1.2.

24. Kuyper, "Conservatism and Orthodoxy," 67. This was Kuyper's reason for delivering a sermon on the relationship between the incarnation of Christ and the church at the occasion of his first sermon in the Utrecht church on 10 November 1867. The title of the sermon is: *De menschwording God's het levensbeginsel der kerk* [*The Incarnation of God: The Life Principle of the Church*].

25. Kuyper, "Conservatism and Orthodoxy," 67, 69.

26. Kuyper criticized the 1816 Synod of The Hague for overlooking Christ's present royal power as well as the Holy Spirit's presiding. Cf. Kuyper, "Tract on the Reformation," §52, 44, f.n. 44.

27. Kuyper, "State and Church," §10, 393; §11, 395.

28. Kuyper, §10, 393–94.

government did not allow it."²⁹ In Kuyper's eyes, this meant that the church had become a subject of the state. For this reason, he appealed for a return not just to the conditions prior to the implementation of the 1816 General Regulations, but to the Church Order of Dordt from 1618–19.

5.1.2 Diverse Theological Strands

The second complex factor relating to the issue of the church elections concerned the diverse theological strands existing within the DRC. As a general framework, two big camps can be discerned: an orthodox camp and a progressive camp.³⁰ However, the demarcating line between the adherents of each strand is not always crystal clear. Each strand emerged at a different time and had its own heyday, gaining more supporters. Furthermore, Kuyper's own life demonstrates how it was possible for a person to move from one position to the other. In what follows, we will observe the emergence of some of the major theological strands in the Netherlands.

The first strand was that of rational supernaturalism. While accepting the principles of rationalism and biblical higher criticism, the adherents of this school maintained the belief that God could surpass the laws of nature. They therefore accepted the historicity of miracles, although they at the same time tried to account for them using natural explanations.³¹ Kuyper's father Jan F. Kuyper (1801–82) was a moderate orthodox theologian, with an inclination to this supernaturalist school.³² Its origins lie in the late eighteenth century, and it dominated the DRC up to the 1820s.

---

29. Kuyper, §13, 399–400.

30. Generally, while the orthodox camp did not welcome the principles of the Enlightenment and the French Revolution, the progressive camp wanted to adopt them. The Enlightenment emphasized the supremacy of reason, and the French Revolution advanced it with the slogan of liberty, equality, and fraternity. The Enlightenment also influenced theology and resulted in so-called theological liberalism. This theology attempted to update Christianity for the modern era. Its followers promoted higher biblical criticism, which in turn resulted in the denial of traditional doctrines.

31. Wintle, *Pillars of Piety*, 13; Bratt, *Abraham Kuyper*, 27; Heslam, *Creating a Christian Worldview*, 27.

32. Before studying theology at Leiden University (1825–28), Jan Kuyper had engaged in a project to translate several English tracts for the Dutch Religious Tract Society. The leader of this society, Algernon S. Thelwall (1795–1863), might have influenced him to adopt supernaturalism. For the details of Jan Kuyper's life, see Bratt, *Abraham Kuyper*, 17; Bruijn, *Abraham Kuyper*, 3; Praamsma, *Let Christ Be King*, 23. See also http://www.dbnl.org/tekst/bie_005biog05_01/bie_005biog05_01_0159.php, accessed 2 March 2018.

The Groningen school succeeded the supernaturalists as the dominant stream in the 1830s. Following in the line of Schleiermacher, theologians of this school rejected the intellectual textual criticism of the rationalists and developed a theology of feeling.[33] They set religious feeling as the source of faith and focused on the person of Christ. It is in Christ that God raises human beings to find their true life purpose.[34] With such a position, they, while claiming ecclesiology as the core of their theology, nevertheless despised the institutional aspect of the church and opposed the obligation of adherence to traditional church doctrines. Instead, they emphasized the importance of the organic aspect of the church.[35] While the leaders of this school did believe that Christ had come to lead humanity to the will of God, for them Christ was not God, nor God a Trinity. They furthermore refused the notion that Christ died to satisfy divine justice on behalf of sinners. While considering Christianity the best religion, they did not regard it as the only true religion.

The Groningen school claimed that its departure from the Calvinist doctrinal standards was necessary and beneficial for the church. It aspired to develop a Dutch national theology that was rooted in Dutch theologians, rather than foreign theologians like Calvin.[36] The Groningen school made exegesis, not dogmatic theology, the decisive factor for the Christian faith. When the findings of higher criticism diverge from traditional doctrines, one should adapt the latter, not the former. After being subjected to criticism from orthodox believers, the Groningen theologians defended themselves by pointing out that they were the experts, and therefore insisted that they be granted autonomy in doing theology without intervention from the church or its members.[37] The Groningers had numerous disciples across the Netherlands and received support from intellectuals and other members of the upper classes within the DRC and its theological faculties up to the 1860s.[38]

---

33. As we will see in later paragraphs, Schleiermacher influenced not only the Groningers but also the modernists and the ethicals.

34. Bruijn, *Abraham Kuyper*, 65.

35. Bruijn, 77.

36. The Groningers considered Calvin responsible for bringing a foreign element into the Dutch Reformation, and therefore preferred the tradition of Dutch biblical humanists such as Thomas à Kempis, Wessel Gansfort, and Erasmus. Cf. Bos, *Servants of the Kingdom*, 150–51, 164, 169.

37. Praamsma, *Let Christ Be King*, 42.

38. Wintle, Pillars of Piety, 25–26; Blei, *Netherlands Reformed Church*, 64.

As mentioned in chapter 1, Kuyper wrote his "Commentatio" as his entry for an essay competition hosted by Groningen University. While he had predicted the end of the church's function within modern society in his 1859 thesis on papal power, now in his 1860 prize-winning essay he endorsed the notion of a church that was financially independent of the state and could diminish its role. Such a church, however, would still play an important role in society as the organism of believers led by the Spirit of Christ.[39] As Bratt has noted, this change was related to Kuyper's adoption of the ideal of the church as a free and voluntary community from Schleiermacher.[40] Similarly, Vree and Zwaan have argued that

> the 22-year-old Kuyper, in the space of less than a year of very concentrated work, not only discovered Calvin, a Lasco and the Church question, including a whole wealth of knowledge, but also himself and his expectations with regard to the church. . . . Gradually he developed a basic ecclesiological structure inspired in particular by Schleiermacher, to which, despite all the changes it underwent later on, he would remain faithful throughout his life.[41]

Accordingly, in his "Commentatio" Kuyper showed his preference for the "organic" ecclesiology of a Lasco, rather than the "institutional" ecclesiology of Calvin. He praised a Lasco as a forerunner of Schleiermacher,[42] whom he regarded as the one who has successfully "brought to light the truest notion of the church from the dark gloom, and has uncovered the innate strength of the church in Christians' mutual union and closest cohesion in Christ."[43] For Kuyper, the ecclesiology of Schleiermacher brought the innate strength of the church to expression.

The professors of Leiden University criticized the Groningers for failing to embrace theological modernism sufficiently. While the Groningen theology still considered God as a special and supernatural reality who intervenes in the human world from above, Leiden's modernism identified God as a God

---

39. Cf. Bruijn, *Abraham Kuyper*, 34.
40. Bratt, *Abraham Kuyper*, 173.
41. Vree and Zwaan, *Kuyper's Commentatio*, 65.
42. Kuyper, "Commentatio," §167, 16.
43. Kuyper, §167, 16.

who reveals himself in human thought, desire, and feeling.[44] While the Leiden professor Jan H. Scholten (1811–85) did defend the importance of Calvin, he rejected the classical Calvinist doctrine of election. In 1848, he argued for a reinterpretation of Calvinism from particular to universal election. He also stimulated his students to a critical study of the church and its theology.[45] Abraham Kuenen (1828–91) was an Old Testament scholar who, in the line of Scholten, argued for the importance of redefining Christianity in the light of scientific development. He therefore rejected supernaturalism and regarded Christianity as a product of evolution in the religious thinking of human beings. Lodewijk W. Rauwenhoff (1828–89) was another provocative figure by his public denial of the bodily resurrection of Christ.[46]

From the perspective of theological position, Leiden University formed the center of the modernist movement in the nineteenth century.[47] The professors of its theological faculty therefore influenced Kuyper in many ways. He joined other students in applauding Rauwenhoff,[48] while Kuenen was one of the examiners for his dissertation and Scholten his doctoral supervisor. While this first generation of modernist theologians caused Kuyper to embrace theological modernism, the second generation of scholars such as Conrad B. Huet (1826–86) and Allard Pierson (1831–96), led him to fight against it. In line with their powerful theological modernist convictions, Huet and Pierson ended up resigning from their ministerial positions in the DRC and embraced agnosticism.

Although theological modernism failed to gain many adherents in the lower levels of society, it did prove attractive to the elites at the universities and the synods of the DRC. Despite their small numbers, they still managed to bring many changes to church life.[49] Most of the changes represented

---

44. Blei, *Netherlands Reformed Church*, 68.

45. See Vandenberg, *Abraham Kuyper*, 22, who rightly points to Scholten's significant influence on Kuyper. Kuyper continued by studying ecclesiology for his dissertation and even set ecclesial issues as his life-long theme.

46. For a further elaboration of Leiden modernism, see Vandenberg, *Abraham Kuyper*, 19; Praamsma, *Let Christ Be King*, 16–17; Puchinger, *Abraham Kuyper*, 11–12.

47. However, it is worth noting that Cornelis W. Opzoomer (1821–92), professor at Utrecht, was also one of the prominent figures of theological modernism.

48. Kuyper, "Kuyper: His Early Life," 29; Vries, "Biographical Note," iv.

49. For example, the synod published a book of evangelical hymns in 1866 and the new translation of the New Testament in 1867. It also saw to new forms for baptism, profession

signs of progress for them, but aberration for the more orthodox camps. The result was a number of different responses. One powerful reaction came in the form of the Secession of 1834, as we saw in section 5.1.1. This group will be discussed at greater length later in section 5.3. Suffice it to say here that they were also known as "confessionals" for their cries for strict observation of the Reformed confessional documents and their teachings. Adherents of this group were mostly merchants, workers, daily laborers, and small farmers who lived in the northern provinces.

Another class within the orthodox camp, whose members mostly came from the aristocratic level in Amsterdam and The Hague, remained in the DRC. They were adherents of the Réveil, which was initially a religious revival movement that started in French-speaking Switzerland as a reaction to German rationalism. Leaders of this movement in the Netherlands included Willem Bilderdijk (1756–1831), Isaac da Costa (1798–1860), and Guillaume Groen van Prinsterer (1801–76). The Réveil movement had pietistic and individualistic tendencies. It also attempted to reform the churches, but had no agenda for seceding.[50] Similar efforts for the church's reform without secession can be detected in Kuyper's ecclesiology. Kuyper's departure from the ecclesiology of the Réveil can be seen in the way he opened the door to the possibility of leaving a corrupted institutional church and in the greater emphasis he placed on the community of believers. He opposed the principles of the French Revolution and suggested an anti-Revolutionary movement. As we will see in section 5.2, Kuyper would cooperate with Groen in the so-called School Struggle and turn the anti-revolutionaries into a more powerful movement.

From the Réveil emerged the so-called Utrecht School, which attempted to oppose theological modernism but still refused to pay full loyalty to the Reformed confessions. The leaders of the Utrecht School, such as Jan J. van Oosterzee (1817–82) and Jacobus I. Doedes (1817–97), advocated the position

---

of faith, and ordination in, respectively, 1870, 1880, and 1880. For further details, see Wintle, *Pillars of Piety*, 44.

50. Praamsma, *Let Christ Be King*, 13. As Praamsma has pointed out, the Réveil was a unique revival movement. While a revival usually takes place in a particular part of a country and lasts for only a limited period of time, the Réveil appeared in several regions of Europe, including Switzerland, France, Germany, The Netherlands, and Scotland. It manifested itself there about the same time, that is, during the first half of the nineteenth century.

that faith is more important than doctrine. Hence, Christians are to focus on the person and work of the Lord Jesus. This theological strand convinced neither the modernists nor the confessionals.[51]

Another theological strand that cooperated with the Réveil was the ethical school. Its leaders, Daniel Chantepie de la Saussaye (1818–74) and Johannes Hermanus Jr. (1829–1905), were friends of da Costa and Groen, respectively.[52] Ethical theologians aspired to establish a mediating theology between Scholten's modernism and the confessionalism of the 1834 Secession group. Adopting the thought of Schleiermacher, this school prioritized the importance of the person of Christ above Christian doctrine, and therefore emphasized pious experience and ethical concerns.[53] The ethical theologians accepted all critical theories regarding the origin, composition, and reliability of the Bible. They argued that Scripture becomes the word of God for an individual when it speaks to their conscience. The adherents of this school rejected the traditional notion of the sinful nature of human nature. Instead, they held to the autonomy of human moral consciousness. From this perspective, one can say that they had a low view of institutional matters such as the church as institution and the confessions.[54]

For the period of his study, Kuyper can be considered a follower of the ethical school. He even worked together with the ethical theologians in the association for the Christian National Schools (CNS) in the context of the School Struggle (see section 5.2). However, the ethical theologians did not agree with Kuyper's insistence on the removal of the word "Christian" from the Education Act of 1857. After the 1869 convention of the CNS accepted Kuyper's suggestion, they resigned from the CNS. To oppose Kuyper's position, Chantepie established the periodical *Protestant Contributions* in 1870. In 1872, as the chairperson of the Zeist Missionary Conference, Chantepie was so irritated by Kuyper, who had started a conflict with the supporters of

---

51. Harinck and Winkeler, "Nineteenth Century," 475.
52. Wintle, *Pillars of Piety*, 51.
53. Heslam, *Creating a Christian Worldview*, 137.
54. Cf. Bratt, *Abraham Kuyper*, 53; Bruijn, *Abraham Kuyper*, 66. Bratt puts it as follows: "the Ethicals gave Christian experience priority over Christian doctrine, put less stock in institutions than in individuals, and vested their hopes for church and nation in the free play of the gospel from person to person." Bratt, *Abraham Kuyper*, 46.

the ethical movement, that he publicly broke off all relations with Kuyper.[55] In 1873, Kuyper wrote that although he had initially found the works of the ethical school's leaders fascinating, he then concluded that they were "too relative, too uncertain of definition, too fluid and accommodating, too bubbling and drifting to give my spirit stability."[56] In 1914, Kuyper confessed that he had once "leaned strongly towards the 'ethical' wing of the church and therefore tended to be anti-Reformed."[57] By the 1880s, Kuyper's primary opponents were no longer the modernists, but this ethical-Irenical group. The term "irenical" indicated that they were not willing to take radical action, especially in breaking with the DRC. From their perspective, Kuyper's actions were not only too political but also reprehensible.[58]

The other group that influenced Kuyper were the pietistic Calvinists. The members of this group devoted themselves to the Further Reformation, a movement from the seventeenth and eighteenth centuries that had sought to apply the Reformation principles in daily life and society.[59] Kuyper encountered one such group of pietists in Beesd, who considered Kuyper a modernist preacher and therefore did not want to listen to his preaching.[60] Although they consisted of uneducated peasants, they were well-versed in Calvinistic principles. At the suggestion of a young woman called Pietje Baltus (1830–1914),[61] Kuyper reread Calvin's *Institutes*. In contrast with his earlier experience of reading Calvin during his student days, Kuyper now gratefully found the concept of God as Father and the church as the mother of believers in Calvinism.[62] It aroused in him a passion not only for ecclesial matters, but

---

55. Bos, *Servants of the Kingdom*, 347–48; Wintle, *Pillars of Piety*, 51.

56. Kuyper, "Confidentially," 57; See also Bruijn, *Abraham Kuyper*, 90.

57. *De Standaard*, 30 March 1914, cited from Kuyper, "Confidentially," 59; Cf. Bruijn, *Abraham Kuyper*, 51–52.

58. Bruijn, 66, 71, 88; Bratt, *Abraham Kuyper*, 45.

59. Bratt, 50.

60. Kuyper, "Confidentially," 55–61.

61. *De Standaard*, 30 March 1914, cited from Kuyper, "Confidentially," 58–59. On her death, Kuyper wrote about his first encounter with her as follows, using the third person: "He [Kuyper] suddenly grasped *the power of the absolute* in this woman and broke with all half-heartedness. Then he got acquainted with the spiritual legacy of the fathers. Dordt, which had first repelled him, from that time on became attractive to him. Also from Calvin he absorbed rays of light."

62. Kuyper, "Confidentially," 56. He wrote, "The orthodox faith was presented to us in such a ludicrous, caricatured way that it seemed a luxury and waste of money for students of modest means to spend anything on such misbegotten writings. I had become acquainted with

also for Calvinism. He had a similar experience with *The Heir of Redclyffe*, which caused him to set a new goal for life, that is, the restoration of the church as the mother of believers.[63] It is also worth noting that Kuyper's numerous, future followers generally came from the lower ranks of society, as had been the case in Beesd.

After his conversion to Calvinism, which elicited a high view of the church in him, Kuyper became a strong opponent of theological modernism.[64] From his perspective, theological modernism had weakened the church institution in many ways. As we saw in chapter 4, his distinction of the organic-institutional church and his concept of the believers' church represented an effort to revive the institution of the church to its proper condition.

Nonetheless, Kuyper was also critical of the trait within this camp of pietistic Calvinists to establish mystical conventicals. As he put it, "they didn't give me enough."[65] The Calvinism of these pietists was a Calvinism that fit the situation of the Reformation era, but could not fully and appropriately respond to the growing influence of Enlightenment ideals.[66] As Puchinger puts it, "Kuyper was not only a restorer, he also was an innovator. After he discovered, like no other theologian, that the Reformed element in society could not be eliminated, he understood that it had to be *restored* and made *decent*, in other words, it had to be *thought through* again."[67] Accordingly, Kuyper also determined himself to revitalize Calvinism for the challenges of the present time.[68]

Interestingly, Kuyper attempted to revitalize Calvinism by drawing on modernism. His opposition to modernism did not mean he rejected the modernist endeavor entirely. Kuyper thus made use of history to criticize

---

Calvin and a Lasco, but in reading them it never occurred to me that this might be the truth." Cf. McGoldrick, *God's Renaissance Man*, 37.

63. Kuyper, "Confidentially," 60.

64. For Kuyper's criticism of modernism, see Kuyper, "Modernism," 91–98.

65. Kuyper, "Confidentially," 56. In Puchinger's words, "Kuyper understood that this faith [of the pietist Calvinist] had to be reformulated in contemporary language." Puchinger, *Abraham Kuyper*, 27.

Similarly, Bratt states that Kuyper wanted to "upgrade Calvinism from an old dogma to an active life, to put Modernist methods to orthodox ends, and to redefine the church to make it fit, and challenge, the contemporary world." Bratt, *Abraham Kuyper*, 42–43.

66. Wagenman, "Kuyper and the Church," 126.

67. Puchinger, *Abraham Kuyper*, 28. Emphasis original.

68. Kuyper, *Lectures on Calvinism*, 40.

the claims of the Modernist movement. As Bratt puts it, Kuyper adopted the method of Scholten, but the contents of their respective theologies were opposites.[69] Although he recognized the danger in the thought of German modern philosophers, Kuyper acknowledged the importance of their principles.[70] Hence, he attempted to utilize their thought for revitalizing orthodox Calvinism. Kuyper's ecclesiology was likewise a mix of Reformed scholasticism with nineteenth-century Idealism and Romanticism.[71]

Having said that, Kuyper took orthodoxy as his anchor. His dependence on modern philosophers did not hinder him in departing from them. As Wagenman has noted, while Hegel suggested a humanistic development process from lower to higher religion, Kuyper did not hesitate to acknowledge the sinfulness of human beings. Consequently, he emphasized the degeneration of the human race and thus the need for God's saving grace in Jesus Christ for present human life. Kuyper's ecclesiology is inseparable from this orthodox hamartiological and soteriological view.[72] In a similar vein, Bratt admits that although Kuyper never discarded Hegelian method, which regards the essence of history as an intelligible process moving toward a certain state, he denounced Hegel's notion of the state as the true divine incarnation.[73]

In sum, the issue of the new election system revealed the complex relationship between the church and the state. Both parties expected support from each other. At the beginning of the nineteenth century in particular, the state imposed regulations placing the DRC under its control, in return for such privileges as the payment of the salary of the ministers and the maintenance of church property. These privileges, together with the desire of church leaders to maintain the position of a national church (if not a state church), made the church reluctant to discharge itself from the control of the state, even

---

69. Bratt, *Abraham Kuyper*, 47, 49. He concludes that Kuyper confronted modernism "on its own grounds of human religious experience."

70. Kuyper, "Modernism," 87–124.

71. Zwaanstra, "Kuyper's Conception of the Church," 153; Bratt, *Abraham Kuyper*, 183.

72. Wagenman, "Kuyper and the Church," 138; Cf. Kuyper, *Lectures on Calvinism*, 55–59.

73. Bratt, *Abraham Kuyper*, 31–32. Bratt also argues that Kuyper's theological method came from Fichte and his epistemology from Kant. To support this emphasis, Bratt refers to Kuyper's "Blurring of the Boundaries" from 1892. See also Bratt, *Abraham Kuyper*, 174. Bratt states that "[t]he German's presence at the heart of Kuyper's ecclesiology never disappeared. His project going forward was to make Schleiermacher safe for Calvin under the rubric of Reformed orthodoxy."

though the state had already yielded the separation of church and state in 1848. At the same time, it is already apparent how Kuyper's suggestions for the problem of church elections were related to his concept of the office of believers as we have discussed in the previous chapter (section 4.2.3). Kuyper urged church members to use the function of their general office to elect the special office bearers.

As noted, the complex relationship between the church and the state is the primary context for Kuyper's concept of a free church. This concept was a suggestion to solve the life-long ecclesiological problems in the DRC, which was subjected to the state and ecclesial hierarchy. The free church concept can help the church to become aware of the state's attempt to control it, even when the state has already decided on church-state separation. Instead of placing the church above the state, or vice versa, a free ecclesiology argues for freedom from the bond of, and dependence on, the state. Furthermore, a free church ecclesiology can remind the church not to depend on the state for its protection and support. The state can support an institutional church, based not on a particular confession, but on equality as a free institution that indirectly brings benefits to society. From this perspective, Kuyper's suggestion of the free church concept can be seen as a kind of third-way solution to the complicated relationship between the church and the state.

Furthermore, by distinguishing between the church as organism and the church as institution, Kuyper attempted to overcome the church's inclination to isolate itself from public life, while still remaining a free church. While the concept of the church as institution, in combination with the concept of the believers' church, secures the endeavor to maintain the purity of the church, the concept of the church as organism encourages the members of the church to engage actively with society. Hence, Kuyper's ecclesiological suggestions can be said to have aimed also at solving the problem of the free church's inclination to withdrawal.

The issue of the new election system also revealed the existence of diverse theological strands in the DRC. Kuyper had unique encounters with those strands, and finally settled in the orthodox Reformed camp. His ecclesiology suggested a return to a Calvinistic concept of the church. However, he saw the need to update orthodoxy so as to make it capable of answering the challenges of the current age. This is a characteristic not only of Kuyper's ecclesiology, but of his entire theology.

5.2 The School Struggle

The *Schoolstrijd* (School Struggle) refers to a long fight in the nineteenth century for the freedom of *bijzonder* (private or denominational) school education and its right to public funding equal to that of *openbaar* (public) schools.[74] The origin of this struggle can be traced back to the change in the educational system after the collapse of the Dutch Republic in 1795. That year, the Netherlands fell under the power of the French and adopted a constitution that implemented the principles of the French Revolution. Whereas education in the past had been under the responsibility of the church, now it became the concern of the state. The purpose of this principle was the maintenance of the unity of the nation, rather than Christianity. These changes, in the minds of conservative Christians, meant that they had lost the ideal education system for their children.

Protests against this liberal national education system started soon after the School Law of 1801 and the School Law of 1803 came into effect, calling the new educational direction to life. Catholics and orthodox Calvinists protested the modern education system, calling it an imposition of false doctrine. To soothe their voices, the government issued the Education Law of 1806, which replaced Enlightenment terms with more traditional Christian terminology. This new law defined the purpose of the public school as nurturing children to develop all social and Christian virtues.[75] Moreover, the 1806 law did not prohibit Christian denominational schools, but did require them to gain recognition from the local government.

However, even this new Education Law did not satisfy orthodox Calvinists. For one, it prohibited the teaching of denominational Christianity in public

---

74. While some historians prefer to translate the term *Schoolstrijd* as Battle of the School, School Conflict, or School War, I follow the terms used by Wendy Naylor, who approaches this theme from the perspective of education and Abraham Kuyper. Naylor, "School Choice," 245–74.

Furthermore, while *bijzonder* literally means "special," I prefer to use the terms "private" or "denominational" as a reference to the founder and operator of the schools. Others translate it as confessional, religious, or free. Cf. Essen, "Struggle for Freedom Education," 55–77; Hooker, *History of Holland*, 126; State, *Brief History of Netherlands*, 167–68; Arblaster, *History of Low Countries*, 187.

75. Onderwijswet van 1806, Reglement, Art. 22: "Alle Schoolonderwijs zal zoodanig moeten worden ingerigt, dat onder het aanleeren van gepaste en nuttige kundigheden, de verstandelijke vermogens der kinderen ontwikkeld, en zij zelven opgeleid worden tot alle maatschappelijke en Christelijke deugden" [All School education will have to be implemented in such a way that, while learning appropriate and useful skills, the intellectual abilities of the children are developed, and they are trained to all social and Christian virtues].

schools.[76] All state-funded schools were to be free from any and every color of a particular denomination. The term "Christian virtues" thus referred to a generic Christianity that would neither take the side of nor offend any denomination. Furthermore, in reality, local governments often refused to grant recognition to denominational schools. When a denominational school did receive recognition, it usually encountered difficulties competing with public schools. Funded by the state, public schools had better facilities and did not have to collect tuition fees from the pupils. In addition, all parents, including those who sent their children to private schools, were required to pay taxes for funding the public schools.[77]

The struggle for freedom and equal funding for denominational schools escalated when the government issued the Primary Education Law in 1878. Following the 1857 Education Law, which had made it difficult to operate denominational schools, the 1878 Law prescribed a further, higher standard for all schools.[78] The government arranged for funds to implement the improvement for public schools alone. Along with this, the government also sought to make school attendance compulsory for all children. Since the private schools had already found themselves in a difficult situation, it was almost impossible for them to implement the law.[79] This meant that they had to stop operating. As a result, the children of the denominational schools had to attend public schools. In other words, Christian parents had no choice but to send their children to a public school, where the teaching was not in line with their religious convictions.

The various concepts for religious education at schools and the efforts undertaken in this School Struggle will be examined in greater detail in section 5.2.2 and following. Suffice it to say here that the struggle led by Kuyper

---

76. Reglement, Art. 23: "Terwijl vastgesteld wordt het nemen van maatregelen om de Schoolkinderen van het onderwijs in het Leerstellige van, het Kerkgenootschap, waartoe zij behooren, geenzins verstoken te doen blijven, zal het geven van dit onderwijs niet geschieden door den Schoolmeester" [While it is established that measures are taken upon the School Children, not in any way to keep them away from the doctrinal teaching of the Denomination to which they belong, the teaching of this education will not be done by the school teacher].

77. Wintle, *Pillars of Piety*, 63; Essen, "Struggle for Freedom Education," 57; Hooker, *History of Holland*, 126; State, *Brief History of Netherlands*, 167.

78. For detailed descriptions of the development of the constitutions and school laws before the Primary Education Law of 1878, see Essen, "Struggle for Freedom Education," 56–61; Naylor, "School Choice," 248–54.

79. Wintle, *Pillars of Piety*, 66.

succeeded in convincing many Dutch people as well as the government not only to grant recognition to all qualified private schools of any religious conviction, but also to subsidize the denominational schools. The struggle finally ended in 1917, when the government amended the constitution, guaranteeing the constitutional right of freedom and full funding for qualified denominational schools, equal to that of public schools.[80] Today, the national education system in the Netherlands still follows in the line of the amendment of 1917, a system that is unique even among other Western nations.[81] It subsidizes all qualified denominational schools, whether Catholic, Protestant, Muslim, Hindu, or Jewish. Furthermore, the underlying concept extends beyond the field of education, also becoming the basis for the tolerance politics in the present-day Netherlands.[82]

The issue of the School Struggle is of vital importance for this dissertation on multiple fronts. Whereas the issue of church elections intensified Kuyper's correspondence with Groen van Prinsterer, the leader of the Réveil movement (cf. section 5.1.2), the issue of the School Struggle made him Groen's co-worker as he continued his project.[83] The School Struggle was the issue that led Kuyper to engage simultaneously and intensively with fields outside the church walls, namely education, journalism, and politics. Accordingly, this topic not only supplies us the context of Kuyper's ecclesiology, but also yields several examples of his engagement with political issues in line with

---

80. Grondwet (1917), Art. 192: "Bij die regeling wordt met name de vrijheid van het bijzonder onderwijs betreffende de keuze der leermiddelen en de aanstelling der onderwijzers geerbiedigd. Het bijzonder algemeen vormend lager onderwijs, dat aan de bij de wet te stellen voorwaarden voldoet, wordt naar denzelfden maatstaf als het openbaar onderwijs uit de openbare kas bekostigd" [In particular, the freedom of special education regarding the choice of teaching materials and the appointment of teachers is respected. Particularly general primary education, which meets the conditions set by law, will be funded from public funds according to the same standard as public education].

81. The establishment of denominational schools triggered the pillarization of Dutch society, which lasted up to the 1960s. Every segment of society, namely Reformed, Catholic, Socialist, and Liberal, had a pillar so that its members could sustain their lives from birth to death without the need to interact with other segments of society. For an exploration of pillarization, see Wintle, *Pillars of Piety*, 62–68; Kwaasteniet, *Denomination and Primary Education*, 231–34.

82. Wintle, *Economic and Social History*, 252.

83. Although they first communicated with each other after Kuyper published a Lasco's work in 1864, their correspondence intensified after Kuyper published a pamphlet on Article 23 in 1867 (see section 5.1). Groen praised Kuyper's piece as "the most remarkable thing to see the light of day on this burning question." Bruijn, *Abraham Kuyper*, 55–56; Bratt, *Abraham Kuyper*, 71.

those ecclesiological concepts. After presenting the two contrasting positions on religious education in public schools, I will discuss Kuyper's position and detail several steps he undertook to bring his thoughts to realization.

5.2.1 Political Liberalism

Many Dutch political elites in the nineteenth century welcomed the principles of the French Revolution. They wanted to modernize the Netherlands by separating the establishment of church and state. Since they sought to turn the nation into a strong state, they introduced changes to the educational system as detailed at the beginning of section 5.2. Although King William I hindered the efforts of the liberals by placing the DRC under his power and restoring several state church traits to the DRC, the advance of political liberalism continued unabated. After his father's abdication in 1840, King William II had no option but to accept the liberal constitution in 1848.

One prominent figure within the liberal camp was John Rudolf Thorbecke (1798–1872), who drafted the Constitution of 1848. Along with the shift from a tyrannical monarchy to a constitutional monarchy, Thorbecke designed the constitution to guarantee the freedom of association, press, religion, and education. In the section on freedom of education, Thorbecke inserted the clause "with respect for everyone's religious concepts."[84] This meant that the constitution guaranteed the freedom of denominational education, making the requirement of government recognition easier to obtain.

However, other liberal politicians did not entirely agree with Thorbecke, preferring to place education under the monopoly of the state. For them, freedom for denominational schools would only repeat the divisions among religious people. Hence, they wanted all children to study at the same secular school, without any religious imposition. They believed that this system would nurture patriotism and foster in children the intellectual ability to decide on religious matters.[85] Accordingly, the liberalists opposed the idea

---

84. Grondwet (1848), Art. 194: "De inrichting van het openbaar onderwijs wordt, met eerbiediging van ieders godsdienstige begrippen, door de wet geregeld. Er wordt overal in het Rijk van overheidswege voldoend openbaar lager onderwijs gegeven. Het geven van onderwijs is vrij, behoudens het toezigt der overhead." [The institution of public education shall be regulated, with respect for everyone's religious concepts, by law. Everywhere in the Kingdom the government shall provide adequate public primary education. The provision of education is free except for supervision by the government.].

85. Hooker, *History of Holland*, 126; State, *Brief History of Netherlands*, 143.

of subsidizing denominational schools in the Education Bill of 1857 as it had been proposed by a sympathizer of the conservative camp. As a compromise, the government decided to allow denominational teaching by the church at the public schools, but only outside school hours.[86]

Therefore, one can conclude that in the perspective of the political liberals, freedom of religion and freedom of education imply the removal of religion from public schools. If public school teachers want to teach a doctrine, they cannot but choose one particular interpretation, which would be doing injustice to the positions that they do not choose. Therefore, the best option is to choose no religious doctrine at all. This was the logical conclusion drawn by many liberals in Kuyper's time. And it is precisely what Kuyper considered the danger of liberalism.[87]

Although the Catholics had protested the state's takeover of education from the church at the beginning of the nineteenth century, they took the side of the liberals once they realized that the king would not allow them to have Catholic private schools. To their mind, it was better to send their children to schools without any religious teaching at all than to schools with Bible stories interpreted from a Protestant perspective. They retained this inclination until the early second half of the nineteenth century.

5.2.2 Conservatism

In contrast to the liberals, the conservatives opposed the removal of Christian teaching from education. Conservatism manifested itself in two forms in nineteenth-century Dutch church history.

The first type of conservatives were those who accepted the influence of modernism in theology, but rejected it in politics. Thus, while they fall into the modernist category of section 5.1.2 (on religion), they are conservatives according to the present section (5.2.2, on politics). Although these conservatives had no intention to obliterate Christianity from public schools, they did support a Christianity that would not offend any other denomination

---

86. Onderwijswet van 1857, Art. 23: " Het geven van onderwijs in de godsdienst wordt overgelaten aan de kerkgenootschappen. Hiervoor kunnen de schoollocalen buiten de schooluren ten behoeve van de leerlingen, die er ter school gaan, beschikbaar worden gesteld" [Teaching religion is left to the denominational church. To this end, school classrooms can be made available outside of school hours for the benefit of pupils attending school].

87. Cf. Kuyper, "State and Church," §3, 382.

or religion. Their inclination to theological modernism meant they had no problem with the term "Christian" as a reference to a generic Christianity. For that reason, they did not oppose the education laws mentioned in the section 5.2, as long as they still retained the term "Christian." Furthermore, most Protestant politicians supported these education laws in part because they did not want Catholic schools to emerge.

Petrus Hofstede de Groot (1802–86), the pioneer of the Groningen School, was a prominent example of the first type of political conservatives. He was upset with the development of a religionless public school and sought to revive the religious element in state schools. However, what he and fellow Groningers wanted to teach was not Christ the Savior, but Christ the perfect teacher; not repentance and regeneration, but education and development; not a corrupted humanity, but a human race bearing the seed of perfection which could be developed through proper education.[88]

The second type of political conservatives were those who were conservative in both theology and politics. They refused a religionless education as well as a generic Christian education. Hence, in contrast to the first type who accepted the education laws, this second type of conservatives opposed them. From their perspective, the position of the former hardly differed from that of political liberalism.[89]

The theological conservatives fought actively during the early stage of the School Struggle. Orthodox Calvinists who had joined the Secession of 1834 believed that they had the obligation to teach their children about the Bible at school. They opposed the national education system by starting several parental or parochial denominational schools. As a result, many were persecuted and heavily fined. This was one of the driving forces behind the mass migrations to the United States in the 1840s. Those who remained in the Netherlands continued their fight by establishing the Association for Reformed Primary Education in 1868.

Apart from the 1834 Secessionists, the theological conservatives also included the proponents of the Réveil Movement. Since most of them were aristocrats, they could cause the voice of theological conservatives to be heard in Parliament. Under the leadership of Groen, they established the association

---

88. Essen, "Struggle for Freedom Education," 57.
89. Wintle, *Pillars of Piety*, 64.

for Christian National Schools (CNS). At the outset, the association insisted that the Netherlands was a Calvinist country and should therefore teach Calvinism in the public schools. However, after experiencing disappointment with the first type of conservatives in Parliament, they turned to focus their fight on the right to establish denominational schools. As noted briefly in section 5.1.2, this caused a division at the national convention of 1869, breaking the association into ethical and anti-revolutionary camps.[90] While the former preferred to maintain the term "Christian" in the Education Law, the latter insisted on its removal. Since the convention ended up adopting the position of the latter, the ethical camp left. The principles of this anti-revolutionary party form the topic of section 5.2.3.

5.2.3 Anti-Revolutionary

As their name suggests, the anti-revolutionaries considered the concepts of the French Revolution godless principles. Hence, Groen and his followers firmly resisted the efforts of the political liberals, in whom they detected heavy influence from the French Revolution. As has been mentioned, the anti-revolutionaries changed their fight, first insisting on the teaching of Calvinism in public schools and later focusing on the right to establish denominational schools. This turn also led them to pursue the removal of the term "Christian" in the education law.

Kuyper played a vital role in that change. He delivered a speech entitled *Het beroep op het volksgeweten* (The Appeal to the National Conscience) at the general public meeting before the 1869 convention of the CNS, where Groen figured as the prominent leader.[91] Kuyper proposed: (1) the removal of the term "Christian" in the education law; (2) the disbanding of the system of employing public school teachers as church staff; and (3) the collection of school fees from all students, except the poor. These three suggestions corresponded with Articles 23, 24, and 33 of the 1857 Education Law, which proved advantageous for public schools and disadvantaged denominational schools.[92]

---

90. See Wintle, 65.

91. For a more detailed description of Groen's fight in the School Struggle, see Essen, "Struggle for Freedom Education," 57–65.

92. This was the first time Kuyper and Groen met in person. Both were delighted with this meeting. Kuyper's appeals were in line with the fight Groen had waged for years. While Kuyper wrote, "from that hour I became his [Groen] spiritual associate, no, more, his spiritual

Kuyper emphasized the freedom of religious education. For him, Christian education is not the territory of the state and so it should not intervene. However, Kuyper did not stop there. He continued with his advocacy for the equal status of the denominational schools, arguing that the state should grant all faith-based schools funding equal to that of the public schools. He insisted that education is the constitutional right of every citizen and at the same time the responsibility of the state. If the church, or Christian parents, help the state in providing qualified education to its citizens, they should be eligible to receive funding from the state. The basis for this funding should not be the charity of the state, but the legal right of education guaranteed by the constitution.

One can see similarities here between Kuyper's proposals above and his free church concept as discussed in chapter 4. Just as the church should be free from the state, so too education should be free from the state. Since Kuyper delivered his sermon "Rooted and Grounded," in which he proposed the notion of the free church and the distinction between the organic and institutional church, one year after this speech, it is no exaggeration to say that the School Struggle represented one of the important contexts for his organism-institution model and his free church concept. As we will see in section 5.2.4, the struggle also represented an application of Kuyper's view on influencing society through the organic church.

Kuyper appealed to the conscience of Dutch people for justice and fairness in primary education. When he advocated the freedom of religion as well as equal funding for denominational schools, he did not just speak for his denomination but, as we will see in the following section, also for other denominations.

5.2.4 Mass Mobilization

The School Struggle led Kuyper to involve himself in many other related matters. He saw that while many Christians wanted to have Christian schools, they had no idea how to realize their aspirations. He also observed that their desire was often mixed with an agenda to turn Christianity into a sort

---

son," a few months later Groen pointed to Kuyper as the future leader of the Anti-Revolutionary movement. Cited from Vandenberg, *Abraham Kuyper*, 53.

of state religion. This convinced Kuyper of the need of mass education for these Christians.

Kuyper himself supplied this need by writing articles in mass media. In 1869, he was invited to become an associate editor for the orthodox weekly *De Heraut*.[93] This invitation meant that he began to write both religious and political articles on a regular basis from October 1870.[94] Kuyper considered his new position an opportunity to educate and train his readers. On 6 January 1871, he became the editor-in-chief, after his predecessor met an untimely death.[95] Kuyper turned the magazine into an organ for his program, with the following motto: "a free church and a free school in a free Netherlands." In April 1872, he also accepted the opportunity to become editor-in-chief of *De Standaard*, a daily newspaper of the Anti-Revolutionary movement. He used this newspaper to expound on and spread Reformed opinion nationwide.[96] Many of Kuyper's well-known works were originally written as series of articles for these papers.

Kuyper's efforts led many orthodox Christians to understand the essence of the issue. They came to support his ideas; they became aware of what was happening and wanted to take part in the struggle. In the awareness that they needed to fight the School Struggle also in the parliamentary context, Kuyper agreed in December 1873 to run for a vacant seat in the Second Chamber of Parliament.[97] With the added support of Catholics, Kuyper was elected by the constituency of Gouda on 21 January 1874.[98]

---

93. *De Heraut* was a semi-religious and semi-political weekly, whose editor-in-chief was Carl Schwarz (1817–70).

94. Bruijn, *Abraham Kuyper*, 68, 82. Kuyper published his first article in *De Heraut* on the issue of church inspection in Utrecht, on 9 July 1869. After that, Kuyper wrote regularly, not only on church and theology, but also on politics, such as the Primary Education Law, higher education, and suffrage. The publishing of newspapers became more affordable with the removal of the newspaper tax on 1 July 1869.

95. Vandenberg, *Abraham Kuyper*, 63.

96. Bratt, *Abraham Kuyper*, 61; Bruijn, *Abraham Kuyper*, 83. Kuyper wrote approximately 16,800 short but sharp, daily "three-star" articles for *De Standaard*. He also wrote longer lead articles.

97. The Dutch Second Chamber of Parliament is similar to the House of Representatives in the US and the House of Commons in the UK.

98. Bratt, *Abraham Kuyper*, 63; Bruijn, *Abraham Kuyper*, 87, 91, 95. According to de Bruijn, in 1874 the second chamber had 80 members: 38 liberals, 16 conservatives, 16 Roman Catholics, and 10 anti-revolutionaries. Kuyper filled the vacancy left by M. A. F. H. Hoffman, Groen's brother-in-law, who had resigned due to his diminishing health. Since the law at that time prohibited active ministers from being parliamentary members, Kuyper had to resign from

In Kuyper's mind, the School Struggle required a political platform. In 1872, he cooperated in founding the Anti-School Law Union. This union coordinated the election campaigns for the anti-revolutionaries. This was the seed for the Anti-Revolutionary Party (ARP) which Kuyper established in 1878 and which became the vessel for orthodox Christians with political talents to gather and fight together in a constitutional way. With respect to this "constitutional way," it is worth noting that Kuyper persuaded his followers to submit to the king's decision to proceed to the ratification process of the 1878 Education Law, despite their success in obtaining many signatures for their petition. He did not want the struggle to take place outside the constitutional route.

The success of the School struggle was not due to orthodox Protestants alone, since they were aided by their coalition with the Catholics. As we have already noted, once Catholics realized that King William I would not allow them to establish Catholic schools, they inclined themselves to the political liberal camp because the liberals provided them a place equal to that of the Protestants in politics, law, economics, society, and culture. In the 1870s, however, the Catholics changed their attitude toward the liberals for several reasons. First, with the papal encyclical "Quanta Cura" of 1864, Rome took an anti-liberal stand. Furthermore, the Dutch bishops pronounced a prohibition preventing Catholic parents from sending their children to Dutch public schools. And, finally, the liberals put an end to the Dutch donations to the Vatican. These factors led the Catholics in the Netherlands to stop their alliance with the liberals. Their desire for Catholic schools caused them to become allies of the anti-revolutionaries instead, who shared a similar vision. The coalition was made possible on the Catholic side by the efforts of Herman Schaepman (1844–1903), a priest and poet who also became a politician, and on the anti-revolutionary side by Kuyper.

The coalition succeeded several times in gaining a majority in Parliament between 1885 and 1925. Along with mass education and the mobilization of people for supporting the coalition, the alliance managed to obtain government approval for a partial subsidy for denominational schools in 1889 and achieved full funding in 1920. This full funding was the implementation

---

the pastoral ministry. Kuyper officially accepted his seat on 10 February 1874, resigned from the pastoral ministry on 16 March, and was installed in Parliament on 20 March.

of an amendment of the Constitution in 1917, guaranteeing funding as a constitutional right.[99]

To conclude this section, one can see similarities between the issue of the School Struggle and the new church elections system discussed in section 5.1. The School Struggle also revolved around the issue of church-state relations, although the matter here was focused more on the side of the state.[100] We saw how Liberals wanted to sever the relationship of church and state, this time in the field of primary education, but Christian conservatives were unwilling to part with the establishment between the Reformed Church and the state. Kuyper criticized both parties. He did not agree with the attempts to nullify the influence of religion in civil society, nor did he support the efforts to "gather everybody into one church and to 'baptize' society institutionally."[101] Hence, we once again see Kuyper suggesting a third-way solution. Instead of privileging his denomination, or adopting the liberal position which attempted to remove all denominations from the public schools, he proposed to grant justice and equity to all denominations.

From the perspective of Kuyper's ecclesiology, his proposals for the School Struggle reflected his concepts of the believers' church and the pluriformity of the church. It is no exaggeration to say that his activities were both implied by, and served to fortify, his distinction between the organic church and the institutional church. Kuyper did not gather institutional churches for his political party, but he assembled Christians. While the church as institution is to concentrate on the church's tasks, the church as organism should bring the light of the gospel outside of the church's walls and windows to all fields of life. Kuyper's efforts to mobilize and organize orthodox Christians for the School Struggle was unavoidably also a political engagement.[102] He believed that political engagement was an inevitable responsibility of Christians.

---

99. Kwaasteniet, *Denomination and Primary Education*, 229; Hooker, *History of Holland*, 127; State, *Brief History of Netherlands*, 170.

100. Wintle rightly observes that education "was the main battlefield between the government of Willem I and the Roman Catholics in the south, it was a subject of constant concern for the orthodox Calvinists throughout the century, and it was to be the principal conflict zone between the liberal left and confessional right towards the end of the century. Wherever there was confessional debate, there was educational debate, and theological issues became political ones through the medium of education policy." Wintle, *Pillars of Piety*, 62.

101. Kuyper, "Common Grace," 196–97.

102. Cf. Vandenberg, *Abraham Kuyper*, 53.

The issue of the School Struggle also reveals that political engagement is never easy. Since Kuyper's time, there have been a variety of political positions, even among conservative Christians. As with the issue of the new church election system discussed in section 5.1, here too one can recognize a desire among orthodox Christians to make their denomination, or at least Christianity, a kind of state religion. This is why having a concept of the church as organism was no more than just the first step toward political engagement. This step was to be followed by political education, organization, and mobilization. As such, those with different positions could probably agree and be found willing to fight together for the same, or at least a similar, position. The greatest number of Kuyper's followers emerged only after such energy-consuming efforts.

5.3 The Doleantie of 1886

The term "Doleantie" refers to the schism that took place within the DRC in 1886. The term comes from *dolere*, a Latin word meaning "to complain" or "to object." The followers of the Doleantie emphasized that the reason for the schism was not a spirit of rebellion, but rather their objections to the unfaithfulness and injustice of the DRC's ecclesiastical hierarchy. The immediate cause of the Doleantie was the expulsion of four ministers and seventy-five elders of the Amsterdam church, including Kuyper, by the national synod in December 1886.[103] The expelled office-bearers then declared themselves the "*wederopgetreden wettige kerkeraad van Amsterdam een Nederduitse Gereformeerde Kerk (Dolerende)*."[104] They chose the term *Nederduitse Gereformeerde Kerk*, which had been the name of the DRC up to the new regulation of 1816, to identify themselves as the true and loyal form of that historical Reformed Church. Thus, they emphasized that they were not separating from the historical Reformed Church, but were remaining in it by throwing off the yoke of synodical hierarchy. About 25,000 members of the Amsterdam church followed in this movement.

---

103. The number of expelled elders decreased from eighty to seventy-five because five elders stated that they had changed their mind. Cf. Blei, *Netherlands Reformed Church*, 74.

104. While Allan Janssen translates the term as "reappeared legitimate church council of Amsterdam," David McKay translates it as "reconstituted lawful church council of Amsterdam." Cf. Bos, *Servants of the Kingdom*, 378; Blei, *Netherlands Reformed Church*, 74.

Prior to that, several consistories together with many congregation members had already separated from the DRC synod. In February 1886, the consistory of Kootwijk church had cut its ties with the ecclesiastical boards of the DRC. The church council there had been asking for permission to call an orthodox minister, but the classical board took very long in responding. Finally, at the advice of Kuyper, the consistory decided to appoint a minister without the permission of classis. Other churches followed the decision to separate, as consistories began to separate from the higher boards and congregation members broke with the consistory.[105] In January 1887, the representatives of these congregations gathered in Amsterdam and decided to call themselves *dolerenden*, following the example of the Amsterdam church.[106]

The Doleantie caused the DRC to lose its position as a majority church in the Netherlands, as 76 ministers and 167,000 members from 200 local churches left between 1886 and 1889.[107] Estimating the loss at 9 percent of the DRC's total membership, Blei describes the Doleantie as a "heavy bloodletting."[108] Similarly, Harinck and Winkeler state that the Doleantie caused the DRC to become a minority church.[109] The term "minority" here indicates that DRC membership had fallen to below half of the total national population. Nevertheless, the DRC still remained the largest church institution in the country.[110]

Compared to the Secession of 1834 in its early years, the Doleantie represented a much bigger schism. The Secession had led a dozen ministers and about 20,000 congregation members to leave the DRC within a year. In 1836, there were about 130 churches that attended the first synod of the Secessionists.[111] In 1892, the churches of the Doleantie and the Secession

---

105. Within the space of one month, the congregations of Voorthuizen and Reitsum separated from the hierarchy of the DRC. Bouma, *Secession, Doleantie, and Union*, 23; Bos, *Servants of the Kingdom*, 379.

106. Blei, *Netherlands Reformed Church*, 75.

107. Bos, *Servants of the Kingdom*, 379; Blei, 77.

108. Blei, 77.

109. Harinck and Winkeler, "Nineteenth Century," 498.

110. Kok, *Nederland op de breuklijn*, 292–93. According to De Kok, the DRC had come to embrace 54.74% of the total population as its members in 1879. By 1889, this number had become 48.88%. In contrast, orthodox Reformed denominations grew from 3.48% to 8.21% of the population.

111. Harinck and Winkeler, "Nineteenth Century," 461; Cf. Blei, *Netherlands Reformed Church*, 65. It is estimated that there were 20,000 adherents in April 1836, and 100,000 adherents

managed to effect a church union, which took the name *Gereformeerde Kerken in Nederland* (Reformed Churches in the Netherlands). Its membership represented 7 percent of the nation's total population.[112]

The surrounding context of the Doleantie of 1886 is essential for understanding Kuyper's ecclesiology. It is no exaggeration to say that his 1883 "Tract on the Reformation of the Churches," which is the most systematical elaboration of his ecclesiology, was a preparation for the Doleantie. Accordingly, an investigation of the Doleantie will not only reveal the context of Kuyper's ecclesiology, but also show us how he applied his concept of the church in practice. For one, the Doleantie sheds light on Kuyper's struggle to liberate the church from what he called the synod's yoke. At the same time, given the later union between the churches of the Secession and the Doleantie, one also can observe his efforts in establishing a federation for churches with similar confessions. Since the Free University in Amsterdam also was a controversial issue in the context of the Doleantie and the Union, I will discuss the Free University issue after elaborating on the relationship between synod and local churches in Kuyper's time. The issue of the Free University will reveal the interconnection between the Doleantie and Kuyper's organism-institution church distinction. Finally, I will conclude section 5.3 by dealing with the union of the Doleantie churches and the Secession churches.

5.3.1 The Church and the Synod

The root of the above disputes between local church council and higher church boards can be traced back to the early nineteenth century. The Enlightenment replaced doctrinal debate with a spirit of tolerance. In 1816, the DRC decided to allow anyone from any Protestant denomination to participate in the Lord's Supper. Moreover, its synod no longer required future ministers to subscribe to or teach the doctrine taught in the classical Reformed forms and confessions.[113] Furthermore, as early as 1819, the synod welcomed all members of

---

(with 328 congregations and 232 ministers) in 1869. Cf. Rasker, *De Nederlandse Hervormde Kerk*, 67; Putten, *Zoveel kerken, zoveel zinnen*, 199; Wintle, *Pillars of Piety*, 29.

112. Bos, *Servants of the Kingdom*, 380.

113. The synod confirmed this position in 1841 by stating that one need not consider all teachings of the classical Reformed documents as being entirely in agreement with God's word. The candidates need only agree with their essence and main teaching. In 1888, after the Doleantie, the synod even replaced the reference to the Reformed confessions. Cf. Blei, *Netherlands Reformed Church*, 62–63.

all Protestant denominations as members of the DRC. However, this tolerance also developed into a hostility toward the orthodox members who had deep convictions regarding their own beliefs and therefore considered the beliefs of others false. As leadership positions were dominated by modernism, the alienation of orthodoxy followed as a result.

The reaction of the orthodox camp led to factional conflicts in the DRC.[114] In Amsterdam and The Hague, the orthodox Reformed camp protested the calling of modernist ministers and formed an association called the Friend of the Truth. In 1863, this association merged with other associations and established a nation-wide organization.[115] This meant that the protest against modernism was spreading across the entire country. In 1864, Groen and others created the Confessional Association, with the purpose of removing the modernists from the DRC. Two years later, this association called for a boycott of modernist ministers. The confessionals had been sending petitions to the synod, which nevertheless continued to refuse to intervene in doctrinal issues. At the same time, the modernists formed the Association for the Preservation and Promotion of Liberalism. One of its purposes was to keep modernist theology in existence. In contrast to the confessionals, the modernists pursued doctrinal freedom.[116]

As we saw in section 5.1, the new system of church elections introduced in 1867 changed the balance of power within the councils of local churches. By the 1870s, the orthodox camp had obtained a majority in the consistories of urban areas, including Amsterdam, The Hague, Rotterdam, Groningen, and Leiden.[117] There its adherents conducted more explicit attempts to counter the influence of modernism. In 1869, an elder of the Amsterdam church protested against a modernist minister, charging that his teaching was not from God but the devil. In 1871, the consistory decided to bring charges before the regional church board against a minister who had denied the authenticity of the bodily resurrection of Christ.[118]

---

114. For an elaboration of the theological modernists and conservatives, see section 5.1.2.
115. Bos, *Servants of the Kingdom*, 345.
116. Bos, 346; Blei, *Netherlands Reformed Church*, 71.
117. Bos, 351.
118. Bos, 352.

The regional board did not, however, respond positively to the charges. After ruling once again in 1875 that it bore no responsibility for maintaining doctrine, the synod decided in 1878 that church membership could not be denied on the basis of religious conviction. Those seeking adult membership in the church were required only to accept the spirit and essentials of the church's confessions. Furthermore, in 1883, the synod changed the requirements for ministerial candidates, replacing adherence to the forms of unity with a commitment to promote the interests of the kingdom of God. With this change, Bos has argued, the synod of the DRC seems to have wanted to prevent an exodus of progressive members and ministers to other denominations which had explicitly declared their acceptance of modernism.[119]

The above details reveal how the modernists still held power at the higher level of the church boards. While the orthodox conservatives sought to preserve the purity of orthodoxy by rejecting every form of deviation, the modernists wanted to welcome all positions. The principles of the conservatives and the modernists collided, and the gulf separating them only became greater with the increasing power of the orthodox camp. Although the orthodox conservatives already dominated the councils of the local churches, their efforts proved in vain when the higher bodies intervened. For the church councils at Kootwijk and Amsterdam, the negative responses of the ecclesiastical boards justified a separation from those hierarchies (section 5.3).

The case of the Amsterdam church is worthy of further elaboration. As one of the members of the Amsterdam consistory, Kuyper created a forum for the orthodox Calvinist faction in 1882. To educate the members of this forum, he gave a series of lectures on the reformation of the churches in 1883. There he introduced them to the term *doleren*, to call themselves congregation members lamenting the yoke of the DRC's synodical bodies. In 1884, these orthodox members of the Amsterdam church council refused to register new members who had followed catechism classes not with an orthodox minister, but with a modernist minister. However, the provincial board condemned this action, and the national synod later took its side as well. In December 1885, the church council of Amsterdam reacted by revising the regulation of church property, seeking to arrange matters such that they would retain the right to the church property in case they broke with the ecclesiastical

---

119. Bos, 377.

hierarchy. After the regional board suspended those who had voted for the revision, the provincial synod raised their suspension to an expulsion. Finally, the national synod confirmed the decision of the provincial synod.[120]

Therefore, there are two aspects to the Doleantie. First, it was a culmination of the response of orthodox Calvinists to the changes made by the modernists.[121] At the same time, it represented a collision between the autonomy of the local churches and the authority of the ecclesiastical hierarchy.[122] This is in turn the context for Kuyper's suggestion that the local church be kept free from the bonds of the ecclesiastical hierarchy and for his notion of the pluriformity of the church.

5.3.2 The Church and the Free University

As we have seen in the previous section, factional conflicts within the DRC often took place in relation to the appointment of a minister. A consistory dominated by modernists usually chose a progressive minister. However, since the majority of congregation members were still orthodox, their preference went out to a conservative or less progressive potential candidate. The change in the system of church elections in 1867 had enabled the orthodox members to vote for orthodox consistory members and orthodox ministers.

In spite of this, the fact that the professors at the faculty of theology accepted theological modernism meant that orthodox graduates remained few in number.[123] The Higher Education Law of 1876 secured the continuation of the theological faculty at the public university.[124] However, the curriculum now became a religious studies curriculum. The law allowed the DRC to appoint two of its professors at the expense of the state for teaching dogmatics and practical theology. Since the DRC synod usually appointed non-orthodox

---

120. Bos, 377–78; Harinck and Winkeler, "Nineteenth Century," 492–93; Wintle, *Pillars of Piety*, 56.

121. Wintle, 41, 53–54. He states that the "Doleantie was the most notable manifestation of this confrontation [between the progressive camp and the orthodox camp]."

122. Cf. Arblaster, *History of Low Countries*, 196, who argues that the Doleantie happened because the control of synod was not in accordance with the presbyterian system and because of the prevalence of private judgments on doctrinal matters.

123. Wintle, *Pillars of Piety*, 54–55.

124. For the debate surrounding the position of the theological faculty at the public university before this Law, see Bos, *Servants of the Kingdom*, 368–74.

men to these positions, this development was of no advantage to the orthodox Calvinists.[125]

To solve that problem, Kuyper established the Free University of Amsterdam. He saw the possibility and necessity of a university for educating orthodox ministers.[126] The successful gathering of more than 305,000 signatures from orthodox Protestants convinced Kuyper to organize Reformed orthodoxy independently.[127] The Higher Education Law of 1876 had also made allowances for the establishment of a private university. This made it possible for Kuyper, together with Frederik L. Rutgers (1836–1917) and Philippus J. Hoedemaker (1839–1910), to establish the Free University in 1880. The Free University was a private university based on Reformed principles. Kuyper hoped that the orthodox faith would be able to penetrate intellectual life. In particular, he tied the faculty of theology to the Calvinist confessions.[128]

As Kuyper explained in the oration he delivered at the opening of the Free University, the basic concept for the university was sphere sovereignty.[129] He argued for a university that had its own sovereignty, that is, freedom from the intervention of both state and church. As such, Kuyper set the theological faculty of the university free from the church.[130] Here one encounters similarities with his articulation of the concept of the free church. The concept of the Free University was undoubtedly a development from his notion of a free church. Moreover, the distinction of the church as institution and organism also played a significant role in maintaining both the freedom and the Christian nature of the university. Kuyper founded an association of Christians to support the university. Its members were not bound to a single institutional church; their bond was that they were orthodox Christians.

To Kuyper's surprise, the synod of the DRC refused to welcome graduates of the Free University as ministers. In 1882, the professors of the Free University asked the synod to permit their graduates to take the examination

---

125. Harinck and Winkeler, "Nineteenth Century," 505.

126. Kuyper had been arguing for private religious universities since 1870. Cf. Bos, *Servants of the Kingdom*, 375.

127. Harinck and Winkeler, "Nineteenth Century," 492.

128. Harinck and Winkeler, 506.

129. See Kuyper, "Sphere Sovereignty [1880]," 461–90.

130. The emphasis on the theological faculty's freedom from the church was to become a problematic issue in the process of unification between the Doleantie and Secession churches. See section 5.3.3.

for ministerial candidacy. Despite the many vacant pastorates and the scarcity of theological students, the synod rejected their requests. In 1885, the synod refused again, even though the regional church board of Rotterdam had submitted a massive petition. The synod only allowed Free University graduates to the positions of a missionary or an evangelist, not a minister. This was the context for the dispute between the consistory of Kootwijk and the regional church board mentioned at the beginning of section 5.3. Kuyper encouraged the church council of Kootwijk to call Jan H. Houtzagers (1857–1940), the first graduate of the Free University, as its minister.[131] By following Kuyper's advice, the church of Kootwijk became the first Doleantie church.

The Doleantie group split from the DRC, but in 1892 went on to unite with the churches of the 1834 Secession. This union forms the topic of the next section.

5.3.3 The Union of 1892

Although the union took place in 1892, it is important to note that the desire for union had already existed in the early stages of the Doleantie. The Secession churches had been observing the growing influence of the orthodox members in the DRC, and to some extent even admired the achievements of Kuyper.[132] While keeping an appropriate distance to avoid all possible blame for taking advantage of the situation of confusion, they hoped for union with the Doleantie churches. The Doleantie churches were for their part also open to such a union, while still harboring some concerns that we will discuss in the following paragraphs.[133] Therefore, after some initial correspondence as early as 6 October 1887, representatives from both sides started provisional discussions for union in Utrecht.[134]

The next steps were nevertheless not easy. Despite many similarities, the two sides were aware of the big gulf dividing them. From the side of the Secession, they were not interested in Kuyper's endeavors for establishing Christian organizations for Christian action. They did not agree with the

---

131. Bos, *Servants of the Kingdom*, 376; Cf. De Jong, "1886 – A Year to Remember," 283. Willem van den Bergh (1850–90), minister of Voorthuizen and Nijkerk, also played an important role in the process of this calling.

132. Harinck and Winkeler, "Nineteenth Century," 495.

133. Bouma, *Secession, Doleantie, and Union*, 15–27.

134. Bouma, 41.

concept of the Free University, particularly its theological faculty, which was placed under an association rather than the church. They also had a different view when it came to Kuyper's notion of presumptive regeneration. Furthermore, they found it difficult to reconcile their pietistic mentality with Kuyper's modern-look optimism. After all, they were actually disappointed that Kuyper had formed the Doleantie churches, rather than joining the Secession church groups which had united to form the *Christelijke Gereformeerde Kerken in Nederland* (Christian Reformed Churches in the Netherlands/CRC).[135] From the perspective of CRC ecclesiology, this meant that the Doleantie did not acknowledge the CRC as a true church.[136] These objections remained without a satisfactory solution, even at the last synod for the union of the Secession churches held in Amsterdam from 7 to 16 June 1892.[137] Bouma has criticized the synod of the CRC in Amsterdam as follows:

> Yet on certain points the answer given by the Synod was not convincing either: sometimes the Synod did not really address the issue. Especially when it came to the matter of confessional faithfulness, the Synod should have done more: it should have sought firm assurances about faithfulness to the confessions on the part of the Doleantie congregations and their broader assemblies. If the Synod had pursued such a role, it might well have proven impossible to bring about a union in the year 1892. But then there would have been more unity in the long run – and in any case, more clarity regarding the issue.[138]

From the side of the Doleantie churches, there were also objections, for instance, against the Regulation of 1869 which was in use in the CRC. Since

---

135. The Secession churches formed two groups, the *Christelijke Afgescheiden Gemeenten* (Christian Separated Churches) and the *Gereformeerde Kerken onder het Kruis* (Reformed Churches under the Cross). These two groups merged to form the CRC in 1869.

136. Harinck and Winkeler, "Nineteenth Century," 495.

137. Bouma, *Secession, Doleantie, and Union*, 191–99. The synod dealt with the following objections: (1) the local church councils had never summoned a congregational meeting to vote on the stipulations of the synod of Leeuwarden concerning the union; (2) the laxity of the Doleantie toward the DRC; (3) the membership book of the Doleantie, which regarded all the members of the DRC as members of the Doleantie; (4) the absence of love in the "marriage" between the CRC and the Doleantie group; and (5) the differences in teaching on regeneration and baptism.

138. Bouma, 202.

this regulation recognized a national church as an entity apart from the local churches, it was not in line with the Church Order of Dordt, which only allowed for the federation of churches without such a national entity.[139] The Doleantie also had concerns about the position of a theological school owned by the church for the education of its ministers, possibly infringing upon the freedom of study.[140]

Despite these difficulties on both sides, the efforts of Kuyper from the side of the Doleantie and of Herman Bavinck (1854–1921) from the side of the CRC made it possible for the union to take place. On Friday, 17 June 1892, the two synods held a joint synodical meeting and ratified the union. They chose the name *Gereformeerde Kerken in Nederland* (Reformed Churches in the Netherlands), which had been the name of the Reformed Church in the sixteenth century. They also used opening sentences for the Acts of Synod which were identical to the opening found in the Acts of the Synod of Dordt from 1618. With these arrangements, they wanted to show that they were no sect, but the true continuation of the historical Reformed churches of the sixteenth century and the Synod of Dordt.[141] The Doleantie brought 306 local churches, 120 ministers, and more than 180,000 members; the CRC 394 churches, 305 ministers, and 190,000 members.[142]

It is worth noting that not all CRC churches joined the union.[143] Some did not feel satisfied with the synod's answers to their objections, and remained as the CRC.[144] Apart from the objections mentioned above, they also considered the Doleantie to be determined neither by Scripture nor the Reformed confessions, but by Kuyper's tract written in 1883. They also did not regard the Doleantie as a successful movement, because a large number of members had chosen to remain in the DRC.[145]

Kuyper himself was probably not satisfied with the result of the Doleantie, either. The orthodox ministers and church members far outnumbered those who had separated. In 1878, Kuyper had succeeded in obtaining more than

---

139. Bouma, 161.
140. Bouma, 162.
141. Bouma, 212.
142. Harinck and Winkeler, "Nineteenth Century," 495.
143. For a detailed elaboration, see Plantinga, "Dissenters of 1892," 217–19.
144. Plantinga, 220–21.
145. Plantinga, 216.

305,000 signatures from orthodox Protestants.[146] Although the distribution of Doleantie members was similar to the distribution of those who had signed the petition, the number of the former was much lower than that of the latter.[147] This meant that many orthodox Protestants had decided to remain in the DRC, despite their opposition to the modernism prevalent in it.[148] The 80 ministers who left only amounted to 6 percent of all DRC ministers. Of the eleven orthodox ministers in Amsterdam, only four decided to follow the Doleantie. It was only in several villages that the entire congregation joined. Elsewhere, congregations became divided. Nationwide, only 7.6 percent of DRC members joined the Doleantie.[149] In addition, in 1888 the Dutch court ruled that the followers of the Doleantie could lay no claim to church property.[150]

One of the reasons for the low number of adherents was the lingering disagreement with Kuyper's thought. Among the DRC's orthodox Calvinist members, two positions could be found regarding the method for reforming the church. Both positions had the desire to reform the DRC. However, while Kuyper concluded that the DRC had deformed to the level that internal reform was impossible, others such as Hoedemaker wanted to continue fighting for reformation from within. As we saw in section 5.3.2, Hoedemaker had joined Kuyper in establishing the Free University, but he now became an advocate of a national church in a Christian state. Many other orthodox Calvinists in the DRC preferred Hoedemaker's approach as well.[151]

Another reason for those orthodox Calvinists not joining the 1886 Doleantie related to Kuyper's method. The act of Kuyper and several of his followers in sawing the panel off the door to the consistory room at the Nieuwe

---

146. Essen, "Struggle for Freedom Education," 69; Cf. Naylor, "School Choice," 269. While van Essen speaks of 305,102 Protestant signatures on behalf of 114,375 children aged six to twelve, as well as 306 DRC consistories and 108 CRC consistories, Naylor mentions "305,869 Protestant signatures, 164,000 Catholic signatures, and the support of 42 church councils."
147. Bos, *Servants of the Kingdom*, 379.
148. Wintle, *Pillars of Piety*, 56.
149. Bos, *Servants of the Kingdom*, 379–80.
150. Harinck and Winkeler, "Nineteenth Century," 493.
151. Harinck and Winkeler, 498–99. It is worth noting that Gunning, the prominent leader of the ethical school mentioned in section 5.1.2, joined the initiative of Hoedemaker for the reorganization of the DRC in the 1900s. The concept of Christianizing the whole country as a Christian state became one of the core ideas for the establishment of the Christian-Historical party. Cf. Wintle, *Pillars of Piety*, 57.

Kerk in Amsterdam caused people to shift their attention from the Doleantie's religious claim to the material aspect.[152] Moreover, Kuyper seems to have been overconfident because of the support of the masses. His focus on the *kleine luyden* (little people) led to his failure in gaining support from among the aristocrats, like Hoedemaker did. Wintle has suggested that the similarities in the position and status of Hoedemaker and Groen attracted the adherents of the Réveil movement, who were aristocrats, to follow Hoedemaker rather than Kuyper.[153] Moreover, the 1892 Union had almost failed when Kuyper hastily criticized the decision of the 1888 CRC synod in Assen without having the official letter of its decision at his disposal.[154] He wrote carelessly that the synod of Assen had destroyed the plan for union. Although Bavinck and others quickly wrote him to explain his misunderstanding, Kuyper did not change his mind. It was only after the publication of the approved letter of the synod of Assen, as well as an in-depth conversation with Bavinck, Rutgers, and Alexander de Savornin Lohman (1837–1924), that Kuyper finally admitted his error.[155]

Nevertheless, it is also possible to appreciate the positive aspects of the Doleantie followed by the church union of 1892. The union was an application of Kuyper's ecclesiology, in particular his emphasis on the need for churches of similar confession to establish one federation. As Bouma put it, the union of 1892 can function as an example for evangelical churches in present times, which on the one hand feel the need to cooperate with other churches, but on the other hand also feel a certain reluctance toward the twentieth-century ecumenical movement.[156] One of the key factors which had made the union possible was the mutual acknowledgment of the other party as a true church.

---

152. Bos, *Servants of the Kingdom*, 378.

153. Wintle, *Pillars of Piety*, 57.

154. Bouma, *Secession, Doleantie, and Union*, 99–102. The synod, which took place from 14 to 30 August 1888, expressed the desire for union and responded to the suggestions from the Doleantie's Synod of Utrecht as follows: (1) the CRC was willing to remove the Regulation of 1869 by discussion with the deputies of the Doleantie synod in Utrecht; (2) the Doleantie was to break completely with the DRC and acknowledge the CRC as a lawful manifestation of the body of Christ; (3) the CRC was to be allowed to maintain its theological school for training future ministers.

155. Bouma, 106–13.

156. Cf. Bouma, 212.

Another factor was their similarity in adherence to the Reformed confessions and the church order of Dordt.[157]

One of the objections that raised its head in the process toward union was Kuyper's notion of presumptive regeneration. As we already noted in chapter 4 (section 4.2.4), since the topic had not been satisfactorily resolved, it continued to be a matter of controversy after the union. While the Utrecht Synod of 1905 attempted to settle the issue, it too ended in an unsatisfactory manner. Its decisions, commonly known as the Conclusions of Utrecht, made a compromise by endorsing Kuyper's view, with the gentle correction that the ground for baptism is not the infant's presumed regeneration but God's promise and ordinance.[158] In the 1930s, the polemic was to surface again, resulting in the schism of 1944.[159]

To sum up, the issue of the Doleantie reveals the top-down structure of the DRC in the nineteenth century. Since 1816, the synod had become the authority above the local churches but under the king. Despite the removal of state control in 1848, the synod retained its power. The condition worsened when the broader assemblies imposed regulations and decisions that, from the perspective of the local church council, were not in harmony with Holy Scripture and the Reformed confessional documents. Kuyper suggested ecclesiological thoughts, especially those articulated in the "Tract of the Reformation of The Churches," to confront this very situation. In other words, the Doleantie was an implementation of Kuyper's ecclesiology in reforming a degenerated church.[160] Naturally, this reform related closely to his concepts of a believers' church and the free church.[161] Blei notes that the starting point for what Kuyper did was his concept of the antithesis, that is, the fundamental difference between Christians and non-Christians. A Christian could and should utilize the Spirit of Christ in every sphere of life, including church life. Since the church is in essence the gathering of true believers, an institutional church should take the confession of faith seriously. When the

---

157. Bouma, 182.

158. Mouw, "Baptism and Salvific Status," 246–47; Cf. Bratt, *Abraham Kuyper*, 169.

159. Mouw, 248–49.

160. It should be observed that Kuyper had already considered the synod unlawful and requested the government to remove the General Regulations of 1852 when he was still a minister in Utrecht. Cf. Bos, *Servants of the Kingdom*, 354.

161. Cf. Bos, 355–56.

church's administrative bodies no longer stand on the truth, believers are no longer obligated to submit to them.[162] In his concept of a free church, Kuyper also proposed freedom from ecclesiastical hierarchy. Although he located autonomy with the local church, he at the same time asserted the importance of federation with other churches of similar confession. As such, he avoided the risk of autonomous local churches falling into isolation.

Kuyper's ecclesiology was quite robust, managing to mobilize a significant number of orthodox members in the DRC to separate from the ecclesiastical hierarchy. It also proved powerful enough to secure the union between the Doleantie and Secession churches. However, it was not convincing enough for other orthodox members, not to mention the liberals, who decided to remain in the DRC. This also related to the way in which the separation took place. In the eyes of many, Kuyper's ways were too harsh.

Another probable problem related to the timing of the separation. Despite Kuyper's intention and ambition to influence the entire congregation, he failed to convince all orthodox members that the time to separate had now come. Many still preferred to reform the church from within, rather than to separate. Although a decision concerning timing will always be difficult to make on the basis of a theological concept, the Doleantie events indicated that one would need to supplement Kuyper's ecclesiology to maximize the number of supporters for the reformation of the church.

Furthermore, although Kuyper's ecclesiology proved to be compelling enough to encourage a union between churches with similar confessions, again one needs to be aware of his recklessness in the process of union as mentioned above. Kuyper also seemed to neglect the relationship with the aristocrats. He had too much confidence in the power of what he called the "little people" and thus forgot to deal respectfully with the members of the elite.

Conclusion

After noting three major issues and their surrounding contexts in the nineteenth century Netherlands, one can conclude that Kuyper's ecclesiology has the following characteristics.

---

162. Blei, *Netherlands Reformed Church*, 72.

First of all, it is evident that Kuyper's ecclesiological concepts represented a series of thoughts for dealing with specific issues that emerged in nineteenth-century Dutch church history, such as church elections, the School Struggle, and the influence of modernism in the church. Kuyper was a person with a passion for renewing the church. This passion caused him to devote his entire life to ecclesiastical matters, both theoretically and practically.[163] Rather than developing his ecclesiology as a pure academic endeavor, Kuyper articulated it as efforts to solve specific and real issues. The three issues we have discussed in this chapter revealed many interrelated contexts of Kuyper's ecclesiology, such as the complex relationship between the church and the state and the increasing dominance of modernism in both theology and politics, which marginalized the orthodox position in church and societal life. This contextual character means that Kuyper's ecclesiological concepts are no timeless ecclesiology. The effectiveness of his ecclesiology is contingent on its contexts. In a similar situation, Kuyper's ecclesiology may bring similar benefits. But in a different condition, its effectiveness may be questionable. Understanding the contextual nature of Kuyper's concepts should therefore push anyone who wants to apply them in another context to consider whether that other context shares essential similarities with Kuyper's context.

Furthermore, considering the gap separating Kuyper's first engagement with the issue of the School Struggle in 1869 and its settlement in 1917, one can understand how much time such sociopolitical engagement really demands. This can serve as a gentle reminder that Kuyperian principles and actions, including his ecclesiology, were no magic that could change a situation instantly. It took a lot of time and effort.

The second characteristic of Kuyper's ecclesiology is its attempt to develop third-way solutions. The term "third" here does not literally mean that there are only two other options. As we have seen throughout this chapter, Kuyper faced more than two different theological and political positions in each issue. He never just chose or rejected existing options. Instead, he attempted to maintain their positive elements and to eliminate their negative elements. Describing his method as "true conservatism" or "genuine orthodoxy," Kuyper sought new forms while preserving the essence of old forms.[164]

---

163. Cf. Wood, *Going Dutch*, 155.
164. Kuyper, "Conservatism and Orthodoxy," 69, 79–83.

On the one hand, Kuyper attempted to restore the DRC to its origin, which in his perspective meant a return to the three forms of unity and the Church Order of Dordt. On the other hand, Kuyper sought to update the church in order to answer the challenges of the times.

Kuyper developed a series of third-way alternatives. We saw in chapter 4 how the organism-institution distinction was intended to keep the church focused on its task, while continuing the engagement of Christians with society, including the political sphere. In this chapter, we saw that this organism-institution distinction represented a third-way solution for the problem of the modernist concept, which stripped the church of its supernatural character, and the conservative inclination to mysticism, which destroyed the institution.[165] The concept of a free church opens the way for a religious state to be able to detach itself from its religious bonds, without neglecting the role of the church in the public square. The church can also separate from the state, while still exercising influence on society. Kuyper's concept of the believers' church, combined with the concept of the pluriformity of the church, was a third-way solution to the problems of a national church and a sectarian church, as well as the problems of both synodical hierarchy and congregationalism.[166] In a similar vein, one can see it as a third-way solution to the ideal of the catholicity of the church and the reality of a variety of different churches.[167]

Third, this chapter has also shown us the polemical nature of Kuyper's ecclesiology. To some extent, this is a result of his attempts to suggest third-way solutions. For, in doing so, he countered many existing positions. Kuyper confronted the modernists, who thought that the state should replace the church. At the same time, he troubled the orthodox conservatives, who mostly agreed with Kuyper's idea regarding church reformation, but nevertheless did not want to separate from the DRC. He even challenged the members of the mystical conventicles, who chose to withdraw to worship in private and did not engage with ecclesio-political issues at all.

---

165. Wood, *Going Dutch*, 12; Cf. Kuyper, "Rooted and Grounded," 49. Kuyper himself stated that it was an alternative to the Roman Catholic's paralysis and the Spiritualist's drought.

166. Cf. Wood, 77, 174.

167. The term "colony of heaven" also has this nuance of a third alternative solution to the views of the Moderates and the Anabaptists. De Bruijne has suggested that while the former commingled the earthly and the heavenly homeland, the latter neglected the fact that the earthly homeland is also part of the will of God. Bruijne, "Not without the Church," 79–80; Bruijne, "'Colony of Heaven,'" 452–54.

As we also saw in chapter 4, Kuyper's doctrine of presumptive regeneration likewise contributed to the complexity of the problem. The matter had already been debated in Reformed circles. If this doctrine is brought outside Reformed circles, it will form a hindrance to the acceptance of Kuyper's ecclesiology, particularly for those who refuse infant baptism. In this chapter, we saw how Kuyper's personality only worsened this polemical aspect. Similarly, in section 5.3.3, on the union between the 1886 Doleantie and the 1834 Secession groups, we found Kuyper criticizing the results of the synod of the Secession camp without carefully reading the official documents. Moreover, he at times used *ad hominem* arguments, rather than attacking the arguments themselves.

In the fourth and present chapters, we discussed Kuyper's ecclesiology and its surrounding contexts. We also observed how Kuyper implemented his ecclesiological concepts to address ecclesio-political issues in his time. Can Japanese evangelical Christians benefit from Kuyper's concept of the church? We will investigate the possibilities in the next chapter.

CHAPTER 6

The Possibilities of Kuyper's Ecclesiology for Japanese Evangelical Christians

In chapter 2, we surveyed three political issues in contemporary Japan as well as the response from Japanese evangelical Christians. Although the issues of the Yasukuni Shrine, constitutional amendment, and disaster countermeasures are three distinct problems, at a deeper level they are all interconnected with problems of nationalism. Like other Japanese people, evangelical Christians in Japan also encounter inherent difficulties in dealing with these nationalism-related problems, and therefore tend to adopt an attitude of indifference and withdrawal. A small number of Christians have initiated and participated in significant protest activities. Nevertheless, encouraging the rest of evangelical Christians to join in sociopolitical engagement remains a challenge. Furthermore, although the resistance movement of evangelical Christians has made a contribution in preventing the further development of right-way conservatism, it remains difficult to work toward satisfying solutions for those deadlocked issues. Chapter 3 observed traumatic events in Japanese church history that shaped the Japanese Christians' tendency to indifference and withdrawal. I outlined several characteristics of Japanese Christians, namely their loyalty to communal authority, the dualism of private and public life, and denominationalism.

To what extent can Kuyper's ecclesiology offer theological motives to Japanese Christians for dealing with political issues? To answer this question, we considered Kuyper's ecclesiological concepts as well as their contexts in chapters 4 and 5. I attempted to systematize his concepts under four headings: (1) the organism-institution distinction; (2) the believers' church; (3) a free church; and (4) the pluriformity of the church. This is a series of ecclesiological suggestions to answer challenges that emerged in the particular Dutch context of Kuyper's time, including those of the church elections, the School Struggle, and the Doleantie.

As I mentioned in chapter 1, this dissertation does not intend to impose Western theology onto non-Western worlds. Instead, it is based on the understanding that Christians of different cultures and ages can mutually benefit from one another. Today's Japanese evangelical Christians can thus learn from Kuyper's ecclesiology. Although the aim of this dissertation has led us to pay more attention to the benefits of Kuyper for Christians in Japan, his ecclesiological concepts were not treated as timeless suggestions but as basic guidance that can and may be appropriated. In this chapter, we will therefore use the results of the previous chapters to discuss elements of Kuyper's ecclesiology that will be useful for evangelical Christians in Japan. I will also interact with several figures who have already been appropriating Kuyperian ecclesiological principles in their contexts. Since several Japanese theologians with concerns similar to those informing this dissertation recommend a Hauerwasian ecclesiology, I will also provide some evaluations of this solution, even though a study of Hauerwas itself lies beyond the scope of this dissertation.[1]

6.1 The Organism-Institution Distinction

As we saw in chapter 4, the most prominent element in Kuyper's ecclesiology is his distinction between the church as organism and as institution. He understood the notion of the visible church to be not just limited to local churches, but to extend also to Christian associations and organizations. While the local churches are the church as institution, the associations and

---

1. Stanley Hauerwas (b.1940) is a former professor of theological ethics at the University of Notre Dame, Duke Divinity School, and the University of Aberdeen. Besides ethics, he is also famous for his political theology. As we will see later on, his ecclesiology emphasizes the need for the church to be aware of the danger of Constantinianism and to contribute to the world, not by getting involved in politics but by being the church.

organizations are the church as organism. Through the latter, the church can engage with sociopolitical issues.

It hardly needs to be said that Japanese evangelical Christians are not familiar with this organism-institution concept. As I detailed in chapter 1, the first Japanese translation of Kuyper's *Lectures on Calvinism* was published as early as 1932, but the interest in his thought remains limited to the small circle of the Reformed group.[2] Most evangelical Christians may be familiar with the distinction of the invisible and visible church, but would only associate the visible church with local churches. As Inagaki puts it, Japanese churches are still not mature enough to have a theological understanding of the organic church.[3] Thus, Kuyper's distinction between its organic and institutional aspects would serve to deepen their ecclesiological understanding.

Furthermore, although evangelical churches have been willing to implement the 1974 Lausanne Covenant emphasizing the importance of both evangelism and social responsibility, they in reality still find it difficult to do. As discussed in chapter 3, most of the evangelical churches can be located on the side of the *kyōkai-ha* (church-centered faction). This camp considers the *shakai-ha* (social action faction) to have abandoned the traditional understanding of evangelism and neglected the church's primary task by its active involvement in sociopolitical engagement. By distinguishing between the church as institution and organism, Kuyper created room for accommodating the above concerns of the evangelicals. While the institutional church concentrates on the ministry of the word, the organic church expands its engagement with society. As we noted in section 4.1.3, Kuyper's suggestion to limit the church as institution to the ministry of the word was to secure the full implementation of this task of the church as institution. As such, the concerns of Japanese evangelical Christians find an answer in this organism-institution concept. Inagaki is thus right to see that the organism-institution model can be meaningful for evangelicals in reorganizing their diversified and therefore confused ecclesiologies.[4] Moreover, the combination of this organism-institution distinction with concept of the believers' church (section 6.2) and free church ecclesiology (section 6.3) serve to ensure that the energy

---

2. Inagaki, "Yakusha no Atogaki," 302.
3. Inagaki, "Kyōkai no Jichi," 329.
4. Inagaki, "Kirisutokyō Tetsugaku," 21; Inagaki, *Kōkyō no Tetsugaku*, 76.

of the pastor, elders, and church members can be focused on implementing the tasks of the institutional church.

At the same time, the distinction between institution and organism also gives room to encourage evangelical Christians to get involved in sociopolitical engagement. As we observed in chapter 3, one of the main reasons for many evangelical churches not to involve themselves in political engagement is the dualism of sacred and secular life; while church life is considered sacred, life outside the church is deemed secular. Kuyper's organism-institution model provides a theological framework for dealing with the dualism of private and public life. Christians are to glorify God not only at church on Sunday, but also every day, everywhere, and in every aspect of life, such as family, work, and political engagement.

More importantly, this model encourages Christians to organize various Christian associations. Christian organizations would keep Japanese Christians from being isolated from Christians of other local churches, and from being alone in broader, mostly non-Christian Japanese society. The social action faction may not be satisfied with the organism-institution model, because they demand the church's direct participation in sociopolitical engagement. However, the organic church model answers their primary concern, namely bringing Christians together with other Christians so as to engage with sociopolitical problems. With the organic church model, Christians do not act individually. As we have observed in chapter 2, while individual engagement is also commendable, its scope and longevity are limited to that one person. In contrast, organizations or associations would be able to provide wider and longer engagement.

These Christian associations or organizations would give the opportunity to think about the Christian way in specific life spheres. This practice will help those Christians to be aware of and avoid the tendency to submit to communal authority identified in chapter 3. In the professional world, submission to the communal authority is expressed through following the customs in the field at stake. Hence, associations of professional Christians can be given a chance to articulate a third way, not choosing between either a Christian "or" professional way, but establishing a Christian "and" professional way. By continuing this endeavor, evangelicals may overcome their inclination to keep their faith in the private realm and make every effort to articulate Christian and professional solutions.

As a result, all issues will be treated based on both Christian principles and professional standards of the relevant field. These associations' leaders and members can proceed to plan and execute sociopolitical engagements according to the field of the respective association. Education associations consist of Christians who have the duty of educational engagement, examine the educational needs of society, and attempt to find ways based on biblical principles to fulfill that need. One can expect a more comprehensive engagement as a result. This point is particularly crucial for the political issues examined in this dissertation, since they are complex and require comprehensive engagement to find satisfactory solutions.

Furthermore, evangelical Christians can understand that the indirect involvement of the church institution serves to protect the institutional church. In case of undesirable developments during this indirect engagement, the damage to the church institution would also be limited to indirect damage, not direct damage. For example, if it happens that a Christian political party is required to change its position or compromise on the topic of abortion in parliamentary deliberations, an institutional church that rejects abortion does not need to change its convictions regarding abortion. At least, the church institution does not need to change immediately. As Heslam puts it, engagement through the organic church gives the institutional church safety from world secularization.[5] In other words, the distinction of the church as organism and as institution opens a way for engaging with various life spheres without being absorbed into the issue at stake.

Moreover, a strong and healthy institutional church would be a place that provides Christians who engage with society strength amid their comprehensive engagement. As we have seen in section 4.1.4, many Kuyper scholars criticized Kuyperian cultural engagement for its marginalization of the church institution. I have argued that Kuyper's concept itself did not necessarily lead to such marginalization. The ideal interconnection of the organic and institutional church in Kuyper's concept will create a virtuous circle: the stronger the institutional church, the more active and productive the organic church, and vice versa. Hence, if one wants to implement Kuyper's organism-institution model, it is crucial to emphasize this interconnection.[6] While

---

5. Heslam, *Creating a Christian Worldview*, 133.
6. Cf. Bruijne, "'Colony of Heaven,'" 463; Bruijne, "Not without the Church," 83.

encouraging the organic church's cultural engagement, Kuyper emphasized the abnormality – that is, fallen nature – of the present state. As Wagenman has put it, since "without the church [institution], the independent life of each believing Christian would expire in the end," "both concentration [by the institution] and extension [by the organism] must take place in a living, dynamic rhythm for the image to work and the meaning to remain intact."[7] Severing the interconnection would be an act of suicide.

This interconnection is crucial for the Japanese context. As we have seen in chapters 1 and 3, many Christian humanitarian works and educational institutions in Japan were set up by missionaries and had thin relations with the church institution. As they pursued professionalism in their fields and sought government funds, the relationship with the church gradually wore thinner and eventually even disappeared. From the perspective of professionalism and government subsidies, the church connection is not attractive to the organizations. By severing their interconnection with the church, many such organizations have ended up becoming prestigious organizations and had significant cultural impact on Japanese society. However, as we saw in section 1.1, their contribution to Japanese local churches is questionable.

The interconnection between the institutional and organic church will also help Japanese Christians to have a more proportional loyalty toward their community. In section 3.1, we saw the refusal of a large number of Hidden Christians to rejoin the Roman Catholic Church. Although the prohibition of Christianity was lifted, they decided to remain as Hidden Christians and to continue their rituals. Similarly, in sections 3.2 and 3.3, we observed how various Christian denominations in Japan, planted by diverse mission bodies in a way that related strongly to their sending countries and denominations, had difficulties cooperating with other denominations, even when these denominations shared many similar similarities. Inagaki rightly points out that Japanese churches do not have a theological concept that enables them to cooperate, while respecting the differences between the many denominations, and that they therefore need the concept of the organic church.[8] This organic church concept will help them to step out of their isolated understanding of Christianity, and recognize the existence of other Christians outside their

---

7. Wagenman, "Kuyper and the Church," 137–38.
8. Inagaki, "Kyōkai no Jichi," 329.

community and the significance of cooperating with them. As we will see in section 6.4, Kuyper's doctrine of the pluriformity of the church would serve to enrich this notion.

One predictable difficulty for this model is represented by the small number of Christians in Japan. This circumstance is the most contrasting factor that emerges when one compares the Japanese Christian's context to Kuyper's context. De Bruijne argues that Kuyper's organic church worked well because there were many Christians who could join and contribute to the various organizations that he established.[9] He emphasizes that Kuyper himself designed the application of the church as organism only for a particular situation, that is, halfway secularization or de-Christianization.[10] When the secularization got worse, a different strategy would be needed. That, along with the declining number of committed Christians in the Netherlands since the 1960s, is in De Bruijne's view why many Kuyperian organizations dissolved or turned into different organizations.[11] Instead of establishing Christian organizations outside a local church, Timothy Keller encourages the church institution to establish vocation groups consisting of twelve to twenty-four people to discuss the particular challenges and opportunities in their fields.[12]

Admittedly, the small number of Christians in Japan makes it difficult to expect sociopolitical engagements at the same scale achieved by Kuyper's Christian organizations. However, I would argue that it is precisely because of their small number that Christians in Japan need this organism-institution church model. First, as I noted in the previous paragraphs, specific Christian associations would help Christians find ways to integrate their faith with their specific professions. They can share their struggles and learn from other Christians with similar vocations. Second, as we saw in chapter 1, the average church attendance in Japan is only 34.23. In some churches, especially those below the average, they do not even have an organist or pianist for their

---

9. Bruijne, "'Colony of Heaven,'" 456; Bruijne, "Not without the Church," 80–81.

10. Bruijne, "'Colony of Heaven,'" 456–57.

11. Bruijne, 477. For an analysis of the change on the church's side that contributed to the change of Christian organizations, see Harinck, "Shot in the Foot," 50–71.

12. Keller and Alsdorf, *Every Good Endeavor*, loc. 3077–83.

Sunday worship services.[13] Moreover, Japanese churches also are faced with aging society issues. Under such conditions, it is difficult to establish various vocation groups of members from only one local church, as Keller has recommended. His practice requires a significantly larger number of members in the church institution. It is much more feasible for one local church to cooperate with other local churches or for them to establish Christian associations which members of other churches can join.

Moreover, as mentioned in the previous paragraphs, since the organization consists of Christians who are experts in their respective fields, that organization, rather than the church institution, has more potential for developing Christian principles for that particular field. Indeed, the complexity of the problems for engagement relating to nationalism, as well as the diverse biblical interpretations of evangelical Christians in Japan, may make it difficult for them to come to the same conclusions. Nonetheless, one may still expect more developed engagements in various fields than if such engagement were carried out directly by only a single church institution.

It is also important to remember that, as we have seen in chapter 3, although Japanese Christians are few in number, their influence on Japanese society has exceeded the expectations for their small number.[14] Many schools, hospitals, and welfare facilities in Japan were started by Christian missionaries. Although those institutions are now operated by non-Christians and can no longer be called Christian organizations *per se*, several Christian concepts are still inherent in them.[15] Although the non-Christians may not fully understand or agree with the original Christian concepts, it is no exaggeration to say that there still is room for Christian associations in this non-Christian Japanese society.

Besides the legacy of those missionaries, there are also cooperatives that were established by the Japanese Christian social activist Kagawa Toyohiko.[16] Although these associations are not Christian organizations, they continue holding the basic principles that Kagawa considered, based on such biblical

---

13. Cf. Shibata, "2025-nen Mondai," 1. Shibata believes that the data of the UCCJ, which reported that as of 2014 the average age of its members was 62.9 years old and approximately 48% of them are older than 70 years old, reflects the condition of most Japanese churches.

14. Cf. Mullins, "Christianity in Contemporary Japanese," 140.

15. Inagaki, "Kyōkai no Jichi," 338.

16. Inagaki, *"Hatarakukoto" no Tetsugaku*, 252–72.

teachings as freedom, independence, and autonomy.[17] As we saw in section 2.2.3, these organizations are interested in concepts of Inagaki's Kuyperian public philosophy that relate also to public welfare and to Kagawa Toyohiko. They have several cooperation projects with Inagaki to study those concepts at greater length.

Considering the small number of Christians in Japan, cooperation with or participation in these cooperatives as well as the institutions founded by missionaries can be a feasible stepping stone in applying the principle of the organic church in Japan. Such engagements would in turn facilitate the establishment of Christian associations interconnected with the church institution. Besides, as I will discuss in section 6.3, the further spread of these bottom-up associations independent of the state would also help them to overcome the top-down culture in Japan.

Having said that, defining a healthy interconnection between the church institution and Christian organizations is not easy, and depends on the way the situation develops. In his time, Kuyper was worried about the danger of both church and state being overarching institutions that impede the effective development of other life spheres. Mouw rightly observes that, while the danger of the church intervening and subjugating other life spheres is significantly declining nowadays, other life spheres such as the family have become severely weakened. In this condition, the church can and should provide some support to compensate for the decline in other spheres.[18] He suggests that North America may still be in a "pre-Kuyper" phase, meaning that there are no Christians who are competent to operate the ministry of the organic church. Hence, the contemporary institutional church needs to take an intentional trans-spherical nurturing role in the teaching ministry. Although an institutional church might only be able to provide a thin address, if it does so, one can hope for the emergence of Christians who are able to establish Christian sphere-specific associations, which in turn can provide a robust "thick" address to complex issues.[19] Mouw calls this a "compensatory strategy" for adapting Kuyper's concept of sphere sovereignty and the institutional church to the needs of the day. As we have discussed in section

---

17. Inagaki, 229.
18. Mouw, "Culture, Church," 56–61; Mouw, *Abraham Kuyper*, 122.
19. Mouw, "Culture, Church," 62–63.

4.1.3, behind the phrase "compensatory strategy" lies an assumption that Kuyper's ecclesiology marginalizes the institutional church. I have argued that such an assumption does not do justice to Kuyper. In that line, I now argue that Mouw's compensatory strategy is already covered by Kuyper's original ecclesiology: Kuyper also emphasized the role of the institutional church institution for nurturing the organic church.

This nurturing role is vital for the Japanese context. However, it is difficult for the institutional church to start that task. If Mouw regards Christianity in the US as still being in a "pre-Kuyper" phase, it would be no exaggeration to say that Japanese Christians still find themselves in a "pre-pre-Kuyper" phase. Asaoka rightly understands that many Christians in Japan think that the church should not get involved in politics because the church in the past did get involved and got miserably wounded. For this reason, Asaoka has cooperated with several parachurch organizations and hosted different events to help the younger generation (high school and university students, as well as young professionals) understand the political situation in Japan in light of biblical teaching. He has also established pastors' associations to gather signatures for petitions to be submitted to the Diets.[20] He uses the experience of the 2011 disaster to encourage many evangelical Christians to become aware of the need to pay more attention to the church's diaconal task. Asaoka insists that the time has come for the Japanese church to examine itself and to renew itself as a church that serves society. Noting the inseparable connection between the tasks of *koinonia* and *diakonia*, he argues that if a church only conducts *koinonia* tasks, it will be inclined to be a closed and conservative church. He believes that by doing both *koinonia* and *diakonia*, the Japanese church can become more lively and its capacity broader and deeper.[21] Besides humanitarian diaconal work, Asaoka also argues for political diaconal task. Since politics relates closely to the dignity and sanctity of human beings, the church can be a bringer of peace by crying out to the rulers for justice and equity for the oppressed.[22]

Asaoka's concepts and practices are compatible with Kuyperian ecclesiology. As we have seen in section 2.2, he was significantly influenced by

---

20. Asaoka, *Kyōkai ni Ikiru Yorokobi*, 204–5.
21. Asaoka, 182, 189–93.
22. Asaoka, 197–98.

Watanabe, a Calvinist ecclesiologist. From the perspective of Kuyper's ecclesiology, what Asaoka has done constitutes suitable preparations for implementing the political role of the organic church. Since the number of evangelical Christians who are able to be active in political engagement is low, it is essential to start by nurturing Christians in their understanding of the biblical teachings related to politics. Christians in Japan need to cooperate, not only across the borders between institutional churches and denominations, but also with parachurch organizations. With an understanding of the organic church, this cooperation would not stop at a pragmatic strategy for dealing with a particular sociopolitical situation. It will have deeper theological foundations and therefore last longer. As a result, the churches in Japan will also be more experienced and will be able not only to publish protest statements, but also suggest more comprehensive solutions.

As we saw in chapter 4, Kuyper emphasized the diaconal work of the church institution. Since many Christian organizations also conduct diaconal work, there is some overlap. Here Keller's suggestions are useful. He distinguishes three types of diaconal ministries and allocates the ministry of "relief" inside and around the community to the jurisdiction of the institutional church, and describes the ministries of "development" and "social reform" as the task of the organic church.[23] This categorization is of help for the division of tasks, while also retaining the interconnection between the church as organism and institution.

6.2 The Believers' Church

The church institution, in Kuyper's view, is a gathering of regenerated and confessing individuals who form a society to live in submission to Christ as their king. Thus, Kuyper called for a believers' church and rejected the concept of a national church. Developing the doctrine of the priesthood of all believers, Kuyper put believers in the position of an army that can and

---

23. Keller, *Generous Justice*, loc. 1794. Keller understands *relief* as "direct aid to meet immediate physical, material, and economic needs," *development* as "giving an individual, family, or entire community what they need to move beyond dependency on relief into a condition of economic self-sufficiency." Emergency medical treatment, food, and clothing aid are examples of the former; education and job training are examples of the latter. Further endeavors to change the conditions and social structures that cause the need for *relief* or *development* is what Keller calls *social reform*. Keller, loc. 1588.

must participate actively in church life and in the fight against Satan and his power in this world. At the same time, Kuyper maintained infant baptism based on the doctrine of the covenant and introduced the concept of presumptive regeneration.

This concept of the believers' church is vital because of the inclination in Japanese Christianity to closely fall in line with the ruler of the time. This inclination, which we detailed in section 3.1, manifested itself in the first Catholic missionaries in the early modern period, in the Christian leaders of the imperial period, as well as in some Christian leaders from the beginning of the post-war period. While rulers first welcomed Christianity, they afterward turned to persecute or oppress it. Considering those bitter experiences, it is understandable that evangelical Christians in Japan are determined not to repeat those same mistakes.

This determination has led some evangelicals to welcome Hauerwasian principles. Using Hauerwas's warning about the dangerous tendency of each and every church to attempt to become the ruling church, Tsukada has detected a Constantinian inclination in Japanese Christianity from its beginnings in the early modern period to its reintroduction during the imperial period and even after Japan's defeat in the Asia-Pacific War.[24] Time and again, Japanese Christian leaders were seduced to be close to the ruler of the time. For this reason, he concludes:

> Christians are . . . to keep order in it for the church to be able to proclaim the gospel of her Lord Jesus Christ. Thus, one of the most urgent and challenging missions for the church in this generation is to reclaim the world as Jesus' [world] from the nation states, without owning or controlling or manipulating it, so that the world may come to see who the true king is [that is, Christ alone].[25]

In the same vein, Fujiwara endorses the views of Yoder and Hauerwas who emphasize that the church's primary task is to be faithful and imitate God, instead of controlling the world.[26] Hauerwasian ecclesiology offers a substan-

---

24. Tsukada, "Whose Politics?," 143, 171–74, 220–29.

25. Tsukada, 237.

26. Fujiwara, "Theology of Culture," 154. It is worth mentioning that Fujiwara supports Yoder and Hauerwas, "with some modifications such as the necessity for other authorities

tial warning to Japanese Christians to be cautious in their inclination toward Constantinianism.

I will discuss the Hauerwasian approach in greater detail below. First, at this point, I would like to argue that Kuyper, like Hauerwas, saw church-state disestablishment as the way to strengthen the church. Kuyper's emphasis on the church institution, along with his concepts of the believers' church and the free church, would yield the same implication as Hauerwas's ecclesiology. Thus, Tsukada's and Fujiwara's recommendation to implement Hauerwas's ecclesiology in Japan is also valid for Kuyper's ecclesiology, at least for its emphasis on the importance of the church institution as a pure church and the rejection of a national church.[27]

In his concept of the believers' church, Kuyper also emphasized the principle of the church as an army of God. Kuyper introduced this term as an elaboration of the militant church concept. As a result, Japanese evangelical Christians will have a more in-depth understanding of the church as the militant church. The church as an army of God implies a readiness to fight against Satan in this world. It is therefore not an isolated or inward-looking institution in this world. The institutional church should be a place to train and send Christians to the battle raging in the world. Christians become cognizant of the presence of Satanic powers working in Japanese society, at the level of both personal-accidental and structural-systematic evil. This outward orientation can help them overcome their inherent inclination to withdraw from engagement with society.

The concept of the church as an army of God is also meaningful for evangelicals in dealing with their Japaneseness. Although the term "army of God" may carry negative shades of meaning for some, particularly in countries with experiences of religious war, in Japan the term would help Japanese Christians to become aware of the ungodly element in their Japaneseness and to confront it properly. As we have seen in chapter 3, the sense of Japaneseness is incredibly strong and can also be found in Japanese Christians. This term would

---

besides the Jesus of the New Testament, the affirmation of coercion to some degree, and need for the awareness of human fallibility." He also suggests modifying their "alternative society" to a "normative or essential community." See Fujiwara, 151–52.

27. For a detailed comparison between the ecclesiology of Hauerwas and Kuyper, see Chung, "Ecclesiology and Social Ethics," 137–65. See also Bruijne, "'Colony of Heaven,'" 454; Bruijne, "Not without the Church," 81; Mouw, *Abraham Kuyper*, 70, 115–16.

help them understand the urgency of being militant. Although the authorities try to persuade them that Japanese traditional rituals are non-religious in nature, Christians in Japan would be able to resist that narrative. They would conscientiously see through the religious, if not demonic, elements mingled in those rituals. They would endeavor to contribute to Japanese society, not only by following the demands of authority but also by resisting the ungodly demands. As Idogaki shows, practicing such resistance in Japan is a desperate struggle.[28] By training as an army of God so as to be aware of and fight against satanic power in peacetime like that experienced by today's Japan, they would be enabled to hold firm in difficult times like those experienced during the Tokugawa and imperial periods.[29]

This principle empowering church members is particularly important for Christians in Japan. As Watanabe has shown, congregants do not understand their calling as congregants. They therefore need to be trained to see their daily workplace as a place to encounter the reality of Christ. Listening to the word of God and prayer are usually limited as in-church activities.[30] What Watanabe called the need for the doctrine of laity can be fulfilled by today's implementation of the Kuyperian notion of the church as an army of God.

At this point, Kuyper differs from Hauerwas. Kuyper suggested an ecclesiology that can also motivate Christians to fight in a more direct way against existing structural evil. Luke Bretherton, professor of theological ethics at Duke University, criticizes Hauerwas for reducing political witness to a subcultural resistance and lacking concern for and commitment to the prosperity of the earthly city.[31] Similar to Kuyper, Bretherton emphasizes the task of the church in addressing political problems. However, more in the line of Hauerwas, he also emphasizes the importance of focusing on the church institution. Using the Augustinian concept of the two cities, he describes civil society as the place where the two cities are mixed and can pursue common objects of love. By doing so, Bretherton attempts to develop a Christian political witness that is consistent with church life, while also being open to cooperating with and learning from those outside the church. For example, he

---

28. Idogaki, *Shinkyō no Jiyū*, 157.
29. Cf. Idogaki, 151–52.
30. Watanabe, *Kyōkai-ron Nyūmon*, 111–13.
31. Bretherton, *Christianity and Contemporary Politics*, 191.

describes how a church in London helps poor citizens by bringing protests to the housing association and addressing the city's major.[32] His concept can be viewed as an attempt to combine Kuyper and Hauerwas. However, the church institution in the model of Bretherton might have a hard time avoiding the immediate effect of a compromise or consensus that ought to be taken in the course of political engagement.

Despite the aforementioned differences, the affinity between Kuyper and Hauerwas on their understanding of the church as a believers' church can serve as a bridge for cooperation between Reformed and Anabaptist camps in Japan. Many evangelicals have Anabaptist roots and share the view that Reformed churches had not fully reformed because of their cooperation with the magistrates. Kuyper's and Hauerwas's similar emphasis on the believers' church would gain the favor of many evangelicals. It may function as a stepping stone for mutual understanding and for developing a theological common ground for cooperation between the two camps. For the Japanese context, where most of the population is not Christian, there should be greater attention given to this side of Kuyper's ecclesiology.

Having said that, one may expect that Kuyper's insistence on infant baptism will irritate evangelicals of non-Reformed background that reject infant baptism. As we saw in chapters 4 (section 4.2.4) and 5 (section 5.3.3), even for some Reformed circles, Kuyper's concept of presumptive regeneration as a justification for infant baptism has proved controversial. An overemphasis on presumptive regeneration can cause laxity in guiding children toward a personal faith.

Another element that Kuyper stressed in his concept of the believers' church is the office of believers, or the priesthood of all believers. With this concept, Kuyper did acknowledge the importance of the special offices, but also cried out for voluntary obedience and rejected absolute obedience to the ecclesiastical hierarchy. Obedience to any hierarchy should be practiced within the context of obedience to God, which restricts not only the office of believers but also the special offices. Combining it with the free church concept, Kuyper extended this principle of the office of all believers to a condition where local congregations should not be subjugated under any ecclesiastical organizations, including classis as well as synod.

---

32. Bretherton, x–xi.

Chapter 3 has shown one dominating aspect of Japaneseness, namely loyalty to communal authority. While many Christians in the early modern period submitted to their leader by outward apostasy while still keeping their faith in secret, many in the imperial period followed the decision of their church leader to support the government's imperialistic and fascist agenda. In the post-war period, there have been several reports of power abuse by church leaders on their congregants in evangelical circles.[33] One of the main reasons for this personality cult is the abuse of the inherent loyalty to communal authority among the Japanese. This character trait may have led both leaders and church members to fail to perceive this abuse. Thus, practicing the Kuyperian teaching of the general office will be useful for the Japanese evangelical churches to eschew possible power abuse. Furthermore, the ability to avoid the cult of personality in church may help Christians to prevent other forms of the leader's personality cult in other life spheres. For most Japanese in the post-war period, the phrase "above authority" has come to refer to the workplace and its leaders. The inability to discern and resist inappropriate demands from this "above authority" has resulted in many social problems in contemporary Japanese society, including workaholism and *karōshi* (death by overwork).[34]

Kuyper also applied his rejection of a hierarchical body to the relationship between church and state. I will elaborate on this topic more extensively in section 6.3. Here it suffices to note that there is consistency in Kuyper's rejection of hierarchy. He not only rejected hierarchy between the church and the state, but also among ecclesiastical bodies themselves. This consistency is also valuable because it can help evangelical Christians to avoid a dualism where they reject submission to the state but still insist on obedience to the higher ecclesiastical institutions.

6.3 A Free Church

Kuyper proposed the separation of church and state. For him, this represents the genuine way for the church to flourish. With the motto "A free church in a free State," Kuyper rigidly prohibited the church from pursuing political

---

33. Cf. Idogaki, *Shinkyō no Jiyū*, 60.
34. Inagaki, *"Hatarakukoto" no tetsugaku*, 4, 31.

authority and rejected the intervention of the state in ecclesiastical matters. Although Kuyper also proposed freedom from every ecclesiastical hierarchy, since we have already discussed that issue earlier, in what follows we will focus on the freedom from the state.

As we saw in chapter 2, despite the Japanese churches' desire to be close to the nation's rulers, they have from the beginning received no government subsidies. They instead have depended on funding from missionary bodies and parishioners. From this perspective, Japanese churches are independent of the state. Although many evangelical missionaries who came right after Japan's defeat in 1945 received several privileges from the US-led Allied occupation government, they were in principle independent of government intervention.

In general, Japanese evangelical figures uphold the strict separation of church and state. In their view, in order to guarantee religious liberty, the government should not get involved in any religious organizations or activities. Any aid would show a preference for a particular religion and therefore violate the principle of separation between the state and religion as prescribed in the constitution.

It is interesting to note that this emphasis of evangelical Christians shares affinities with the liberal view of religion in Kuyper's time. In chapter 5, we saw how Dutch liberals in the nineteenth century, under the influence of the French Revolution, preferred a strict separation between state and religion. The conservative Christian leaders, in contrast, felt that the disestablishment of church and state during the Napoleonic occupation had been harmful to church life. For this reason, they welcomed the re-establishment of special relations between the state and the church as decreed by the king's General Regulation of 1816. They also accepted the requirement of introducing a generic Christianity in all public schools. Similarly, in chapter 3, we saw that the right-wing conservatives in Japan considered changes introduced by the Allied occupation government harmful to the uniqueness of Japan. They wanted to revive the establishment between the State Shinto and the state, as well as the narrative of the State Shinto as a non-religious ideology. Many Christians in Japan protested this movement using a logic similar to that of Dutch liberalists, crying for a strict separation between religion and the state.

Probing the perils of the liberals and the conservatives, Kuyper criticized the positions of both. For him, church and state each have their own sovereignty directly from Christ. Hence, the state should not subjugate the church, nor vice versa. Kuyper rejected the re-establishment of church and state and saw disestablishment as the way to strengthen both. At the same time, he also rejected the view of the liberals which was influenced by the French Revolution's stance on religion as a danger to the state and that religion and its communities should be denied public function. Therefore, for Kuyper, although the state and the church should be separated, the church should not be removed from the public square, provided that the state maintains equal distance from all denominations. Kuyper thus developed a third-way approach between the liberal and conservative views. This approach may offer a stimulus for Japanese evangelical Christians to contribute solutions to the issues in which the nation has met a deadlock.

As we saw in chapter 2, some prominent evangelical figures have been resisting the government's attempts to return to the imperialist era. Their protest has mainly been based on the principle of the freedom of belief, as well as the separation of religion and state. Considering the small numbers of Japanese Christians, these resistance efforts are commendable. However, they have failed to provide solutions to complex issues like those discussed in chapter 2. While the struggles of Japanese Christians have proved valuable in decelerating the nationalist-conservative movement, they offer no help for solving the deadlock. Establishment and strict separation are two opposing poles.

Kuyper provided a way to understand that strict separationism ironically violates neutrality toward religion. His appeal caused Dutch people to be aware of the religiosity of the liberal or secular worldview, so that they came to develop a different separation, a separation that was fair to all ideologies, including secularism. The present-day Dutch government subsidizes religious organizations such as Muslim schools and Christian hospitals, not based on their religious affiliation, but for their contribution to society in the relevant field. As long as the organizations fulfill the standard requirements, they are eligible to receive public funds regardless of their religious orientation. This is the Dutch version of neutrality or separation between religion and the state. For Kuyper, religious freedom concerns not only individuals, but also groups and communities. Neutrality does not mean avoiding all accommodations for religious communities, but it means supporting all groups equally. This was the reason behind his struggle to obtain state funding for denominational schools. Monsma and Soper rightly acknowledge this to be the "Dutch contribution to a more complete understanding of religious liberty."[35]

Chapter 2 also showed that it is was this understanding of Kuyper regarding the separation of state and religion that enabled Inagaki to offer suggestions different from those made by other evangelical figures. Many long-standing and deadlocked political issues in Japan are linked to a Japanese nationalism closely related to the doctrines of the State Shinto. Inagaki correctly understands the dissatisfaction of the proponents of Japanese nationalism with a strict separation between church and state. Hence, in a departure from other evangelical figures, he suggests solutions that enable all worldviews to practice their beliefs, including Shintoistic nationalism. Evangelical Christians need to acknowledge their freedom fairly, too.

But why do many Japanese evangelical Christians insist on strict separation? Idogaki argues that, given Japan's history of using religion for war mobilization as well as the firm entrenchment of this mentality in Japanese politicians, the separation between state and religion should be stricter in Japan than in any other country.[36] As we have seen in section 3.1, the government harshly persecuted Christians in Japan for over two centuries. Afterward, in section 3.2, we observed how the government oppressed Japanese Christians. We also saw in section 3.3 and in chapter 2 how the Japanese government in the post-war period often trampled on the personality of individuals despite the freedom of thought, conscience, and religion guaranteed by the constitution. These traumatic experiences caused Japanese people, including Christians, to find it difficult to express their disagreement with the government. Many are either afraid or indifferent to politics. A few evangelical Christians have shown the courage to protest the government. Although these three attitudes differ in appearance, what they have in common is a negative view toward the government and the state. Although evangelicals acknowledge that the government is an instrument of God as taught in Romans 13, they tend to emphasize the government's tendency to corruption. As a result,

---

35. Monsma and Soper, *Challenge of Pluralism*, 216. For them, "pillarization in the Netherlands has changed radically in recent decades, but in their public policy the Dutch have retained the idea that it is appropriate for the state to accommodate both secular and religious organizations because people naturally want to express their principles, secular or religious, within and through groups." (Monsma and Soper, 216.)

36. Idogaki, *Shinkyō no Jiyū*, 47, 51.

they focus on the discussion on the right of resistance.³⁷ From this perspective, it is no exaggeration to say that Japanese evangelicals have a low view of the state. The main reason why evangelical Christians fight for the strict separation between the state and religion lies in this low view of the state.

In chapter 4, we saw that although Kuyper also sounded warnings about the inherent dangers of the state, he still did have a high view of the state. With his concept of common grace, he could pay more attention to the positive side of the government as an instrument of God in this world. A higher view of the state would similarly help Japanese Christians to recover from their traumatic experiences with it. Evangelicals can also develop various political engagements other than just protesting activity. Kuyper neither despised the state nor encouraged Christians to withdraw from political engagement. Instead, as we have seen in section 6.1, he urged the church to influence society by nurturing the conscience of its members. Through Christian associations, they can propose well-developed programs to the government or political party that can benefit society from a biblical perspective.

A similar argumentation can be identified in the appeals of Idogaki and Asaoka to learn from the Confessing Church in Germany.³⁸ They emphasize the importance of the Confessing Church movement in preparing evangelicals for resisting the ungodly government. Like ecumenical Christians who had already done so earlier,³⁹ they also recommend the Barmen Declaration and the resistance of Dietrich Bonhoeffer.⁴⁰ Considering the similarities between Nazi Germany and imperial Japan, their arguments have a certain validity. Nonetheless, without denying the importance of the Confessing Church movement, one must comprehend the limits of that approach, as detailed in this dissertation. By just emphasizing the movement for the right of resistance and faith confession, it will be difficult to go beyond the act of protesting. A higher view of the state, in combination with the concept of the organic

---

37. For example, see Watanabe, *Shinkō ni Mototzuku*; Idogaki, *Shinkyō no Jiyū*, 68–84.

38. Idogaki, 40, 84; Asaoka, "Barumen Sengen."

39. For example, Mori, *Fukujū to Teikō*; Miyata, *Kokka to Shūkyō*, 208–46; Miyata, *Barumen Sengen*; See also Kazuaki, "Bonhoeffer's Social Ethics," 47–60.

40. Since there are many affinities between the ecclesiologies of Bonhoeffer and Kuyper, the acceptance of Bonhoeffer in Japan could also be indicative of possibilities for Kuyper in Japan. Cf. Dekker and Harinck, "Position of the Church," 86–98. However, many evangelicals do not agree with Bonhoeffer's attempted use of violence. See, for example, Idogaki, *Shinkyō no Jiyū*, 84.

church as mentioned in section 6.1, can encourage the evangelicals in Japan to establish Christian associations for analyzing the political issues at stake and articulating third-way solutions based on a Christian view of the state, as Inagaki has already been doing.

Moreover, the Kuyperian high view of the state, which is closely related to, if not rooted in, his free church ecclesiology, will help Christians to articulate Japanese Christian political engagement using biblical principles, rather than Japaneseness as their anchor. This stance is vital for evangelicals. As we saw in section 2.2, Christian leaders in Japan had attempted to articulate a Christian political theory that placed greater weight on Japaneseness, resulting in a Christianity that sacrificed the church's freedom and supported the government's fascist and imperialistic agenda. Many evangelicals have avoided all political engagement because they do not want to repeat similar mistakes. From this perspective, Kuyper's view of the state provides a more balanced position. His high view does not sacrifice the freedom of the church in particular or of religion in general.

While emphasizing the high value of the state, Kuyper also sounded warnings about the dangerous tendency of the state to subjugate all fields, including the religious sphere. This warning should not be neglected when implementing and developing a Kuyperian high view of the state in Japan. As noted by Wagenman, the value of Kuyper's ecclesiology is not only its tremendous cultural impact, but also "the ability of his concepts to equip the church even today to seek greater faithfulness to Christ" and "helping the church of any age rediscover its mandate, discern the spirits of age, and engage the whole of the culture for Christ."[41] In other words, Kuyper's suggestion for political engagement is not the end. It is an instrument in the broader context of glorifying Christ in all sectors of human life. This "not without Christ" political engagement satisfies the evangelicals' concerns.

6.4 The Pluriformity of the Church

Kuyper advocated unity in diversity within the institutional church. Based on the creational order and the way of revelation, Kuyper believed that variegation is part of the beauty of human life, rather than a problem. Moreover,

---

41. Wagenman, "Kuyper and the Church," 138.

as finite human knowledge cannot fully comprehend and articulate infinite divine matters, a single institutional church cannot be the only manifestation of the richness of salvation in Christ.[42] Furthermore, Kuyper viewed ecclesial disputes not merely as a consequence of human sin, but also as protection from God against evil uniformity which would harm the creational diversity. Hence, what Kuyper rejected was not unity but uniformity. He demanded of churches of the same confession that they pursue organic unity, which allows for pluriformity within the confederation. Thus, he suggested appreciating other churches and denominations, while still having a firm conviction in one's own confession.

This kind of pluralism is relevant for contemporary Christians. Mouw rightly understands the relevance of this concept for today's situation. He sees that while many Christians tend to affirm many-ness simply without seeing any overall coherence, not a few others have the inclination to remove some or all of that many-ness. Kuyper suggested something different.[43] With his pluriformity concept, Kuyper affirmed many-ness as unity in diversity.

In Japan, Kuyper's concept of the pluriformity of the church can function as a theological justification for acknowledging different denominations. The coalition of different conservative groups and the union of church groups, as discussed in sections 5.2.3 and 5.3.3, also provide examples of how to implement the concept of church pluriformity. As we saw in sections 3.2 and 3.3, one characteristic of Japanese Christianity is the existence of various denominations. This variety relates not only to different biblical emphases, but also to the country of origin of the missionary sending bodies. This condition is intensified by the intrinsic sense of loyalty Japanese people feel toward their group. Like the large number of underground Christians who did not want to rejoin the Catholic Church (section 3.1), evangelical Christians too show such adherence to their groups. Although they face such problems as small membership, a shortage of ministers, as well as limited financial resources, they prefer to maintain their local church and denomination rather than considering a merger or cooperation with other denominations, even if they are very similar. Amid such a situation, the concept of pluriformity would serve to offer a more robust theological view of the doctrine of the

---

42. Kuyper, *Lectures on Calvinism*, 101.
43. Mouw, *Abraham Kuyper*, 18–22.

body of Christ, which is one but has many different parts. This will help the evangelicals to view other denominations as comrades and thus open the way for cooperation.

Unification or cooperation between different denominations is a long-standing issue in Japan. As early as 1885, there was already an agenda among Protestant churches in Japan to cooperate and merge. Although the discussion re-emerged in 1906, 1923, and 1937, it never actually came to a realization. Unification only happened when it was forced on them by the government in 1941. Accordingly, it was a unification under political pressure. It was a unification that neglected the uniqueness of each denomination. During the post-war period, while mainstream churches were active in promoting the ecumenical movement, evangelical churches were not enthusiastic. They regarded the movement as a pursuit of unity at the expense of fundamental doctrines, a unity that tended to welcome all theological positions with the one exception of the orthodox theology held by the evangelicals. Hence, evangelicals in Japan had two bitter historical experiences relating to unification or cooperation, namely the unification in 1941 and the post-war ecumenical movement.

Watanabe sees an ecclesiological problem behind the above issues of church unification and the ecumenical movement. For him, the unification of Japanese churches during the imperial period happened because Japanese churches showed themselves weak in the face of governmental authority and because they did not have a deep understanding of the church and their own denomination.[44] This lack of understanding even caused some leaders to perceive the forced unification as God's grace for them in bringing their long desire for church unification to realization. They only prioritized unity, without discerning whether or not the unity was based on the authority of Christ. For Watanabe, this same shortcoming characterizes the figures who promoted the ecumenical movement in Japan. Instead of a superficial ecumenism, Watanabe suggests that Japanese churches ought to devote themselves to the uniqueness of their own denomination and to contribute to the other denominations from the perspective of that uniqueness. For him,

---

44. Watanabe, *Kyōkai-ron Nyūmon*, 149–50.

that is the real meaning of ecumenism.⁴⁵ Watanabe's proposal is in line with Kuyper's concept of the pluriformity of the church.

Kuyper went further than Watanabe by also encouraging churches and denominations with a similar confession to cooperate and even merge. This point is crucial for Japanese churches. According to Idogaki, while many splits in Japanese churches related to non-doctrinal issues, some church mergers were conversely conducted without serious consideration for agreement on the confession of faith.⁴⁶ Cooperation between churches with similar confessions is also significant for the survival of the churches in Japan. It will be difficult for Japanese churches to survive in the near future, given the small numbers and old age of their membership. The combination of Kuyper's organism-institution model and the pluriformity concept will help church members avoid unnecessary inclination to have excessive loyalty to one institutional church. With a deeper understanding of the uniqueness of one's own denomination, one can see essential similarities in other denominations. Instead of only working hard to maintain their church institution at the expense of some of the church's other tasks, Japanese evangelicals can establish a federation of churches of similar confession. They may even consider taking the "difficult" decision to dissolve and to merge with other church institutions of similar confession, so as to be able to implement the entire task of the institutional church properly.

As we noted in section 4.4.4, this unification should moreover allow diversity proportionate to the distinction between fundamental and nonfundamental matters. This Kuyperian insight of unity in diversity can serve as a boundary during and after the unification process. However, as we saw in section 5.3, the merger of church groups is never easy, even for Kuyper in the 1892 Union. Furthermore, the schism that later took place in 1944 within the unified Reformed Churches in the Netherlands (RCN) denomination also serves as a reminder about the difficulties of maintaining unity in diversity within a denomination.⁴⁷ It is an arduous task because it relates to the ten-

---

45. Watanabe, 151–53.

46. Idogaki, *Shinkyō no Jiyū*, 144–45.

47. It is worth noting that the RCN merged in 2004 with the DRC and the Evangelical Lutheran Church in the Kingdom of the Netherlands to form the present-day Protestant Church in the Netherlands.

sion between creation and fall, such that cooperation and disputes, mergers and schisms, will continue to take place until the second coming of Christ.

Finally, the concepts of pluriformity and the free church would help evangelical Christians develop their political engagement. Langley appreciates Kuyper's attitude of mutual respect within a pluralist framework for creating a climate of trust and political stability.[48] Furthermore, Inagaki believes that such Kuyperian principled pluralism will allow Japanese Christians to showcase to the broader Japanese society how to accept and utilize other, different groups.[49] Acceptance and equal treatment of others is an essential principle in reflecting on solutions for the deadlocked political problems in Japan.

First, therefore, the evangelicals can implement Kuyper's notion of pluriformity by having confidence in their own convictions, while still respecting other, different positions. As we saw in chapter 5, although Kuyper strongly believed in Calvinism and his theological position therefore opposed that of the Catholics on many points, he could still cooperate with them for political engagement. Kuyper's political agenda, for example, in the issue of the School Struggle (section 5.2) was not to give his denomination privileges, but to provide equal support to all denominational schools.[50] Since evangelicals are few in number in Japan, cooperation with other Christians is necessary for political engagement. With this Kuyperian principle and example, they could take courage to cooperate with other denominations, even with non-evangelicals as well as non-Christians.

Second, based on the concept of unity in diversity which they practice in ecclesial life, Japanese Christians can attempt to implement that concept in devising solutions for the sociopolitical issues with which they engage. The evangelicals can use this principle of equal distance and equal support to all religions as a basic direction. One might therefore hope that their equity may contribute to progress for solving the deadlocks. As we saw in chapter 2, those issues are interconnected with the nationalism of the imperial period. This nationalism forced people, including people from surrounding Asian countries, to conduct Shinto rituals by describing them as non-religious practices. The current pursuits for a return to that nationalism have raised concerns

---

48. Langley, *Practice of Political Spirituality*, 78.
49. Cf. Inagaki, *Kokka, Kojin, Shūkyō*, 141.
50. Kuyper, *Pro Rege 3*, IV.18.§4,150.

not just for Japanese people, but also for people from other Asian countries. Awareness of others who consider State Shinto doctrines and rituals to be religious and having the ability to treat them equally, will help Japanese people to move forward from those deadlocks.

Third, as we saw at the end of section 3.3.3, Japan now needs to employ migrant workers because of its economic development and aging society. This need allows Japanese society to live in harmony with people of different cultures and religions. A strong sense of Japaneseness based on the familial system in Japan tends to make Japanese people exclusive and leads them to reject outsiders. This means that the challenge for Christians to be an example for Japanese society in respecting people of different groups has become more urgent.

Conclusion

The research question for this dissertation was: *How could Kuyper's concept of the church equip Japanese Christians in their political engagement as Christians?* This chapter has discussed how the combination of the organism-institution model, the believers' church, the free church, and the pluriformity of the church can serve to answer the needs of evangelicals for their political engagement as evangelical Christians. They can be active in political engagement through Christian organizations without neglecting the ministry of the church institution. While remaining firm in their convictions, evangelicals can cooperate mutually with those of similar confessions in a federation as well as with those of different convictions. By doing so, they will be able not just to continue their protest movements, but also build their sociopolitical engagement in more comprehensive ways.

Although the sociopolitical problems in contemporary Japan are different from the problems experienced in Kuyper's time, one can safely say that the core of the problem is similar, that is, the complex relationship between religion and the state. The state, in Kuyper's time as well as in contemporary Japan, attempts to intervene in the religious realm. The types of responses to this problem also share several affinities: there is a politically conservative camp which would like to re-establish the close relationship between the state and religion, and there is the camp of the political liberals who prefer strict separation. While many Japanese evangelicals opt for the latter position, many orthodox Christians in Kuyper's time preferred the former. The preference of the latter resembles the nationalist-conservative agenda in contemporary Japan.

Instead of choosing between existing options, Kuyper suggested a third-way response, arguing for equal distance from and treatment of all religious or ideological currents. After a long struggle, his suggestion was accepted in the Netherlands. Considering the similarities in the problems as detailed above, one may expect that Kuyper's proposals will offer a similar breakthrough to Japan's long-deadlocked sociopolitical issues.

Kuyper's concern to provide alternatives between responding to new challenges and preserving precious principles has some similarities with the character of Japanese people. They try to accommodate new trends without throwing away their old ways. However, while Japanese use Japaneseness as their anchor, Kuyper anchored his third-way solution in biblical values. This anchor can be a model for Japanese evangelical Christians in developing their political engagement.

As mentioned in chapter 4, Kuyper did not stop at ecclesiology. He also developed the concepts of antithesis, sphere sovereignty, and common grace to justify his engagement and to mobilize his followers. On the one hand, this indicates a limitation of Kuyper's ecclesiology. Just as one cannot construct a building with only the cornerstone, so the implementation of Kuyper's ecclesiology in sociopolitical engagement should be accompanied by other thoughts he developed, as detailed above. On the other hand, the advantages of Kuyper's ecclesiology also manifest themselves, as he also provided the correlates to his ecclesiological proposals. Kuyper himself had experiences both as a church minister and a state minister. Hence, his concepts of political engagement were rooted in his ecclesiology. These correlate views to Kuyper's ecclesiology can help Christians in advancing their involvement in related life spheres. When the concept of a free church is combined with the principles of sphere sovereignty, common grace, and the antithesis, one can have a theological framework for formulating solutions to many political issues in Japan based on Christian perspectives.

In other words, Kuyper's ecclesiology, along with its correlate concepts, can offer a new direction for the political engagement of evangelical Christians in Japan, from strict separation to equal distance separation. Evangelicals can also develop engagement in other life spheres such as science, education, and the arts. Inagaki sees this as an opportunity to transform the top-down political culture in Japanese society into a more democratic society and greater civil participation.[51] For him, democracy in Japan still only exists at the surface level, since in reality Japanese people surrender their freedom to be used by politicians, bureaucrats, and business administrators.[52] Thus, the implementation of Kuyperian ecclesiology and its correlated principles will contribute not only to the independence of churches in Japan, but also to Japanese society at large. The engagement of churches will be more positive, broadening the involvement of civil society and thus reducing the long-established tendency to self-annihilation for the state. The greater involvement of civil society in various life spheres will serve to prevent the state from acting tyrannically in the relevant spheres and to transform it to a more bottom-up culture.

As we saw in chapter 2, Inagaki has been attempting to provide solutions to several contemporary political issues from a Kuyperian perspective. Some non-Christians have showed an interest in this approach. It is still an ongoing process and will undoubtedly require further deliberation. One path for future research to take is the development of more comprehensive solutions based on a Kuyperian ecclesiology and its correlative principles. Along with politics, Kuyper also addressed other specific life spheres such as education, charity, and economics. Since Japan also faces many problems in these areas, the potential of a Kuyperian approach for those fields will also be of interest to future scholarship.

Finally, it is worth recalling that any Kuyperian endeavor should be conducted with a humble heart and in readiness for a long struggle which does not bear instant fruit. Engaging with church life and politics is never easy. It depends on various elements, and it will take a long time and requires much energy. Mouw reminds us that the triumphant Christ is still a grieving Savior who will accomplish the restoration of all creation at his second coming.[53] Similarly, De Bruijne also alerts us to Kuyper's warning about the negative developments against Christianity, which will render Christian engagement hard to implement.[54] Therefore, one should avoid all excessive

---

51. Inagaki, "Kyōkai no Jichi," 340; Inagaki, *"Hatarakukoto" no tetsugaku*, 226–29.

52. Inagaki, "Kirisutokyō Tetsugaku," 23–24.

53. Mouw, *Abraham Kuyper*, 135–36.

54. Kuyper, "Twofold Fatherland," 306; Bruijne, "'Colony of Heaven,'" 455–58; Bruijne, "Not without the Church," 81.

optimism. Nonetheless, as this dissertation has shown, Kuyper's ecclesiology is worth adopting in the attempt to equip Japanese evangelicals for political engagement.

Bibliography

Abe, Takao. *The Jesuit Mission to New France: A New Interpretation in the Light of the Earlier Jesuit Experience in Japan*. Leiden: Brill, 2011.

Akiyama Yoshihisa. "Hisaisha Shien to Kyōkai: Tōhoku Herupu no Hataraki o tōshite Kangaeta koto [Survivor Support and The Church: Thoughts through The Work of Tohoku Help]." In Tokyo Christian University Faith and Culture Center, *Hisai-chi Shien to Kyōkai*, 7–48.

Ambros, Barbara. "Mobilizing Gratitude: Contextualizing Tenrikyō's Response after the Great East Japan Earthquake." In Mullins and Nakano, *Disasters and Social Crisis*, 132–55.

Arase, David M. "The Impact of 3/11 on Japan." *East Asia: An International Quarterly* 29, no. 4 (2012): 313–36.

Arblaster, Paul. *A History of the Low Countries*. 2nd ed. Basingstoke: Palgrave Macmillan, 2012.

Asaoka Masaru. *"Barumen Sengen" o Yomu: Kokuhaku ni Ikiru Shinkō* [Reading the Barmen Declaration: Faith that Lives the Confession]. Tokyo: Inochi no Kotobasha, 2011.

———. *Ken o suki ni yari o kama ni: Kirisutosha toshite kenpo o kangaeru.* [Turning Swords into Plowshares, Spears into Pruning Hooks: Thinking about the Constitution as a Christian]. Tokyo: Inochi no Kotobasha, 2018.

———. *Kyōkai ni Ikiru Yorokobi: Bokushi to Shinto no tame no Kyōkai-ron Nyūmon* [The Joy of Living in a Church: An Introduction to Ecclesiology for Pastors and Lay People]. Tokyo: Kyobunkwan, 2018.

———. "'Shinjitayōni Ikiru' Mono tonaru [Be the Person Who 'Lived as What I Believed']." In *Kurisuchan Toshite "Kenpō" wo Kangaeru* [Thinking about the "Constitution" as Christian], edited by Kurisuchan Shinbun [Christian Newspaper], by Asaoka Masaru, Kataoka Terumi, Naitō Shingo, Che Son-e, Okada Akira, Yohena Chōshū, and Tsuboi Setsuko, 10–23. Tokyo: Inochi no Kotobasha, 2013.

———. "'Tsukaeru Kyōkai' e no kaikaku [Reformation toward 'Serving Church']." In *Hisai-chi to Kokoro no Kea*, edited by Tokyo Christian University Faith and Culture Center, 45–78. Tokyo: Inochi no Kotobasha, 2014.

———. "'Tsutaeru Kyōkai' kara 'Tsukaeru Kyōkai' e: Kyōkai no Sasshin no tame ni ["From 'Teaching Church' toward 'Serving Church': For the Renewal of the Church"]. In *Higashinihon Daishinsai kara Towareru Nihon no Kyōkai* [Questioning the Japanese Church from the Great Eastern Japan Disaster], edited by Shinshū Kaki Senkyō Kōza, 35–53. Tokyo: Inochi no Kotobasha, 2013.

Asō, Tarō. "Yasukuni ni Iyasaka Are! [Long Live Yasukuni!]." *Asō Tarō Official Website*. Accessed 22 March 2017. www.aso-taro.jp/lecture/talk/060808.html.

Ballhatchet, Helen J. "Modern Missionary Movement in Japan: Roman Catholic, Protestant, Orthodox." In Mullins, *Handbook of Christianity in Japan*, 35–68.

Belcher, Jim. *Deep Church. A Third Way beyond Emerging and Traditional*. Downers Grove: InterVarsity, 2009.

Berkouwer, Gerrit C. *The Church*. Translated by James E. Davidson. Studies in Dogmatics. Grand Rapids: Eerdmans, 1976.

Bevans, Stephen B. *Models of Contextual Theology*. Maryknoll: Orbis, 1992.

Blei, Karel. *The Netherlands Reformed Church, 1571–2005*. Translated by Allan J. Janssen. Grand Rapids: Eerdmans, 2006.

Bolt, John. *A Free Church, a Holy Nation: Abraham Kuyper's American Public Theology*. Grand Rapids: Eerdmans, 2001.

Bos, David. *Servants of the Kingdom: Professionalization among Ministers of the Nineteenth-Century Netherlands Reformed Church*. Translated by David McKay. Leiden: Brill, 2010.

Bosch, David J. *Transforming Mission: Paradigm Shifts in Theology of Mission*. Maryknoll: Orbis, 1991.

Bouma, Hendrik. *Secession, Doleantie, and Union, 1834–1892*. Translated by Theodore Plantinga. Neerlandia: Inheritance, 1995.

Boxer, Charles R. *The Christian Century in Japan 1549–1650*. Berkeley: University of California Press, 1951.

Bratt, James D. "Abraham Kuyper: His World and Work." In *Abraham Kuyper: A Centennial Reader*, edited by James D. Bratt, 1–16. Grand Rapids: Eerdmans, 1998..

———, ed. *Abraham Kuyper: A Centennial Reader*. Grand Rapids: Eerdmans, 1998.

———. *Abraham Kuyper: Modern Calvinist, Christian Democrat*. Grand Rapids: Eerdmans, 2013.

Breen, John. "Popes, Bishops and War Criminals: Reflections on Catholics and Yasukuni in Post-War Japan." *The Asia-Pacific Journal* 8–9, no. 3 (March 1, 2010): 1–15.

———. "'The Nation's Shrine': Conflict and Commemoration at Yasukuni, Modern Japan's Shrine to the War Dead." In *The Cultural Politics of Nationalism and Nation-Building: Ritual and Performance in the Forging of Nations*, edited by Rachel Tsang and Eric Taylor Woods, 133–50. Abingdon: Routledge, 2014.

———. "Voices of Rage: Six Paths to the Problem of Yasukuni." In *Politics and Religion in Modern Japan: Red Sun, White Lotus*, edited by Roy Starrs, 278–304. Basingstoke: Palgrave Macmillan, 2011.

Bretherton, Luke. *Christianity and Contemporary Politics: The Conditions and Possibilities of Faithful Witness*. Chichester: Wiley-Blackwell, 2010.

Brinkman, Martien E. "Kuyper's Concept of the Pluriformity of the Church." In *Kuyper Reconsidered: Aspects of His Life and Work*, edited by Cornelis van der Kooi and Jan de Bruijn, 111–22. VU Studies on Protestant History 3. Amsterdam: VU Uitgeverij, 1999.

Bruijn, Jan de. *Abraham Kuyper: A Pictorial Biography*. Translated by Dagmare Houniet. Grand Rapids: Eerdmans, 2014.

Bruijne, Ad de. "'Colony of Heaven': Abraham Kuyper's Ecclesiology in the Twenty-First Century." *Journal for Markets and Morality* 17, no. 2 (2014): 445–90.

———. "Not without the Church as Institute: The Relevance of Abraham Kuyper's Ecclesiology for Christian Public and Theological Responsibilities in the Twenty-First Century." In *The Kuyper Center Review, Vol. 5: Church and Academy*, edited by Gordon Graham. Grand Rapids: Eerdmans, 2015.

———. "Volume Introduction." In *On the Church*, edited by John H. Wood Jr. and Andrew M. McGinnis, by Abraham Kuyper, xxv–xxxvii. Bellingham: Lexham, 2016.

Bunka-chō [Agency for Cultural Affairs], ed. *Shūkyō Nenkan Reiwa Gan'nenban* [Religious Year Book 2019]. Tokyo: Bunka-chō, 2019. Accessed 5 August 2020. https://www.bunka.go.jp/tokei_hakusho_shuppan/hakusho_nenjihokokusho/shukyo_nenkan/pdf/r01nenkan.pdf..

Cabinet Office. "Heisei 24 Nenban Bōsai Hakusho [White Paper on Disaster Management 2012]," 24 June 2011. Accessed 14 April 2016. http://www.bousai.go.jp/kaigirep/hakusho/h24/bousai2012/html/honbun/4b_8s_14_00.htm.

Calvin, John. *Institutes of the Christian Religion*. Edited by John T. McNeill. Translated by Ford L. Battles. Louisville: Westminster John Knox Press, 1960.

Cary, Otis. *A History of Christianity in Japan: Protestant Missions*. New York: Fleming H. Revell, 1909.

Chung, Kwang-Duk. "Ecclesiology and Social Ethics: A Comparative Study of the Social and Ethical Life of the Church in the Views of Abraham Kuyper and Stanley Hauerwas." PhD diss., Theological University Kampen, 1999.

Colson, Charles, and Nancy Pearcey. *How Now Shall We Live?* Wheaton: Tyndale, 1999.
De Jong, Peter Y. "1886 – A Year to Remember." In *Secession, Doleantie, and Union: 1834–1892*, by Hendrik Bouma, 255–99. Neerlandia: Inheritance, 1995.
———. "The Dawn of a New Day." In *Secession, Doleantie, and Union: 1834–1892*, by Hendrik Bouma, 237–54. Neerlandia: Inheritance, 1995.
Dekker, G., and G. Harinck. "The Position of the Church as Institute in Society: A Comparison between Bonhoeffer and Kuyper." *The Princeton Seminary Bulletin* 28, no. 1 (2007): 86–98.
Doak, Kevin M. "Introduction: Catholicism, Modernity, and Japanese Culture." In *Xavier's Legacies: Catholicism in Modern Japanese Culture*, edited by Kevin M. Doak, 1–30. Vancouver: UBC Press, 2011.
Dohi Akio. *Nihon Purotesutanto Kirisutokyō-shi*. [History of Japanese Protestant Christianity]. Tokyo: Shinkyō Shuppansha, 1994.
Eglinton, James. *Trinity and Organism: Towards a New Reading of Herman Bavinck's Organic Motif*. London: T&T Clark, 2012.
Egmond, Adrianus van. "Kuyper's Dogmatic Theology." In *Kuyper Reconsidered: Aspects of His Life and Work*, edited by Cornelis van der Kooi and Jan de Bruijn, 85–94. Amsterdam: VU Uitgeverij, 1999.
Essen, Jantje L. van. "The Struggle for Freedom Education in the Netherlands in the Nineteenth Century." In *Guillaume Groen van Prinsterer: Selected Studies*, translated by Herbert D. Morton, 55–77. Jordan Station: Wedge, 1990.
Fire and Disaster Management Agency. "Heisei 23 nen (2011) Tōhoku Chihō Taiheiyō Oki Jishin (Higashi Nihon Daishinsai) nitsuite Dai 151 Hō [Report No. 151 on the 2011 Great Eastern Japan Disaster]," 8 September 2015. Accessed 14 April 2016. www.fdma.go.jp/disaster/higashinihon/assets/jishin151.pdf.
Fujiwara, Atsuyoshi. "Theology of Culture in a Japanese Context: A Believer's Church Perspective." PhD diss., Durham University, 1999.
Furuya Yasuo. "Naze Nihon ni Kirisutokyō wa Hiromaranainoka [Why does Christianity Not Prosper in Japan?]." *Nihon no Shingaku* [Japan's Theology] 53 (2014): 167–71.
———. "Nihon no Kyōkai [The Japanese Church]." *Shingaku* [Theology] 53 (1991): 20–37.
Goheen, Michael W., and Craig G. Bartholomew. *Living at the Crossroads*. Grand Rapids: Baker Academic, 2008.
Graf, Tim. "Buddhist Responses to the 3.11 Disasters in Japan." In Mullins and Nakano, *Disasters and Social Crisis*, 156–81.
Haight, Roger. "Comparative Ecclesiology." In *The Routledge Companion to The Christian Church*, edited by Gerard Mannion and Lewis S. Mudge, 387–401. New York: Routledge, 2008.

Hanko, Herman C. *For Thy Truth's Sake: A Doctrinal History of the Protestant Reformed Churches*. Grandville: Reformed Free Publication Association, 2000.

Harefa, Surya. "First Rooted, Then Grounded: The Position of The Church Institution in Kuyper's Ecclesiology." *Verbum Christi* 7, no. 1 (April 2020): 25–40.

———. "Resistance to Japanese Nationalism: Christian Responses to Proposed Constitutional Amendments in Japan." *Evangelical Review of Theology* 43, no. 4 (October 2019): 330–44.

Harinck, George. "A Shot in the Foot: The Change of Protestant Churches in Post-War Society in the Netherlands." *Church History and Religious Culture* 94, no. 1 (2014): 50–71.

Harinck, George, and Lodewijk Winkeler. "The Nineteenth Century." In *Handbook of Dutch Church History*, edited by Herman J. Selderhuis, 435–520. Göttingen: Vandenhoeck & Ruprecht, 2014.

Hastings, Thomas J. "Japan's Protestant Schools and Churches in Light of Early Mission Theory and History." In Mullins, *Handbook of Christianity in Japan*, 101–24.

Heslam, Peter S. *Creating a Christian Worldview: Abraham Kuyper's Lectures on Calvinism*. Grand Rapids: Eerdmans, 1998.

———. *Kindai Shugi to Kirisutokyō: Aburahamu Kaipa- no Shisō* [Modernism and Christianity: The Thought of Abraham Kuyper]. Translated by Inagaki Hisakazu and Toyokawa Shin. Tokyo: Kyobunkwan, 2002.

Heywood, Andrew. *Key Concepts in Politics and International Relations*. London: Palgrave Macmillan, 2015.

Hiebert, Paul G. *Anthropological Insights for Missionaries*. Grand Rapids: Baker, 1986.

Higashibaba, Ikuo. *Christianity in Early Modern Japan: Kirishitan Belief and Practice*. Leiden: Brill, 2001.

Hooker, Mark T. *The History of Holland*. Westport: Greenwood Press, 1999.

Ichikawa, Yasunori. "21 Seiki o Mukaeta Karuvinizumu: JCA no Shimei no Keishō to Tenbō [Calvinism Welcoming 21st Century: The Inheritance and Prospect of JCA's Mission] (2002)." In *Karuvan and Karuvinizumu: Kirisutokyō to Gendai Shakai* [Christianity and Contemporary Society], edited by Japan Calvinist Association, 413–27. Hitomugi Shuppansha, 2014.

Idogaki Akira. *Shinkyō no Jiyū to Nihon no Kyōkai* [Religious Freedom and Japanese Church]. Tokyo: Inochi no Kotobasha, 1983.

Ikejiri Ryōichi. "Oshiyoseru 'Kokka Shintō' no Nami: Seiji-Shihō Reberu de no Senzen Kaiki no Ugoki [Surging Wave of the 'State Shinto': The Regression Movement to the Pre-War State at Political and Judicial Level]." In *Kokka Shūkyō to Kurisuchan: Futatabi Junan no Toki wa Kuru no ka* [State Religion *and Christian: Will a Time of Suffering Come Again?]*, 16–45. Tokyo: Inochi no Kotobasha, 1988.

Inagaki, Hisakazu. *"Hatarakukoto" no tetsugaku: Dī-sento wa-ku to wa nanika* [The Philosophy of "Working": What is Decent Work]. Tokyo: Akashi Shoten, 2019.

———. *Jissen no Kōkyō Tetsugaku: Fukushi, Kagaku, Shūkyō* [Practice of Public Philosophy: Welfare, Science, and Religion]. Shunjūsha, 2013.

———. *Kaiken Mondai to Kirisutokyō* [The Problem of Constitutional Amendment and Christianity]. Tokyo: Kyobunkwan, 2014.

———. "Kami no Kuni to Kōkyō-sei no Kōzō Tenkan [The Kingdom of God and The Structural Transformation of the Publicness]." In *Kami no Kuni to Sekai no Kaifuku: Kirisutokyō no Kōkyō-teki Shimei* [The Kingdom of God and Restoration of the World: Christian Public Mission], edited by Inagaki Hisakazu, 159–241. Tokyo: Kyobunkwan, 2018.

———. "Kirisutokyō Sekaikan kara no Nihon Shingaku no Saihensei [Reorganization of Theology from Christian Worldview]." *Kirisuto to Sekai* [Christ and the World] 24 (March 2014): 140–64.

———. "Kirisutokyō Tetsugaku to Gendai Shisō (IV): Aburahamu Kaipa- to Jiyū no Mondai[Christian Philosophy and Modern Thought (IV): Abraham Kuyper and the Problem of Freedom]." *Kirisuto to Sekai* [Christ and the World] 9 (March 1999): 10–31.

———. *Kokka, Kojin, Shūkyō: Kingendai Nihon-no Seishin* [State, Individual, Religion: The Spirit of Present-Modern Japan]. Tokyo: Kōdansha, 2007.

———. "Kokumin-teki Fukushi to Heiwa: Yasukuni ni kawaru Tsuitō Shisetsu no Mondai [National Welfare and Peace: The Problem of a Memorial Facility for Replacing Yasukuni]." *Kirisutokyō Shakai Fukushigaku Kenkyū* [Christian Social Welfare Science] 48 (January 2015): 4–16.

———. *Kōkyō Fukushi to iu Kokoromi: Fukushi Kokka kara Fukushi Shakai e* [Attempts of Public Welfare: From Welfare State to Welfare Society]. Tokyo: Chūō Hōki Shuppan, 2015.

———. *Kōkyō no Tetsugaku no Kōchiku o Mezashite: Kirisutokyō Sekai-kan, Tagen Shugi, Fukuzatsu-kei*. Tokyo: Kyobunkwan, 2001.

———. "Kyōkai no Jichi [Self-Governance of the Church]." In *Jichi kara Kangaeru Kōkyōsei* [Publicness from the Perspective of Self-Governance], edited by Nishio Masaru, Kobayashi Masaya, and Kim Tae-Chang, 320–40. Kōkyō Tetsugaku [Public Philosophy] 11. Tokyo: Tokyo University Press, 2004.

———. "Memory and Reconciliation in Japanese History." *Diogenes* 57, no. 3 (2010): 41–51.

———. "Nihon ni Sanka-gata Mishushugi o Tsukuru [Creating Participatory Democracy in Japan]." *Kyōdō Kumiai Kenkyū-shi Niji*, no. 63 (Spring 2018): 2–12.

———. *Shūkyō to Kōkyō Tetsugaku: Seikatsu sekai no Supirichuariti* [Religion and Public Philosophy: The Spirituality of the Living World]. Tokyo: Tokyo Daigaku Shuppankai, 2004.

———. "Yakusha no Atogaki [Translator's Afterword]." In *Kindai Shugi to Kirisutokyō Aburahamu Kaipa- no Shisō* [original title: Creating a Christian Worldview: Abraham Kuyper's Lectures on Calvinism], edited by Peter S. Heslam, translated by Inagaki Hisakazu and Toyokawa Shin, 299–305. Tokyo: Kyobunkwan, 2002.

———. *Yasukuni Jinja 'Kaihō'-ron: Hontō no Tsuitō towa Nanika?* [The "Liberation" Theory for Yasukuni Shrine: What is the Genuine Commemoration?]. Tokyo: Kōbunsha, 2006.

Ion, A. Hamish. "The Cross Under an Imperial Sun: Imperialism, Nationalism, and Japanese Christianity, 1895–1945." In Mullins, *Handbook of Christianity in Japan*, 69–100.

Izuta Akira, and Kim Son-Do. *Nihon no Fukuin-ha: 21 Seiki ni Mukete* [The Evangelicals in Japan: Towards the Twenty-First Century]. Tokyo: Nihon Fukuin Dōmei, 1989.

Jong, Marinus de. "The Church Is the Means, the World Is the End: The Development of Klaas Schilder's Thought On the Relationship between the Church and the World." PhD diss., Theological University Kampen, 2019.

Kärkkäinen, Veli-Matti. *An Introduction to Ecclesiology: Ecumenical, Historical & Global Perspectives*. Downers Grove: InterVarsity, 2002.

Kawakami, Naoya. "Cooperation of Christians Following the Great East Japan Earthquake." In *The Church Embracing the Sufferers, Moving Forward: Centurial Vision for Post-Disaster Japan: Ecumenical Voices*, edited by Atsuyoshi Fujiwara and Brian Byrd, translated by Richard Mort, 103–14. A Theology of Japan Monograph Series 7. Ageo: Seigakuin University Press, 2014.

———. "Kyōkai no Minisutori- toshite no Tomurai to Supirichuaru Kea [Mourning and Spiritual Care as the Church Ministry]." In Tokyo Christian University Faith and Culture Center, *Hisai-chi Shien to Kyōkai*, 49–118.

Keller, Timothy. *Center Church: Doing Balanced, Gospel-Centered Ministry in Your City*. Grand Rapids: Zondervan, 2012.

———. *Generous Justice: How God's Grace Makes Us Just*. Kindle version. New York: Dutton, 2010.

Keller, Timothy, and Katherine L. Alsdorf. *Every Good Endeavor: Connecting Your Work to God's Work*. Kindle version. New York: Dutton, 2012.

Kerr, George H. *Okinawa: The History of an Island People*. Boston: Tuttle Publishing, 2000.

Kingston, Jeff. "Downsizing Fukushima and Japan's Nuclear Relaunch." In Mullins and Nakano, *Disasters and Social Crisis*, 59–80.

Kirisutokyō Nenkan Hensyūbu, ed. *Kirisutokyō Nenkan 2014* [Christian Year Book]. Tokyo: Kirisuto Shinbun-sha, 2013.

Kok, Johannes A. de. *Nederland op de breuklijn Rome-Reformatie: numerieke aspecten van protestantisering en katholieke herleving in de noordelijke Nederlanden 1580–1880*. Assen: Van Gorcum, 1964.

Kondō Yoshiya. *Hisaichi kara no Tegami: from Iwate* [Letter from Disaster Areas: from Iwate]. Tokyo: Inochi no Kotobasha, 2012.

Kramer, Hans M. "Beyond the Dark Valley: Reinterpreting Christian Reactions to the 1939 Religious Organizations Law." *Japanese Journal of Religious Studies* 38, no. 1 (2011): 181–211.

Kuyper, Abraham. "Commentatio [1860]." In *On the Church*, edited by John H. Wood Jr. and Andrew M. McGinnis, translated by Todd M. Rester, Harry Van Dyke, Nelson D. Kloosterman, Todd M. Rester, and Arjen Vreugdenhil, 3–39. Bellingham: Lexham, 2016.

———. "Common Grace [1902–1905]." In Bratt, *Abraham Kuyper: A Centennial Reader*, 165–201.

———. *Common Grace: God's Gift for A Fallen World, Volume 2: The Doctrinal Section [1903]*. Edited by Jordan J. Ballor and J. Daryl Charles. Translated by Nelson D. Kloosterman and Ed M. van der Maas. Bellingham: Lexham, 2019.

———. "Confidentially [1873]." In *Abraham Kuyper: A Centennial Reader*, edited by James D. Bratt, translated by Reinder Bruinsma, 45–61. Grand Rapids: Eerdmans, 1998.

———. *Confidentie. Schrijven aan den Weled. Heer J. H. van der Linden. [1873]*. Amsterdam: Höveker & Zoon, 1873.

———. "Conservatism and Orthodoxy: False and True Preservation [1870]." In Bratt, *Abraham Kuyper: A Centennial Reader*, 65–85.

———. *De Gemeene Gratie. Derde Deel. Het Practische Gedeelte [1905]*. Amsterdam: Höveker & Wormser, 1904.

———. "De Uitverkiezing," in *Uit het Woord. Stichtelijke Bijbelstudiën*, vol. 2, Uit het Woord. Amsterdam: J. A. Wormser, n.d.

———. *Encyclopedia of Sacred Theology: Its Principles [1898]*. Translated by J. Hendrik de Vries. New York: Charles Scribner's Sons, 1898.

———. *Lectures on Calvinism [1898]*. Grand Rapids: Eerdmans, 1999.

———. "Lord's Day 21 [1893]." In *On the Church*, edited by John H. Wood Jr. and Andrew M. McGinnis, translated by Arjen Vreugdenhil, Nelson D. Kloosterman, Harry Van Dyke, Nelson D. Kloosterman, Todd M. Rester, and Arjen Vreugdenhil, 317–72. Bellingham: Lexham, 2016.

———. "Modernism: A Fata Morgana in the Christian Domain [1871]." In Bratt, *Abraham Kuyper: A Centennial Reader*, 87–124.

———. *On the Church*. Edited by John H. Wood Jr. and Andrew M. McGinnis. Translated by Harry Van Dyke, Nelson D. Kloosterman, Todd M. Rester, and Arjen Vreugdenhil. Bellingham: Lexham, 2016.

———. *Our Program: A Christian Political Manifesto [1916–1917]*. Edited by Harry Van Dyke. Translated by Harry Van Dyke. Bellingham: Lexham, 2015.

———. *Our Worship [1911]*. Translated by Harry Boonstra. Grand Rapids: Eerdmans, 2009.

———. *Pro Rege: Living under Christ's Kingship, Volume 1: The Exalted Nature of Christ's Kingship [1911]*. Edited by John Kok and Nelson D. Kloosterman. Translated by Albert Gootjes. Bellingham: Lexham, 2016.

———. *Pro Rege: Living under Christ's Kingship, Volume 2: The Kingship of Christ in Its Operation [1911]*. Edited by John Kok and Nelson D. Kloosterman. Translated by Albert Gootjes. Bellingham: Lexham, 2017.

———. *Pro Rege: Living under Christ's Kingship, Volume 3: The Kingship of Christ in Its Operation [1912]*. Edited by John Kok and Nelson D. Kloosterman. Translated by Albert Gootjes. Bellingham: Lexham, 2019.

———. "Rooted and Grounded (1870)." In *On the Church*, edited by John H. Wood Jr. and Andrew M. McGinnis, translated by Nelson D. Kloosterman, 42–73. Bellingham: Lexham, 2016.

———. *Rooted and Grounded: The Church as Organism and Institution [1870]*. Edited by Nelson D. Kloosterman. Translated by Nelson D. Kloosterman. Grand Rapids: Christian's Library Press, 2013.

———. *Separatie en Doleantie [1890]*. Amsterdam: Wormser, 1890.

———. "Sphere Sovereignty [1880]." In Bratt, *Abraham Kuyper: A Centennial Reader*, 461–90.

———. "State and Church [1916]." In *On the Church*, edited by John H. Wood Jr. and Andrew M. McGinnis, translated by Arjen Vreugdenhil, Nelson D. Kloosterman, Harry Van Dyke, Nelson D. Kloosterman, Todd M. Rester, and Arjen Vreugdenhil, 375–438. Bellingham: Lexham, 2016.

———. "The Blurring of the Boundaries [1892]." In Bratt, *Abraham Kuyper: A Centennial Reader*, 363–402.

———. *The Work of the Holy Spirit [1888–1889]*. Translated by Henri De Vries. New York: Funk and Wagnalls, 1900.

———. "Tract on the Reformation of the Churches [1883]." In *On the Church*, edited by John H. Wood Jr. and Andrew M. McGinnis, translated by Arjen Vreugdenhil, Nelson D. Kloosterman, Harry Van Dyke, Nelson D. Kloosterman, Todd M. Rester, and Arjen Vreugdenhil, 76–280. Bellingham: Lexham, 2016.

———. "Twofold Fatherland [1887]." In *On the Church*, edited by John H. Wood Jr. and Andrew M. McGinnis, translated by Nelson D. Kloosterman, Harry

Van Dyke, Nelson D. Kloosterman, Todd M. Rester, and Arjen Vreugdenhil, 281–314. Bellingham: Lexham, 2016.

———. "Uniformity: The Curse of Modern Life [1869]." In Bratt, *Abraham Kuyper: A Centennial Reader*, 19–44.

———. "Wedergeboorte en bekeering [1876]." In *Uit het Woord. Stichtelijke bijbelstudiën. Derde bundel*, 1–106. Amsterdam: J. H. Kruyt, 1879.

Kuyper, Catherine M. E. "Abraham Kuyper: His Early Life and Conversion." In *On Kuyper: A Collection of Readings on the Life, Work and Legacy of Abraham Kuyper*, edited by Steve Bishop and John H. Kok, 27–32. Sioux Center: Dordt College Press, 2013.

Kwaasteniet, Marjanne de. *Denomination and Primary Education in the Netherlands (1870–1984): A Spatial Diffusion Perspective*. Nederlandse geografische studies 117. Amsterdam: Koninklijk Nederlands Aardrijkskundig Genootschap, 1990.

Langley, McKendree R. *The Practice of Political Spirituality: Episodes from the Public Career of Abraham Kuyper, 1879–1918*. Jordan Station: Paideia, 1984.

Lee, Samuel. *Rediscovering Japan, Reintroducing Christendom: Two Thousand Years of Christian History in Japan*. Lanham: Hamilton Books, 2010.

Lillback, Peter A. "Interview of Dr. Stephen Tong." *Unio Cum Christo* 1, no. 1–2 (Fall 2015): 289–300.

Marshall, Paul. *Thine Is the Kingdom: A Biblical Perspective on the Nature of Government and Politics Today*. Grand Rapids: Eerdmans, 1984.

Matsunaga, Kikuo. "Theological Education in Japan." In *Preparing for Witness in Context: 1998 Cook Theological Seminar*, edited by Jean S. Stoner, 295–311. Louisville: Presbyterian Publishing House, 1999.

McGoldrick, James E. *God's Renaissance Man: The Life and Work of Abraham Kuyper*. Darlington: Evangelical Press, 2000.

McGrath, Alister E. *Evangelicalism & the Future of Christianity*. Downers Grove: InterVarsity, 1995.

———. *The Future of Christianity*. Oxford: Blackwell, 2002.

McLaughlin, Levi. "In the Wake of the Tsunami: Religious Responses to the Great East Japan Earthquake." *CrossCurrents* 61, no. 3 (2011): 290–97.

Mikkel, Douglas. "The Contemporary Christian Response to Japanese Nationalism." In *Perspectives on Christianity in Korea and Japan: The Gospel and Culture in East Asia*, edited by Mark R. Mullins and Richard F. Young. Lewiston: Edwin Mellen, 1995.

Miyata Mitsuo. *Barumen Sengen no Seiji-gaku* [Political Science of the Barmen Declaration]. Tokyo: Shinkyō Shuppansha, 2014.

———. *Kokka to Shūkyō: Rōma-sho 13shō Kaishaku-shi, Eikyō-shi no Kenkyū* [State and Religion: A Study of the Interpretation History and Influence History of Romans 13]. Tokyo: Iwanami Shoten, 2010.

Miyazaki, Kentarō. "Roman Catholic Mission in Pre-Modern Japan." In Mullins, *Handbook of Christianity in Japan*, 1–18.

———. "The Kakure Kirishitan Tradition." In Mullins, *Handbook of Christianity in Japan*, 19–34.

Mizukusa Shūji. "Seisho o Megane ni Genpatsu o Yomu [Reading the Nuclear Power Plant by Using the Bible as Glasses]." In *Genpatsu wa Jinrui ni Nani o Motarasu noka: Seisho to Genba kara Mietekuru Mono* [What Does the Nuclear Power Plant Bring to Humankind?: Things Seen from the Bible and Actual Spot], edited by Tokyo Christian University Faith and Culture Center, 9–50. Tokyo: Inochi no Kotobasha, 2014.

Monsma, Stephen V., and J. Christopher Soper. *The Challenge of Pluralism: Church and State in Five Democracies*. 2nd ed. Lanham: Rowman & Littlefield Publishers, 2009.

Mori Heita. *Fukujū to Teikō e no Michi: Bonheffa- no shōgai* [The Road to Obedience and Resistance: The Life of Bonhoeffer]. Tokyo: Shinkyō Shuppansha, 1964.

Mori, Nobuhito, Tomoyuki Takahashi, and The 2011 Tohoku Earthquake Tsunami Joint Survey Group. "Nationwide Post Event Survey and Analysis of the 2011 Tohoku Earthquake Tsunami." *Coastal Engineering Journal* 54, no. 4 (January 2012): 1–32.

Mouw, Richard J. *Abraham Kuyper: A Short and Personal Introduction*. Grand Rapids: Eerdmans, 2011.

———. *Aburahamu Kaipa- Nyūmon: Kirisutokyō Sekai-kan Jinseikan e no Tebiki* [Introduction to Abraham Kuyper: A Guide to Christian Worldview and Life View]. Translated by Inagaki Hisakazu and Iwata Mieko. Tokyo: Kyobunkwan, 2012.

———. "Baptism and the Salvific Status of Children: An Examination of Some Intra-Reformed Debates." *Calvin Theological Journal*, no. 41 (2006): 238–54.

———. "Culture, Church, and Civil Society: Kuyper for a New Century." *The Princeton Seminary Bulletin* 28, no. 1 (2007): 48–63.

———. *When the Kings Come Marching In: Isaiah and the New Jerusalem*. Rev. ed. Grand Rapids: Eerdmans, 2002.

Mullins, Mark R. "Christianity in Contemporary Japanese Society." In *Handbook of Contemporary Japanese Religions*, edited by Inken Prohl and John Nelson, 133–58. Leiden: Brill, 2012.

———, ed. *Handbook of Christianity in Japan*. Leiden: Brill, 2003.

———. "Japan." In *Christianities in Asia*, edited by Peter C. Phan, 197–215. Oxford: Wiley-Blackwell, 2011.

———. "Japanese Responses to Imperialist Secularization: The Postwar Movement to Restore Shinto in the Public Sphere." In *Multiple Secularities beyond the West: Religion and Modernity in the Global Age*, edited by Marian

Burchardt, Monika Wholrab-Sahr, and Matthias Middell, 141–67. Berlin: De Gruyter, 2015.

———. "Neonationalism, Politics, and Religion in Post-Disaster Japan." In Mullins and Nakano, *Disasters and Social Crisis in Contemporary Japan*, 107–31.

Mullins, Mark R., and Kōichi Nakano. "Introduction." In Mullins and Nakano, *Disasters and Social Crisis*, 1–20.

———, ed. *Disasters and Social Crisis in Contemporary Japan: Political, Religious, and Sociocultural Responses*. Basingstoke: Palgrave Macmillan, 2016.

Murayama-Cain, Yumi. "The Bible in Imperial Japan, 1850–1950." PhD diss., University of St. Andrews, 2010.

Naitō Shingo. "Kirisuto-sha toshite 'Genpatsu' o Dō Kangaerunoka [How to Think of Nuclear Power Plant as a Christian?]." In *Genpatsu wa Jinrui ni Nani o Motarasu noka: Seisho to Genba kara Mietekuru Mono* [What Does the Nuclear Power Plant Bring to Humankind?: Things Seen from the Bible and Actual Spot], edited by Tokyo Christian University Faith and Culture Center, 51–75. Tokyo: Inochi no Kotobasha, 2014.

Nakamura, Satoshi. *Nihon Kirisutokyō Senkyō-shi: Zabieru Izen Kara Konnichi Made* [The History of Japanese Christian Mission: From before Xavier to the Present]. Tokyo: Inochi no Kotobasha, 2009.

———. *Nihon ni Okeru Fukuin-ha no Rekishi: Mōhitotsu no Nihon Kirisutokyō-shi*. [History of Evangelicals in Japan: Another Japanese Christian History]. Tokyo: Inochi no Kotobasha, 2000.

Naylor, Wendy. "School Choice and Religious Liberty in the Netherlands: Reconsidering the Dutch School Struggle and the Influence of Abraham Kuyper in Its Resolution." In *International Handbook of Protestant Education*, edited by William Jeynes and David W. Robinson, 245–74. International Handbooks of Religion and Education 6. Dordrecht: Springer, 2012.

Neda Shōichi. "Maegaki [foreword]." In *Kurisuchan Toshite "Kenpō" wo Kangaeru* [Thinking about the "Constitution" as Christian], edited by Kurisuchan Shinbun [Christian Newspaper], by Asaoka Masaru, Kataoka Terumi, Naitō Shingo, Che Son-e, Okada Akira, Yohena Chōshū, and Tsuboi Setsuko, 3–6. Tokyo: Inochi no Kotobasha, 2013.

Nishikawa Shigenori. *Watashitachi no Kenpō: Zenbun kara Dai 103-jō made* [Our Constitution: Preamble to Article 103]. Tokyo: Inochi no Kotobasha, 2005.

———. *Yūji Hōsei-ka no Yasukuni Jinja: Kokkai Bōchō 10-nen, Watashi ga Mita Koto Kiita Koto* [Yasukuni Shrine under Emergency Legislation: What I Have Seen and Heard from Ten Years Hearing the National Assembly]. Tokyo: Nashinoki-sha, 2009.

Oliai, Mohammad H. "The Japanese and Christianity: A Complex Relation." PhD diss., Vrije Universiteit, 2013.

Olson, Roger E. "Free Church Ecclesiology and Evangelical Spirituality: A Unique Compatibility." In *Evangelical Ecclesiology: Reality or Illusion?*, edited by John G. Stackhouse, 161–78. Grand Rapids: Baker Academic, 2003.

Ono Shizuo. *Nihon Purotesutanto Dendō-shi* [History of Protestant Evangelism in Japan]. Takehara: Nihon Kirisuto Kaikakuha Kyōkai Seibu Chūkai Bunsho Iinkai, 1989.

Ōsawa Masachi, and Inagaki Hisakazu. *Kirisutokyō to Kindai no Meikyū* [Christianity and Modern Labyrinth]. Tokyo: Shunjūsha, 2018.

Plantinga, Cornelius. *Engaging God's World: A Christian Vision of Faith, Learning, and Living*. Grand Rapids: Eerdmans, 2002.

Plantinga, Theodore. "The Dissenters of 1892." In *Secession, Doleantie, and Union: 1834–1892*, edited by Hendrik Bouma, 213–21. Neerlandia: Inheritance, 1995.

Praamsma, Louis. *Let Christ Be King: Reflections on the Life and Times of Abraham Kuyper*. Jordan Station: Paideia Press, 1985.

Puchinger, George. *Abraham Kuyper: His Early Journey of Faith*. Edited by George Harinck. Translated by Simone Kennedy. Amsterdam: VU University Press, 1998.

Putten, Jan van. *Zoveel kerken, zoveel zinnen: een sociaalwetenschappelijke studie van verschillen in behoudendheid tussen Gereformeerden en Christelijke Gereformeerden*. Kampen: Kok, 1968.

Rasker, Alber J. *De Nederlandse Hervormde Kerk vanaf 1795: haar geschiedenis en theologie in de negentiende en twintigste eeuw*. 2nd ed. Kampen: Kok, 1981.

Reconstruction Agency. "Hinanshasū no suii [Change of Evacuee Number]," 8 April 2015. Accessed 14 April 2016. www.reconstruction.go.jp/topics/main-cat2/sub-cat2-1/20150408_hinansha_suii.pdf.

Reid, David. *New Wine: The Cultural Shaping of Japanese Christianity*. Berkeley: Asian Humanities, 1991.

Rekishi Shiryō Hensan Iinkai [Historical Materials Compilation Committee]. *Nihon Kirisuto Kaikakuha Kyōkai-shi: Tojō ni Aru Kyōkai* [The History of the Reformed Church in Japan: A Church on the Road]. Hiroshima: Seikei Jusansho Shuppanbu, 1996.

Rothacher, Albrecht. *The Japanese Power Elite*. Chippenham: Rowe, 1993.

Rots, Aike P. "Ambiguous Identities: Negotiating Christianity and 'Japaneseness.'" In *Handbook of Contemporary Japanese Religion*, edited by Inken Prohl and John Nelson, 309–44. Leiden: Brill, 2012.

Samuels, Richard J. *3.11 Disaster and Change in Japan*. Ithaca: Cornell University Press, 2013.

Sasakawa Norikatsu. "Jimintō 'Kenpō Kaisei Sōan' no Bunseki: Omoni Ten'nōsei ni Sokushite [Analysis of LDP's Amendment Draft: With a Main Focus on the Emperor System]." *Hōritsu Ronsō* [Law Journal] 87, no. 6 (March 2015): 51–97.

Satō Nobuyuki. "Higashinihon Daishinsai to Gaikokujin Hisaisha [The Great Eastern Japan Disaster and Foreign Victims]." In *Higashinihon Daishinsai kara Towareru Nihon no Kyōkai* [Questioning the Japanese Church from the Great Eastern Japan Disaster], edited by Shinshū Kaki Senkyō Kōza, 103–26. Tokyo: Inochi no Kotobasha, 2013.

Satō, Seizaburō, Ken'ichi Kōyama, and Shunpei Kumon. *Postwar Politician: The Life of Former Prime Minister Masayoshi Ōhira*. Tokyo: Kodansha International, 1990.

Schilder, Klaas. *Pictoralia: A Series of Lectures by K. Schilder/Part 2: The Church*. Edited by Gerardus van Rongen. Translated by Gerardus van Rongen. Miniatures 10. Kelmscott: Western Australia: G. van Rongen, 2002.

———. "The Main Points of the Doctrine of the Covenants." Translated by T. vanLaar, 31 August 1944. http://spindleworks.com/library/schilder/covenant.htm.

Sherrill, Michael J. "Christian Churches in the Postwar Period." In Mullins, *Handbook of Christianity in Japan*, 163–80.

Shibata Hatsuo. "2025-nen Mondai to Kirisuto Kyōkai [The 2025 Problem and the Church]." *JMR Nihon Senkyō Nyūsu* [JMR Japan Mission News] 13 (September 2018): 1–2.

Shinohara, Motoaki. "The Church as God's Missionary Community: Towards an Evangelical Missional Ecclesiology with Implications for the Japanese Church." PhD diss., Trinity Evangelical Divinity School, 2012.

Shinto no Tomo Henshūbu, ed. Sonotoki, *Kyōkai Wa: 3.11 Go o Ikiru* [The Church at That Time: Living after 3.11]. Tokyo: UCCJ Board of Publications, 2012.

Son, Bong-Ho. "Relevance of Sphere Sovereignty to Korean Society." In *Kuyper Reconsidered: Aspects of His Life and Work*, edited by Cornelis van der Kooi and Jan de Bruijn, 179–89. Amsterdam: VU Uitgeverij, 1999.

Sonoda, Kōyū, and Delmer M. Brown. "Early Buddha Worship." In *The Cambridge History of Japan: Volume 1: Ancient Japan*, edited by Delmer M. Brown, 359–414. Cambridge: Cambridge University Press, 1993.

State, Paul F. *A Brief History of the Netherlands*. New York: Facts on File, 2008.

Statistics Bureau Ministry of Internal Affairs and Communications. *Final Report of the 2015 Population Census: Population and Households of Japan*. Tokyo, 2018. Accessed 5 August 2020. https://www.stat.go.jp/english/data/kokusei/2015/poj/pdf/2015ch01.pdf.

Steele, M. William. "Christianity and Politics in Japan." In Mullins, *Handbook of Christianity in Japan*, 359–82.

Subeno, Sutjipto, Solomon Yo, Benyamin Intan, and Jessy Siswanto, eds. *70 Years of Blessing 1940–2010: Dr. Stephen Tong Life and Ministries in Pictures*. Surabaya: Momentum, 2010.

Takahashi Kazuyoshi. "Kirisutokyō no Katsudō [Activities of Christianity]." In *Shinsai Fukkō to Shūkyō* [Disaster Recovery and Religion], edited by Inaba Keishin and Kurosaki Hiroyuki, 88–113. Tokyo: Akashi Shoten, 2013.

Takahashi Tetsuya. *Yasukuni Mondai* [The Issue of Yasukuni]. Tokyo: Chikuma Shinsho, 2005.

Takakura Tokutarō. *Takakura Tokutarō Chosaku-shū* [Collected Works of Takakura Tokutarō] Vol. 1. Tokyo: Shinkyō Shuppansha, 1964.

Takenaka, Akiko. "Mobilizing Death in Imperial Japan: War and the Origins of the Myth." *The Asia-Pacific Journal* 13, no. 38/2 (September 2015): 1–13.

Tanaka Nobumasa. *Kenpō Kyūjō no Sengoshi* [Postwar History of Article Nine]. Tokyo: Iwanami Shoten, 2005.

———. *Yasukuni no Sengoshi* [History of Postwar Yasukuni]. Tokyo: Iwanami Shoten, 2002.

Tanaka, Toshiyuki. *Hidden Horrors: Japanese War Crimes in World War II*. Lanham: Rowman & Littlefield, 2018.

Tokyo Christian University Faith and Culture Center, ed. Hisai-*chi Shien to Kyōkai no Minisutori-: Tōhoku Herupu no Hataraki* [Support for Affected Areas and The Church's Ministry: The Work of Tōhoku Help]. Tokyo: Inochi no Kotobasha, 2014.

Tomura Masahiro. "Aa Ware Yasukuni-bito naru kana, Kono Chi no Ronri yori Ware o Sukuwan Mono wa Tare-zo: Ro-ma-bito e no Tegami 7:7–25 [O Yasukuni Man That I Am! Who Shall Deliver Me from This Logic of Blood: Romans 7:7–25]." In Tomura, *Tennō-sei Kokka to Shinwa*, 188–98.

———. "Nihon no Nashonarizumu to no Tatakai: Yasukuni, Gengō, Daijōsai [Struggling with Japanese Nationalism: Yasukuni, Regnal Year, New Emperor's Food-offering Ritual]." In Tomura, *Tennō-sei Kokka to Shinwa*, 11–25.

———. "Shibarareta Te: Shito Gyōden 26:1–32 [Bound Hands: Acts 26:1–32]." In Tomura, *Tennō-sei Kokka to Shinwa*, 179–87.

———, ed. *Tennō-sei Kokka to Shinwa: "Yasukuni," Shisaku to Tatakai* [Emperor System State and Myth: "Yasukuni," Thought and Struggle]. Tokyo: Nihon Kirisuto Kyōdan Shuppan-kyoku, 1982.

———. "'Yasukuni' to Fukuin: Piripi-bito e no Tegami 2:6–8 ['Yasukuni' and Gospel: Philippians 2:6–8]." In Tomura, *Tennō-sei Kokka to Shinwa*, 199–210.

Toren, Benno van den. "Can We See the Naked Theological Truth?" In *Local Theology for the Global Church: Principles for an Evangelical Approach to Contextualization*, edited by Matthew Cook, Rob Haskel, Ruth Julian, and Natee Tanchanpongs, 91–108. Pasadena: William Carrey Library, 2010.

———. "Intercultural Theology as Three-Way Conversation: Beyond the Western Dominance of Intercultural Theology." *Exchange* 44, no. 2 (2015): 123–43.

Tsuchiya, Hiroshi. "Nihon ni okeru Kirisutokyō no Senkyō [Christian Mission in Japan]." *Higashi Ajia Bunka Kōshō Kenkyū Bessatsu* [East Asian Cultural Interaction Studies Supplemental] 6 (31 July 2010): 77–90.

Tsukada, John Jutaro. "Whose Politics? Which Story?: A Critical Engagement with Constantinianism and Theological Accommodationism with Stanley Hauerwas, with a Special Focus on the Churches in Japan." PhD diss., University of Aberdeen, 2016.

Van Leeuwen, Petrus A. *Het Kerkbegrip in de Theologie van Abraham Kuyper*. Franeker: T. Wever, 1946.

Vandenberg, Frank. *Abraham Kuyper*. Grand Rapids: Eerdmans, 1960.

Vree, Jasper, and Johan Zwaan. *Abraham Kuyper's Commentatio (1860): The Young Kuyper about Calvin, a Lasco, and the Church*, Vol. I. Leiden: Brill, 2005.

Vries, John Hendrik de. "Biographical Note." In *Lectures on Calvinism*, by Abraham Kuyper, i–vii. Grand Rapids: Eerdmans, 1999.

Wagenman, Michael R. "Abraham Kuyper and the Church: From Calvin to the Neo-Calvinists." In *On Kuyper: A Collection of Readings on the Life, Work and Legacy of Abraham Kuyper*, edited by Steve Bishop and John H. Kok, 125–39. Sioux Center: Dordt College Press, 2013.

Walls, Andrew F. "The Ephesian Movement: At a Crossroads in Christian History." In *The Cross-Cultural Process in Christian History: Studies in The Transmission and Appropriation of Faith*. Maryknoll: Orbis, 2002.

Walsh, Brian, and Richard J. Middleton. *The Transforming Vision*. Downers Grove: InterVarsity, 1984.

Watanabe Nobuo. "Daiichi no Haisen to Daini no Haisen: 3.11 kara Miete kita Mono [The First War-Defeat and The Second War-Defeat: Things That Are Seen from 3.11]." In *Higashinihon Daishinsai kara Towareru Nihon no Kyōkai* [Questioning the Japanese Church from the Great Eastern Japan Disaster], edited by Shinshū Kaki Senkyō Kōza, 9–34. Tokyo: Inochi no Kotobasha, 2013.

———. "Kenpō Kyū-jō no Seishin-teki Shichū [Mentally Pillar of Article 9]" Presented at the Tokyo Kokuhaku Kyōkai Shūkyō Kaikaku Kinen Kōkai Kōen-kai [Reformation Remembrance Open Seminar of Tokyo Confession Church], Tokyo, 31 October 2005. Accessed 4 April 2019. http://www7b.biglobe.ne.jp/~tokyokokuhakukyoukai/kouen/kennpoukyuujounoseishinntekisityuu.html.

———. *Kyōkai-ron Nyūmon* [Introduction to Ecclesiology]. Tokyo: Shinkyō Shuppansha, 1970.

———. "Sensō Seikan-sha no Heiwa Kenpō Yōgo-ron [Advocacy of Peace Constitution by a War Survivor]" Presented at the Tokyo Kokuhaku Kyōkai Heiwa Kōen-kai [Seminar on Peace of Tokyo Confession Church],

Tokyo, 12 August 2004. Accessed 4 April 2019. http://www7b.biglobe.ne.jp/~tokyokokuhakukyoukai/kouen/kouen29.html.

———. *Shinkō ni Mototzuku Teikō-ken* [Faith-based Resistance Right]. Tokyo: Inochi no Kotobasha, 2016.

Wilson, Jonathan. "'Staying In': Engaging Japanese Culture with the Authentic Gospel." In *The Church Embracing the Sufferers, Moving Forward: Centurial Vision for Post-Disaster Japan: Ecumenical Voices*, edited by Atsuyoshi Fujiwara and Brian Byrd, 80–81. A Theology of Japan Monograph Series 7. Ageo: Seigakuin University Press, 2014.

Wintle, Michael. *An Economic and Social History of the Netherlands, 1800–1920: Demographic, Economic and Social Transition*. Cambridge: Cambridge University Press, 2000.

———. *Pillars of Piety: Religion in the Netherlands in the Nineteenth Century 1813–1901*. Hull: Hull University Press, 1987.

Wolters, Albert M. *Creation Regained: Biblical Basics for a Reformational Worldview*. Grand Rapids: Eerdmans, 1985.

Wood, John H., Jr. *Going Dutch in the Modern Age: Abraham Kuyper's Struggle for a Free Church in the Netherlands*. New York: Oxford University Press, 2013.

Yamaguchi Yōichi. "Hon Bukkuretto no Atogaki [Afterword of This Booklet]." In Tokyo Christian University Faith and Culture Center, *Hisai-chi Shien to Kyōkai*, 119.

Yamaguchi Yōichi, and Shibata Hatsuo. *JMR Chōsa Repo-to (2018 Nendo)* [JMR Investigation Report 2018]. Inzai: Tokyo Christian University Japan Missions Research, April 2019. http://www.tci.ac.jp/wp-content/uploads/2015/08/JMR_report_2018.pdf.

Yamasaki, Kazuaki. "Bonhoeffer's Social Ethics and Its Influences in Japan." In *Interpreting Bonhoeffer*, edited by Clifford J. Green and Guy C. Carter, 47–60. Historical Perspectives, Emerging Issues. Minneapolis: Augsburg Fortress, 2013.

Zwaanstra, Henry. "Abraham Kuyper's Conception of the Church." *Calvin Theological Journal* 9, no. 2 (1974): 149–81.

"Disaster Overview." *NHK (Japan Broadcasting Corporation)*. Accessed 14 April 2016. https://www.nhk.or.jp/ashita/english/status/overview.html.

"LDP Announces a New Draft Constitution for Japan." *Jimintō* [Liberal Democratic Party]. Last modified 7 May 2012. Accessed 21 February 2017. www.jimin.jp/english/news/117099.html.

Langham Literature, with its publishing work, is a ministry of Langham Partnership.

Langham Partnership is a global fellowship working in pursuit of the vision God entrusted to its founder John Stott –

> *to facilitate the growth of the church in maturity and Christ-likeness through raising the standards of biblical preaching and teaching.*

Our vision is to see churches in the Majority World equipped for mission and growing to maturity in Christ through the ministry of pastors and leaders who believe, teach and live by the word of God.

Our mission is to strengthen the ministry of the word of God through:
- nurturing national movements for biblical preaching
- fostering the creation and distribution of evangelical literature
- enhancing evangelical theological education

especially in countries where churches are under-resourced.

Our ministry

Langham Preaching partners with national leaders to nurture indigenous biblical preaching movements for pastors and lay preachers all around the world. With the support of a team of trainers from many countries, a multi-level programme of seminars provides practical training, and is followed by a programme for training local facilitators. Local preachers' groups and national and regional networks ensure continuity and ongoing development, seeking to build vigorous movements committed to Bible exposition.

Langham Literature provides Majority World preachers, scholars and seminary libraries with evangelical books and electronic resources through publishing and distribution, grants and discounts. The programme also fosters the creation of indigenous evangelical books in many languages, through writer's grants, strengthening local evangelical publishing houses, and investment in major regional literature projects, such as one volume Bible commentaries like the *Africa Bible Commentary* and the *South Asia Bible Commentary*.

Langham Scholars provides financial support for evangelical doctoral students from the Majority World so that, when they return home, they may train pastors and other Christian leaders with sound, biblical and theological teaching. This programme equips those who equip others. Langham Scholars also works in partnership with Majority World seminaries in strengthening evangelical theological education. A growing number of Langham Scholars study in high quality doctoral programmes in the Majority World itself. As well as teaching the next generation of pastors, graduated Langham Scholars exercise significant influence through their writing and leadership.

To learn more about Langham Partnership and the work we do visit **langham.org**

www.ingramcontent.com/pod-product-compliance
Lightning Source LLC
Chambersburg PA
CBHW070235240426
43673CB00044B/1802

This is an important piece of research – a thorough and thoughtful study of the beliefs and practices of a particular group of Muslims, with a focus on their experience of spiritual powers. Judy Wang'ombe has observed and listened to both leaders and "ordinary" practitioners of that group, but has also investigated how they relate to their more orthodox Muslim kin, and how the more orthodox Muslim leaders view them. She offers rich insights into motivations and perceptions, and into a complex web of social, medical, family, and spiritual factors.

Ida Glaser, PhD
International Academic Coordinator and Founding Fellow,
Centre for Muslim-Christian Studies, UK

Dr. Judy Wang'ombe's in-depth study into Borana Muslims' involvement in the *Ayyaana* cult unearths their lived experiences of the spirit world. The research findings exhibit the cognitive and epistemological disparities between the official Islamic teacher's interpretations and the ordinary Borana Muslims' understanding of the spirit world they experience in everyday life. While conventional Islamic studies have been focused mainly on other classical issues rather than ordinary Muslims' lived experiences, her research illustrates the unpretentious, religiocultural lenses through which Islam is perceived and lived out among ordinary Muslims. Dr. Wang'ombe speaks loudly that academics interested in Islam should consider ordinary Muslims' experiences and expressions of Islam in dynamic local contexts that comprise of multiple cultural and psychological elements beyond a monolithic religious system. Thus, this book is a must-read for those looking seriously into Islamic phenomena in a specific cultural context.

C. S. Caleb Kim, PhD
Coordinator of the Center for the Study of Religions,
Institute for the Study of African Realities,
Africa International University, Kenya

It is a privilege to write an endorsement for this excellent study. I have been to Kenya once, and I teach courses on Folk or Popular Islam. It was therefore fascinating to learn about the *Ayyaana* cult among Kenyan Borana Muslims.

I especially appreciate Dr. Wang'ombe's excellent use of literature, including the Qur'an and Hadith, to explain general Islamic views of jinn and spirit possession. It was then fascinating to compare this with what she found in her careful field study among *Ayyaana* cult members. Her time in the field helps us see life through Borana eyes.

While this careful and comprehensive study focuses narrowly on one Muslim group, the way in which she carried out the research serves as a very helpful template for similar research in other contexts. I highly recommend this book.

John Jay Travis, PhD
Affiliate Faculty in Islamic Studies,
Fuller Theological Seminary, California, USA

The *Ayyaana* cult is one of those ambiguous religious phenomena that both straddles the Borana cultural milieu and is embedded in local understandings of Islam in northern Kenya. Marsabit Borana-speaking communities share similar cultural and religious affinities with their co-ethnics across the Ethiopian border. *Ayyaana* is one of the many things that connect and enrich their cross-border religious and spiritual worldviews. The *Ayyaana* cult, existing at the fringe of mainstream Islam, is often cast as the syncretic and heretic version of the faith followed by illiterate peri-urban poor, and it is often least understood. No recent or previous studies bring such clarity to the mystical world of this spirit possession cult as Judy's work does. Its richness is its in-depth survey of the imaginaries and territorialities of the spiritual entities as perceived, debated upon, and believed in by both mainstream Muslim scholars and adherents of *warra ayyaana*. This pioneering work is based on a solid ethnographic methodology, enriched with analyses of lyrical *Ayyaana* songs and terminologies, and it offers refreshingly original exploration of the world of spirit management that oscillates between exorcism and adorcism as imagined by diverse religious actors. Students of ethnography, sociology, Islam, and Christian-Muslim relations studies would definitely find this work highly informative and useful in understanding the lived experiences of Muslim Borana in northern Kenya.

Halkano Abdi Wario, PhD
Senior Lecturer in Religious Studies,
Senior Volkswagen Foundation Humanities Research Fellow,
Egerton University, Kenya
Associate Director, Center for Study of Terrorism, Violent Extremism and Radicalization,
HORN International Institute of Strategic Studies, Kenya